Native American Herbalist's Bible

14 Books in 1

500+ Herbal Remedies & Medicinal Plants to Restore Your Natural Wellness.
Grow Your Own Garden and Build Your Apothecary Table &
Herbal Dispensatory

Natalie Hathale

Table of Contents

Native American Herbal Apothecary

The Basics of Native American Herbal Medicine

BOOK 1 of "The Native American Herbalist's Bible"

Natalie Hathale

Introduction

"As you develop your awareness in nature, you begin to see how we influence all life and how all life influences us. A key and critical feature for us to know"

Wanbli Nata'u – Ogala Lakota

We are all sons and daughters of Mother Nature. Even if our society tries to make us forget about our true nature, we must always remember we are links in a complex chain that involves every creature on this earth.

Our ancestors knew this simple truth and lived by it. They were aware of their true nature, and were connected with Mother Nature at a level that could seem impossible for us to understand. They were conscious of the gift that she generously provides us for our own prosperity.

In fact, our forest, meadows, and hills are full of herbs and flowers that can seem insignificant to you but if correctly treated and prepared, can heal many of the ailments that we suffer, and improve our overall well-being.

Western society has lost that knowledge. The tendency in the medicine field, dominated by the economic interests of the pharmaceutical industries, has always been to create, in sterilized laboratories, chemical compounds that can rapidly treat symptoms of specific ailments to make you happy in the short time. Many of these commonly used medications are only palliatives that do not solve the root problem and have indeed undesired side effects, some of them unknown.

Medicine and science have become increasingly interested in the last decades in the healing power of herbs and flowers, rediscovering most of the ancient knowledge of the Native Americans, giving scientific foundation to the many rituals and cures known by centuries by my people.

In this book series, my purpose is to guide you in rediscovering this ancient wisdom through a structured learning approach that will make you become a proficient herbalist starting from zero.

In detail, in this first book, I will introduce Native American Medicine, with its methods and preparations. You will know where to find the plants, how to harvest them, and how to treat and store them.

The other books of this series are designed to give you the missing pieces to know your way in Native American Herbal Medicine.

In particular, in the second book of the series, you will have access to the Herbal Encyclopedia of the most important herbs and flowers used in traditional Native American medicine.

Finally, in the third book, we will close the circle, learning what herb to use and the correct preparation techniques to create herbal remedies for the most common ailments and diseases you can encounter.

I tried to join two worlds in this book, by providing you pieces of my ancient culture with its holistic character in a well-structured learning course.

I hope you find this interesting, that you **get your bonuses on the last page of the book,** and that reading this book will be just the beginning of your journey…

Native American Medicine

It is not uncommon nowadays to resort to alternative medicine practices to treat common ailments. Naturopathy and phytotherapy are chief among these practices that aim to cure disease using the healing power of herbs and plants.

This tendency reflect the desire in people to resort to a more natural way to heal and to avoid the introduction in their body of synthetic chemical substances that merely replicate the natural ones and whose long-term side effects are not totally known. Find a less toxic alternative to such chemical substances is a priority for our society and Native American plant-based medicine could be a suitable option.

Healing properties of herbs

Herbs have been used for medical purposes since the dawn of time by all the cultures, from Asia to Europe, to America. The benefits of white willow bark decoction to reduce fever or Echinacea poultice to treat an infected wound were widely known all over the world by many ancient cultures, as well as the poisoning properties of other plants like hemlock or thorn

Phytochemicals are the chemical substances produced by plants due to their metabolism. Some of the phytochemicals normally used by Natives are powerful antioxidants, immune system stimulators, and are known to be effective in managing cholesterol levels in the blood:

- Triterpenoids: they are known to be powerful tools for liver detoxification and they are useful to prevent dental cavities and ulcers. Licorice has plenty of it.
- Diterpenes: Romero is the main source of these powerful antioxidants.
- Anthocyanidins: Mainly to be found in berries.
- Salicin: you can find it in the white willow (Latin name: Salix Alba) bark; it is known to

apple. This knowledge was the result of direct experience passed from generation to generation. Today science can provide an explanation on why a certain herb can be effective to treat a certain disease, that was unknown by our ancestors. The secret is to identify the chemical substances contained in the herbs: Phytochemicals and Enzymes.

be effective for flu, fever, and chronic pain relief.
- Lipoic Acid: removes heavy metals from your blood and helps to prevent heart diseases and stabilizing blood sugar.
- Omega-3 and Omega-6 Fatty Acids: because of the fact that these substances cannot be made by our body it is of crucial importance that they are taken through food. They help in the preservation of the nervous system and improve cholesterol levels.
- Eleutherosides: These substances have a positive effect on one's stamina and overall body strength. They are proven effective to stimulate appetite, improve the immune system and boost metabolism.
- Flavoglycosides: they fight free radicals and improve blood pressure.

- Ginkgolic Acid: as the name suggests this substance can be found in Ginkgo Biloba; it is widely known for its antioxidant and anticancer properties. Not many people know that it can improve mood swings and mental clarity.
- Monoterpenes: the powerful antioxidant of Ginkgo Biloba.
- Hesperidin: Liver disease and capillaries strengthening are the main benefits of this substance. You can find it in the thistle seeds.
- Saponins: Powerful anti-inflammatory, antibacterial, and antifungal substance group; you can find them in ginseng root.
- Isothiocyanates: this substance can be found in horseradish; it is a powerful antioxidant.
- Glycyrrhizinis: This chemical substance, mainly present in licorice, have powerful anti-inflammatory and antiviral properties
- Hypericin: Good for mood swings.
- Alkaloids: They prevent yeast formation in our bodies preventing infections of the bladder (like cystitis), candida, and bloating.
- Phenolic Acids: Mainly to be found in berries and flowering plants, these substances stop the formation of nitrosamines which can cause tumors.
- Phthalides: powerful detoxifying and anticancer substances found in parsley.
- Chlorophyll: Antibacterial substance, which is obviously present in all the green herbs, it helps in healing burns and wounds in general.
- Gingerols: as the name suggest this substance can be found in Ginger; they help digestion and fight liver toxicity.
- Lactones: they are powerful boosters of metabolic autophagy, thus helping in cancer prevention. Kava-kava root is full of them.
- Proanthocyanidins: these antioxidants can be found in the elderberry. They have been proven to be useful to fight flu and high cholesterol levels.
- Quercitin: You may recall it because it is one of the main substances that the trendy "Sirtfood Diet" indicates as a metabolism booster. Quercetin belongs to a wider class of substances called flavonoids, which have antihistamine, anti-inflammatory and anticancer properties. They also strengthen the capillaries.
- Rosmarinic Acid: obviously found in Romero, this substance fights nausea, bloating, and migraine.
- Silymarin: Liver protector and antioxidant. Widely present in the milk thistle.
- Tannins: this group of substances is widely present in the plant kingdom and it is renowned for its antioxidants, antiviral properties, and the positive effect on the capillaries' strength. Also, you may recall them because they are one of the substances that the trendy "Sirtfood Diet" indicates as a metabolism booster.
- Polyacetylenes: these powerful anticancer substances promote metabolic autophagy and regulate the production of prostaglandins. Parsley is the main source of them.

Enzymes are the natural complement to the Phytochemicals, whose action is started and enhanced by them.

Enzymes are of chief importance to determine the overall effectiveness of herbal remedies. For this reason, it is of fundamental importance not to destroy them by exposing the herbs to high temperature or alcohol.

Native American Herbalism

The use of herbal remedies by the Native Americans is lost in the mists of time. Since the tribes had no written history the first documented use of herbs for medical purposes

between Native Americans dates back to the first half of the 17th Century, with the beginning of contacts between the Europeans and the Native Americans in the North-East of the United States.

Native Americans generously shared with them what they had learned in centuries of trial and error about the use of their proper indigenous herbs for healing.

Among these remedies, many have found application in most of the over-the-counter medicines you can find today in your pharmacy or grocery store. The main example of this phenomenon is the White Willow bark that was used by Native Americans to treat colds and that today is used to produce acetylsalicylic acid, commonly known as aspirin.

The message that Native Americans lived by is being discovered again in recent days: humans are just a link in a more complex chain that involves all the beings who live on this earth and everything they need to thrive is within the grasp of their hands. The land he lives in is his mother and provides him with shelter, food, and medicine. The only state of being in which he realizes his full potential and achieves the maximum happiness is when he lives in perfect harmony with the surrounding nature.

Native American tribes put healers in high consideration. They were always among the more trusted counselor of the chief and were renowned for their wisdom and honesty. Not only they took care of the health of the tribe by providing medications and help but also they were entrusted with the ancient rituals, and with passing on histories and legends that gave the tribe its specific identity among the other ones.

The healing process for the Native Americans consists of two parts: physical healing and spiritual healing. For Natives these two aspects were inseparable: medicine, which was the cure for the physical body, was given during ceremonies that were done to cure the spirit. This holistic approach can be found in many cultures and modern medical science is now re-discovering what our ancestors had sensed centuries ago: the intertwined connection between spirit and body and how each other can influence our healing process.

For Native Americans, the cure for the disease was both on the spiritual plane, evoked by the ceremony and physical plane, which is only the tangible manifestation of the spirit.

With this idea in mind, herbs were not only used for healing but they had a ceremonial purpose. Tobacco and Sage chief among them.

It is also widely documented the burning of herbs to clear the mind, to assist visions, to chase away evil spirits, or in sweat lodges to detoxify mind and body.

It was believed that the « spirit » of the plant is the one who operates the healing. To preserve the spirit a certain set of rules must be observed during the gathering of the herb.

Interesting fact, these rules, which we can superficially ascribe to Native American religious folklore, are almost the same in each tribe, even if they were very far away from each other.

The learning process of herbal medicine

Native Americans learned which herbs and flowers to use through the empirical approach. They used an herb to treat disease and if it worked, they would have used it again.

They based their approach on the profound sense of attunement they felt with Nature and the interesting thing is they were not the only ones: Hippocrates, pre-Confucian Chinese Medicine men, and African shamans used the same method to heal people. Red fruits were associated with the treatment of blood-related issues, or Ashwagandha root to treat male sexual problems (due to its phallic shape).

This approach is based on what is called the "Doctrine of Signatures" by which the medical properties of a plant or an herb can be revealed by its appearance, mainly color or shape.

Other commonly used methods for choosing the herbs to use were the nature observation of what berries, herbs or roots animals ate (especially bears due to the fact that they resemble humans when walking on two legs).

Although these methods may seem unreliable from a scientific point of view, the fact is that Native Americans were one of the "healthiest" civilizations ever lived. Their strength and resistance shocked Europeans. In addition, archeological analyses on bones and skeletons of ancient Native Americans confirm that almost none of them suffered bone problems such as arthritis or rheumatism. Also, the chronicles of the first Europeans report that they were less prone to suffer heart, respiratory diseases, or for women to die during childbirth.

For sure, they know their way with herbal medicine: they knew what plants to pick, the correct season to harvest them, how to store them in the most effective way and how to prepare them to heal certain conditions.

It is not by chance that the most sold herbal supplements nowadays, were also used by Native Americans for the same healing purposes: Ginseng, Echinacea, St. John's worth, Cranberries, Goldenseal, and Evening Primrose were widely used by almost all the tribes that inhabited North America to heal from various ailments.

About Herb Supply

Native American knowledge about healing is deeper than it is widely known: through a slow process of trial and error, over centuries they gathered information about, not only herbs and their healing power but also how and when to harvest them to maximize their effect.

As already stated, they were more attuned with the surrounding nature and they quickly understood that the harvest and the treatment of the herbs must be done according to the plant's lifecycle.

Not only that, they developed a preference for the specific indigenous plants of each zone. They understood that each plant is an optimized living thing, specifically designed to thrive in a specific environment; foreign species, introduced from other countries, are in some way lessened in their virtues and properties due to the fact that they have grown in an environment different from the one they were designed for.

As you can see, Native American herbal medicine is much complex than it seems. It is a holistic system of healing very different from the one adopted by western society.

Native Americans based their medicine on prevention and, when disease happens, on encouraging the body's own response.

Herbs are allies and friends and they must be treated with respect and not as mere resources to be exploited. According to this point of view, it is of primary importance for the responsible herbalist to make sure to take only what is needed, minimizing the waste, restore the plant's habitat and eventually replant what has been taken, in full accordance with the Native American approach to the foraging.

Growing your own herbs

No matter how black your thumb has been until now, I decided to write this section to give you practical advice on how you successfully can grow your own herbs.

Although you may feel that this is a daunting task, it is easier than it seems and for sure is less time-consuming than wildcrafting.

The secret is starting small: many plants are very easy to cultivate and can thrive even in a pot beside a sunny window in your city apartment. Among these plants, there are many that can be used for medical purposes such as mint, thyme, or sage.

Below you can find a list of plants that you can easily grow and that will give you the confidence to start your own medical plants

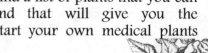

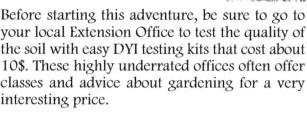

garden with more daring herbs, even if you have no room in your flat: Garlic., Rosemary, Basil, Mint, Lemon, Fennel, Lovage, Oregano, Cilantro, Horseradish and Thyme.

Advice on Buying Herbs

I understand that not anyone has access to a forest or a meadow in the proximity of his/her home, so I decided to write this paragraph as a guide to the conscious purchase of herbs. Although you may find the herbs you need for your preparations in the grocery store or herbal shop, my advice is to rely on local producers: they may be more expensive but the quality is higher and generally worth the price.

When purchasing herbs you must look at three key factors to determine the quality:

- Soil: ask where the herbs have been cultivated, and research that country's regulation regarding pollution. This task may seem complicated but many big retailers already offer this certification of conformity in their products. If you are interested in urban farms, ask them if they use clean soil and if they have water filtration systems
- Growing Practices: the aspects you have to take care of when inquiring about growing practices are :
   o Fertilizers
   o Insects management
   o Outdoor/Greenhouse/Hydroponic cultivation

Before starting this adventure, be sure to go to your local Extension Office to test the quality of the soil with easy DYI testing kits that cost about 10$. These highly underrated offices often offer classes and advice about gardening for a very interesting price.

- Drying: Drying temperature is very important. If too high, it will burn the leaves and you will lose all the precious substances contained in it. Look at the color of the leaves and discard them if it is brown-black.

My go-to advice, in this case, is trusting your senses: if the herbs have a vivid color, and give off a fragrant aroma, then their quality is almost certainly good.

Being someone who wildcrafts and dries her own herbs, I have found the sweet spot is a temperature between 77°F and 86°F in a dark environment with the plants widely spaced or hung upside down from the ceiling. Using these low temperatures, I found that leaves and flowers are completely dry in roughly one week and roots in one month. Real drying times depend on the plant itself, its water percentage, and obviously the size, so my advice is to always check if leaves and flowers are "crunchy" and if roots are dry on the inside by cutting a specimen.

Wild crafting

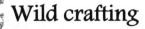

The experience of waking up early in the morning, hike into the wild, and harvesting your own herbs is for sure a satisfactory one.

However, as always, you should be aware of what you are going to do. Sometimes this is not your best choice: overharvesting endangered plants or destroy the habitat of plants is a big problem nowadays. You can easily check the list of the endangered species on unitedplantsaver.org. Often the best solution is to grow your own herbs or to buy them from trusted producers who operate in the fair trade circuit.

This is particularly important because the use of some plant may cause damages to the producers (strangled by the big companies) or to the populations that have « silently » used them for

centuries and that become damaged by the spike of prices followed by some random increase in popularity due to some trend.

It is the case of the Lepidium Meyenii, a plant grown by Andeans for food purposes under the name of Maca. This plant has also the reputation to be an aphrodisiac and a testosterone booster. Not many years ago, big companies discovered this plant and its reputation. To make money out of it, they started offering the producers, more money than the locals did. These latter, could not afford it anymore and suffered severe famine problems.

In the next chapter, you can find a complete go-to guide to wildcraft in total safety and without risks of damaging plant species or their habitat.

Wild Crafting 101

Wildcrafting is probably the most ancient activity men have ever done. It consists of harvesting plants from the wild, for food or medicinal purposes. When done sustainably this is a win-win for both men and plants: men can receive food or medicinal herbs from nature, and in exchange they take care of the surrounding environment by taking only what is necessary, replanting plants and seeds, removing dead branches to help the plant grow faster and stronger.

Win-Win Wildcrafting

There are techniques and gathering methods that allow the plant and the surrounding environment to benefit from the harvesting. This is important to minimize the impact we have on our planet and to ensure that we have access to

the benefits nature gives us for many generations to come. Below some of the most used techniques to adopt in the different situations:

- Shrubby plant: when cutting a branch or a stem, cut above a leaf node to encourage the plant to grow more.
    Cut at a 45° angle about 6mm above the node. In case you have a plant with opposite leaves, cut straight across.
- Replant root crowns whenever you can.
- Harvest roots only during fall. In this season, leaves tend to die and all the nutrients tend to fall back to the roots.
- Harvest branches that are already broken but still attached to the plant. This will give you the parts you need and will set the plant free from a possible source of infection and disease. Be sure to leave a flat surface.
- When harvesting branches, make a two-inch deep cut under it before sawing from the top. This will assure that you do not strip the bark at the end of the cut when the branch falls to the ground in the latter part of the cut.

Rules for Ethical Wildcrafting

The Rocky Mountains Herbalist's Coalition, from Colorado, selected a set of rules to live by, when wildcrafting. These rules may seem

obvious and common sense but if followed religiously, will assure that everyone would benefit from the local flora for generations.

1. Never pick endangered species.
2. Before harvesting, be sure of the plant identification.
3. Ask permission and thank the plants.
4. Leave mature plants who stay in a higher position untouched so they can indeed repopulate the picking zone with the down-slope rolling of seeds.
5. Gather only from abundant stands and no more than 10% of the plant.

How to select the site for wildcrafting

- Obtain permission from your local authority with a regular license to pick plants.
- Follow the guidelines of your local authority of where to pick, and what zones to avoid.
- Stay far away from pollution sources: Roadsides, Electric wires, and farms or gardens that may use chemical fertilizers. Be sure to be upwind or upstream from these areas.
- Do not pick from a fragile environment.

When to pick

- Flowers: Pick them at the beginning of the blooming, possibly during a full moon phase, between 6 and 10 a.m.
- Leaf: pick them before the flowering phase of the plant between 6 and 10 a.m.
- Roots picking: to be done after the seeding phase of the plant during the new moon, and early in the morning to avoid deep dirt to dry. For plants with a biannual living cycle, harvest during the autumn of the second year.
- Barks: Pick during spring, in the three-quarter waning moon, and never strip the whole tree. Be sure to leave the healthiest plants untouched. If you strip branches be sure to avoid branches too near to the ground to avoid fungal rot on the plant. Pick the inner bark (cambium) and be sure to adopt pollarding techniques for the short branches and coppicing for low stumps.
- Pitch and Sap: the favorite season for harvesting is winter.

- Seeds and Fruits: harvest when mature according to the natural rhythm of the plant.

How to manage your picking sites

- Do not wear hard-soled shoes, to avoid damages to the ground
- Be aware of the plant's proper lifecycle. Be sure not to harvest the same spot year after year. Observe the picking spot and evaluate through comparative pictures if your impact on the zone is too much. Eventually, avoid the harvesting for a year or two.
- Provide food to the remaining plants. I use Native American traditional cornmeal, which is handy, but your organic waste such as an apple peel will also do the job.
- Treat the spot as it would be your garden: tend to it, remove weeds, and make manual pollination if needed.
- Use appropriate wildcrafting techniques and tools described in this chapter to be sure to cause minimal damage to the area.
- Digging to find medical roots may cause damages and erosion to the ground. Be sure to cover the holes, and to replace the foliage and dirt on the digging spot.
- If you are harvesting leaves or flowers, do not eradicate the whole plant.

Wildcrafting Ritual

The picking was one of the most important phases for the Native American healers. It was the most spiritual and intense part for sure, where you connect with mother nature and you engage with the deities who inhabit the world.

Phyllis Hogan, the founder of the Arizona Ethnobotanical Research Association, is a skilled herbalist. During her forty years of experience in the field, she worked with many Native American tribes (especially Navajo and Hopi) and she adopted their gathering rituals:

- Be sure to wear nice clothes and jewelry as a sign of worthiness in the eyes of the deity.
- You always pick early in the morning. You begin by burning a juniper twig, then collect the soot and smudge some of it in a

vertical line in the middle of your forehead while praying to the sun

- Once you find the plant you want to collect, you tell it your name and offer cornmeal to the picking spot.
- Select a plant in the immediate proximity of the one you want to pick and ask permission to pick the surrounding plants explaining that you want to use them for healing purposes. Then you wait for permission.
- It may happen in various forms: a blowing of the wind, the rustling of leaves, or just a feeling. If you do not receive permission, you do not pick.
- Once you receive permission, give cornmeal offerings to the four directions (starting from the east and working clockwise), the middle, and place a pinch of cornmeal on your head. This is an

important sign of connection to the spiritual world.

- IMPORTANT: Do not pick the plant you asked permission for. It is your emissary in the plant world. If a plant resists picking, then don't force it. Pick only the plants that come out easily.
- Never take more than you need, pick 10% of the plant maximum.
- Place what you pick on a clean linen or cotton sheet. Be sure to align all the plants in the same direction and do not mix the species. Place some other cornmeal in the sheet and welcome the plants openhearted. Tell them again why you picked them and why they are needed.
- Do not process them immediately. When you come back home, remove them from the sheet, line them on a table and let them rest for another day. Thank them again before processing.

Wildcrafting essentials

The right tool for the job. This is an essential concept to understand in any crafting activity, from woodworking to cooking.

When you have the right tool, you work faster and better. You are less exposed to accidental cuts or wounds and, more important, you create fewer damages to the environment and the plants by making clean cuts or more surgical diggings.

Below you can find a list of the essentials you need to start wildcrafting in safety and with ease.

1. A Plant Identification Handbook:

This is probably the most important tool you need. Clear identification of a plant will tell you if it is edible or poisonous if it is

endangered or not and the parts to pick for medicinal or food purposes.

2. Scissors, Clippers, and a sharp Knife:

Scissors and clippers are valuable tools. They allow clean cuts and minimize the damages to the plant. My advice is to invest and buy good quality tools because they will allow you to make clean cuts with less effort and will minimize the possibility that you accidentally cut yourself (even with more hard plants or roots like Echinacea). Ultimately, they will make the job easy and will endure for decades. Another valuable tool is a sharp knife that will allow you to make an accurate 45° cut on the plant that scissors and clippers can't do.

3. Gloves:

Essential tools when you deal with thorny and stinging plants and when using a knife to protect your hands.

4. **Trowel and Folding Shovel:** These two are unevaluable when digging roots. For most roots, the trowel will be enough but for deeper ones, it is necessary to have in your backpack a folding shovel. They come in every size and cost and, when folded they do not occupy much space.

5. **Saw:** This one is essential when harvesting branches for obvious reasons. It will make clean cuts in the trunk and the tree will be less exposed to diseases and infection

6. **Paper Bags and Clean Linen Sheets:** Although Native American traditions allow only clean sheets to store the plants from the picking place to your home, brown paper bags are a good substitute. The main function they must have is to absorb moisture and facilitate transpiration of the herbs. Plastic bags are to be avoided at all costs because they encourage mold formation.

Becoming an Experienced Wild Crafter

Only time will give you the tools to know your way with the plants and the environment in your surroundings or in your picking spots. Of course, there are some tips to speed up the process:

- Observation: take your time with the plants. Look at them with curiosity, and use your nose and touch as well as your eyes. You will begin to notice new things even in the most common plant. How it changes from season to season and from year to year in some cases.

- Take notes: whenever you identify a plant, note where it lives, its neighbor plants, the insects you found. In no time, you will be able to understand the patterns and easily

you will know where to look to find the plant you need.

- Keep a sketchbook: even if you are not Leonardo Da Vinci, and you barely know what a pencil is, I encourage you to keep a sketchbook of the plants you identify. It will help you take the habit of deep and careful observation of the plants.

- Build your own herbarium by preserving flowers, leaves, and buds in the middle of a book for some time to make it dry. Then stick it in a notebook.

- Take photos: today technology makes this task easier than when I started wildcrafting. You can easily take a picture with your phone and write notes on it.

Safe Wildcrafting Rules

Be sure to follow these simple rules when wildcrafting. It will assure that you get your feet

wet in the safest way possible in this fascinating world. In time, you will develop confidence and

knowledge with your environment and you will know what to pick and what to leave:

- Clearly identify the plant before harvesting. There is plenty of poisonous plants that look exactly like medical ones.
- If you have some doubt, do not harvest. Take a picture and check while at home or with your local Extension Office.
- Do not "taste test" plants you do not know.
- Be sure to know the endangered plants in your surroundings.
- Attain to the 10% rule: only harvest the 10% or less of what you find, to be sure to do not damage the environment.
- Never harvest near urban environments such as high-tension trellis, or roadsides, or railways.
- Caution: you could be allergic or intolerant to some plant and you don't even know. When you try a new plant, be sure to take small amounts and try <u>only one</u> new plant at the time.
- Keep your eyes open: even if wildcrafting may seem like hiking, it is more different from that. There are many hidden dangers when you go deep into the woods such as thorns, stinging plants, or holes in the ground that can make you sprain your ankle.
- **Avoid plants with white sap:** this is a big red flag that indicated that the plant is poisonous.
- **Flowers in umbels:** Be careful with this one. Many curative plants such as yarrow form flowers in an umbel, but also many poisonous lookalikes do that. Be 100% sure of what you are picking.
- Exercise additional caution with mushrooms, they could be extremely poisonous.

- Many herbs look like mint but they do not smell or taste minty. Many unexperienced wildcrafters have been in trouble by eating poisonous lookalikes.
- If you see an animal eating a certain herb, this is not a sign that the herb is edible. Some animals have developed tolerance to some poisonous plants.

Free Apps for Plant Recognition

Today technology makes the job easier than when I began. On the internet, there is plenty of websites and apps that will help you identify the various plants you will encounter. Below my favorite free apps:

- **Like That Garden**: You can upload your picture and it will give you immediate recognition of the plant. Recognition is not always 100% reliable and works better with flowering plants, so use your own judgment
- **Leafsnap**: You can upload the picture of the leaf and it will give you immediate recognition of the plant. The picture must be taken on a white background, and this can be unpractical
- **ID Weeds**: Developed by the University of Missouri. It will recognize the plant after the input of some attributes. Less practical than the two above but more reliable. You can also check from their pictures database.
- **Vtree**: Developed by Virginia Tech, gives you a list of plants available in your surroundings by acquiring your GPS position. It provides also plant pictures and descriptions.
- **About Herbs**: it is a database of herbs and plants with pictures, descriptions, and simple medical preparations. My advice is to use it in combination with one of the other apps listed above.

AMAZING BONUSES FOR ALL THE READERS:

Just Scan the QR-Code on the right to get them!

Herbal Preparations

The science of distilling and extract phytochemicals from plants has been perfecting techniques and tools since the dawn of time. Alembics, chemical extractions, and industrial maceration processes are way too much diffused in the pharmaceutical (and in the herbal) industry nowadays.

Kitchen Essentials

Contrary to the common belief, it is not difficult to obtain high-quality herbal preparation using common kitchen tools.

Here the essentials you need:

- Mason Jars with screw lid or an airtight lid
- Glass Bottles with screw lid (preferably blue or amber color)
- Small glass bottles with a dropper lid
- Strainers
- Cheesecloth or unbleached coffee filters
- Measuring cups and spoons
- Funnels
- Sticky labels
- Blender

Besides these essential tools, there are many others that definitively make the job easier and faster:

- French press coffee maker

Techniques for Herbal Preparations

For Native Americans, disease and healing were holistic processes that involved both the spirit and the body, so it was essential to them to pray and thank the plant and its spirit for their sacrifice when preparing a remedy, thus converting it into medicine.

Native Americans assumed medications in the following forms:

- Natural form
- Poultice / Powder
- Through Tea/Infusions
- As Tinctures
- As Salves

I decided to add some more preparation techniques that can be prepared in the comfort

In the next paragraphs, we will go over the essentials you need, the ingredients required and the most simple herbal preparations you can do in the comfort of your kitchen to wet your feet in the herbalism world. Lastly, I will give you some advice to make your way easier and safer.

- Thermos
- Herb grinder or Mortar and Pestle
- Kitchen planetary mixer

Ingredients

Besides herbs and water, below you can find the list of the other ingredients that you need to prepare powerful herbal remedies:

- Alcohol
- Honey (possibly from a local supplier to avoid contaminants)
- Beeswax
- Coconut Oil
- Oils (both from vegetal and animal source)
- Capsules (00 sizes)
- Rosewater
- Sea Salt or Epsom Salt
- Apple Cider Vinegar

of your kitchen that will bring this ancient knowledge to the 21st century.

Raw herbs consumption

Herbs can also be consumed in their natural or dried state. They can be eaten (like Osha for respiratory issues) or if finely powdered applied on wounds and burns to facilitate healing (like Echinacea).

Cold Infusion

An **Infusion** is made by mixing cold or hot water with herbs.

Essential for the success of this preparation is the quality of water. Rainwater, spring water, well

water, will be my best choice but if they are not available distilled water is the best option.

If the herb has a strong fragrance it can be infused in cold water, but most of the infusions work better with a warm one. Due to the low temperature of the water, the preparation time is long, from an hour to overnight.

The general rules when managing herbs for infusions are :

- Leaves: 1 oz. of dried herbs for 32 oz. of hot water. Let rest 4 hours minimum in mason jars with the lid screwed on.
- Flowers: 1 oz. of dried herbs for 32 oz. of hot water. Let rest 2 hours minimum in mason jars with the lid screwed on
- Seeds: 1 oz. of dried herbs for 16 oz. of hot water. Let rest 1 hour minimum in mason jars with the lid screwed on.
- Barks and Roots: 1 oz. of dried herbs for 16 oz. of hot water. Let rest 8 hours minimum in mason jars with the lid screwed on.

Cold infusions can be kept in the fridge for a maximum of 2 days.

Hot Infusion / Tea

Preparing a **Hot Infusion or a Tea** just consists of pouring "just off the boiling" water over the soft part of fresh or dried herbs (flowers/leaves). It follows the same rules of the cold infusion regarding the proportions between water and herbs but the preparation times drastically reduce to half an hour to an hour.

Hot infusions can be kept in the fridge for a maximum of 2 days.

Decoction

A decoction is a solution obtained by boiling the hard part of the herbs (stems, seeds, roots, bark) in the water for at least 10 minutes. The high temperature allows the phytochemicals to dissolve in the water and to be extracted even from the hardest of the roots.

Recommended dosages for each cup of water is 1 tsp. dried root/bark or 4 tsp. fresh root/bark.

The general rule of thumb regarding the preparation timings is that the mixture must be boiled until it is reduced by half.

An important feature to take care of is to never prepare decoction into aluminum containers.

Also, decoctions can be kept in the fridge for a maximum of 2 days.

Poultice

This method is just one step over the raw consumption of the herb. It obviously consists of the pounding and of fresh herbs. Alternatively, the maceration of dried herbs with some water can be considered a poultice too. It is the most indicated preparation for topical applications.

Powder

Powders are simply made by grinding the dried part of the herbs. This preparation is then put into gelatin 00 capsules for direct ingestion.

A simple example you can use in no time regarding this preparation technique is probably one of the best available treatments of diarrhea. In fact, you can simply put the cinnamon powder into 00 capsules. Take four maximum per day. Once in the stomach gelatin will dissolve and the powder will absorb water, making an astringent action. Cinnamon with its emollient phytochemicals will soothe the inflamed part of your bowels.

Powders can be obtained at home with the simple pounding in a mortar for the dried soft part of the plant. In case you want to powder roots or barks, my go-to advice is to buy the powder in your herbal shop or to use your kitchen planetary mixer toolbox (many have grinding tools to attach to the central body of the machine).

Fomentation

This preparation simply consists of the application on a wound or injury of a linen or cotton rag soaked in a warm decoction.

Single Extraction

The method to obtain an herb extraction is quite simple. You just need a non-metallic, dark container with an airtight lid (I use an amber glass bottle with a screw lid) and the herb or root of your choice.

Chop the herb or the root, put it in the amber glass bottle, and cover it with a 50% alcohol-water solution. A rough dosage for this preparation is to prepare 8 oz. of alcohol-water solution for each oz. of fresh herb or root. Of course, you have to adjust on the spot the effective quantity needed to cover the chopped herb.

To ensure airtightness, use plastic wrap: cut a small four inches strip, fold it in four by length, place it on the bottle mouth just and then tighten the screw lid. The thin plastic wrap will seal completely the bottle.

Then the container must seat in the fridge for 2 weeks. Be sure to shake it once a day minimum for optimal result.

Lastly, at the end of the two weeks, strain the solution filter paper. If you don't have access to filter paper you can simply use unbleached coffee filters.

Double Extraction

Double extraction is a preparation method that uses the waste of the single extraction. Place the residuals you found in your unbleached coffee filter, in a saucepan. Add 8 oz. of distilled water for every ounce of the residual and put it on high heat. Once it gets to a boil, reduce the heat to low and let simmer for half an hour. Let the decoction cool down, strain it, and add it to the single extraction.

Percolation

This preparation consists of dripping water or alcohol over powder of dried herbs. To give you a practical example, it is what happens in your coffee machine. The recommended weight ratio between powdered herb and water is 1:10.

Tincture

Moving to more advanced techniques, we found the tincture, which consists of the maceration of minced herbs with alcoholic solutions (usually 95% or 50% alcohol).

The recommended weight ratio between herbs and the 50% Alcohol solution for tinctures preparation is 1:5 in case you use dried herbs and 1:2 in case you use fresh herbs.

Be sure to use amber jars when preparing tinctures. The soaking time for tincture is 2 weeks in a shadowy place, to avoid any contact with the sunlight. After two weeks, tinctures can be filtered using cheesecloth or unbleached coffee filters and put into an amber glass bottle with a dropper lid. Be sure to label them with the exact preparation date and to preserve them in a shadowy place.

If preserved this way, tinctures may endure for years.

Oils

In this preparation, herbs are "cooked" in warm oil to extract the phytochemicals. The combination of temperature and chemical compatibility between the oil and the phytochemical makes this method one of the bests to extract and concentrate the medical principles of the plant.

Instructions for Dried Herbs

- Finely pound your dried herbs of choice with mortar and pestle. The use of these tools are preferred because they do not overheat the herbs like a blender preserving their phytochemicals
- Transfer them into a glass dish and submerge them with the oil of your choice (olive, canola…). No part of the herb must be exposed.
- Cook in the oven at low temperature for 10 hours at 170°F

- Let them cool and strain it using cheesecloth.
- Be sure to squeeze out all the oil from the cheesecloth.

Instructions for Fresh Herbs

- Chop the herbs, put them in a mason jar and cover them with oil so no part of them is exposed. Close the lid.
- Let sit in the sun for 2 weeks
- Strain the mixture using cheesecloth, squeezing out all the oil.
- Let the oil rest one day. The water contained in the herbs will naturally go to the bottom of the jar and can be easily discarded when decanting

Salves

Once you get your oil infusion, preparing Salves is relatively easy. You just have to pour the oil into a stainless steel cooking pan and heat very gently on a stove. When the oil is warm, add beeswax and stir.

The recommended weight ratio between beeswax and oil is 1:2.

When beeswax is melted, place a few drops of the mixture on the plate to check consistency and, if needed, add more beeswax/oil if it is too soft/hard.

Once you reach the perfect consistency, pour the mix in a mason jar and let it cool uncovered.

IMPORTANT: heat destroys the precious phytochemicals, so do not ever surpass 170°F temperature

Tips for Success

Lastly, I want to write five essential tips that will make the job easier for you, and that will

prevent you from commit mistakes and errors that could compromise the results and the effectiveness of your remedies.

- Label: it is essential to label everything to be sure what you are taking in.
- Start small: Begin with small batches of each remedy. You will test what works for you and what doesn't and you will not break the bank. Once you learn, scaling up is always easy.

About Drying Herbs

Regarding the supply of the herbs, if you want to resort to wildcrafting it is essential that you learn how to dry properly your harvest. In this paragraph I prepared a list of 9 points to follow to be sure that you preserve your herbs in the best way possible, so they will maintain intact their medical properties:

1. Preparation :
   o Never wash leaves or flowers. Just shake them to remove dust or insects. Separate leaves and flowers from stems and spread them on a clean table on a single layer.

   If you want to dry big plants, you can hang them upside down in your cellar.

   o Wash carefully underwater roots and barks to remove mud and dirt. Then spread them on a clean table on a single layer.

Preservation times of preparations

Mason jars are for sure the best containers to preserve your herbs and preparations: they are cheap, available in every store, and with an airtight lid.

The only problem with them is that they are transparent and allow sunlight to radiate directly to the herbs, thus compromising their medical properties. Amber or cobalt glass would be the best for the preservation of herbs and herbal remedies but unfortunately, amber glass bottles are quite expensive and not widely available.

- Prepare every remedy in the proper size. Do not prepare too much of them or you will risk wasting it because they went bad.
- Consult your doctor or herbalist if you are assuming pharmaceutical drugs: the combined effect of drugs and herbs can cause unpleasant side effects.
- Check the substances before using: look for signs of mold and always check the integrity of the packages before using a certain remedy.

2. Cover the herbs with cheesecloth. This will shield them from insects or bugs and will ensure proper ventilation.
3. Scrape the outer layer in case you use barks (in jargon, tossing)
4. Dry your herbs in a well-ventilated, shaded area such as an attic.
5. Herbs drying time: usually one week. If the herbs have a fragrant smell and brittles when pinched, then it is ready.
6. Roots and Barks drying time: three weeks to a month. Cut a specimen in half and check if the inside is completely dry.
7. Once the herbs are dried store them in mason jars with the lid well closed and label them. Preservation time of dried herbs is 1 to 4 years.
8. Be sure to store your herbs and preparation far from sunlight and excessive heat.
9. Try to dry whole, uncut herbs because they will have more intense healing properties.

The trick you can use, as a beginner, to avoid this problem is to use common mason jars but to store them in a cellar or any place far away from direct sunlight. With this single trick, you will increase the endurance of your herbs or preparation by 5 times.

Below the typical endurance times, you can expect using this method

- Dried herbs: 1 to 4 years
- Tinctures: 7 years
- Oils and salves: 6-12 months

Native American Herbal Apothecary

Spirituality and Practices of Native American for Today's Medicine Men

BOOK 2 of "The Native American Herbalist's Bible"

Natalie Hathale

Spirituality in Native American Medicine

No matter what your beliefs are, when studying Native American traditional medicine, soon or later a discussion on spirituality is always necessary.

Natives believed in the healing of the body through the healing of the spirit and a reunion of it with a higher power.

The name of this higher power can change from tribe to tribe but all the stories agree on the fact that it created everything we can see: from the meadows to the rivers, to the mountains, to the animals that inhabit the lands. To each of its creations, it granted gifts for its own sustainment,

thriving, and well-being. Each creation (and us among them) is in perfect balance with the others. In this view, it is easy to understand why the healers of the tribes were also religious figures and healing was ceremonial in nature. The healing process involved not only drinking a decoction or applying a poultice but also a deep reconnection to our most profound nature, to tap into the spiritual power within and around us to be born again. Among Native Americans, it was a common belief that sickness comes from men forgetting their place in nature, without periodically renewing their connection with the Mother.

In this experiencing and re-experiencing the connection with nature men can find their balance in life, knowing exactly their place and being aware of the greater picture. We will see the most important ceremonies in the next paragraphs but, before that, it is important to state that herbs, being the purest expression of nature, granted the practitioner the power to experience the awareness of the deep connection between men and nature.

Smudging

Smudging was the mandatory preparation for more complex ceremonies.

It simply consisted of burning a bundle of herbs and « bathing » in its smoke and ashes. Both the healer and the other participants must attend this event. It is the sign that what will follow is sacred.

The herbs commonly used for smudging were cedar, sage, thyme, and peppermint.

The ceremony simply consists of the healer preparing a bundle of the dried herbs and setting it on fire. Then, he

extinguishes the fire and lets the bundle reduce to embers, fanning the smoke toward himself and towards each person the takes part in the ceremony, bathing them in the sacred smoke.

Sacred Pipe

The pipe is an undeniably important sacred object for all the Native American tribes. It was used in many healing and sacred ceremonies; its presence enhanced the effect of the medicine and called to gather all the spirits of the earth.

The pipe, in all its parts, has a deep meaning: the bowl represents the female nature of life, the nurturing, the Mother Earth; the stem represents the male part, the Father Sky; the tube that connects stem and bowl, represents the connection between the visible and material world with the invisible and spiritual one.

As a complete object, it represents the thin line the man must walk to live in balance with nature. Once assembled, the pipe is the joining of all the aspects of life in one single object; it reconnects the multi-faced aspects of reality into a single entity.

The healer had the right to choose the herbs to be smoked during the ceremony (usually they were tobacco, uva ursi, sage, thyme, raspberry, and willow). Before smoking, the healer offered small pinches of tobacco to the four directions, the plants and the animal kingdom, the sky, the earth, the mother, the sun, and the moon. With this, all the elements witnessed and were invited to the ceremony.

The one who carries the pipe is not its owner, but rather he is its keeper. He is the one who is entrusted by the whole tribe to be the intermediary with the Great Spirit, and due to this power is was taken into great consideration. Smoking was praying: each inspiration of smoke was a prayer to the Great Spirit and all its manifestation in the world.

The keeper and the pipe were deeply connected. The pipe spoke to him and created the connection between the material and the spiritual world. The more experienced the keeper, the stronger was this connection.

The Sacred Pipe Ceremony

The Sacred Pipe Ceremony is a moment of profound reconnection with the deepest nature that lies within ourselves. During the ceremony, we surpass our senses and achieve a deeper sense of meaning.

Although each tribe has its own specific rituals and peculiarities regarding the sacred pipe ceremony, the essence is very similar between all of them. Each part of the ceremony has a proper etiquette, motivated by an important, sacred meaning.

The first step of the ceremony is smudging: the bundle is lit and the participants (pipe keeper first) are smudged using a bird feather.

When all the people have been smudged, it is the turn of the parts that will be assembled to form

the pipe: first the stem north to south and then west to east, then the bowl in the same way.

Smoke must penetrate all the cavities of the stem and the bowl to purify the pipe in each of its parts.

This part of the ceremony is very evocative and it gives you the possibility to concentrate on the healer and to calm your inner dialogue so you will be prepared for what comes next.

Once the smudging is completed, the bowl and stem are held up high, respectively in the left and in the right hand, and permission to smoke is requested to the Great Spirit.

Here the pipe keeper acts as an intermediary between the spiritual and the material world for the first time: he evokes the Spirit and attunes with It, looking for signs of the granted

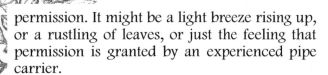

permission. It might be a light breeze rising up, or a rustling of leaves, or just the feeling that permission is granted by an experienced pipe carrier.

Granted permission, the healer joins the two parts of the pipe. As already stated, this is a very important and sacred moment because it represents the joining of all the parts of life and the reconciliation of all the dualisms. The entire universe becomes one single entity.

After the junction of the two parts, it comes the filling part. The stem is laid down on the lap of the healer and the bowl on the ground.

The healer takes four pinches of the smoking mixture one at a time, he holds them up high and puts them inside the bowl with the right hand.

Each time he fills the bowl he asks an entity to join the Sacred Pipe. In order, he calls for the Great Spirit, the spirits of trees and greens, the spirits of the animals that walk, swim, or fly, and finally the four elements of fire, water, air, and stone.

With each pinch, he invites a part of the material and spiritual world to join the ceremony.

A lot of experience and practice is requested from the carrier to actually feel these elements joining the ceremony and to be able to talk with them.

In the next phase, each one of the attendants places his prayers into the pipe holding the bowl of the pipe with the left hand. The first is the pipe keeper, and then the one on his left, and so on until the circle is completed. Prayers might not be necessarily requests or desires but also tanks or worries that the participants want to share with others and the spirits.

Once the circle is completed, the pipe comes back to the healer who lights it with big puffs of smoke without inhaling. Then, the carrier holds it up high, stem higher, and offers the pipe to the Creator, the first to smoke.

Also in this phase, the sensitivity of the carrier is vital because he must sense the Creator to come and smoke the pipe. Once the Creator accepted the first smoke, the pipe is lowered down and passed to mother earth, and then to the four directions.

Once all the spirits had their smoke, it is the healer's turn to smoke, and subsequently, the others, starting from the left.

The inhalation of the smoke is a moment of deep connection between the one who smokes and the Spirit: each prayer that has been placed inside the pipe, becomes smoke and it blends with the smoker. With the exhalation of smoke, the prayer diffuses in the universe, towards the Creator, but a part of it remains with the one who expressed it.

The pipe passes to the left until all the smoking mixture is gone. Once the pipe is empty, the carrier expresses his final thanks to the Great Spirit for generously gave them permission to smoke and then he cleans and puts the pipe away.

Medicine Wheel

As the Sacred Pipe, also the **Medicine Wheel** is an ancient notion of the Native Americans (and not only them), which purpose was to reconcile the different parts of one reality to their oneness.

We are made by different personalities, which coexist, in the same body. Inside you, there is the child, the nurturing mother, the wise, the hot-tempered teenager, the hunter, and many others.

Each one is part of you, and you cannot be you without any of them. There will be parts angry with you for not having given them the proper consideration and attention in the past, and parts of you that are taking the stage too much often.

Over time, it is important that you can establish a good relationship with all of your parts, giving them the proper space to express themselves so they are happy and feel appreciated.

You want them to be your partner in life, without working against your interests because they are upset or unsatisfied. This wholeness is crucial for the actions you take in life.

It is incredible how this ancient and intuitive concept of the Native Americans, resembles the Analytic Psychology of Carl Gustav Jung. According to Jung, the subconscious was not the place where the removed memories and complexes were "stored", but rather, using a

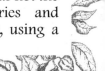

metaphor, an intricate bundle of many archetypal personalities.

Each personality has its own desires and capacities, and it interacts with others and with the conscious Ego. The psychic dynamics of everyone derive from the relationships and the clashes among personalities and between each personality and the consciousness.

Phenomena like self-sabotage and any psychological inversion behavior can be easily explained with this concept.

Native Americans were widely aware of this concept before Jung and most of their religious practices were oriented to the reconciliation of the opposites into the oneness of your person.

As an example, I recall here an ancient Hopi exercise to start establishing a dialogue with your inner selves. It may take some time a day for some months, but the results and the improvement you will experience in your day-to-day life will be astonishing:

- Find a quiet spot in which you can stay uninterrupted for some ten minutes a day. Seat comfortably and take two or three deep breaths to relax.
- Imagine you are walking in a meadow. It is a sunny, beautiful day and the sky is clear and blue. The only noise you hear is the blowing of the wind and the rustling of the grass when you cross it. There is only you.
- After walking some time you find an old house in the middle of the fields. You open the front door and you find yourself in a very big room with a big round table in the middle.
- The table has seats. Many are taken by other people or animals, many not. This is your inner circle.
- Find yourself a comfortable chair. Seat down and talk in turn to all the other people you find there.
- Who they are? What's their story? What do they want? How can you help them?
- Be sure to find an agreement with all of your personalities. You will be surprised how fast your life will change without any more self-sabotages and with single-minded actions.

The medicine wheel expresses this concept: we are a wholeness of different parts and we must find a way to be in a good relationship with all of them if we want to thrive in this life with balance and harmony.

This concept can be extended from the oneness of yourself to the oneness of your family and your community and so on to the whole universe.

Native Americans knew the simple truth of the many that are one and indeed they created the Medicine wheel ceremony to restore the wholeness of life.

In this ceremony, the practitioner must build a circle with stones. This simple act creates an upward spiral of positive energy and all the forces of life participate in this wheel of life in order to create this holy place of unity and harmony.

By creating himself a place of harmony and peace, the practitioner is giving back to the Creator some of the order and harmony he received.

Each stone represents a member of the community or a member of your personality, who can come freely and be heard in what he/she has to say.

At the center of the Circle, there is the biggest stone of all, which represents the Spirit, the core of everything.

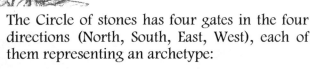

The Circle of stones has four gates in the four directions (North, South, East, West), each of them representing an archetype:

- South: Represents beginning, childhood, spring, hope, and vitality. It symbolizes renewal

- West: Struggle, Adolescence, research for meaning and identity. It represents the quests into the darkest traits of our personalities, the passage "through the shadow", as Jung said, to find who we really are. In this sector of the circle, we suffer from the deprivation of the things we think are important. The west is the symbol of the painful deconstruction.

- North: It is the time of middle age, maintaining balance, taking care of the others, and altruism

- East: it is the time of old age, time of rest, wisdom, and enlightenment. It is the phase when you abandon the entire material world and you are more sensitive to the spiritual one.

As for the sacred pipe, also for the medicine wheel, there is more below the surface. Each element has a deeper meaning and purpose and all can be used to reach the well-being of the individuals.

How to Build a Medicine Wheel

Medicine Wheels are not other than "circles" of stones put in specific places to symbolize specific elements of the personality. Similar ceremonial constructions can be found all over the world and throughout human history: Stonehenge and the Japanese Karesansui gardens are examples of what I am talking about.

Building a Medicine Wheel is indeed quite easy.

First, you have to find a suitable place to build your medicine wheel. Do not worry too much about the space you have available. As with most of the Native American ceremonies, the effectiveness depends on the intention of the practitioner. As long as you are really committed to the construction of a Medicine Wheel, you deeply understand the meaning behind what you are doing, and you do it with purpose, a quiet corner in your yard or even in your flat will be enough to ripe the benefits.

When you feel a place is good, smudge it with sage, thank the place for having revealed to you and declare your intention to build a medicine wheel there.

Now the real work begins: you have to gather and select the rocks for your medicine wheel. You can simply go to the woods or to the seaside to find rocks of all sizes, suitable for your purpose.

Pray for the place to help and guide you; declare your intention to build a Medicine Wheel while looking for suitable stones around you.

Medicine Wheels require a minimum of 25 stones: a big one for the center, two to mark each gate, and four stones between each gate.

Select the rocks' size depending on the space available in your yard or flat, and smudge each stone you find, thanking the spirit for its help. Whenever you decide to pick a stone, leave a tobacco offering to the place as compensation.

Once you have all your stones in the place you want to build your medicine wheel, thank them for their help in building your Medicine Wheel and ask each of the stones where they prefer to be put and place there.

You will be surprised by the sense of accomplishment you will feel once you complete your Medicine Wheel.

Remember, Medicine wheels are living things: you have to take care of the wheel with proper maintenance (removing weeds, brushing the stones to remove the dirt) and you can always rearrange the circle or add more stones.

The Wheel is a metaphor for yourself, your life, your family, and your community. Taking care of it is taking care of each of them.

Sweat Lodge

Sweat Lodges "healing tools" diffused in all the Native American Tribes. They are essentially

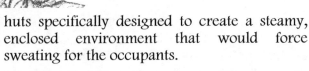
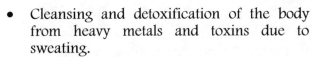
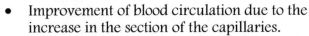

huts specifically designed to create a steamy, enclosed environment that would force sweating for the occupants.

Traditionally they allow ten to fifteen people inside, in complete darkness. The steam is produced by the healer who pours water over hot stones, placed at the center of the hut.

The healer is of fundamental importance in this ceremony because it controls the atmosphere inside the hut and accompanies the spiritual healing process by chanting and praying.

The recommended timing to pass inside a sweat lodge is fifteen minutes; after that, the healer opens the door of the hut and encourages participants to go out and cover themselves with blankets inside a normal tent. After half an hour, the participants have to have a cold bath or shower.

If properly conducted the sweat lodge ceremony can bring many benefits:

- Immune System Boost due to the increase in body temperature

- Cleansing and detoxification of the body from heavy metals and toxins due to sweating.
- Improvement of blood circulation due to the increase in the section of the capillaries.
- Clearing of the airways from mucus and phlegm by the steam. The moist helps in the treatment of minor airway dysfunctions and colds. Warning: do not use in case of serious lung diseases such as pneumonia
- Liver detoxification and improvement of digestion and nurturing substances absorption.

Each tribe used their own technique to build the sweat lodge: they could be almost subterranean structures or they could be real huts made with the materials available in their environments like wood, mud, or animal pelts.

WARNING: Sweat lodge ceremonies can be dangerous for people who suffer from blood pressure problems (both Hypo and Hypertension), heart problems and in case of epilepsies, pregnancy, menstruation, fever, dermatological ailments, and local or general inflammations.

Build Your Own Sweat Lodge

As already stated, sweat lodges are essentially huts to promote sweating. For this purpose, you can use a sauna, if you have one, or you can build your own hut in your backyard. The « standard » dimensions for a sweat lodge are 10 feet in diameter, with a dome 2 to 3 feet tall.

It is easier than it seems, you only have to put in some hard work.

Below the list of the recommended materials but you can use your creativity in case you don't have exactly these items:

- 16 flexible poles, 3 to 4 feet long. My go-to choice for the material would be white willow saplings but you can use whatever you find suitable for the application.
- Canvas to create the sidewalls.

The first thing you have to take care of when building a sweat lodge is to be sure to have a source of freshwater near-by to cool the body after the ceremony. A river or a lake would be perfect but a shower or a bath could do the job quite easily. Once you identify a suitable spot, clear the ground from rocks and leaves and

trace a circle roughly ten feet in diameter. Cut the circle by tracing also the North-South direction and the East-West direction. Use this trace as a reference for the next work phases.

Dig a pit in the center of the circle. Recommended dimensions for the pit are diameter 3 feet – depth 2 feet.

Plant the poles on the external perimeter of the circle, one foot deep in the ground, equally spaced. Be sure to leave room for the entrance of the lodge aligned to the east and the rising sun.

After that, join the ends of the poles to create a dome. Use canvas or any other material to create the walls of the hut, shielding the lodge from light and heat dispersion. Be sure to leave an entrance and to have something to cover it once all the participants to the ceremony are in.

Lastly, create a fire pit just outside of the lodge to heat the stones.

Now all the hard work has been done and the real ceremony can start. First, light the fire on the outside fire pit, which will be symbolic of the sun. Once it is well hot, offer it a pinch of

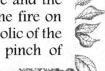

tobacco and place the stones in it to get hot. The rocks themselves are symbolic of mother earth.

In the meantime, bring some water to a boil. Water should be enough to prepare herbal tea for all the participants. The traditional Navajo recipe includes peppermint, chamomile, catnip, sage, and powdered ginger root (1 tsp of each for every 2 cups).

Once the stones are hot enough, use some thick leather gloves to avoid burning your hands while bringing them inside the pit of the sweat lodge.

When all the stones and participants are inside the sweat lodge, close the door and pour water on the hot stones. Water is the symbol of life and the steam, produced when it touches the hot stones, is symbolic of the Spirit.

Drink your herbal tea during the ceremony, it will help you increase sweating and keep you hydrated.

Be sure to stay in the sweat lodge for no more than 15 minutes. Then wrap up in a blanket and cool down outside the lodge for about half an hour. When you feel comfortable, take a cold shower or bath in the nearby stream.

Build Your Own Removable Sweat Lodge in the Wilderness

You don't need to have access to a yard or permanently dig your garden to ripe the benefits of the sweat lodge ceremony.

It is indeed quite easy to make a small, removable sweat lodge in the wilderness that can easily welcome four people inside.

You only need an old dome tent and have some extra care and you can do it safely and with minimal effort:

- Choose a suitable spot for assembling your sweat lodge: choose a flat, rocky surface near to a stream or a lake. Avoid muddy spots.

- Cut a circle on the bottom of an old dome tent leaving at least 10 inches from the edge. With this trick, you will have a tent that maintains its shape once assembled with a rocky floor in the middle.

- Follow the instruction in the previous paragraph to conduct properly a sweat lodge ceremony, being cautious to avoid any contact of the hot rocks with the plastic parts of the tent.

AMAZING BONUSES FOR ALL THE READERS:

Just Scan the QR-Code below to get them!

Native American Herbalism in practice

Now that you have the basic knowledge of Native American herbal remedies, I think it is time for you to get your feet wet and start looking at some interesting herbs you can easily find in your herbal shop. With these herbs you can start preparing simple herbal remedies for you and your family.

Ashwagandha (Indian Ginseng)

The tea obtained by mixing 1 tsp of powdered root in 1 cup of boiling water is effective in case of stomachache and indigestion. Another effect of it is related to the treatment of stress and anxiety. The recommended use of the above tea is one cup maximum, to be drunk three or four times throughout the day. Another use of the Ashwagandha is related to the poultice obtained from pounding the fresh leaves. This can be used as an antibiotic and anti-inflammatory remedy for topical application on wounds. Warning: Due to its sedative characteristics, it may interact with the following drugs: Anticonvulsants, Antipsycotcs, Benzodiazepine, Sedatives, Fenitonine, Antidepressive drugs.

Blackberries

Leaves of blueberry can be reduced in a poultice with mortar and pestle and applied on swollen joints for anti-inflammatory medication or to stop bleeding.

They are also an excellent emergency medication in case you hurt yourself in the woods. Just chew blackberry leaves and apply the poultice in the wound to stop the bleeding and for an antiseptic action.

The tea you obtain from dried leaves is perfect for treating diarrhea and minor intestinal disorders.

Finally, a less-known use of the blackberry is a remedy for sore throats created by its roots: after accurately wash them to remove the dirt, reduce them to poultice with mortar and pestle; Mix this poultice with honey to create an effective syrup for sore throats and cough.

Black Gum

This deciduous tree can grow up to eighty feet tall. The wide central trunk is covered by scaled and deeply indented brown-red bark. Many leafy brown-reddish branches depart from the central trunk in any direction. Leaves are alternate and lance-shaped with smooth edges. The yellow flowers are both male and female and grow in round clusters on elongated peduncles. The decoction obtained from black gum bark will help in the treatment of minor respiratory conditions. Bark decoction was also effective as a wash during difficult childbirth. Finally, the "jelly juice" of the root was used as an eyewash.

Cattails

This Long, spear-shaped plant can grow up to 8 feet tall and is widely diffused in wet environments (lakeshores, bogs, streams…) all over the North American continent. It produces two flowers during spring that resemble hot-dogs on a stick. The thicker one, located in the lower part of the plant is the female one; the upper one is the male flower, which disappears after the dispersion of all the pollen. Native Americans widely used the decoction of roots as a topical treatment for sunburns due to its emollient characteristics. Also, the flowers were used to treat wounds because they stop the bleeding and absorb excessive moisture. In addition, ashes obtained by burning leaves are antiseptic and were used to seal wounds and burns. Besides the medical application of the plant, natives used it as food: in detail, roots were dried and grinder to obtain flour for bread and porridge, while hearts were boiled and eaten as vegetables.

Ceanothus Cuneatus (Buck Brush)

This wonderful herb was used by natives to treat mouth and throat inflammation and also cysts.

Its leaves if reduced in poultice are perfect for treating burns, blisters, and wounds in general.

Also, the decoction of its roots has cleansing properties on kidneys and liver and will help reduce high blood pressure.

Devil's claw

The decoction of Devil's Claw is useful for fever and digestion ailments. Also, salves from this herb can help in the treatment of skin conditions.

A poultice from this fresh plant will help with joint pain and arthritis.

Green Briar Root

The decoction obtained from this root is helpful for blood detoxifying and has anti-inflammatory properties.

Preparing salves from this root will help to relieve joint pain.

Honeysuckle

The decoction of this fresh herb is used to treat mild respiratory diseases such as asthma, while its poultice is applied on swollen or arthritic joints to reduce the pain.

Native Americans used the tea obtained from flowers to treat diarrhea and fever, due to its astringent qualities. The said tea was used also as a gargle in the treatment of sore throat and laryngitis and as a topical wash to soothe common skin ailments like eczema and rash.

Finally, the bark tea was used in the treatment of Urinary Tract Infections and as a lenitive for the symptoms of gonorrhea and other Sexual Transmitted Diseases such as syphilis.

Licorice root

Native Americans widely used the licorice for medical purposes, mainly related to stomach conditions. In fact, the decoction prepared with the peeled, dried root was used for laxative purposes in case of constipation. Another use of this tea was to reduce the fever because the diaphoretic substances contained in it induced sweat on the patient.

Other medical uses of the wild licorice were related to the tea of leaves, used as a topical medicament for earache, and the raw root consumption for toothache and sore throat.

Finally, the poultice obtained from the fresh root was used topically on swollen joints in case of rheumatism or gout.

WARNING: it increased blood pressure, so it is not advised in case of hypertension.

Mint

This small plant emerges from the basal rhizome as a straight green stem with a square section, bearing many lance-shaped leaves. These are bright green, aromatic, and with serrated margins. The small flowers appear in whorls at the top of the plant in different colors, depending on the species (white for peppermint, blue or purple for other species of mint).A decoction of mint leaves will soothe an upset stomach. Also chewing fresh leaves will have a positive effect on it.

Mullein

The demulcent effect of the mullein (leaves and flowers) were widely known by Native

Americans who used it in decoction and teas to treat mild respiratory conditions, from cough to nasal congestion.

The action of mullein was frequently paired with the one of other plants like thyme and rosemary.

The poultice obtained from fresh leaves was used to treat wounds, swellings, and skin ailments such as rashes, while dried ones were smoked to induce cough and expectorate the phlegm.

Note: Mullein is particularly indicated for beginner gardeners because it can easily grow in yards.

Prickly Pear Cactus

Also, this plan was used for both sustainment and healing.

The poultice obtained from the pads with mortar and pestle is an effective antiseptic and can be used to treat wounds and burns in general.

The tea obtained by boiling its pads is wonderful for UTI and for lowering cholesterol levels.

Romero

A decoction of Romero leaves will soothe an upset stomach. Also, if drunk frequently, it has positive effects for pain relief on sore joints, muscle pain, and on your cardio-circulatory system.

Red Clover

This wonderful herb is perfect if prepared as a tea to deal with minor respiratory conditions due to its strong anti-inflammatory properties. The benefits that this tea will bring to your life also regard the cardio-circulatory system because it is proven that it helps in reducing cholesterol levels and in strengthening the capillaries walls.

Sage

This is probably the most common sacred plant among Native Americans. It is used in any smudging or pipe ceremony as an intermediary with the Creator and to purify from negative energies.

Also, its decoction has healing properties for stomach pain and colds.

Saw palmetto

This plant was used both for sustainment and for medical purposes. Its decoction helps digestive problems and helps lowering excessive fever.

Slippery Elm

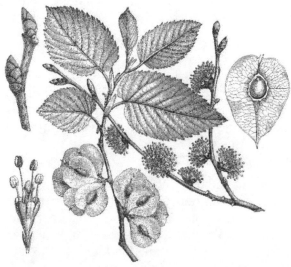

The decoction obtained from its inner bark or the tea obtained from its leaves is used to treat toothaches and mild respiratory conditions.

The poultice obtained from the leaves can be used to relieve insect bites, while on the fields.

Sumac

Sumac thrives in forests and fields all over the South-Eastern United States. Complex preparations of this herb were used by Natives to treat eye problems like conjunctivitis but many other problems could be treated by the decoction of its leaves.

In fact, gargling the decoction will help with a sore throat and the drinking of it has astringent properties.

Furthermore, the poultice you can create from fresh leaves or berries has anti-inflammatory properties in the treatment of skin rash and urticaria.

Uva ursi

Leaves of Bearberry were widely used by natives both for medical and ceremonial purposes. It was a sacred plant used in every important Native American ceremony, especially in the sacred pipe one.

Also, its medical applications are many: from the topical application of leaves poultice to treat wounds and stop bleeding due to its astringent characteristics, to the decoction of leaves and berries, used to treat bladder and kidney problems or as a mild analgesic.

Also, the salve obtained from leaves was used for rashes and sores: leaves were cooked at very low temperature in animal fat for one day. To reach the right thickness, beeswax was added to the strained melted fat.

A simple preparation you can do in the comfort of your kitchen to benefit from this incredible plant is the Phytochemicals Alcoholic Extraction. By simply soaking the leaves in alcohol for one week in a mason jar, shielded from the light you can obtain a powerful analgesic for headaches. The recommended dosage is one teaspoon of the alcoholic extraction in a cup of water two times a day.

Wild ginger

The most common use of wild ginger among Natives was the preparation of oils to treat ear infections.

The decoction obtained from the roots helps in digestive ailments, intestinal gas, nausea, and mild bronchial problems.

Wild rose

The wild rose tea is perfect as a preventive cure for seasonal, common colds. It has diuretic properties and an anti-inflammatory effect on sore throats if gargled.

Yarrow

This herb derives its Binomial Name (Achillea millefolium) from the Greek hero Achilles which legend says used her to cure his wounds.

In fact, it has very powerful anti-hemorrhagic properties.

The best way to use it is fresh: using a mortar and a pestle, create a poultice from the leaves, and apply it directly on the wound to stop bleeding.

Another less known application of the Yarrow is related to the treatment of diarrhea and other simple intestinal disorders.

In fact, simply extracting its juice from the leaves (with a juicer) and mixing it with water or by preparing a tea with fresh leaves, will soothe an upset stomach.

AMAZING BONUSES FOR ALL THE READERS:

Just Scan the QR-Code below to get them!

Conclusion

In this second book, we have covered the basic knowledge of Native American Herbal medicine, with a deep focus on the preparation techniques and the storage methods.

We have seen the most common plants that Natives used for their day-to-day healing and we provided useful tips and tools for you to gather your wild plants by yourself. Lastly, I described to you the most important sacred and healing ceremonies of the Natives with details on the meaning behind each of them, giving you the basics to understand the Native American spirituality.

I sincerely hope that this will be just the beginning of your journey and that you will increase your knowledge on Native American medicine for a healthier and better way to treat the common disease without relying on industrial drugs and medication.

If you have enjoyed this book, feel free to leave a review to share your experience.

Just scan the QR code on the right, it will take 30 seconds!

My best wishes and may the Spirit guide your journey!

Native American Herbal Encyclopedia

The Complete Abies to Zizia Field Book of North American Medicine Plants Used by Natives.
Find, Gather, Grow and Harvest Your Own Medical Herbs

BOOKS 3, 4 and 5 of "The Native American Herbalist's Bible"

Natalie Hathale

Introduction

"The Circle has healing power. In the Circle, we are all equal. When in the Circle, no one is in front of you. No one is above you. No one is below you. The Sacred Circle is designed to create unity. The Hoop of Life is also a circle. On this hoop, there is a place for every species, every race, every tree, and every plant. In this completeness of Life must be respected in order to bring health on this planet"

Dave Chief, Oglala Lakota

Nature is a generous mother and gives her sons all the tools they need to thrive in harmony with each other.

This is the philosophy that stands behind the Native American way of life and that gave motive to their everyday actions.

They respected plants and animals and revered them as brothers and sisters. They never forgot to express gratitude to nature whenever they gathered fruits or killed an animal for sustenance.

It was usual for Natives to leave offerings of their precious tobacco whenever they picked fruits from a tree or to wear the fangs of a bear to show respect for the life and the strength they were forced to take from the earth.

They reflected this holistic approach also to medicine. A remedy must not be the mere solution to a symptom of a disease but it must correct the unbalance on one's body that manifested itself as that disease.

In this view, their approach was very different from western medicine that heavily relies on pharmaceutical drugs.

These substances, although brought us many advantages, take a high price in terms of our long-term well-being. They rely on chemical compounds that force the body to respond in a certain way rather than helping our body to tap into its own healing resources.

The body is passive and gradually impaired by using medications that solve the problem in the short term but that don't make you stronger by forcing you to face the disease and win.

Native American healers worked differently, assisting the body <u>and</u> the spirit to react by itself rather than offering an immediate cure.

Nature, being a generous mother, gave men all they need to heal within the reach of their hands filling the lands, meadows, and mountains with herbs and flowers that contained within themselves the power to stimulate the healing process.

In this second volume of the series, we will provide you a complete encyclopedia of the herbs used by Native North-Americans to cure their bodies and their souls and restore their natural balanced harmony with nature. I also added some other herb commonly used in the herbal medicine as a valuable substitute in case you can't find the Native ones.

In my book series, my purpose is to guide you in rediscovering this ancient wisdom through a structured learning approach that will make you become a daring herbalist starting from zero.

That's why I provide also a botanical and a medical glossary at the end of the book to facilitate your learning and understanding.

In detail, in the first book, I introduced Native American Medicine, with its methods and preparations. You will know where to find the plants, how to harvest them, and how to treat and store them.

Finally, in the third book, you will close the circle, learning what herb to use and the correct preparation techniques to create herbal remedies for the most common ailments and diseases you can encounter.

I tried to join two worlds in this book, by providing you pieces of my ancient culture with its holistic character in a well-structured learning course.

I hope you find this interesting and that reading this book will be just the beginning of your journey...

A

Abies Balsamea

Binomial Name: Abies Balsamea.

Habitat: North of the United States or South of Canada in forests.

Characteristics: Evergreen tree up to 65 ft. tall. The gray bark frequently leaks sap and changes its appearance depending on the age of the plant: smooth for younger trees, coarse for older ones. Leaves are needle green on the upper part, white on the bottom. Cones are 4 inches long and red/purple.

Parts to collect for medical purposes: Sap, Roots, Barks, and Leaves.

Preferred solvent: Boiling Water.

Main effect: Analgesic and Antiseptic.

Native American Use:

The decoction of barks was used to reduce fever and stimulate sweating to detoxify the body. Also, needle tea was used to cure respiratory problems and colds due to its astringent characteristics.

Finally, the sap is used directly to treat burns and close wounds. Raw consumption of it is used to prevent colds and sore throats.

Minor use of this balsamic sap was during the sweat lodge ceremony: the sap was dripped on the hot stones to create aromatic steam.

Agave

Binomial Name: Agave Americana.

Habitat: Southern United States (mainly in California, Arizona, and Nevada) and Mexico.

Characteristics: A squat central stem, barely visible, composes this perennial plant. The succulent leaves are long, pointed, and green-grayish. At the time of its sexual maturity (it can take up to twenty years), it creates a single flower from a central spike and then it dies.

Parts to collect for medical purposes: Leaves.

Preferred solvent: Water or Alcohol.

Main effect: Diuretic, Anti-inflammatory.

Native American Use:

The sap is very sticky and can bond together the edges of a deep wound for emergency medication.

Leaves if assumed in big quantities can result in poisoning. Due to this characteristic, Natives of the South Western states used agave leaves for fishing: they put the leaves in a pond or in a closed area of a river; the poison contained in them temporarily paralyzed fishes that swam that area, so they floated on the surface and became easy pickings.

The juice was used for its anti-inflammatory and diuretic characteristics.

Modern use:

Agave hearts are renowned to be used for tequila production.

Not everyone knows that the Progesterone hormones typically prescribed during pregnancy to help the proper fetal development, are extracted from Agave leaves.

Also, roots are commonly used in the production of natural soaps due to their high content of Saponins: you can indeed create excellent, all-natural soap and shampoo by extracting juice from grating and squeezing agave roots.

Lastly, Agave nectar is used as a sugar substitute due to its low glycemic effect on the body and reducing the fat-burning stop effect that sweet substances have on the body.

Agrimony

Binomial Name: Agrimonia Eupatoria.

Habitat: All over the United States, at the margin of woods and in meadows.

Characteristics: Agrimony is a perennial infesting flower. From the small rhizome a single, erect stem emerges from the ground and can reach up to 30 inches. Leaves are lance-shaped with a serrated margin and have two smaller leaflets with a slightly different shape. Clusters of small yellow flowers with five petals and protruding stamens are located on top of the plant. Fruit is a small achene with hooks to attach to animals who pass nearby.

Parts to collect for medical purposes: Flowers.

Preferred solvent: Water.

Main effect: Astringent, Diaphoretic, Febrifuge.

Native American Use:

Iroquois and Cherokee used root decoction to treat diarrhea and reduce fever, while the tea prepared from leaves and flowers was used to treat Urinary Tract Infections.

Alder

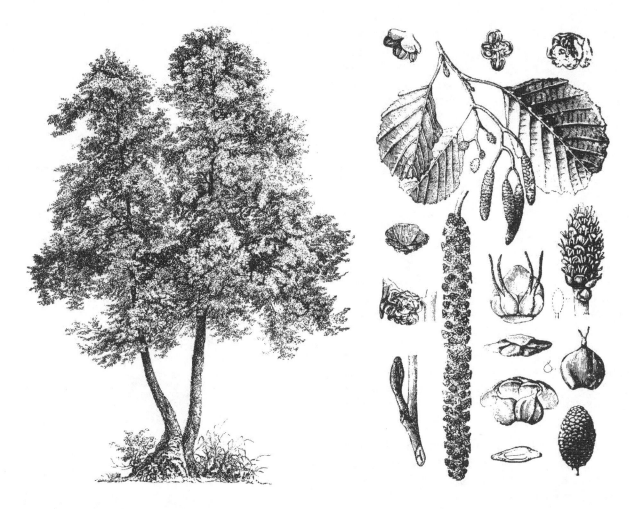

Binomial Name: Alnus Rubra.

Habitat: All the wet and moist areas of the United States and Canada.

Characteristics: Alders are trees of medium height (about 70 feet tall). The bark that covers the wide trunk has changing characteristics depending on the age of the tree. It can be smooth and gray for a young one or coarse and whitish for an old one. Leaves are oval-shaped with a pointy end and serrated margins. Flowers are catkins of different dimensions depending on the sex: male green-yellow flowers are long and protruding downward; female ones are small and red cones. The latter, generate, when pollinated, cones with flat seeds.

Parts to collect for medical purposes: Bark.

Preferred solvent: Water.

Main effect: Astringent, Cathartic, Tonic.

Native American Use:

Female ament decoction was used to treat Sexual Transmitted Diseases such as gonorrhea.

Male flower poultice was eaten to stimulate bowel movement in serious cases of constipation.

Fresh leaves poultice was used to cure wounds and skin infections, while the ash obtained from the leaves combustion was used as toothpaste.

The tea prepared with dried leaves has an anti-inflammatory effect if used to wash the skin area in case of urticarial or rash.

The decoctions from boiling barks have a febrifuge and astringent effect. Also, it is still used nowadays as a gargle for sore throat. Use fresh, inner bark to maximize the effect.

Aloe Vera

Binomial Name: Aloe Vera.

Habitat: the Southern United States, especially Southeastern ones.

Characteristics: At the base of the plant, there is a basal rosette of long, pointed succulent leaves with toothed edges. Color is olive green, sometimes mottled in yellow. It creates a group of red or yellow tubular flowers from a central spike.

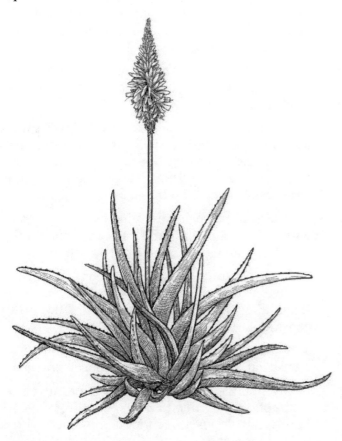

Parts to collect for medical purposes: Leaves juice.

Preferred solvent: Water.

Main effect: Tonic, Emmenagogue, Vermifuge, Cathartic, Depurative

Native American Use:

The poultice of fresh leaves was used to treat wounds, insect bites, and burns in general. A mostly unknown use of these fresh leaves poultice is the following: poultice was put into cheesecloth to dry. The dried poultice was then ground to obtain a fine powder that was used as a topical treatment for open wounds to stop bleeding and for blisters to absorb the moisture and avoid infections. If diluted into water, the powder was used to regulate the menstrual cycle or to expel intestinal worms.

WARNING: Do not give in case of pregnancy, liver or gallbladder conditions, or hemorrhoids

Amaranth

Binomial Name: Amaranthus Retrolexus.

Habitat: Diffused almost all over the United States and Canada in meadows and prairies.

Characteristics: This flowering plant is roughly 4 feet tall and has gray-green, oval-shaped, rough leaves. At the end of the branches, the flowers are hairy aments red or purple depending on the species. Inside the flowers, during fall you can find numerous, small, black seeds. The taproots are red.

Parts to collect for medical purposes: Leaves and Flowers.

Preferred solvent: Water.

Main effect: Astringent.

Native American Use:

The decoction or raw consumption of leaves was used for its astringent characteristic and to reduce excessive menstruation (hypermenorrhea). The decoction of leaves was also used as gargling for throat inflammation.

Seeds were used as food for sustainment. You grinding them and prepare bread or cakes. Leaves (raw and cooked) and roots (boiled) are edible too.

Angelica

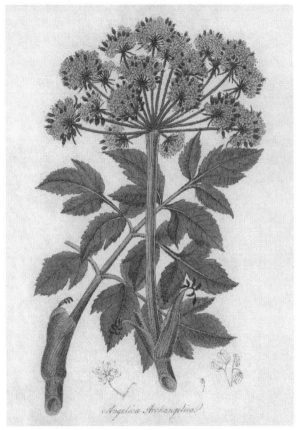

Angelica Archangelica

Binomial Name: Angelica Atropurpurea.

Habitat: Wet lowlands in the North-Eastern States.

Characteristics: Six feet tall plant with thick, purple stems. Leaves are large and divided into three to five minor, smaller, oval-shaped leaves. Flowers are grouped in umbels and are small and white. It is really similar to the hemlock but this one is poisonous so, to be sure of the identification, the best advice is to smell the roots or the seeds. If these have the typical angelica smell, almost like celery, then it is angelica. Another method for double-checking is to break a branch or a leaf and smell. If it smells like urine, then it is hemlock.

Arsemart

Binomial Name: Persicaria hydropiper.

Habitat: All over the United States, in wet environments.

Parts to collect for medical purposes: Roots, leaves, flowers, seeds.

Preferred solvent: Boiling Water.

Main effect: Carminative, Expectorant, Diuretic, Emmenagogue.

Native American Use:

The application of the fresh root poultice on swollen joints or any kind of contusion from mild to severe had an anti-inflammatory and pain relief effect on the part treated.

The decoction was the preferred way for Natives to extract the phytochemicals and to use Angelica for healing purposes.

In detail, the decoction of leaves and flowers was used to cure all sorts of diseases: rheumatism, sore throats, fevers, ulcers, Urinary Tract Infections, and headaches. It was considered a panacea for every condition.

It is also a powerful carminative and helped with intestinal gas and a powerful anti-inflammation gargle in case of sore throat.

The raw consumption of leaves was used for its astringent characteristic to treat diarrhea. The same effect has been ascribed to the raw consumption of roots.

Seed decoctions were used to treat increase menstrual flow, in the case of hypermenorrhea.

In my opinion, the handiest way for Angelica assumption is by tinctures: the tincture of roots (dosage: 40 drops, three to four times a day) or seeds (dosage: 20 drops, three to four times a day) is beneficial in treating the condition listed above in a timesaving manner.

Other uses of Angelica in the Native American culture, besides the medical purpose, are related to religion (dried leaves and flowers were used to be smoked in the sacred pipe ceremony).

In addition, seeds were used as food for sustainment. You can create flour by grinding them and prepare bread or cakes, in many South American typical dishes. Leaves (raw and cooked) and roots (boiled) are edible too.

Characteristics: Also known as Water Pepper or Marsh pepper Smartweed. This annual plant can grow up to 30 inches and likes wet environments such as marshes and alluvial meadows. Its taproot sinks into the ground up to 3 feet in general, so it is difficult to eradicate.

The green-reddish, smooth stems emerge straight from the ground with alternate, lance-shaped leaves covered with thin hair. The inflorescence is located at the top of the stem as a vertical cluster of small pink flowers. It blooms in summer. After the pollination, the plant produces a small, triangular black seed at the base of each dried flower.

Parts to collect for medical purposes: Whole plant.

Preferred solvent: Water, Alcohol.

Main effect: Diuretic, Diaphoretic, Tonic, Vermifuge, Analgesic.

Native American Use: Poultice and juice of the herb were used on ulcers and swollen joints, both topically and internal due to its mild analgesic characteristics. For the same reason, the chewing of the root was used to treat toothache.

One of the most common uses was related to the treatment of parasite worms: the tea obtained from leaves and flowers is effective in the case of sepsis and intestinal worms. The recommended dosage is 1 tsp. of the dried herb infused in 1 cup of boiling water for half an hour; the infusion must be drunk throughout the day two or three tablespoonfuls at the time. The topical application of drops of diluted tincture inside the ear was used to kill worms within.

Ashwagandha (Indian Ginseng)

Binomial Name: Withania Somnifera.

Habitat: This plant is not Native American but it is widely diffused and cultivated in India, Nepal and Pakistan and in some regions of Mediterranean are.

Characteristics: This woody shrub plant can grow up to 2 feet and 7 inches. in shadowy but dry environments like deep forests. From the root, thin a single hairy stem emerge bearing many other sub branches that depart radially. Leaves elliptic, dark green and 5 inches long. From the green, bell-shaped flowers, the red, round fruit evolves.

Parts to collect for medical purposes: Root (dried).

Preferred solvent: Water. Main effect: Sedative, Tonic, Stomachic, Antispasmodic.

Herbal Medicine Use: The tea obtained by mixing 1 tsp of powdered root in 1 cup of boiling water is effective in case of stomachache and indigestion. Another effect of it is related to the treatment of stress and anxiety. The recommended use of the above tea is one cup maximum, to be drunk three or four times throughout the day. Another use of the Ashwagandha is related to the poultice obtained from pounding the fresh leaves. This can be used as an antibiotic and anti-inflammatory remedy for topical application on wounds. WARNING: Due to its sedative characteristics, it may interact with the following drugs: Anticonvulsants, Antipsycotcs, Benzodiazepine, Sedatives, Fenitonine, Antidepressive drugs.

B

Balsam Fir

Binomial Name: Abies Balsamea.

Habitat: North of the United States or South of Canada in forests.

Characteristics: Evergreen tree up to 65 ft. tall. The gray bark frequently leaks sap and changes its appearance depending on the age of the plant: smooth for younger trees, coarse for older ones. Leaves are needle green on the upper part, white on the bottom. Cones are 4 inches long and red/purple.

Parts to collect for medical purposes: Sap, Roots, Barks, and Leaves.

Preferred solvent: Boiling Water.

Main effect: Analgesic and Antiseptic.

Native American Use:

The decoction of barks was used to reduce fever and stimulate sweating to detoxify the body. Also, needle tea was used to cure respiratory problems and colds due to its astringent characteristics.

Finally, the sap is used directly to treat burns and close wounds. Raw consumption of it is used to prevent colds and sore throats.

Minor use of this balsamic sap was during the sweat lodge ceremony: the sap was dripped on the hot stones to create aromatic steam.

Balsam Root

Binomial Name: Balsamorhiza Sagittaria.

Habitat: Foothills of Rocky Mountains.

Characteristics: Small plant (one to two feet tall). Leaves are arrow-shaped and hairy to the touch and are concentrated on the bottom part of the plant (basal). Flowers are yellow both on petals and on florets, with protruding stamens.

remove the bitter taste.

Barberry

Binomial Name: Berberis Canadensis.

Parts to collect for medical purposes: The whole plant.

Preferred solvent: Boiling water.

Main effect: Antibacterial and Antiseptic.

Native American Use:

The raw consumption of leaves stimulates the immune system and is considered a preventive treatment for colds and flu. The poultice of leaves is also excellent to treat wounds and burns and can be an excellent solution for a wound dressing if you hurt yourself in the wood. By chewing some leaves and applying the poultice on the wound you will get both the antiseptic benefits of your saliva and of the balsamroot.

For deeper injuries, you can also use the sticky sap to glue together two edges of the wound.

The decoction of leaves and roots was used to treat colds, stomachaches, and symptoms of Sexual Transmitted Diseases like the burning feeling due to gonorrhea.

As food, the plant can be consumed raw in all its parts, but roots are very bitter. Boiling them will

Habitat: Diffused in forests all over the Northern United States and in the whole of Canada.

Characteristics: This shrub has thorns on its branches and can grow up to 8 feet tall. Leaves are grouped in clusters along the branches. They are succulent, simple with teeth on their edge. Dense clusters of yellow flowers populate the end of the branches. Flowers have six sepals and evolve into scarlet, ovoid fruits after pollination.

Parts to collect for medical purposes: Berries, barks, leaves.

Preferred solvent: Alcohol, Water.

Main effect: Antiseptic, Carminative, Febrifuge.

Native American Use: The decoction obtained from the **bark** is considered a cure for diarrhea attacks and was used as a gargle for sore throat. Bark was also used topically by reducing it to a poultice and applying it directly on mouth sores and wounds. It facilitated the healing of the part due to its antiseptic characteristics.

Fruits were used bot for food (WARNING, excessive consumption can cause diarrhea) and for healing purposes: the decoction of the berries was used to reduce fever when other methods failed.

Decoction of **leaves** was considered effective in liver detoxification.

Bearberry

Binomial Name: Arctostaphylos Uva Ursi.

Habitat: All over Northern and Western United States and in the whole of Canada, in forests.

Characteristics: This low-lying, evergreen dwarf shrub covers the ground of the forests. Leaves are obovate, smooth, and thick. During

Finally, the **roots** were used for medical purposes both raw and cooked: the poultice of fresh roots was used to induce salivation and stimulate the appetite when someone was recovering from a disease, while their decoction was used as a wash for difficult wounds and burns due to its antiseptic properties.

spring small white-pinkish calyx-shaped flowers appear in small groups at the top of the stems. Fruits are round red drupes with on average three hard seeds inside.

Parts to collect for medical purposes: Leaves.

Preferred solvent: Alcohol, water.

Main effect: Diuretic, Astringent.

Native American Use: Leaves of Bearberry were widely used by natives both for medical and ceremonial purposes. It was a sacred plant used in every important Native American ceremony, especially in the sacred pipe one. Lakota called it čhaŋšáša, Ojibwe asemaa, Menominee, but the term that became widely known among Europeans to define it is the Unami Delaware word for "mixture", Kinnikinnick. Besides the ceremonial use of this plant, its medical applications are many: from the topical application of leaves poultice to treat wounds and stop bleeding due to its astringent characteristics, to the decoction of leaves and berries, used to treat bladder and kidney problems or as a mild analgesic.

Also, the salve obtained from leaves was used for rashes and sores: leaves were cooked at very low temperature in animal fat for one day. To reach the right thickness, beeswax was added to the strained melted fat.

A simple preparation you can do in the comfort of your kitchen to benefit from this incredible plant is the Phytochemicals Alcoholic Extraction. By simply soaking the leaves in alcohol for one week in a mason jar, shielded from the light you can obtain a powerful analgesic for headaches. The recommended dosage is one teaspoon of the alcoholic extraction in a cup of water two times a day.

Lastly, Natives used Bearberry for food: dried Kinnikinnick berries were crushed to obtain a powder which is used as a spice; also the fresh berries were boiled and then cooked with

animal fat until they become tender and ready to be mashed.

WARNING: Do not use in case of pregnancy

Beech

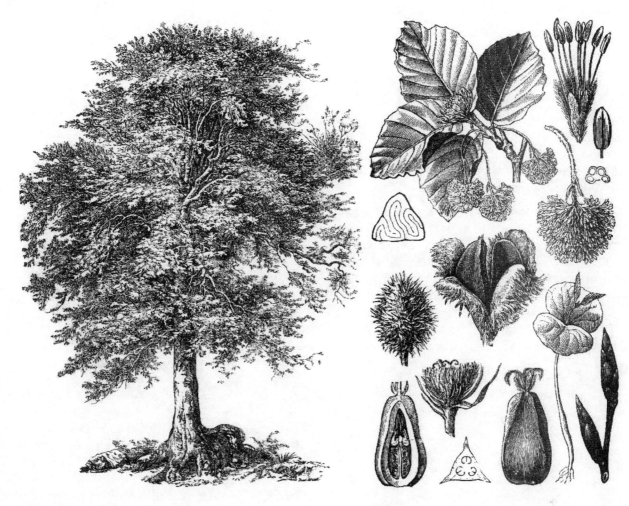

Binomial Name: Fagus Grandifolia.

Habitat: The Eastern United States and Southeast of Canada. It grows in sunny environments.

Characteristics: This beautiful tall tree can grow up to 120 ft. The central trunk is covered by smooth, gray bark and bears long and thick branches, populated by many leaves. These are deeply veined, oval-shaped, and with toothed edges. Leaves fall in autumn, as per all the deciduous trees. Fruits are small four-lobed nuts covered with soft thorn-like red hair.

Parts to collect for medical purposes: Bark, leaves.

Preferred solvent: Water.

Main effect: Antibacterial, Astringent.

Native American Use:

The decoction of beech barks and leaves helps in the treatment of dysentery and diarrhea due to its astringent characteristics. This decoction was also used to treat liver conditions (also modern doctors use it to treat diabetes) and bladder infections. The recommended dose and use for this treatment is 1 tsp of dried leaves or bark for each cup of boiling water, to be drunk three tablespoonfuls at the time before the main meals.

Black cohosh

Binomial Name: Actaea Racemosa.

Habitat: Forests, meadows, and prairies of the Northern United States and Southern Canada.

Characteristics: This evergreen plant emerges from a black-green rhizome as a straight green stem that reaches 6 feet tall at its best. Leaves are basal, broad, and grouped in compounds of three leaflets with toothed margins. Flowers are grouped in densely populated racemes and are composed by a central stigma surrounded by protruding stamens with no petal nor sepal.

Parts to collect for medical purposes: Root.

Preferred solvent: Boiling water.

Main effect: Diuretic, Diaphoretic, Expectorant, Sedative, Emmenagogue.

Native American Use: Black Cohosh root decoction was widely used by Natives to cure cough and as a blood purifier. Another wide use was the treatment of hypo-menorrhea (poor menstruation flow) and to induce abortions.

A simple preparation of the black cohosh you can do in no time is the Alcoholic infusion. This preparation is highly effective in curing rheumatism. The instructions to prepare it are quite simple: just soak black cohosh fresh root in alcohol with a weight ratio of 1:8 for one week. The recommended dose for the assumption is one tsp of the alcoholic extraction in a cup of water two times a day.

WARNING: Do not use during pregnancy.

Black Gum

Binomial Name: Nyssa Sylvatica.

Habitat: From the Eastern coast of the United States to East Texas, in wet environments.

Characteristics: This deciduous tree can grow up to eighty feet tall. The wide central trunk is covered by scaled and deeply indented brown-red bark. Many leafy brown-reddish branches depart from the central trunk in any direction. Leaves are alternate and lance-shaped with smooth edges. The yellow flowers are both male and female and grow in round clusters on elongated peduncles.

Parts to collect for medical purposes: Bark and roots.

Preferred solvent: Boiling water.

Main effect: Diuretic, Diaphoretic, Expectorant, Sedative, Emmenagogue.

Native American Use: The decoction obtained from black gum bark will help in the treatment of minor respiratory conditions. Bark decoction was also effective as a wash during difficult childbirth. Finally, the "jelly juice" of the root was used as an eyewash.

Black Haw

Binomial Name: Viburnum Prunifolium.

Habitat: Diffused all over North America (the United States and Canada both) mainly in the eastern cost zone.

Characteristics: On average, this tree can reach 20 ft. in height. It has a gray-brown outer bark and deep green, oval-shaped, teethed leaves. Roots are brown-reddish color and flowers are grouped in small white clusters. Fruits are deep black berries with a sweet taste.

Parts to collect for medical purposes: Barks and root bark.

Preferred solvent: Water, Alcohol.

Main effect: Diuretic, Astringent, Nervine, Antispasmodic.

Native American Use: Native American healers used Black Haw root bark decoction to prevent miscarriages in women who had shown a tendency to it by their previous history or by having symptoms of uterus contractions. The prescription was to take the root bark decoction three weeks before the timing when the last miscarriage happened and continue for three weeks after. If no miscarriage of other uterus contractions happened after the three weeks, the cure could be stopped.

The benefits of the root bark decoction did not limit to the prevention of miscarriages: it is known for its use also as a powerful febrifuge and in case of diarrhea when other treatments failed.

Lastly, it has positive effects on heart palpitation issues, menstrual disorders, and cramps.

Bloodroot

Binomial Name: Sanguinaria Canadensis.

Habitat: Diffused all over the eastern part of North America. From the Eastern coast of Canada in the North to the Great Lakes region, down to the Mississippi River in the South.

Characteristics: This small low-lying plant can reach at its best 7 inches in height. The stem emerges from a twisted, red rhizome that releases a red sap if squeezed (hence the name), bearing usually four to five leaves. These are green-grayish and many lobes (five to seven). The flower is white with ten to twelve petals and central yellow stamens.

Parts to collect for medical purposes: Root.

Preferred solvent: Water, Alcohol.

Main effect: Antibacterial, Expectorant, Sedative, Emetic.

Native American Use: Bloodroot was renown by natives to be a powerful emetic and it can cause vomit if eaten in excessive quantities. It was used in case of food poisoning.

Another use for this the root is the topical application of its juice to treat warts. The double extraction of root is used in moderate quantities to treat respiratory disease from mild to severe, such as cough, laryngitis, and bronchitis, and asthma.

The root alcoholic extraction contains sanguinarine, which is nowadays used for the topical treatment of skin cancer.

Another, non-medical use of this root extraction is as a repellent for mosquitos and insects. Natives applied it on their bodies to prevent insect bites and that's why Native Americans were called red skins by the first Europeans.

Blueberry

Binomial Name: Vaccinium.

Habitat: All over North Unites States and Canada, in plains and forests.

Characteristics: This family of plants grows near to the ground for the majority of species. The height of the different species of this shrub can vary greatly, from a few inches up to fifteen feet. The leaves that populate the woody branches are alternated and are oblong. Flowers are white-pinkish and bell-shaped, growing in groups at the end of the stems. Fruits are round, deep blue when ripe and sweet.

Parts to collect for medical purposes: Leaves and berries.

Preferred solvent: Boiling water, Alcohol.

Main effect: Diuretic, Astringent.

Native American Use: Natives used to prepare tea from dried leaves as a remedy for diarrhea and used this drink as a topical wash for skin conditions like dermatitis and rashes of all sort.

An interesting application of this shrub was the consumption of the powder of dried leaves to immediately reduce the sensation of nausea.

Regarding the fruits, besides the obvious raw consumption, a simple preparation you can make, also in the comfort of your kitchen is the alcohol infusion to treat spasmodic diarrhea and Irritable Bowel Syndrome. The instructions are quite simple: just place dried blueberry in a glass bottle and covered it with 95% Alcohol. Let the bottle rest for at least one month in a shaded place. The recommended dosage for this remedy is 1 tbsp. of the alcoholic infusion in four oz. of distilled water.

Blue False Indigo

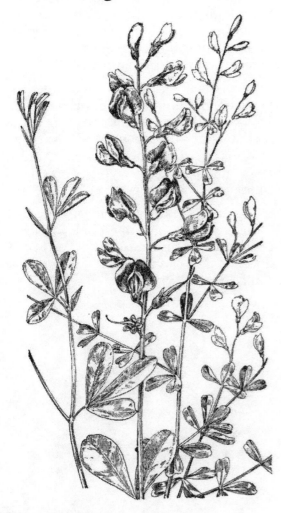

Binomial Name: Baptisia australis.

Habitat: Diffused all over the Eastern to the Mid-western United States, at the sides of the forests and in the meadows.

Characteristics: This perennial plant can grow up to 5 feet. The pale green stem emerges straight from the central rhizome, with alternate leaves, composed of three obovate leaflets. Flowers bloom in June and are assembled in racemes. They resemble the pea flowers and are blue/purple. Fruits resemble inflated peapods with a sharper point and bear yellow pod-like seeds inside.

Parts to collect for medical purposes: Roots.

Preferred solvent: Water.

Main effect: Emetic, Purgative, Astringent.

Native American Use:

Natives used the tea obtained from the roots to treat nausea, diarrhea, and toothache or as a topical wash in case of conjunctivitis.

On the contrary, the raw consumption of the plant can cause vomit and nausea due to its mild toxicity.

WARNING: Do not assume during pregnancy or lactation.

Boneset

Binomial Name: Epatorium Perfoliatum.

Habitat: All over the Eastern United States and Canada, in wet environments.

Characteristics: This perennial shrub can grow up to 5 feet tall. The stems that emerge from the ground bear opposite, long, pointed leaves with teethed margins. It almost seems as the stem pierces one wide big leaf. The white-pinkish flowers are grouped in clusters at the top of the stems.

Parts to collect for medical purposes: Leaves and flowers.

Preferred solvent: Water, Alcohol.

Main effect: Febrifuge, Diaphoretic, Carminative.

Native American Use:

Native Americans used boneset leaves and flowers in many medical preparations. For example, the tea obtained from the infusion of dried leaves was considered a powerful febrifuge and was used also in the treatment of most severe diseases such as malaria, pneumonia, arthritis, and gout.

Talking about gout and arthritis it is important to report also the topical application of the poultice obtained by pounding of fresh leaves and flowers, as a topical anti-inflammatory treatment on swollen joints and other contusive traumas to the joints.

The double infusion of the roots was used as an emetic in case of food poisoning and to cure sore throat with gargling.

WARNING: if taken in big quantities it may cause vomit and can cause liver damages.

Buckthorn (Cascara Sagrada)

Binomial Name: Rhamnus Cathartica or Purshiana.

Habitat: R. Cathartica can be found on Lake Michigan shores while R. Purshiana is diffused in the North-West of the North-American continent.

Characteristics: These bushes are small and densely populated by leaves and berries. The branches have a gray-brown bark, with white lenticels and are full of thin, oval-shaped, and green-white leaves. Flowers are small, white, and grouped in very dense clusters. Fruits are round and yellow/orange when mature, with three small seeds inside.

Parts to collect for medical purposes: Bark and root.

Preferred solvent: Boiling water, Alcohol.

Main effect: Purgative, Emetic, Vermifuge.

Native American Use:

Ojibway used to prepare the buckthorn bark infusion to stimulate bowel movement and to remove intestinal worm infestation. The plant was renowned to be mildly toxic and the decoction of young branches and fruits was used as an emetic to treat food poisoning.

Native Americans' protocol to collect the barks was based on the natural cycle of the plant. They collected the bark between the end of spring and the beginning of summer when it is softer and easier to remove. Then they dried it for at least one year, in a shaded place to preserve it and concentrate its healing properties.

WARNING: The bark decoction must never be used to remove an intestinal occlusion. Moreover, continuous use is not advised because buckthorn is carcinogenic if assumed constantly.

California Poppy

The sap, like all the poppies, is where the sedative substances are more concentrated. Natives were well aware of that and used to apply topically it on gums to reduce the pain related to toothache.

Native Americans also used to chew the roots to ingest this sedative sap to treat headaches and toothaches.

An unknown use of this plant regards the seedpods, which produce a sticky resin when removed from the plant. This resin promotes lactation if rubbed on nipples.

WARNING: To be avoided during pregnancy

Catnip

Binomial Name: Eschscholzia Californica

Habitat: Western Coast of the United States and Canada, in dry environments.

Characteristics: Small flowering plant, 30 inches tall on average. Leaves are not many, divided into many thin blue-green and pointed leaflets. The single flower that emerges from the ground has four bright yellow-orange petals. Small black seeds are contained in it.

Parts to collect for medical purposes: The whole plant.

Preferred solvent: Water, Alcohol

Main effect: Sedative, Diuretic, Analgesic

Native American Use:

Like all the poppies, also the California poppy is renowned for its sedative effects. Native Americans used to give tea prepared with dried leaves and flowers to reduce anxiety and soothe panic attacks. The tea was also renowned to soothe menstrual pain and facilitate diuresis. In addition, this tea is toxic for insects and parasites and was used as a hair wash in case of head lice.

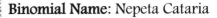

Binomial Name: Nepeta Cataria

Habitat: Diffused all over North America

Characteristics: This perennial, many-branched shrub grows up to 4 feet tall. Leaves are small, ovate, and gray-white, with serrated margins. Flowers are small and lilac. They appear from the top of the stem in large clusters.

Parts to collect for medical purposes: Leaves, stems, and flowers.

Preferred solvent: Boiling water, Alcohol.

Main effect: Carminative, Tonic, Diaphoretic, Emmenagogue.

Native American Use:

Native Americans used the infusion of the whole plant (leaves, stems, and flowers) for intestinal problems. The tonic effect of the plant reduces intestinal spasms and soothes inflammation related to diarrhea and dysentery. The infusion above has also a carminative effect, helping in the treatment of intestinal gas. It was particularly indicated to calm menstrual cramps and dysmenorrhea.

Another use of the tea was related to its diaphoretic character: increased sweating would help in reducing fever states and in promoting overall detoxification of the body.

Another use of the plant was the topical application of the catnip poultice on swollen joints for pain relief in case of gout and rheumatism.

WARNING: do not use during pregnancy.

Cattail

Binomial Name: Typha Latifolia or Typha Angustifolia

Habitat: Cattail is diffused all over North America, in wet environments (lakeshores, bogs, streams…)

Characteristics: Long, spear-shaped plant up to 8 feet tall. It produces two flowers during spring that resemble hot-dogs on a stick. The thicker one, located in the lower part of the plant is the female one; the upper one is the male flower, which disappears after the dispersion of all the pollen.

Parts to collect for medical purposes: Roots, leaves.

Preferred solvent: Boiling water.

Main effect: Anodyne, Emollient.

Native American Use:

Native Americans widely used the decoction of roots as a topical treatment for sunburns due to its emollient characteristics. Also, the flowers were used to treat wounds because they stop the bleeding and absorb excessive moisture. In addition, ashes obtained by burning leaves are antiseptic and were used to seal wounds and burns.

Besides the medical application of the plant, natives used it as food: in detail, roots were dried and grinder to obtain flour for bread and porridge, while hearts were boiled and eaten as vegetables.

Chamomile

Binomial Name: Matricaria matricarioides.

Characteristics: Small flower, 20 inches height at maximum in the wild, that grows mainly along the pathway. The flower has yellow pollen and a corolla of white petals. Leaves are bright green and oblong, with narrow laciniae.

Habitat: Diffused all over North America

Parts to collect for medical purposes: Flower and herb.

Preferred solvent: Water, Alcohol.

Main effect: Nervine, Sedative, Antispasmodic, Carminative.

Native American Use: The infusion of the fresh or dried plant was used to soothe stomachache and to cure excessive intestinal gas. Not only that, but the infusion was effective also on menstrual cramps, dysmenorrhea, and, if topically applied, to relieve skin inflammations, acne, and eczema.

The tea was also used as a tonic for nerves and to calm anxiety and panic attacks. The mild sedative effect of this decoction was also used to treat arthritis and swollen joints pain.

A seemingly unknown use for this wonderful plant is related to meat preservation. In fact, the dried and powdered herb was on meat to absorb moisture and to prevent it from rotting.

WARNING: Chamomile may cause an allergic reaction.

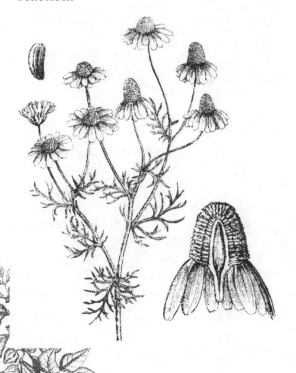

Cicely

Binomial Name: Myrrhis Odorata

Habitat: Diffused all over the United States and Canada in forests and woods.

Characteristics: Two to three feet tall plant with green, thin, long, flavored leaves. Flowers are small and white, grouped in umbrella-like clusters.

In addition, this plant is really similar to the hemlock but smaller. To be sure of the identification, again, trust your nose. If roots smell like anise, then it is safe to pick.

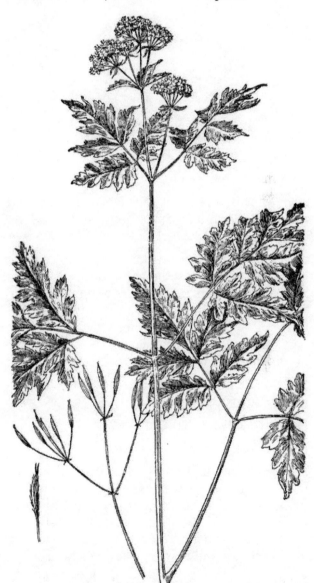

Parts to collect for medical purposes: Roots and leaves.

Preferred solvent: Boiling water.

Main effect: Cleansing, Expectorant.

Native American Use: The decoction of roots is used to treat digestion and airways ailments

Corn

Binomial Name: Zea mays

Habitat: Diffused all over the North-Eastern and the Central United States and in the whole Central and South American continent.

Characteristics: Corn belongs to the Poaceae family. It is one of the most ancient cereals cultivated by men. Corn is a six to nine feet long, spear-shaped, plant that produces two types of flowers. The lower ones are female and are widely known as the corncobs; the ones on top of the plant are the male ones.

Parts to collect for medical purposes: Green pistils, Cornsilk.

Preferred solvent: Diluted alcohol.

Main effect: Diuretic, Emollient.

Native American Use: Besides its well-known uses as food, corn was used also as a medical plant. The decoction of the green pistils, known as "young silk" was impressively effective in treating urethra and kidney problems such as kidney stones and urinary tract infections.

Another use of the young corn silk is related to its tincture. This was obtained by the maceration of minced fresh silk with a 50% alcohol solution. The recommended weight ratio between herbs and the 50% Alcohol solution is 1:2 and the recommended soaking time is two weeks in a shaded place.

(such as Asthma) and has positive effects on anemia due to its high content in iron.

Twenty drops of this tincture, in combination with twenty drops of Damiana tincture, after the main meals, are a panacea against any Urinary Tract Infections.

Cow Parsnip

Binomial Name: Heracleum Maximum.

Habitat: Diffused all over the North-American continent, both in the United States and in Canada, in the inland regions.

Characteristics: This perennial plant can reach six to eight feet tall. It has various vertical, hollow, and hairy stems that pop up from the ground, with opposite and large leaves, divided in pointy lobes. The small white flowers are grouped in umbels, the same as other Apiaceae.

Parts to collect for medical purposes: The whole plant.

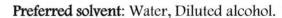

Preferred solvent: Boiling water.

Effects: Anti-inflammatory.

Native American Use: Besides the raw consumption of stems and leaves for food, the medical use of this plant among Native American tribes is widely documented. Fundamental, before any use of this plant, is the removal of the outer skin from the stem to reduce to a tolerable level of toxicity.

Natives used the poultice of the plant for direct topical application on skin inflammation problems such as eczemas and rash. Also, the poultice of roots was effective to reduce swellings, especially on the feet.

Natives also used this plant in combination with the ashes of a campfire as a filter to purify water. By putting a piece of burned wood inside the hollow stem and using it as a straw, water was filtered by the graphite and was less subject to cause intestinal problems.

WARNING: Due to the high toxicity levels, the use of this plant is not advised in any case, especially during pregnancy or lactation. Many substitutes and preparations are available in any herbal apothecary.

Cranberry

Binomial Name: Vaccinium Oxycoccus

Habitat: North of the US, in wet environments

Characteristics: This small, evergreen plant is located at the base of the forests' ground. It can grow up to 15 inches tall at maximum. The woody branches have smooth, dark brown, bark. The flowers are often solitary located at the end of the branches. They are white-pinkish, and bell-shapes with petals curled inward. Fruits are round and deep red.

Parts to collect for medical purposes: Bark, fruits.

Preferred solvent: Water, Diluted alcohol.

Main effect: Diuretic, Astringent, Tonic.

Native American Use: The Natives used the medical properties of cranberries in the treatment of Urinary Tract Infections. This use is still actual nowadays in the case of cystitis and kidney stones.

To absolve to the purpose the berries were consumed raw, juiced, or, if they were only available in dried condition, as a tea. The cranberries have been scientifically proven to low the pH of the urine, thus promoting the dissolution of the sodium accumulations known as kidney stones and reducing the growth of bacterial infection in it that could cause UTIs.

The tea obtained with barks instead of dried berries, was extremely effective in treating menstrual pain and dysmenorrhea and was used also as a topical wash for infected wounds and skin ulcers because, due to its astringent properties, it promoted the formation of scarring tissue.

D

Damiana

Binomial Name: Turnera Diffusa

Habitat: Widely diffused in Texas and in the whole of Central America.

Characteristics: This small shrub can grow up to three feet tall. A halo of branches emerges from the ground, bearing many lance-shaped leaves with serrated edges. Flowers, with five yellow petals and five yellow stamens, originate from the top of the branches.

Parts to collect for medical purposes: Leaves.

Preferred solvent: Water, diluted alcohol.

Main effect: Antiseptic, Antibacterial, Antifungal, Diuretic, Stimulant.

Native American Use: Native Americans used dried leaves to prepare a decoction to treat Urinary Tract Infections and bladder issues in general. Besides this medical purpose, this decoction was also considered a renowned aphrodisiac and it was used to increase sexual stamina for both males and females.

Damiana was also a ceremonial plant and it was said to induce hallucinations if assumed in big quantities. Native Americans said that it allowed the spirits to communicate with the healer, through the hallucinations.

WARNING: do not use in case of pregnancy, lactation, or liver issues. Advised dosage, in any case, is a maximum of 10 grams of dried leaves per day.

Dandelion

Binomial Name: Taraxacum Officinale

Habitat: Diffused all over the South-Eastern United States.

Characteristics: In Europe, it is also known as "lion tooth". This perennial plant can grow up to 20 inches in height. The plant has a taproot and a crown of basal big, green, and deeply toothed leaves. The stems that emerge from the basal leaves are straight and green, bearing flowers on top. These are round, yellow, and with a multitude of petals. Each flower is hermaphrodite, which means that has both male and female characteristics. The flower head, when pollinated evolves into spherical clusters called blow balls, where seeds are grouped. Seeds are dry and umbrella-shaped to be easily moved by wind.

Parts to collect for medical purposes: Roots.

Preferred solvent: Water, Diluted alcohol.

Main effect: Diuretic, Deobstruent, Tonic.

Native American Use: Besides the raw consumption of the leaves for food, Native Americans used dandelion also for its medical properties.

In fact, **root** decoction was used for cleansing and detoxification in case of liver and gallbladder conditions because it helped digestion and had a laxative effect. The diuretic properties of the decoction were widely known and the antispasmodic properties of the dandelion were also used to treat menstrual cramps and Pre-Menstrual Syndrome.

Root decoction was used also to increase lactation and to stimulate the appetite via the promotion of bile production.

Finally, it is scientifically proved that dandelion raw consumption of leaves reduces the cholesterol level in the blood flow. This is due to the fact that reduces the cholesterol absorption from food.

Devil's Club

Binomial Name: Oplopanax Horridus

Habitat: the North-Western States, in wet, shaded environments

Characteristics: This bushy shrub is a close cousin of ginseng. The central stem and the minor ones are full of pointed thorns. Leaves depart in spirals from the stems. They are many-lobed and have thorny peduncles. The small, white flowers are arranged in spherical umbels at the top of the plant. The fruits are bright red drupes.

Douglas Maple

Binomial Name: Acer Glabrum

Habitat: Mainly diffused in the North-West of the United States and Western Canada.

Characteristics: This tree can grow up to 35 feet tall. Leaves are wide, three-lobed with pointy

Parts to collect for medical purposes: Root, barks.

Preferred solvent: Boiling water, alcohol.

Main effect: Tonic.

Native American Use: Natives used this plant for ceremonial and sacred purposes. The root bark decoction was used as a tonic for nerves due to its qualities similar to ginseng. Other than that, the plant was used as a dye for tissues and as a traditional body painting for warriors (ashes of the burnt devil's club were mixed to grease to create the paint that was said to protect during battle).

ends and serrated margins. Flowers are grouped in corymbs of ten and are yellow in color. Seed have horizontal "leaflets" such as a helicopter. These blades help them fly for long distances when they detach from the tree.

Parts to collect for medical purposes: Leaves and barks.

Preferred solvent: Water.

Main effect: Astringent, Anti-Inflammatory.

Native American Use:

Native Americans used the tea obtained from dried barks and leaves to reduce fever and in the treatment of dysentery and diarrhea. It was used as a panacea for all kinds of diseases when specific treatments were not available. The poultice obtained from fresh leaves was used to reduce swelling of joints and rheumatism.

E

Echinacea

Binomial Name: Echinacea Purpurea.

Habitat: Widely spread on flatlands of the Eastern and Central United States.

Characteristics: This plant is made by a single stem, 3 feet tall. The single flower is purple and umbrella-shaped. The stem is covered with a thick pelt of tiny thorns. Leaves are large and rough to the touch. Roots are yellow on the inside with black spots.

Parts to collect for medical purposes: Flower, leaves, roots.

Preferred solvent: Alcohol.

Main effect: Febrifuge, Sialagogue, Analgesic, Diaphoretic.

Native American Use:

The medical properties of Echinacea are widely known all over the world. Ancient Greeks and Egyptians used this plant since the dawn of time as a panacea for every disease. Also, Native Americans were aware of its power and used it to treat many conditions.

Root decoction was used as an analgesic for sore throat, toothache, and stomach pain. The diaphoretic properties of the Echinacea were used to induce sweat, thus cleansing the body and reduce fever.

The poultice obtained by pounding **flowers and leaves** is used to treat wounds, acne, and many skin conditions. Also, the consumption of the raw leaves helps in fighting microbial and fungal infection (such as candida) and it has been proven to be a good antiviral.

WARNING: The assumption of Echinacea is not recommended during pregnancy.

Elderberry

Binomial Name: Sambucus.

Habitat: Diffused all over the United States and Canada.

Characteristics: This bushy shrub can grow up to 33 feet. The stems that emerge from the ground have dark brown bark, often with vertical fissures. The opposite leaves are oval-shaped with a pointy end, bright green, with serrated margins and hairy in the below part. The white (or cream depending on the species) flowers are arranged in large clusters at the top of the plant. Fruit are round berries whose color may vary from one species to another: red for the racemose, blue for the cerulean, and almost black for nigra.

Parts to collect for medical purposes: The whole plant, from root to flowers and fruits.

Preferred solvent: Water.

Main effect: Vomit inducing, Cathartic, Diaphoretic, Diuretic, Demulcent, Febrifuge.

Native American Use:

Native Americans used to prepare tea with flowers to reduce fever and to stimulate diuresis. This tea was also used in topical application in case of itching or painful skin conditions such as urticaria or rash.

The above tea was indicated for many problems of the respiratory system, from mild to severe: it was a treatment for asthma, allergies, sinusitis, and bronchitis.

The bark decoction had different effects, promoting bowel movement for a laxative action.

Finally, the mild toxicity of the berries was used to create a powerful analgesic by preparing a decoction of the berries, which soothed back pain, menstrual cramps, and rheumatisms.

WARNING: excessive consumption of berries (especially the red ones) can be poisoning.

F

Fendlerbush

Binomial Name: Fendlera Rupicola.

Habitat: Diffused all over the Southern United States.

Characteristics: This plant is a small shrub two to three feet tall. Branches are deeply tangled together and are covered with a gray-brownish bark. The small leaves are opposite and oblong. Flowers are made of four white, arrow-shaped petals and a central part with stamens and styles. Fruits are egg-shaped.

Parts to collect for medical purposes: Inner bark.

Preferred solvent: Water.

Main effect: Cathartic.

Native American Use:

Native Americans used the decoction of the inner bark as a laxative or as a hair wash in case of head lice.

Feverfew

Binomial Name: Tanacetum Parthenium.

Habitat: Diffused all over the United States and southern Canada in gardens and meadows.

Characteristics: This small flower can grow up to 20 inches in height at maximum in the wild. It is a very simple plant with a flower with yellow pollen and a corolla of white petals. Leaves are yellow-greenish and pinnate.

Parts to collect for medical purposes: Flower and herb.

Preferred solvent: Water, Alcohol.

Main effect: Nervine, Sedative, Antispasmodic, Carminative.

Native American Use:

As the name suggests, Natives used this plant to help in reducing the fever. The tea obtained from the flower is a powerful febrifuge and was also used to treat headaches due to its mild sedative action.

Frasera

Binomial Name: Frasera Carolinensis.

Habitat: Diffused all over the Southern United States

Characteristics: This perennial plant, can reach 8 feet in height. It is composed, in its flowering state, by a single reddish stem that emerges straight from the ground with lanceolate leaves spreading in the four directions from it at regular intervals. At the top of the plant, the yellow flowers are grouped in clusters.

Parts to collect for medical purposes: Leaves and flowers.

Preferred solvent: Water.

Main effect: Nervine, Sedative, Analgesic.

Native American Use:

Native Americans used to prepare a poultice of Frasera leaves and flowers to treat with a topical application swollen joints and rheumatism pain. The sedative effect of the substances contained in it gave some relief to the pain due to the inflammations.

Leaves and flowers were also decocted and the drink obtained had a calming and nervine effect, used to treat anxiety and panic attacks.

G

Gentian

Binomial Name: Gentiana villosa

Habitat: Diffused all over the Eastern United States.

Characteristics: This small perennial plant can reach up to two feet maximum in height. Leaves are dark-green with the shape of a spear point. Bell-shaped flowers are grouped in clusters and they are white with purple stripes.

Parts to collect for medical purposes: Leaves, flowers, and roots.

Preferred solvent: Water.

Main effect: Analgesic.

Native American Use:

Natives used the mild analgesic effect of the Gentiana Villosa by preparing a poultice from the pounding of the whole plant. The poultice was indicated to snake bites. Also, the root was used in a decoction to give relief from back pain.

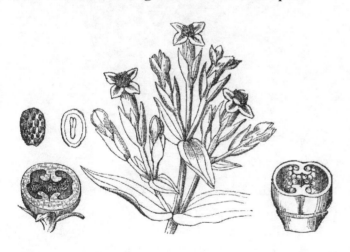

Geranium

Binomial Name: Geranium.

Habitat: Diffused all over the Eastern United States.

Characteristics: This plant produces many branches with single flowers emerging from a central root and two feet maximum in height. Leaves are usually palmate and have seven lobes, each lobe with serrated edges (depends on the specific species). Flowers have five wide petals

of different colors from species to species: purple, pink, red, white.

Parts to collect for medical purposes: Leaves, flowers, and roots.

Preferred solvent: Water.

Main effect: Astringent, Anti-hemorrhagic.

Native American Use: A widely unknown use of the geranium is the one of emergency medication in case of injuries. In fact, it is a powerful anti-hemorrhagic and the whole plant (leaves, flowers, and roots) was pounded in poultice directly on deep wounds to stop the bleeding. Usually, the plant was chewed to create the poultice and to add to the astringent and anti-hemorrhagic action, the antiseptic action of the saliva. Root was used in poultice and decocted: poultice was instead used to treat hemorrhoids, while root decoction was used for toothache.

Ginseng

Binomial Name: Panax Ginseng.

Habitat: Diffused wild on the South-Eastern part of Canada and in the Eastern Part of the United States up to Mississippi. It needs a dry and shaded environment, such as big forests of trees with big canopy.

Characteristics: This small perennial grows in shaded and well-drained zones. From the basal rhizome, the single stem can reach up to 20 inches in height. It divides into three basal leaves, arranged in whorls. Each leaf is made by five, smaller leaflets lance-shaped and with finely serrated margins. At the top of the single stem, there is a cluster of small, yellow/green flowers that develops into a group of bright red round seeds.

Parts to collect for medical purposes: Roots, especially dried.

Preferred solvent: Water.

Main effect: Emollient, Nervine, Stimulant, Febrifuge.

Native American Use:

The ceremonial use of ginseng is widely documented among Native Americans. It was used as a sacred plant to chase the evil spirits away during the most sacred ceremonies such as the Green Corn Dance and funerary ones.

The medical use of the plant is mainly related to the febrifuge effect of the decoction of its dried roots. The drink was also said to have a cleansing effect on the body due to its diaphoretic properties (induce sweating).

Lastly, the decoction had an anti-stress and nervine effect on the nervous system and was used in the treatment of trauma (Nervine).

WARNING: excessive consumption (more than 3g per day) will cause dysentery and insomnia. To be avoided during pregnancy and lactation.

WARNING: because American wild ginseng is becoming very rare, it is considered an endangered species. The cultivated one from China is a good substitute but always remember to wash it accurately because it is sprayed with a fungicide to preserve its freshness throughout the journey.

Goldenrod

Binomial Name: Solidago Canadensis

Habitat: Diffused all over the North American continent, from coast to coast in meadows and on the sides of cultivated fields.

Characteristics: This perennial plant is made by a group of stems that can grow up to 7 feet tall from a central rhizome. These round and thin stems are smooth at the base and slightly hairy on the top. Leaves are alternate, lance-shaped, and serrated margins. The small, yellow flowers are positioned at the top of the stem in racemes.

Parts to collect for medical purposes: Leaves and flowers.

Preferred solvent: Water.

Main effect: Carminative, Astringent, Diaphoretic, Diuretic.

Native American Use: Native Americans used the decoction of Goldenrod flowers and leaves to treat many conditions. It was used as a preventive treatment for colds and fever. This drink was also proven to be effective in case of allergy to pollen and dust to soothe the inflamed mucosae and to have a cleansing effect on the whole body (and kidneys in particular) due to its strong diuretic properties.

Lastly, this tea was used as a topical wash for ulcers and wounds.

Flowers and leaves, once dried and powdered were applied topically on wounds and burns to stop bleeding and absorb their excess moisture.

Goldenseal

Binomial Name: Hydrastis Canadensis.

Habitat: Diffused in forests and well-drained grounds of the Eastern United States and South-Eastern Canada. It usually grows near American ginseng (Ashwagandha).

Characteristics: This small flower reaches 10 inches at best and it can be found in dense colonies in the forests, especially near the American ginseng. It grows from the yellow underground rhizome as a hairy stem with lobed leaves (usually seven) with serrated margins. At the top of the plant, the flower blooms during spring. This is a hermaphrodite flower that bears no petals but only white stamens, that encircle a green calyx. It will fall soon after the blooming, giving space to the round scarlet fruits that bear shiny black seeds.

Parts to collect for medical purposes: Rhizome.

Preferred solvent: Water, Alcohol.

Native American Use: Native Americans used the decoction of dried rhizomes and roots to treat dysentery due to its specific astringent characteristics. This decoction was also used for its emollient and anti-inflammatory properties as a wash for skin inflammation or conjunctivitis. The raw consumption of the root was indicated to benefit from these characteristics also in the treatment of cough and sore throat. The root extraction was widely used for curing scrofula and as a panacea for every liver and gallbladder condition. The powdered dried rhizome was applied on wounds and burns to prevent infections due to

its antiseptic properties. Also, is was considered a powerful anti-fungal.

WARNING: The consumption of this herb is not allowed during pregnancy or lactation. In addition, excessive consumption may result in food poisoning.

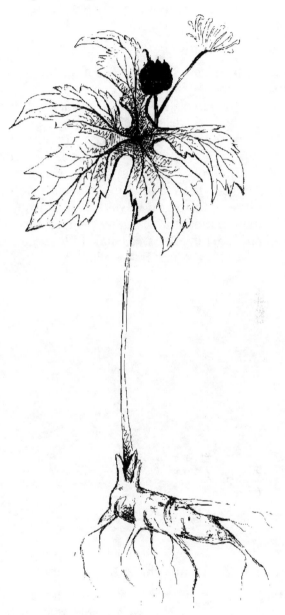

Gooseberry

Binomial Name: Ribes Uva Crispa

Habitat: In the forests of the Middle and Eastern parts of the North American continent. Both in the United States and Canada.

Characteristics: This many-branched perennial shrub can grow up to 4 feet tall and spread widely in forests on low ground. Branches can both have or have not thorns on the same plant and are densely populated by three to five-lobed, palmate leaves. The green-whitish flowers are small, tubular, and grouped in clusters. After the pollination, they develop into round, red, and spiky fruits with many red-brown seeds inside.

Parts to collect for medical purposes: Fruits and roots.

Preferred solvent: Water, Alcohol.

Native American Use: Besides the raw consumption of fruits, Native Americans used the plant for medical purposes. In fact, the tea obtained by the dried fruits was gargles to soothe sore throats. Also, the decoction of roots was used as a wash for eye inflammation or drunk directly, due to its vermifuge characteristics, to treat intestinal worms. Finally, the poultice of fruits and leaves was used to cure skin inflammation due to its emollient feature. It was believed that it cured snakebites because snakes were frightened by the plant.

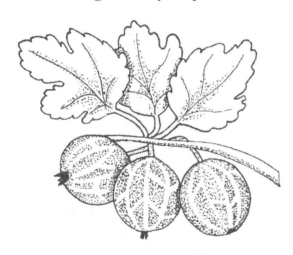

Gravel Root

Binomial Name: Eutrochium purpureum

Habitat: Widely diffused in wet environments of the Eastern part of North America, both in the United States and in Canada.

Characteristics: This perennial shrub can grow up to ten feet tall. The stems grow straight from the central, underground rhizome, bearing many, oblong leaves, grouped in whorls. These leaves have serrated margins and are hairy to the touch. At the top of the stems, pink, bell-shaped flowers grouped in umbrella-shaped clusters.

Parts to collect for medical purposes: The whole plant.

Preferred solvent: Boiling water.

Effects: Diuretic, Tonic, Vermifuge, Febrifuge.

Native American Use: Native Americans used Gravel Root leaves to treat a plethora of conditions. For example, the tea obtained by the dried leaves and flowers was used as a topical wash on infected wounds to reduce inflammation and infections. Also, said tea was drunk to treat all the Urinary Tract Infections and kidney stones, using its diuretic properties. The diaphoretic qualities of this tea also helped in reducing fever and promoting cleansing.

Leaves were also used raw, by pounding them and applying the poultice directly on wounds and burns to promote healing and prevent infections on the injury.

Lastly, Natives used also the Gravel Root rhizome decoction to cure Asthma and menstrual problems, for its anticonvulsant qualities.

WARNING: do not assume this herb during pregnancy or lactation.

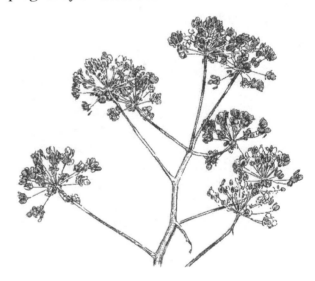

Gutierrezia

Binomial Name: Gutierrezia sarothrae.

Habitat: Diffused all over the flat areas like prairies and plains in the west-central regions of Canada, down to the West-Central United States and Northern Mexico.

Characteristics: This small, perennial bushy subshrub is widely diffused in many environments, from prairies to semi-arid sites. It is made by many an intricate net of green-yellowish stems forming a dome of 60 inches in diameter and 40 inches in height at its best. The alternate leaves that populate the stems are small and almost linear. At the top of the stems, clusters of small, yellow flowers bloom from July to September. After the pollination, the plant develops many achenes, grouped into a small pappus. The seeds are then distributed by the wind.

Parts to collect for medical purposes: Roots, leaves, and flowers.

Preferred solvent: Water.

Main effect: Analgesic, Carminative, Diuretic.

Native American Use:

The decoction obtained from the whole plant was used to treat colds and coughs by both drinking it and gargling it in case of sore throats. The analgesic properties of this decoction of Gutierrezia sarothrae was used by gargling also in case of toothache.

A curious use done by the Navajo was to rub the ashes of the burned plant all over their body to treat headaches.

The poultice of the plant was used as a topical analgesic for swollen joints, insect bites, wounds in general, and in the case of snakebites.

WARNING: the plant is toxic when consumed in large quantities due to its high content of alkaloids. To be avoided in case of pregnancy.

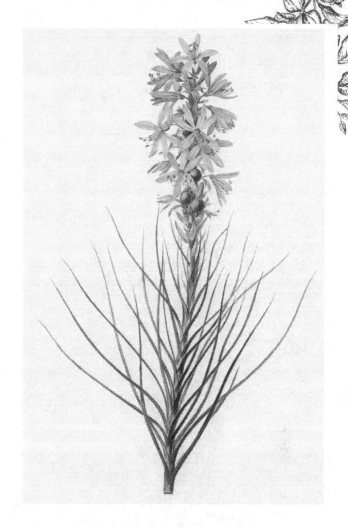

H

Hawthorn

Binomial Name: Crataegus Laevigata

Habitat: Diffused in wet environments and forests, all over the North American continent, both in the United States and Canada.

Characteristics: This shrub can grow up to ten feet tall in an intricate entanglement of branches. These are thorny and widely populated by green-yellowish leaves, five-lobed and with serrated margins. Flowers are located at the end of the branches in white clusters of ten to twenty. After pollination, they evolve into round glossy fruits, black or red in color.

Parts to collect for medical purposes: Leaves and fruits.

Preferred solvent: Boiling water.

Native American Use:

The Natives used hawthorn leaves to treat minor wounds when no other treatment was available. Leaves were simply chewed and the poultice applied on wounds and burns for easy emergency medication.

The plant was also used to prepare a decoction from seeds, that was used to treat diarrhea. The said decoction was also used as a mild sedative, mostly in case of heart palpitation. The medical use of this plant was always associated with heart diseases by Native Americans and surprisingly by many other ancient populations all over the globe. In time, recent studies have proved that it has a positive effect on the main heart disease as tachycardia and hypertension and may help in lowering the cholesterol levels.

WARNING: do not assume this herb during pregnancy or lactation.

Heal-all

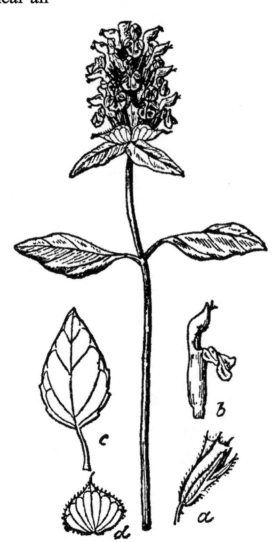

Binomial Name: Prunella Vulgaris

Habitat: Diffused all over the United States and Canada in meadows, fields, and at the edge of forests. It prefers wet, shady environments.

Characteristics: This small perennial can grow up to ten inches in height. The plant is a single vertical stem with opposite, oblong leaves with serrated margins. At the top of the stem, there are blue/purple flowers grouped in a whorled cluster.

Parts to collect for medical purposes: The whole plant.

Preferred solvent: Boiling water.

Effects: Hepatic, Cholagogue, Astringent.

Native American Use: As the name suggests, the Native Americans considered the plant a panacea for a plethora of diseases. The influence of the tea obtained by the whole plant to treat liver and gallbladder dysfunctions is well documented, not only between Native Americans but also in other cultures all over the world. Many tribe healers also used the plant and its decoction, due to its astringent qualities, in the treatment of excessive menstrual flow. Other documented uses of this decoction are many: from mouthwash to treat mouth sores and gingivitis, to the topical wash of wounds and burns, or to the drink of it to reduce fever or diarrhea attacks.

Finally, the raw consumption of the plant is useful for sore throat.

Honeysuckle

Binomial Name: Lonicera Japonica.

Habitat: Diffused all over the United States and Canada. Being invasive, it is widely diffused at the edges of forests and streams.

Characteristics: This small plant is a climbing vine. The leaves that populate the green-reddish branches are oblong and lance-shaped. Flowers have the shape of white or red trumpets, depending on the species with many protruding white/yellow stamens. Fruit obtained after the pollination is round and black.

Parts to collect for medical purposes: The whole plant.

Preferred solvent: Boiling water, Alcohol.

Effects: Febrifuge, Astringent, Antimicrobial.

Native American Use: Native Americans used the tea obtained from flowers to treat diarrhea and fever, due to its astringent qualities. The said tea was used also as a gargle in the treatment of sore throat and laryngitis and as a topical wash to soothe common skin ailments like eczema and rash. Finally, the bark tea was used in the treatment of Urinary Tract Infections and as a lenitive for the symptoms of gonorrhea and other Sexual Transmitted Diseases such as syphilis.

Hops

Binomial Name: Humulus lupulus.

Habitat: Diffused in the inland zone of North West of the United States and South West of Canada.

Characteristics: This climbing perennial is the main aromatic ingredient in the preparation of beer. The climbing green stems are densely populated by opposite leaves, with three to five lobes with serrated edges. The female flowers are small and made of numerous florets, while the male ones are small and yellow. Female flowers evolve into fruits (strobili) with conical shape and gray-yellowish in color.

Parts to collect for medical purposes: Female flowers.

Preferred solvent: Boiling water, Diluted Alcohol.

Effects: Diuretic, Nervine, Sedative, Febrifuge.

Native American Use:

Native Americans' medical use of hops is not widely documented. The common herbal practice advises using the tea obtained with the dried cones to reduce fever and calm nerves.

It is renowned the use of leaves during the sweat lodge ceremony.

WARNING: Hops may cause allergy.

Horsetail

Binomial Name: Equisetum Arvense.

Habitat: Diffused all over the United States and southern Canada, alongside water shores.

Characteristics: This perennial can grow up five feet tall. It is a leafless, segmented stem with an apothecium on top, from which spores can diffuse. In summer, it seems to change into a different plant: many thin, long, needle-like branches grow for the stem in whorls.

Parts to collect for medical purposes: Leaves and roots.

Preferred solvent: Water.

Effects: Emollient, Astringent, Diuretic.

Native American Use: Native Americans used this plant for medical purposes for both humans and horses. In fact, it is interesting to recall the use of it to create a decoction to treat the cough of horses.

The main medical purpose for humans was instead related to its diuretic qualities: the tea obtained with the needle-like branches was used to treat painful urination in case of Sexual Transmitted Disease and Urinary Tract Infections in general. Also, the bath obtained by infusing the branches in hot water was used to treat gonorrhea and syphilis.

The stem, reduced to a poultice, is used in topical applications for skin rash.

WARNING: excessive consumption may be poisonous

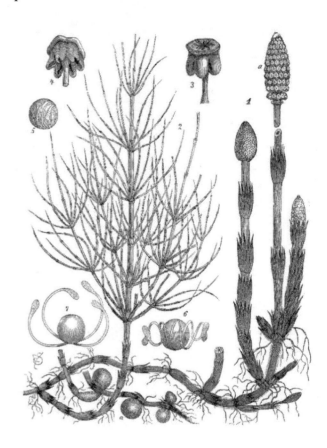

Hyssop (New Mexico Giant)

Binomial Name: Agastache neomexicana

Habitat: Diffused in South-Western States of North America and North-East Mexico, in deep forests and moist environments.

Characteristics: This perennial plant belongs to the mint family. The stems emerge straight from the underground rhizome, to reach up to 3 feet tall. The lance-shaped leaves are bright green, aromatic, and with serrated edges.

Parts to collect for medical purposes: The whole plant.

Preferred solvent: Alcohol.

Effects: Anti-inflammatory, Expectorant, Febrifuge.

Native American Use: The salves and oils obtained by the whole plant were used to treat cough, by dissolving it in boiling water and inhaling the steam. The recommended preparation for the oil extraction plans to first powder the dried plant into a mortar and then transfer it into a glass dish. The powder is then submerged in the oil of your choice (olive, canola, etc…) and cooked overnight in your kitchen oven at low temperature (170°F). The oil extraction is then obtained by straining the mixture using a cheesecloth. The oil is then gently heated on a stove and thickened with beeswax to obtain the salve.

Another use of the hyssop is the preparation of tea from the whole plant to reduce fever. Finally, dried and powdered leaves were used topically on wounds and sores.

I

Ilex Verticillata (Winterberry, Fever Bush)

Binomial Name: Ilex Verticillata.

Habitat: Mostly thriving in wet environments (but it is present also in sandy soles) of North-Eastern to the Central States and South-East of Canada.

Characteristics: This deciduous shrub can grow up to fifteen feet tall. It has glossy, alternate leaves, which fall during autumn. Leaves are lance-shaped and with serrated margins. Flowers are very small and are made of five small white-greenish petals that encircle a green calyx. Fruits are glossy red berries that persist during winter, becoming a food resource for birds and animals in general.

Parts to collect for medical purposes: Berries and leaves.

Preferred solvent: Alcohol.

Effects: Emetic, Febrifuge.

Native American Use: Native Americans widely used this shrub for its medical purposes. The raw consumption of the berries or leaves induces nausea and vomit and was used in case of food poisoning. Medical studies certify that this raw consumption reduces blood pressure.

The main use of this plant is the preparation of a decoction from leaves, that was used to reduce fever, hence the common name, fever bush.

Effects: Astringent.

Native American Use: The Lummi tribe, who inhabited the Northern part of the Washington State, near Bellingham, used the decoction of flowers to stop diarrhea.

British Columbia Natives used attributed to the decoction of berries for the same purpose, along with using it as a wash in case of smallpox and chickenpox among children.

Finally, the poultice of leaves was used to treat wounds and burns.

Ironwood (Ocean Spray, Creambush)

Binomial Name: Holodiscus discolor

Habitat: Widely diffused throughout the Pacific Coast of the United States (especially in California) and Canada. The plant can grow in various habitats, from the coastal moist environments to dry mountain ones.

Characteristics: This shrub can be three to five feet tall. It has small, alternate leaves, lance-shaped, and with serrated margins. From May to July, white clusters of white, sweet-scented flowers droop down from the edge of the branches. Fruits are small and covered by hair.

Parts to collect for medical purposes: Flowers and leaves.

Preferred solvent: Water.

J

Juniper

Binomial Name: Juniperus Comunis

Habitat: Widely diffused all over the North American continent, both in the United States and Canada

Characteristics: This evergreen shrub can grow up to 50 feet tall at its best. Thorn-like green leaves assembled in whorls densely populate the branches of this plant. Female flowers are small,

spherical, and green; male ones are small, yellow and grow in groups of three. They have a catkin shape with whorls of stamens. The highly aromatic berries are deep blue and hard.

Parts to collect for medical purposes: Berries.

Preferred solvent: Boiling water, Alcohol.

Native American Use:

Besides the widely documented application of the dried berries as a spice for game meat, this plant was also widely used for its medical purposes, not only by natives but also by Mediterranean cultures.

For example, the decoction obtained from the berries can help in premenstrual syndrome and dysmenorrhea. Also, it was used for its diuretic and antiseptic properties to treat Urinary Tract Infections and gallbladder conditions. Needles and bark could be added to the decoction to enhance the effect.

WARNING: do not assume this herb during pregnancy or lactation and in case of kidney diseases.

L

Lady's slipper

Binomial Name: Cypripedioideae.

Habitat: Diffused in wet environments all over the Northern United States and Canada.

Characteristics: From the single root of this perennial plant, many stems can grow up to three feet tall. Each stem has basal, opposite, lance-shaped leaves. These are a paler shade of green on the bottom side than the upper side and can reach up to one foot long. The flower on top is pinkish and similar to a slipper orchid.

Effects: Astringent, Antiperiodic.

Parts to collect for medical purposes: Root.

Preferred solvent: Boiling water, Alcohol.

Native American Use:

Native Americans collected the rhizome of this plant for medical purposes usually during fall when the plan was about to let the stem and leaves fall off to endure the winter. This is the best period to collect all kinds of roots, taproots, and rhizomes because all the healing substances are going to concentrate on them due to the winter proximity.

The preferable preparations to achieve the maximum effectiveness from Lady's Slipper roots are the decoction and the tincture. These preparations were both widely used to treat dysentery and diarrhea and to lower fever. They also had a calming effect on nerves.

WARNING: Due to the destruction of its natural habitat, it is an endangered species, so it is recommended to cultivate it and then harvest it.

WARNING: The whole plant is urticant and may cause skin rash and swelling.

Lemon Balm

Binomial Name: Melissa Officinalis.

Habitat: Diffused in gardens and meadows all over the United States and Canada.

Characteristics: This perennial, low-lying plant reaches roughly three inches tall. It grows from the ground in many stems widely populated with oval-shaped, bright green leaves with serrated margins. Flowers are small, tubular, and white. The main characteristic of this plant is the intense fragrance of lemon that it emanates from leaves and flowers, hence the name.

Effects: Carminative, Febrifuge, Analgesic.

Parts to collect for medical purposes: Leaves, Flowers, and Stems.

Preferred solvent: Boiling water, Alcohol.

Native American Use:

Native Americans used the tea prepared with the aerial parts of the plant for its many benefits. The carminative qualities of lemon balm helped with intestinal gas. Moreover, the analgesic effect of it was used to calm nerves and, in combination with the anticonvulsant substances contained in it, helped to treat menstrual cramps. Finally, the diaphoretic substances inside of it induce sweat and promote cleansing of the body and a lowering of body temperature in case of excessive fever.

This plant is perfect for the black thumbs because it is very infesting and rather inextirpable. It covers all the ground it can so its cultivation is advised in pots inside your home. The traditional harvesting period of lemon balm is spring for leaves and summer for flowers.

WARNING: do not use during pregnancy or lactation and in case of hypothyroidism condition.

Licorice (Wild American)

Binomial Name: Glycyrhizza Lepidota.

Habitat: Widely diffused in wet, moist environments of the Western United States or Canada.

Characteristics: This plant grows in intricate root stalks and spread in width rather than growing in height. It can reach up to 5 feet in height at its best, but it can occupy a wide surface on the ground. Odd-pinnate, flat leaves with smooth edges populate the root stalks and, at the top of the stalk, the green-yellowish flowers are grouped in vertical clusters, like red clover. Seeds are contained inside pods, like peas, and are shiny black.

Effects: Emollient, Purgative, Expectorant, Febrifuge.

Parts to collect for medical purposes: Roots (dried) and leaves.

Preferred solvent: Water.

Native American Use: Native Americans widely used the licorice for medical purposes, mainly related to stomach conditions. In fact, the decoction prepared with the peeled, dried root was used for laxative purposes in case of constipation. Another use of this tea was to reduce the fever because the diaphoretic substances contained in it induced sweat on the patient.

Other medical uses of the wild licorice were related to the tea of leaves, used as a topical medicament for earache, and the raw root consumption for toothache and sore throat.

Finally, the poultice obtained from the fresh root was used topically on swollen joints in case of rheumatism or gout.

WARNING: it increased blood pressure, so it is not advised in case of hypertension.

Lobelia

Binomial Name: Lobelia Cardinalis.

Habitat: Widely diffused in wet environments all over the North American continent, both in the United States and Canada.

Characteristics: This small perennial flower can reach up to five inches in height. The green leaves are wide and lance-shaped, assembled opposite at the side of the central stem. The zygomorphic, tubular blue flowers are arranged in vertical clusters at the end of the stems. The blooming period is August to October.

Effects: Emetic, Expectorant, Sedative, Diaphoretic.

Parts to collect for medical purposes: Leaves, stems, and roots. Avoid flowers due to high toxicity.

Preferred solvent: Water.

Native American Use: Native Americans widely knew the mildly toxic properties of lobelia. In fact, they used it to induce vomit to treat food poisoning, by preparing a decoction of the stems.

The tea prepared from leaves was used to induce sweating and lower the fever, while the decoction of only roots was used to treat symptoms of sexually transmitted diseases (such as syphilis and gonorrhea) and to get rid of intestinal worms in case of a parasite infection.

Finally, the poultice of roots was used to treat back pain and insect stings with topical application.

WARNING: Avoid flowers due to high toxicity.

M

Maidenhair Fern

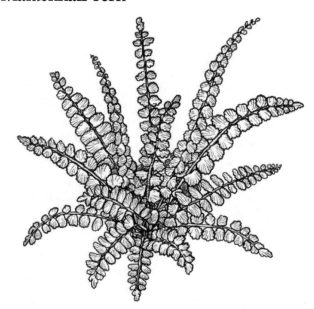

Binomial Name: Adiantum Capillus-Veneris.

Habitat: Diffused mainly in moist environments of the Southern half of the United States, from coast to coast.

Characteristics: This plant can grow up to fifteen inches at its best. The thin and almost black branches arise from a rhizome root. Fronds (large, divided leaves) are very thin. Leaves are cuneiform and insist on the thin, black rachis, the prosecution of the branch.

Effects: Anti-inflammatory, Analgesic.

Parts to collect for medical purposes: The whole plant.

Preferred solvent: Boiling water.

Native American Use:

This plant was used for ceremonial purposes as one of the plants to be smoked in the sacred pipe.

The medical purposes of the Maidenhair Fern are less common: mostly the whole plant decoction was used to reduce swelling in case of insect bites via a topical application.

In addition, drinking the fronds tea was said to cure depression and mental illness.

Mayapple

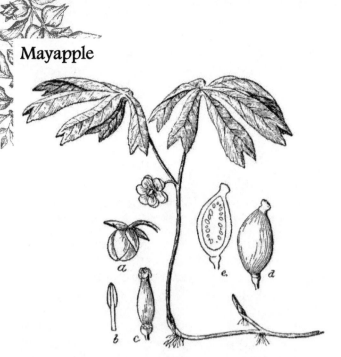

Binomial Name: Podophyllum Peltatum.

Habitat: Diffused in the deep forests in the Eastern United States and Canada.

Maple

Characteristics: This perennial flower grows in the deep, shaded woods. Each stout has two wide and five-lobed leaves. The single flower that grows underneath the leaves is white and with six petals surrounding a central group of yellow stamens. The edible fruit ripens in the latest part of summer.

Effects: Purgative, Cholagogue.

Parts to collect for medical purposes: Sap and roots.

Preferred solvent: Boiling water and Alcohol.

Native American Use: Native Americans used topically Mayapple roots as a poultice or powder to treat warts. Also, the decoction prepared from leaves is a strong emetic and laxative and was used to treat intestinal worms.

NOTE: Root decoction can be used as a powerful natural insecticide for your garden.

WARNING: use only strictly under medical supervision.

Binomial Name: Acer.

Habitat: Common tree, widely diffused all over the North American continent.

Characteristics: This family of deciduous trees includes many species whose height can vary greatly, from 30 to 150 feet tall. Throughout the species, the bark is wrinkled in the older plants, while it is smooth in younger ones. Leaves are many, three-lobed and with serrated edges. Fruits are samaras, a winged achene with horizontal "leaflets" such as helicopter blades. These help the seeds fly for long distances when they detach from the tree.

Parts to collect for medical purposes: Inner bark and leaves.

Preferred solvent: Boiling water.

Effects: Astringent.

Native American Use:

Native Americans widely used the maple in their day-to-day lives. In fact, its sap was the best source of sugar available for them. They collected it during winter and spring and used it as a sweetener. The same process is done today for the harvesting and production of maple syrup.

Besides the sustenance, maple was also used for its healing properties: the leaves infusion was used for detoxification, while the inner bark decoction was used as a wash for conjunctivitis

Milkweed

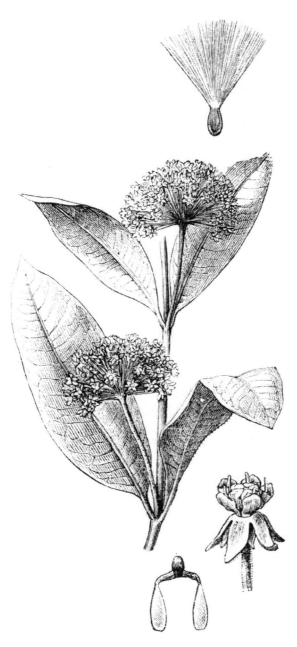

and other eye conditions. If drunk, the inner bark decoction has an expectorant effect helping in removing the phlegm in case of cough and sore throat.

Binomial Name: Asclepias Speciosa.

Habitat: Diffused mainly near the cultivated fields, all over the North American continent, both in the United States and Canada.

Characteristics: This perennial plant is made by a single stem emerging from the ground to reach three to five feet tall. Leaves are opposite, large, and oval-shaped. The pink flowers are concentrated in spherical clusters that grow from the leaf axils. Seeds are contained in seedpods and have a pappus to be easily moved by the wind.

Parts to collect for medical purposes: Flowers, leaves, and roots.

Preferred solvent: Boiling water

Native American Use:

Native Americans used milkweed flowers only after accurate preparation due to their high content in toxic substances (cardiac glycosides). They were used as food, after boiling them. Seeds were crushed to obtain flour to prepare bread.

The medical applications of this plant are many. From the decoction of the dried roots used to increase lactation to the topical application of sap that came out from leaves, to treat warts, urticaria, and insect bites.

Also, the poultice of leaves was used to treat wounds and the dried leaves infusion was used to treat stomach problems.

WARNING: It is strictly forbidden the use without medical advice and supervision because it contains toxic substances for the heart. It may cause infertility.

Mullein

Binomial Name: Verbascum Thapsus.

Habitat: Common plant widely diffused all over the mountain areas of the United States and Canada, from coast to coast.

Characteristics: The Mullein is a biennial straight plant, two to eight feet tall. The single stem is populated by leaves that grow in whorls

around it. The lower ones are wide, long, and hairy. Leaves size decrease from the bottom to the top of the plant. At the top of the spike, there is a vertical cluster of yellow flowers with red pistils.

Parts to collect for medical purposes: Flowers and leaves.

Preferred solvent: Boiling water.

Effects: Emollient, Diuretic, Astringent.

Native American Use: The demulcent effect of the mullein (leaves and flowers) were widely known by Native Americans who used it in decoction and teas to treat mild respiratory conditions, from cough to nasal congestion.

The action of mullein was frequently paired with the one of other plants like thyme and rosemary.

The poultice obtained from fresh leaves was used to treat wounds, swellings, and skin ailments such as rashes, while dried ones were smoked to induce cough and expectorate the phlegm.

NOTE: Mullein is particularly indicated for beginner gardeners because it can easily grow in yards.

N

Nettle

Binomial Name: Urtica Dioica.

Habitat: Widely spread all over the United States and Canada, near cultivated fields, marshes, and wetlands in general.

Characteristics: This perennial plant can grow up to five feet tall from the creeping rhizome. The single stem with a square section is covered with stinging hair. Leaves are dark green, ovate, opposite, and with deeply serrated margins. Dioica means that the male and female flowers are located on different plants: female ones are drooping raceme, while the male flowers are erect ones. Both male and female flowers have four tepals that enclose the reproductive organs (stamens or ovary). The female flower evolves, after pollination in an egg-shaped achene.

Parts to collect for medical purposes: Roots and leaves.

Preferred solvent: Boiling water.

Effects: Diuretic, Astringent, Expectorant.

Native American Use:

Native Americans widely used the nettle to treat many conditions related to the upper respiratory tract. It is widely documented the use of the infusion of fresh leaves and stems to treat allergies, cough, or even asthmatic conditions.

One of the most effective treatments you can do in the comfort of your kitchen using nettle is the tincture of fresh nettle by using a weight ratio between herb and 50% Alcohol solution of 1:2. By simply soaking fresh nettle leaves in the alcoholic solution for 2 weeks in a shadowy place, and straining the liquid, you will have access to a powerful preventive treatment in case of bronchitis, flu, and colds in general. Just assuming 20 drops of the tincture two times a day (I prefer to do it first thing in the morning and just before dinner), in the proximity of the cold season will shield you from the possibility to catch a cold or flu.

Native Americans also used the dried and powdered plant on wounds and burns in topical application to stop bleeding and as a disinfectant. The dried leaves were also used to prepare a diuretic tea recommended in case of Urinary Tract Infections.

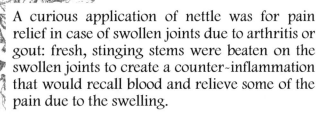

A curious application of nettle was for pain relief in case of swollen joints due to arthritis or gout: fresh, stinging stems were beaten on the swollen joints to create a counter-inflammation that would recall blood and relieve some of the pain due to the swelling.

Another not common application of the nettle was the raw consumption of it to improve the health and beauty of hair.

Note: Nettle, as all the infesting plants can be easily grown into your garden. The difficult part is contain its spreading.

O

Oak

Binomial Name: Quercus.

Habitat: Widely diffused all over the United States and Canada, from coast to coast, in forests and yards.

Characteristics: This family includes many species of trees that can grow up to one hundred feet. The leaves that populate the branches of these towering trees are alternate. Lobes, cuts, margins, and overall shape of the leaves change from species to species. Throughout the species, male flowers are yellow amentia while female flowers are small and green, located at the base of the leaves. After pollination, they evolve into acorns.

Parts to collect for medical purposes: Barks and acorns.

Preferred solvent: Boiling water.

Effects: Antiseptic, Astringent.

Native American Use: The Native Americans' use of the oak was for both medical and sustenance purposes. Acorns were pounded into a paste for food while the tea from barks was used as a wash for mouth (mouth sores or gum inflammation) and for wounds and burns in general.

The dried and powdered bark was used as an antiseptic for topical application on wounds to facilitate the healing.

The decoction of red oak barks was used to treat diarrhea and abdominal pain.

All the medical properties of oak are related to its high content in tannins, an astringent chemical substance that can be used to treat many intestinal disorders and to soothe an inflamed gut.

Orange Agoseris

Binomial Name: Agoseris Aurantiaca

Habitat: Widely diffused in the mountain regions of the Western North America Continent, from California to Canada and Alaska.

Characteristics: This perennial flower is a close sibling to the sunflowers. It is formed by a basal rosette of leaves. It has no stem but it has peduncles that resemble stems that bear the flower. These change from smooth to hairy

towards the top of the peduncle. On top of it, the ligulate head holds the ray florets. It evolves into a ball of achenes with fringed extremities after the pollination.

Preferred solvent: Water.

Effects: Emetic.

Native American Use: Native Americans were aware of the mild toxicity of the plant and used it to their advantage by making tea from flowers, which was a powerful emetic to treat food poisoning.

Other uses of the plant included the cold infusion of the flowers as a wash on wounds and burns, and the poultice of leaves, used on swollen joints as an anti-inflammatory.

Oregon Grape

Binomial Name: Mahonia Aquifolium

Habitat: Evergreen shrub widely diffused at the edge of the forests in the north-western United States.

Characteristics: This evergreen shrub can reach up to seven feet tall. Leaves are pinnate, pointed, and bright green. Flowers are small and yellow-greenish with purple sepals and evolve into blue

berries after pollination. Roots are bright yellow on the inside.

Preferred solvent: Boiling water.

Effects: Purgative, Cathartic.

Native American Use: Native Americans used Oregon Grape in many ways. Above all, fruits

were renowned to induce vomit if eaten in small quantities.

The decoction of stems was used to promote detoxification of the liver and gallbladder. Decoction of bark was used for the same purpose and as an eyewash for conjunctivitis or as a gargle for tonsillitis.

Roots were used both in decoctions to treat upset stomach due to Oregon Grape astringent properties and in extraction as a topical treatment on the skin for ulcers and excessive dryness.

WARNING: do not use during pregnancy or lactation.

P

Pasque Flower

Binomial Name: Pulsatilla.

Habitat: Diffused in prairies and meadows all over the United States, especially in the Northern and Central States.

Characteristics: This family of small flowers grows spontaneously in the meadows of the Northern and Central states. Throughout the species, the common characteristics are the finely dissected, hairy leaves and the elegant flower with purple petals.

Parts to collect for medical purposes: Aerial parts (stem, leaves, and flowers).

Effects: Sedative.

Native American Use:

The Native Americans from Montana widely used tea from flowers to cause uterine contraction and thus abortion or to speed up difficult childbirth. It is strongly advised to do not to use this plant for medical purposes because mistakes in dosages can cause cardiac arrest.

WARNING: Direct ingestion is highly toxic.

Passionflower

Binomial Name: Passiflora.

Habitat: Mainly diffused on forest edges in the South-Eastern United States.

Characteristics: This climbing plant can climb up to forty feet in height. Stems that emerge from the roots are brown-red with alternated, lightly hairy leaves with serrated margins. Flowers are big and definitively recognizable with a blue-white crown of petals near the protruding pistils.

Parts to collect for medical purposes: Leaves and flowers.

Preferred solvent: Alcohol.

Effects: Sedative, Diuretic, Analgesic.

Native American Use:

Native Americans used the tea obtained from fresh or dried leaves and flowers as a mild,

sleep-inducing sedative. The drink helped in stomach pain, intestinal gas and was used as an anticonvulsant for menstrual cramps. The infusion of the crushed root was used to treat earache and in topical application against hemorrhoids. The poultice of the root was used topically on wounds and skin inflammations.

Peppermint

Binomial Name: Mentha piperita.

Habitat: Diffused all over the United States and Canada, often near water streams and pounds.

Characteristics: This small plant emerges from the basal rhizome as a straight green stem with a square section, bearing many lance-shaped leaves. These are bright green, aromatic, and with serrated margins. The small flowers appear in whorls at the top of the plant in different colors, depending on the species (white for peppermint, blue or purple for other species of mint).

Parts to collect for medical purposes: Leaves and stems.

Preferred solvent: Alcohol, Water.

Effects: Carminative, Stimulant.

Native American Use: Native Americans' use as a food of peppermint is widely documented.

The medical one is less known. The tea made with dried or fresh leaves helps with excessive intestinal gas because of the carminative substances contained in it.

The essential oil is an effective stimulant and it can be used to massage sore muscles due to its cooling effect on the part.

During the sweat lodge ceremony, the leaves infusion was dripped on hot stones for effective action against airways congestions.

The poultice was used as a refreshing medicament for burns and skin ailments like urticarial.

WARNING: the essential oil can be aggressive to open wounds and burns.

TIPS FOR BEGINNER GARDENERS: Mint is very infesting, grow them inside steel containers, or soon your garden will be invaded.

Pine

Binomial Name: Pinaceae

Habitat: Widely diffused in forests and woods all over the United States and Canada.

Characteristics: This evergreen tree can grow up to 60 feet tall. The many branches of this plant depart in whorls from the wide, central trunk. The bark is thick and brown. Leaves are green and needle-shaped. The small, tubular, and white-greenish flowers are located at the end of the branches. The pine cones bear seeds inside.

Parts to collect for medical purposes: Inner bark, leaves, and sap.

Preferred solvent: Boiling water.

Effects: Febrifuge, Expectorant.

Native American Use: Native Americans widely used pines for their sticky and antiseptic sap. This can be used to seal the edges of wounds for emergency medication. In addition, the pine needle tea was used to prevent scurvy (due to its content of vitamin C) and is a powerful febrifuge because of the diaphoretic substances contained in the needles. Another use of the needle tea was related to its antiseptic and antimicrobial features: in fact, it was also widely used as a gargle for sore throat.

Pine needle tea can be also a source of energy and minerals and had saved many lives of unprepared backpackers who lost themselves in the woods.

Platain

Binomial Name: Plantago Lanceolata or Marittima.

Habitat: Diffused all over the United States, alongside cultivated fields and along the seashore for the Plantago Marittima.

Characteristics: This small plant emerges from the ground as an upright, straight green stem. Leaves have different shapes dispensing on the species: the Lanceolata species has oblong, pointed leaves, while the Marittima ones are more pointed. A vertical spike of small hermaphrodite flowers composes the inflorescence. Each flower has protruding stamens with thin, hair-like peduncles.

Parts to collect for medical purposes: Leaves and stems.

Preferred solvent: Water.

Effects: Astringent, Antiseptic.

Native American Use: Native Americans used the Plantain both for food and for medical purposes. Leaves were used as food, though not very nutritious.

The tea made with flowers creates a gel-like drink that was used in the treatment of diarrhea and dysentery to reduce the spasmodic attacks and to soothe the inflamed gut. Moreover, the poultice made by chewing the raw leaves of the fresh plant was used topically to treat urticarial and skin inflammations in general, and as an antiseptic medication for wounds.

The fresh leaves were dried during summer and used throughout the year, especially during the cold seasons to treat colds and coughs because the tea obtained from it is a strong expectorant and diuretic.

Finally, the raw consumption of seeds was used in case of constipation due to its strong laxative effect.

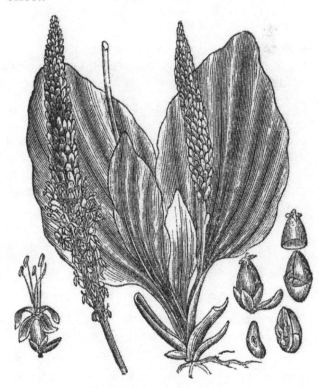

Prickly Pear

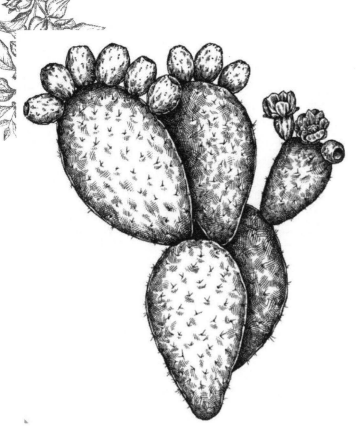

known use of peeled pads is the topical application on breasts to stimulate lactation.

Evening Primrose

Binomial Name: Opuntia-

Habitat: Diffused in dry environments, all over the Southern United States, alongside cultivated fields.

Characteristics: This plant belongs to the family of cactus and has large, drop-shaped, light green pads covered with black dots from which thorns emerge. Flowers are large and yellow, fruits are egg-shaped and in various colors within the same plant (yellow, green, purple, orange).

Parts to collect for medical purposes: Pads, fruits, and flowers.

Preferred solvent: Water.

Effects: Astringent, Antiseptic.

Native American Use: Native Americans of the Southern States widely used pads, flowers, and fruit for food (after peeling of course).

The medical properties of this widely diffused cactus are less known. For example, the tea made from flowers is astringent and is useful for Irritable Bowel Syndrome and dysentery to both calm the spasmodic bowel movement and to soothe the inflammation within. Another use of the plant was the topical application of the peeled pads on burns and wounds to eliminate infections and facilitate healing. Another less

Binomial Name: Oenothera Biennis.

Habitat: Diffused in gardens and fields all over the United States and Canada.

Characteristics: This small plant has a two years life cycle. In the first year, flowers do not appear but the plant is only a basal cluster of leaves. In the second year, the stem emerges from the ground, three feet tall at maximum with serrated, oblong leaves and a flower on top. The yellow flowers open in the evening and they have four petals and protruding yellow stamens. Seeds are black-brown and drop-shaped.

Parts to collect for medical purposes: Roots.

Preferred solvent: Water.

Native American Use: The medical application of the evening primrose includes mainly the pounding of the whole plant or parts of it, to obtain a poultice.

94

In detail, the poultice of the plant was used by Native Americans to treat wounds and burns with topical applications. The astringent and antiseptic properties of the plant helped the injuries to heal faster and to avoid infections. Instead, the poultice of only roots was heated and applied topically to treat hemorrhoids and fissures.

A rather unknown use of the plant in nowadays herbalism includes the power to lower the cholesterol levels by the seed extract: just put the roughly pounded seeds into a non-metallic, dark container with an airtight lid, covering them with a 50% alcohol-water solution. The rough weight ratio is 1:8 but of course, you have to adjust on the spot on the effective quantity needed to cover the seeds. Then the container must seat in the fridge for 2 weeks. Be sure to shake it once a day minimum for optimal result.

WARNING: excessive doses of primrose may cause headaches and nausea. Do not use during pregnancy or lactation or if assuming psychotropic drugs.

Purslane

Binomial Name: Portulaca Oleracea.

Habitat: Widely diffused all over the United States and Canada, in gardens and meadows.

Characteristics: This small, succulent plant is a weed commonly found in any garden. The red/purple stems emerge from the ground in an intricate entanglement and spread in any direction. Leaves that cover the stems are narrow, pointed, and smooth-edged. The yellow or orange flowers have five colorful, heart-shaped petals encircling an explosion of protruding stamens. It blossoms in June.

Parts to collect for medical purposes: The whole plant.

Preferred solvent: Water.

Native American Use:

Native Americans used this small flower in a similar way to the evening primrose: by pounding the whole plant to obtain a poultice.

This was used to treat skin conditions as urticaria or eczemas, or to help in the healing of wounds. A few drops of the juice obtained by squeezing this poultice inside cheesecloth sheets were used topically to treat earache.

The fresh plant was used also decocted as a topical wash for wounds and burns due to its antiseptic characteristics or as a drink to treat intestinal worms. The decoction of only leaves was astringent and emollient for the gut, so it was widely used to treat diarrhea.

Red Clover

Binomial Name: Trifolium Pratense.

Habitat: Diffused all over the United States, in sunny plains and meadows.

Characteristics: This perennial plant is made by a single, hairy stem emerging from the ground. It can reach ten to twenty inches in height. The alternate compound leaves are trifoliate. The lower compound has long petioles which are absent in the upper compound. Leaves are oval-shaped, hairy, and with smooth margins. Leaves have the characteristic arrow-tip-shaped "stain" of light green toward the middle. The plant terminates with a spherical cluster of red or purple tubular flowers that bloom from July to September.

Parts to collect for medical purposes: Leaves and flowers.

Effects: Expectorant.

Native American Use: Native Americans used red clover tea as a tonic and for all the respiratory conditions from asthma to cough. In addition, this decoction was used as a wash for wounds and burns due to its astringent characteristics and as a remedy for menopausal side problems, hot flashes in particular. The diaphoretic effect of the tea helps in cleansing the body and regulates the thyroidal hormone production that causes the hot flash / chilling sensations.

WARNING: If assumed during menstruation, it may cause excessive bleeding, so the consumption must be done after consulting with a medical practitioner.

Redroot

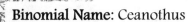

Binomial Name: Ceanothus

Habitat: Diffused all over the Western States of the whole North American continent, from the Pacific Ocean to the Rocky Mountains, from California to British Columbia.

Characteristics: This plant has almost forty varieties. Mainly it presents as a ground plant that grows covering extended areas, but it can be different depending on the species. For example, the Ceanothus Californiana is a small tree six to eight feet tall. The stems are covered in small thorns and have small white (or blue) flowers grouped in clusters at the end. Seeds are small, triangular, and contained in pods. The medical part is the root. The exterior part of it is deep black but, once removed, it reveals an inner red root. The harvesting period for the root is usually autumn. Be sure to cut and peel the root once it is fresh because once dried, it becomes rock hard.

Parts to collect for medical purposes: Root.

Effects: Expectorant, Astringent, Sedative, Febrifuge.

Native American Use: The Native Americans used redroot decoction to treat sore throat, especially in infants. The sedative action of the plant helped in reducing the pain associated with tonsillitis and the expectorant function helped to remove the phlegm, thus speeding up the recovery from the disease. The root decoction was also effective to reduce fever because due to its sweat-inducing substances (diaphoretic) and stimulates the lymphatic system, and then the immune one. The best way to assume the redroot is by the direct ingestion of the tincture. Assuming 20-30 drops of it and letting them "drip" throughout the tonsils and the whole throat will assure relief to a sore throat and fast healing.

Romero

Binomial Name: Thricostema Ianatum.

Habitat: Bushy plant widely diffused in the Southern part of California and in the Pacific coast of Mexico.

Characteristics: This plant grows up to five feet tall from the ground in many intricate branches. Leaves are small and pointed similar to rosemary, for which it was mistaken by the first conquistadores. From March to June, the plant blooms with small groups of blue or purple, goblet-shaped flowers with three petals and protruding purple stamens.

Parts to collect for medical purposes: Flowers and leaves.

Effects: Expectorant, Febrifuge, Anticonvulsant, Analgesic.

Native American Use: Native Americans mainly used the Romero for its properties anticonvulsant properties. The decoction of Romero leaves will soothe an upset stomach and calm menstrual cramps. In addition, if drunk frequently, the decoction has positive effects for pain relief on sore joints, muscle pain, and will give an overall improvement on your cardio-circulatory system due to the increase of capillary section. Another use of the leaves decoction was to treat sore throat and to lower the fever due to its sweat-inducing properties.

Finally, the poultice of flowers was used topically on wounds for emergency medication while in the woods.

S

Sagebrush

Binomial Name: Artemisia Tridentata.

Habitat: Diffused in dry and almost desert environments, all over the Western Unites States, from California to Washington state, from Texas to Montana.

Characteristics: This strongly aromatic plant can grow up to seven feet tall. Its leaves are spatula-obovate with a smooth margin, connected to the branch at the narrow end. The bigger ones usually have three lobes towards the end. Each leaf is covered by thin hair that allows the plant to increase the heat transfer surface and be cool even in the hottest desert environments. Leaves send out a strong sage-like scent but the two plants are not even remotely related. This silvery hair gives the plant its typical silver-green color. The plant blooms in late summer with bright yellow flowers that grow at the end of each stem in vertical clusters.

Parts to collect for medical purposes: Leaves.

Native American Use:

Native Americans considered this plant sacred due to its similarity of scent with sage. They used the plant for the smudging ceremony and to chase demons away. In addition, it was used in the sweat lodge ceremony due to its aromatic properties.

The medical use of the plant mainly relies on the decoction of leaves. It was considered a powerful febrifuge because it induced sweat and promoted the lowering of body temperature. In addition, this decoction was used to help the uterus to contract in difficult childbirths and to treat stomachache.

If used as a gargle, the astringent properties of the decoction helped with sore throat and bronchitis. Moreover, this tea was used as a wash for the eyes in cases of conjunctivitis.

Finally, a small tent was created between a bowl containing the hot decoction of leaves and the head of the patient, using a canvas or a pelt. The steam of the decoction was inhaled by the patient to benefit from the expectorant qualities of the aromatic substances of the sagebrush, to promote the excretion of phlegm and mucus from the upper respiratory tract.

The poultice of fresh leaves was applied over wounds and helped the healing due to its antiseptic properties.

Sassafras

Binomial Name: Sassafras Albidum.

Habitat: Meadows and edges of forests in the Eastern and Midwestern United States. It needs dry areas to grow and thrive.

Characteristics: This tree can grow to almost fifty feet tall. Its leaves are three-lobed and with irregular edges. Roots have been used as natural aromas in many drinks and beverages as for example the root beer, in fact, when broken roots smell exactly like that. Flowers are green-yellowish with six petals that encircle a crown of yellow pistils.

Parts to collect for medical purposes: Root, barks, and leaves.

Native American Use: The Native Americans used the dried leaves as a spice, simply by powdering or roughly crushing them.

The decoction of roots was used as a tonic and for its detoxifying effects. Also, it will cause some relief to the symptoms of Sexual Transmitted Diseases such as syphilis or gonorrhea. The anticonvulsant effect of the root decoction was also an effective treatment for stomachache, menstrual pain, and cramps.

Bark tea was instead used for its diaphoretic effects as a powerful febrifuge.

WARNING: Sassafras roots produce a substance called safrole, which is carcinogenic. For this reason, it must be taken after consulting with a practitioner and with moderation.

Saint John's Wort

Binomial Name: Hypericum Perforatum.

Habitat: Widely diffused all over the United States and Canada, in gardens and meadows.

Characteristics: This officinal, perennial plant can grow to almost four feet tall from the creeping rhizome. The red-brown stems are woody at the base of the plant and become more "tender" towards the top of it. Opposite and stalkless leaves populate the branches. They are bright green and oblong with many small glands attached to the bottom. These can be easily seen in the backlight. The flowers that originate at the end of each stem are made by five ovate, yellow petals that encircle a cluster of long yellow pistils. Seeds are shiny-black and cylindrical, two millimeters long.

Parts to collect for medical purposes: The whole plant.

Native American Use: Saint John's Wort is one of the most used officinal plants in herbal medicine all over the world. Native Americans were aware of its properties and widely used it in many preparations. It was considered a heal-all plant with astringent, anti-inflammatory, and antiseptic characteristics.

The whole plant decoction was used for its emmenagogue properties to treat menstrual problems, such as poor blood flow or Pre Menstrual Syndrome. The stimulating effect on uterus contraction was also used to induce abortions and facilitate difficult childbirth.

Not only that, the tea obtained from flowers was used as a mild sedative to calm nerves and induce sleep in case of traumatic events or insomnia.

Regarding the fresh plant uses, we can mention the poultice of the whole plant was applied over wounds to facilitate healing and avoid infections due to its antiseptic properties. In addition, raw root consumption was used to treat snakebites. Finally, leaves and flowers were used raw as a buffer to treat wounds and nasal epistaxis because they immediately stopped bleeding.

WARNING: do not assume in case of pregnancy or if suffering from bipolar disorder or depression.

SIDE EFFECTS: gastrointestinal irritation and allergic reactions.

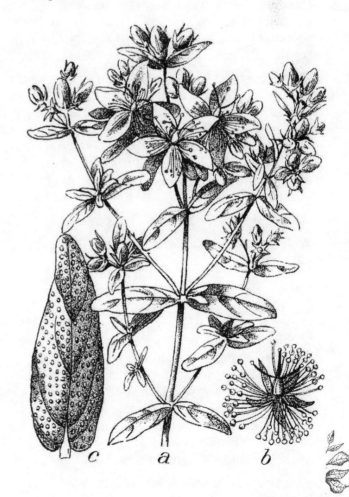

c a b

Saw palmetto

Binomial Name: Serenoa repens.

Habitat: Diffused all over the South-Eastern United States. It typically grows in dense colonies, in plains and sandhills, especially near the coastline. It can also be found in woods under pines.

Characteristics: This fan palm is also called Dwarf American Palm and can grow up to 13 feet tall to its best. From the central trunk, deeply scaled, depart many leaves, composed by a long petiole, full of thorns at its side, which terminates with a fan ten to twenty long leaflets. The leaflets are two to three feet long and pointed. Vertical panicles of flowers with three white petals and six yellow stamens appear between the leaves in spring. Fruits are large red or black drupes, the size of a small olive.

Parts to collect for medical purposes: Leaves.

Native American Use: Native Americans used the palm leaves as a building material, to create roofs of simple shelters. Regarding the medical uses, the only worth mentioning was the decoction of leaves that would help digestive problems and lowering excessive fever.

Modern Use: Saw palmetto has been recently studied for the treatment of prostate cancer and prostate enlargement symptoms. Its assumption regulate the production of testosterone, thus reducing the tendency of the prostate cells to replicate. Many food supplements you find in your drugstore are based on Saw Palmetto extraction.

Senega Snakeroot

Binomial Name: Poligala Senega.

Habitat: Diffused all over the Eastern to the Central United States and Canada, from New Scotland to Saskatchewan, to Mississippi State to South Carolina.

Characteristics: This small plant has two years life cycle, being a perennial. From the root, every year, several stems pop out and grow up to fifteen inches. These are red and smooth and hold whorls of lance-shaped, pointed leaves spirally arranged. At the top of the stem, the white flowers are grouped in vertical, densely populated clusters.

Parts to collect for medical purposes: Root~

Preferred Solvents: Water, Alcohol.

Effects: Expectorant, Febrifuge.

Native American Use: Ojibwa used this root in combination with others to prepare a heal-all remedy mainly used by their warriors. This mixture of herbs was said to give strength and facilitate healing, so Ojibwa warriors used to chew it daily and spread it on wounds and burns. This plant was also used in ceremonies and was said to have the power to chase demons away. The powder of the dried root was applied over wounds and helped the healing due to its antiseptic and astringent properties.

Raw root consumption is recommended in case of cough to help the expectoration of phlegm and in case of fever due to its diaphoretic properties. The poultice of the root can be applied over swelling of any sort and it is effective in reducing the inflammation.

Sumac

Binomial Name: Rhus coriaria.

Habitat: Sumac thrives in forests and fields all over the South-Eastern United States.

Slippery Elm

Binomial Name: Ulmus Rubra.

Habitat: Widely diffused in forests and fields all over the North-Eastern United States and Quebec.

Characteristics: The deciduous tree can grow up to 50 feet on average. The leafy branches spread widely around the central trunk made of reddish wood. The dark green leaves are oblong to obovate-shaped (depending on the species) and with serrated margins. They are rough to the touch in the upper part and velvety on the bottom. Flowers have no petals and are produced in dome clusters of fifteen to twenty each. Fruits are ovoid samaras that can be easily diffused by wind, bearing a red, hairy seed.

Parts to collect for medical purposes: Bark, both inner and outer.

Preferred Solvents: Water, Alcohol.

Effects: Expectorant, Emollient, Diuretic.

Characteristics: This shrub can grow up to 30 feet high from the underground rhizome. The branches grow twisted from the ground and spread in many lesser red-brownish branches. Leaves are pinnately compound, lance-shaped, and bright green with serrated margins. The five-petaled, red flowers are arranged in vertical panicles, densely populated. After pollination, they evolve into red drupes.

Parts to collect for medical purposes: Bark, both inner and outer.

Preferred Solvents: Water, Alcohol.

Effects: Astringent, Anti-inflammatory.

Native American Use: Native Americans used the decoction of sumac bark as a wash to treat conjunctivitis and as a gargle to treat sore throat. This decoction was also drunk to benefit from its astringent properties in case of dysentery and diarrhea. The fresh leaves were pounded to create a poultice with anti-inflammatory properties for the treatment of skin rash and urticarial with topical application.

Native American Use: Native Americans widely used this indigenous species of elm for medical purposes by preparing a decoction of the dried inner bark. The inner bark release a mucilaginous substance that if drunk, can help to treat gastritis and ulcers by protecting the stomach walls; if used as a wash is a powerful emollient for wounds and burns. The same effects were obtained by the infusion of the powdered inner bark.

The outer bark decoction was used differently, to induce uterine contraction and causing abortions or helping difficult childbirths.

The salve obtained by thickening with beeswax the oil of outer bark is useful to treat colds, sore throat, and bronchitis by dissolving it in boiling water and inhaling the steam (fumigation).

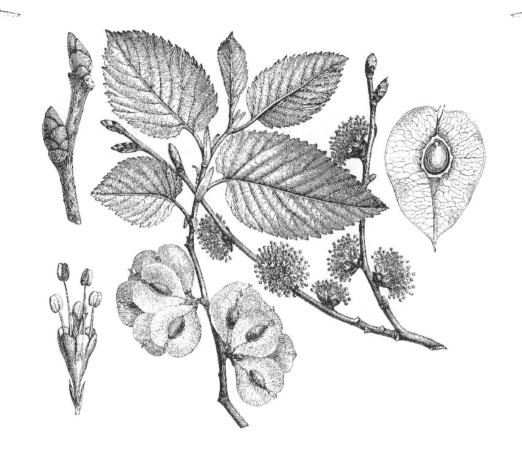

T

Tobacco

 and drawing EPS10

Binomial Name: Nicotiana.

Habitat: It grows wild in the South-Western United States, in desert environments.

Characteristics: This shrub can grow up to thirteen feet tall. Leaves are lanceolate (typical dimensions are 12 inches long by 4 inches wide at the base) and yellow-greenish. Leaves dimensions reduce from basal to upper leaves. The flowers are located on top of the plant and are trumpet-shaped and pink. They emanate an unpleasant flavor.

Parts to collect for medical purposes: Leaves.

Preferred Solvents: Water.

Effects: Antispasmodic, Cathartic, Emetic, Analgesic.

Native American Use: Native Americans used tobacco mainly for ceremonial purposes, by smoking it in the sacred pipe. The plant was also used for some small medical purposes, for its analgesic properties. In fact, the poultice obtained by pounding the fresh leaves was used on joints swelling and scorpion stings to reduce the pain, and as a panacea for skin conditions.

Fresh or powdered leaves were chewed to reduce headaches.

Finally, the leaves poultice, mixed with chalk, was used as a primitive toothpaste to whiten the teeth.

Toothwort

Binomial Name: Cardamine Diphylla.

Habitat: Widely diffused in the moist woodlands of the Eastern United States and Quebec.

Characteristics: This plant belongs to the mustard family, thus it is edible. The single, thin stem, which can grow up to 12" in height, holds lance-shaped leaves with serrated edges, grouped in triplets. At the top of the plant, there is a cluster of white flowers with four petals.

Parts to collect for medical purposes: Roots.

Preferred Solvents: Water.

Effects: Febrifuge, Analgesic, Carminative.

Native American Use: Algonquin Native Americans widely used the root of this small flower for medical purposes. Root infusion was used to reduce fever and as a gargle to treat sore throats, especially in children; the said infusion was also used to treat symptoms related to Sexually Transmitted Diseases such as syphilis and gonorrhea. In addition, the root was consumed raw by simply chewing it to reduce

headaches thanks to its analgesic properties and to reduce stomach gas (carminative effect). Root poultice was also used topically on swellings and arthritic joints.

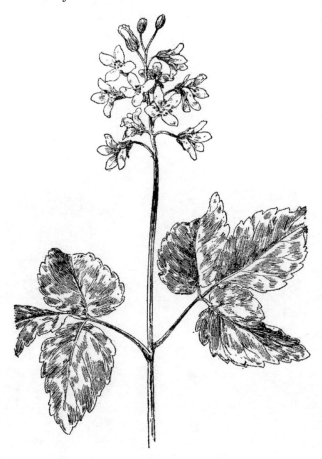

U

Usnea

Binomial Name: Usnea

Habitat: Wild lichen that thrives in wet environments, especially in the North-Western United States and British Columbia.

Characteristics: This lichen is a symbiont of pines, junipers, cypresses, and many others. It grows on their branches and feeds on the tree lymph, giving in exchange nitrogenous substances. It is easy to accurately detect the Usnea (also called "old man's beard"): Usnea has a white central core from which depart the many filaments. Other lichens that may be poisonous do not have this central white axon,

so be sure to check before risking picking venomous look-alikes.

Parts to collect for medical purposes: The whole lichen.

Preferred Solvents: Water.

Effects: Carminative, Antiseptic, Emollient, Antifungal.

Native American Use: Cowichan tribe from South Western part of Canada, used the poultice of the whole lichen for wounds and skin infections. The dried and powdered lichen was used in the same way to absorb the liquid seeping from wounds and burns and to facilitate healing, relying on its antiseptic properties.

Alcohol tinctures of the lichen are used to treat infections (pulmonary in particular, such as tuberculosis). The raw consumption or the tea obtained from the dried lichen are used in the same way.

The tea, used as a vaginal wash is effective in curing any fungal or yeast infection such as candida.

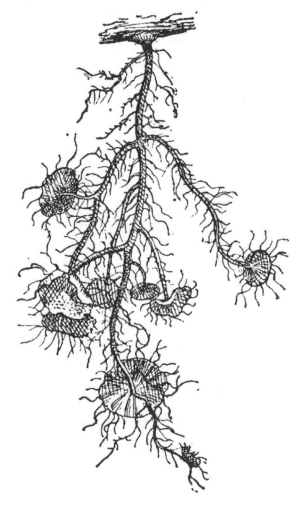

V

Valerian

Binomial Name: Valeriana Officinalis.

Habitat: This plant belongs to the mountain climate. It can be usually found in the north face of hills and mountains, all over the United States and Canada.

Characteristics: This small plant grows to almost sixty inches. From the ground emerges a single green stem with nodes at regular intervals. On each node, two opposite small branches depart and carry seven to nine long, lance-shaped, and smooth-edged leaves. At the top, it divides into three lesser vertical branches with a cluster of small white flowers on top. Flowers are bell-shaped with four white petals and a protruding central stamen. It blooms from April to July.

Parts to collect for medical purposes: Root.

Preferred Solvents: Water.

Effects: Sedative, Nervine.

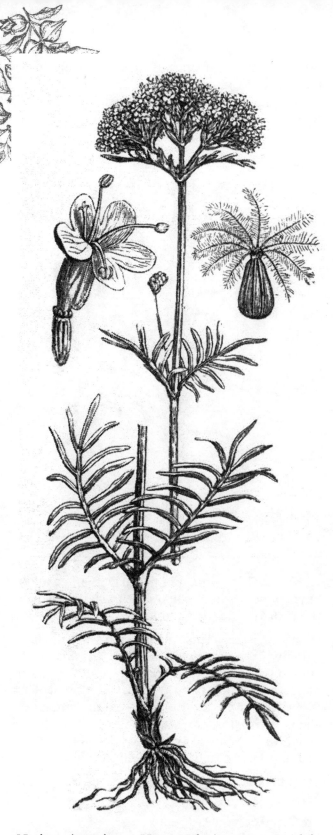

decoction is astringency, so this same decoction was also useful to treat diarrhea and colds.

The poultice of the roots can be used topically to treat wounds, burns, and skin inflammation in general.

The effect of this herb is enhanced when mixed with others, such as peppermint, gentian, and red clover.

Venus's Slipper

Binomial Name: Calypso Bulbosa.

Habitat: This mountain plant is widely diffused all over the United States and Canada, in wet environments

Characteristics: This slipper orchid is a perennial plant that can grow to ten inches in height. It has a single, wide basal leaf, lance-shaped, pointed, and bright green. At the top of the stem, the flower blooms in March into an orchid with protruding purple/pink petals. The labellum is the purple protuberance on the bottom of the flower similar to a slipper.

Parts to collect for medical purposes: Root.

Preferred Solvents: Water.

Effects: Antispasmodic.

Native American Use: The bulb of the flower was consumed raw or the flower sucked as a treatment for epilepsy.

Native American Use: Valerian was widely known, not only among Native Americans but also among many ancient populations for its sedative action. The tea prepared from Valerian roots is a mild sedative and stress-relieving drink. It is sleep-inducing and so it is useful to treat insomnia. A side property of the root

105

Violet

Binomial Name: Viola Odorata.

Habitat: Widely diffused all over the United States and Canada, in damp woods and shady environments.

Characteristics: Perennial small plant that can grow up to 10 inches at its best. Its leaves are heart-shaped with serrated margins and displaced as a basal rosette. At the end of the winter, it blooms in small, violet flowers with five zygomorphic petals.

Parts to collect for medical purposes: Flowers and leaves.

Preferred solvent: Boiling water.

Main effect: Antibacterial, Expectorant, Carminative, Laxative.

Native American Use: Native Americans used violet as a heal-all plant. The violet tea was used to regularize body function and to reduce intestinal gas due to its carminative qualities. Also, it was considered effective in lowering the body temperature.

Gargling the infusion of dried flowers was indicated to reduce conditions related to throat inflammation and excessive mucus production such as sore throat, earaches, cough, and hoarseness.

W

Watercress

Binomial Name: Nasturtium Officinalis.

Habitat: This wild plant thrives in watery environments such as marshes and bogs, all over the United States and Canada.

Characteristics: This plant grows in floating mats with roots immersed into the water. It spreads in width rather than grow in height, in fact, it can reach twenty inches at its best. The plant grows in an intricate entanglement of stems with alternate, ovate, three-lobed leaves. From May to July at the top of the stems, small groups of three to five white flowers bloom.

Parts to collect for medical purposes: Roots and leaves.

Preferred Solvents: Water.

Effects: Detoxifying, Carminative.

Native American Use: The most documented use of this plant by Native Americans is the use of leaves to spice their dishes due to their spicy and acrid taste.

The medical use is less known and indicates the raw consumption of the plant to treat cough, colds, and indigestion, due to its strong expectorant qualities. The astringent and expectorant properties of the plant will facilitate the removal of phlegm and excessive mucus in no time.

The plant has also strong diuretic characteristics and was indicated for cleansing and detoxifying.

TIPS FOR BEGINNER GARDENER: This plant can easily grow in your own backyard, just by collecting it in the field and replanting it. Be sure to provide plenty of water.

Water Birch

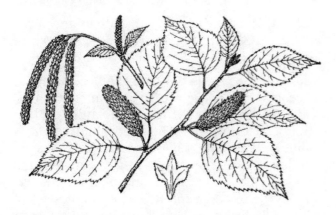

WARNING: Do not use during pregnancy.

White Poplar

1. Schwarzpappel (Populus nigra), Zweig mit Fruchtkätzchen.
2—4. Balsampappel (Populus balsamifera); 2. Zweig, 3. aufgesprungenes Früchtchen, 4. Same.

Binomial Name: Betula occidentalis.

Habitat: Widely diffused in the inland regions of the Western United States and Canada, up to the east part of Alaska.

Characteristics: This small tree can grow up to 35 feet tall, with many trunks from the single rootstalk. From the trunks (covered by a red-brown and smooth bark), depart many branches populated by opposite, ovate leaves with serrated margins. Flower are catkins: the male ones drooping down, the female erect. Seed have horizontal "leaflets" such as a helicopter (samara). This helps them fly for long distances when they detach from the tree.

Parts to collect for medical purposes: Leaves and bark.

Preferred solvent: Alcohol, Water.

Main effect: Anti-inflammation, Febrifuge.

Native American Use:

Native Americans used the Water Birch febrifuge properties by preparing a strong tea from leaves and barks. This drink could also be used as a wash for mild skin ailments, such as pimples.

Binomial Name: Populus Balsamifera.

Habitat: White poplar grows wild in wet environments all over the northern part of the North American continent, from New Scotland and Labrador, west to Alaska.

Characteristics: This massive tree can grow up to 100 feet tall. From the wide central trunk (covered by a gray-green and smooth bark), depart many branches populated by heart-shaped leaves with serrated margins. Flowers are in the shape of white catkins. A resinous, fragrant substance covers new buds, making them sticky.

Parts to collect for medical purposes: Leaves, Barks, and Buds.

Preferred Solvents: Water.

Effects: Diuretic, Febrifuge, Analgesic.

Native American Use: It is not a case that salicin, widely contained in the bark of the popular, is considered a precursor of aspirin. Native Americans benefited from the analgesic and febrifuge properties of this tree by preparing a bark decoction to treat colds, flu, and rheumatism.

In addition, the inner bark decoction was used for its strong diuretic properties as a cleansing and detoxifying drink.

Another interesting use of this plant is the one that involves the sticky resin that covers its buds: the salve obtained from it is perfect to seal wounds and ensure proper healing without infections.

The instructions are quite simple: mix the resin and a vegetable oil of your choice (olive, canola…) in a weight ratio of 1:8 into a non-metallic container; cook the mix in the oven for 10 hours at 170°F. Let the mix cool, transfer it in a pan and gently reheat it; add beeswax to thicken it to the desired consistency.

WARNING: It may cause allergic reaction.

Wild Carrot

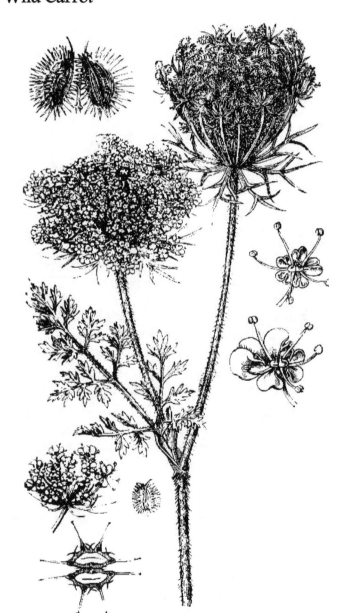

Binomial Name: Daucus Carota.

Habitat: Widely diffused in meadows and fields all over the North American Continent, both in the United States and Canada.

Characteristics: Also known as Queen Anne's Lace or Devil's Plague. This biennial plant is native of Europe but it has been naturalized on American Continent. The root of this plant is white-yellowish and slightly scented. Leaves are pinnately compound and concentrated at the base of the plant. It is an umbrelliferae so flowers are concentrated in umbrella-like clusters at the top of the plant. The center flower is typically purple, while all the others are white or pink. Seeds are brown and flat on one side.

Parts to collect for medical purposes: The whole plant.

Preferred Solvents: Water.

Effects: Diuretic, Deobstruent, Vermifuge.

Native American Use:

Native Americans used tea obtained from the flowers as a treatment for dropsy. Other remedies prepared by Natives, include the powder obtained by pounding seeds and dried roots in the treatment of many diseases, from intestinal disorders to intestinal worms, to urinary tract infections. Said powder has also emmenagogue effects, increasing menstrual flow in case of hypo-menorrhea or amenorrhea.

The poultice of the fresh root was used topically on abscesses and infected wounds.

Willow

Binomial Name: Salix Alba.

Habitat: Widely diffused in wet environments all over the North American Continent, both in the United States and Canada.

Characteristics: This tree can grow up to 100 feet tall. From the wide central trunk, depart many drooping branches widely populated by narrow and lance-shaped leaves with finely serrated margins. The drooping shape of its branches gives the tree its characteristic shape. Flowers, both male and female are in the shape of catkins: yellow for males, green for females.

Parts to collect for medical purposes: Bark.

Preferred Solvents: Boiling water.

Effects: Diuretic, Febrifuge, Analgesic.

Native American Use: Salix bark is known to be rich in salicin, which is the natural molecule from which aspirin is derived. In fact, natives and other ancient populations used Salix bark to treat colds, rheumatism, and headaches, making use of the febrifuge and analgesic properties of this plant.

Salix bark decoction was effective for pain relief in cases of tendinitis, arthritis, and bursitis. Its anti-inflammatory properties helped to reduce the swelling and the pain associated with those ailments.

WARNING: due to its high salicin content it can aggravate preexisting conditions such as ulcers and intestinal bleeding.

WARNING: The willow tree is full of cadmium, which it collects from the surrounding environment. Cadmium is a toxic metal for our bodies.

TIPS FOR THE BEGINNER GARDENER: willow roots spread widely in the surrounding of the tree and may cause the death of the nearby plants.

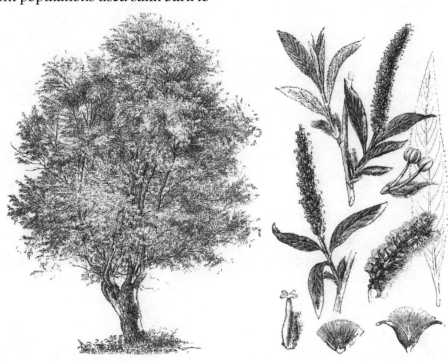

Witch Hazel

Binomial Name: Hamamelis Virginiana.

Habitat: Widely diffused in forest and woods all over the Eastern and Mid-Eastern part of the United States, from the Atlantic shore to the Mississippi River and the Great Lakes Region.

Characteristics: This bushy tree can grow up to 30 feet tall. The bark is peculiar: brown on the outside, bright red on the inside. Many twisted trunks depart from the ground rootstalk, widely populated by alternate leaves with serrated margins. At the bottom of leaves, the flowers emerge in groups typically of seven. The petals of these are narrow, oblong, twisted, and yellow.

Parts to collect for medical purposes: Bark and leaves.

Preferred Solvents: Boiling water, Alcohol.

Effects: Expectorant, Diuretic, Analgesic, Antiseptic.

Native American Use: Native Americans used the tea from fresh or dried leaves as a wash for wounds, burns, eyes, and in the treatment of hemorrhoids. It also was effective in skin conditions such as athlete feet (due to its antifungal properties) and in eczemas. If drunk, the tea helped with phlegm expulsion and was a powerful febrifuge. Also, was used to treat sore throats and as an astringent to cure dysentery.

The inner bark is where the healing properties concentrate the most so decoctions and teas prepared with it may result more effective.

Native Americans used to harvest young buds in spring, to prepare a decoction, considered a powerful tonic.

NOTE: Twigs were used as divining rods. Water diviners selected a branch of witch hazel in the shape of a Y and slowly walked a certain area where water was looked for. When the stick began to move, that was the sign that in that spot, there was water underneath.

Wormwood

Binomial Name: Arthemisia Campestris

Habitat: Widely diffused in dry environments all over the North American Continent, both in the United States and Canada.

Characteristics: The Arthemisia Campestris has a two-year life cycle. In its first year, it appears as a rosette of deeply divided, almost linear, gray-greenish leaves. In the second year, many reddish stems grow from the bottom. These, are covered with smaller and more deeply cut leaves. Stems are covered with hairs and have small, yellow flowers at the top.

Parts to collect for medical purposes: Leaves and flowers.

Preferred Solvents: Diluted Alcohol.

Effects: Vermifuge, Febrifuge, Sedative, Carminative, Emmenagogue.

Native American Use: The medical uses of the Arthemisa Campestris are many and well known. Natives used to chew and swallow the juice of leaves to help with intestinal gas, making use of its anticonvulsant and carminative properties.

The decoction of leaves was a powerful sweat-inducing, fever-reducing drink. This decoction was also useful to kill intestinal worms and other parasites and to increase blood flow in case of poor menstruation.

A bundle of fresh herbs was set to dry and then used in the smudging ceremony as a stick to smudge the participants.

The fresh herb was used also during the sweat lodge ceremonies.

WARNING: Arthemisia is toxic if assumed in excessive quantities.

WARNING: Do not use if you are already assuming anticonvulsants.

Y

Yarrow

Binomial Name: Achillea Millefolium.

Habitat: Widely diffused all over the North American continent in gardens and forests.

Characteristics: This infesting plant is widely diffused all over North America. The plant produces several stems from the ground rhizome that can reach up to 3 feet in height. The hairy, bi-pinnate, cauline leaves, widely populate the stems, and their size decrease moving towards the top of the plant. Dense clusters of twenty to forty white flowers with five petals and yellow stamens are located at top of the plant.

Parts to collect for medical purposes: Leaves, flowers, and stem.

Preferred Solvents: Diluted Alcohol, Water.

Effects: Astringent, Diuretic, Diaphoretic, Analgesic.

Native American Use: Yarrow is one of the most used herbs in Native American medicine, mostly used in combination with others, such as passionflower or sage, to increase its effects.

A not-so-known, but widely adopted among Native Americans, usage of the plant is the snorting of dried and pulverized leaves to stop chronic epistaxis and headaches.

The poultice of leaves has a strong anti-inflammatory effect in case of mastitis, common skin ailments such as eczemas, or burns and wounds. Raw leaves can be used as an emergency medication if you hurt yourself in the woods. In fact, if applied directly onto the wound they can immediately stop the bleeding.

Native Americans also used the tea obtained from the fresh plant to induce sweating and treat fever, inflammations, and infections. This decoction is also a strong diuretic and was considered depurative. This decoction was also used for its analgesic property as a topical wash in case of insect stings.

The infusion prepared with leaves only has a sedative effect and helps in relaxation and sleep, while the decoction of only roots was used as a wash for acne.

Tincture of yarrow is effective in reducing excessive menstrual blood flow (hypermenorrhea).

Salves obtained from yarrow are effective if rubbed on the patient's chest in case of bronchitis.

Smudging of the dried plant keeps mosquitos away.

WARNING: it contains thujone, a carcinogenic substance and so it must be assumed in moderation.

Yellow Dock

Binomial Name: Rumex Crispus.

Habitat: Diffused all over the North American continent in gardens and yards.

Characteristics: This small perennial plant is widely diffused all over North America. It can grow up to 40 inches from the taproot rhizome, which is brown on the outside, and yellow on the inside. This taproot can sink down to 30 inches deep in the ground. The basal leaves are long, narrow, and have curly edges. Flowers are placed on top of the plant in red or white vertical racemes. Seeds can be collected in winter at the top of the plant.

Parts to collect for medical purposes: Rhizome.

Preferred Solvents: Alcohol, Water.

Effects: Astringent, Tonic, Laxative, Anti-inflammatory.

Native American Use: The anti-inflammatory properties of this plant were used by Native Americans to treat swollen joints and arthritis. A

topical application of the poultice of fresh, mashed rhizome was indicated in these cases.

The juice of the rhizome or the roasted seeds features amazing astringent properties in the treatment of diarrhea and dysentery.

The powder obtained by the dried rhizome was used as an anti-hemorrhagic on wounds.

The decoction of the dried rhizome, which is very bitter, is a powerful stimulant of the liver and helps in detoxifying the blood.

WARNING: do not use in case of pre-existing kidney conditions. The high concentration of tannin of the yellow dock can be dangerous if eaten in excess.

Yew

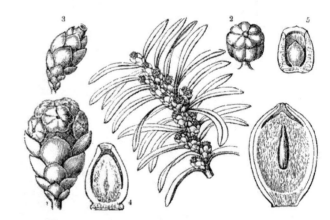

Binomial Name: Taxus Brevifolia.

Habitat: Yew grows wild in the Pacific Coast States, from Northern California up to Graham Island and in the North-Western part of Idaho.

Characteristics: This evergreen tree can grow up to sixty feet in height. Leaves are lanceolate and small to avoid heat dispersion during the cold winter. Fruits are small, red berries in the shape of a cup, with a black seed in the center.

Parts to collect for medical purposes: Fruit, leaves, and barks.

Preferred Solvents: Alcohol, Water.

Effects: Astringent, Tonic, Laxative

Native American Use: Native Americans used the poultice of the fresh needles as a dressing for wounds and burns. These were also used in a decoction, to create an analgesic and antiseptic wash.

Bark decoction was used as an analgesic for stomachache.

Yew berries were consumed raw to procure abortions, stimulate menstruation, or induce uterine contractions in case of difficult childbirths.

WARNING: the plant is toxic so consume it under medical supervision. It may cause abortions.

Yucca

Binomial Name: Yucca Filamentosa.

Habitat: Similar to other succulent plants, it is mainly diffused in the hot, dry desert environments of the Southern United States and Mexico.

Characteristics: This perennial desert plant has no stem but only emerges from the ground in a whorl of basal, long, sword-like leaves. From this whorl of basal leaves pops us straight a single spike that can reach up to sixty inches, bearing a vertical cluster of white, bell-shaped flowers. The flowering period in which this flower can be admired is from late spring to late summer.

Parts to collect for medical purposes: Roots and leaves.

Preferred Solvents: Alcohol, Water.

Effects: Analgesic, Antiemetic, Purgative.

Native American Use: Native Americans used this plant for hygienic purposes. Being rich in saponins, yucca roots extract was used as a natural soap and to remove head lice.

The dried root decoction has been used to relieve gout and rheumatisms and is a powerful laxative. The water obtained by filtering the poultice of leaves is useful to calm uncontrolled vomit.

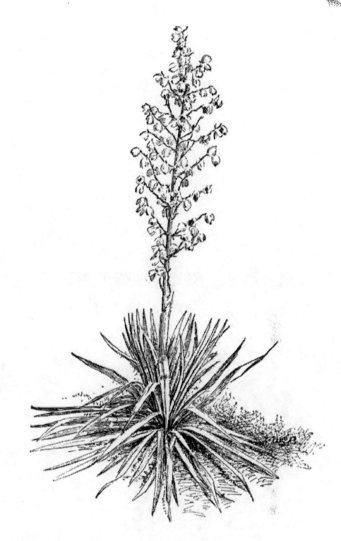

Z

Zizia Aurea (Golden Alexander)

Binomial Name: Zizia Aurea.

Habitat: Golden Alexander is native of the Atlantic regions of the North American continent but it has spread down to the Midwestern of both Canada and the United States. It prefers wet environments.

Characteristics: This perennial flower can grow to a maximum of 3 feet tall. Leaves are lance-shaped, with serrated margins, and are divided into two or three lobes. Lower leaves are bigger and grouped in groups of three. Upper leaves are smaller. Flowers are located on top of the plant and are grouped in umbrella-shaped clusters. Each flower is less than half a centimeter long and has five sepals, five yellow petals, and five stamens. Fruits are small, egg-shaped, and green.

113

Parts to collect for medical purposes: Flower, roots, and leaves.

Preferred Solvents: Alcohol, Water.

Effects: Analgesic, Febrifuge.

Native American Use:

Native Americans used dried root powder as a powerful analgesic in teas and decoctions. The tea from leaves and flowers is used to treat Pre Menstrual Syndrome and menstrual pain.

AMAZING BONUSES FOR ALL THE READERS:

Just Scan the QR-Code below to get them!

Conclusion

In these third and fourth books, we have described in depth more than one hundred herbs used in Native American Herbal medicine, with a deep focus on where to find them, how to identify them without second-guessing, and how they can be used. We have seen how to recognize the curative plants from their poisonous lookalikes and, if possible, how to grow them in your yard or in a pot beside a sunny window in your flat.

I sincerely hope that this will be just the beginning of your journey and that you will increase your knowledge on Native American medicine for a healthier and better way to treat the common disease without relying on industrial drugs and medication.

If you have enjoyed this book, feel free to leave a review to share your experience.

Just scan the QR code on the right, it will take 30 seconds!

My best wishes and may the Spirit guide your journey!

Glossary of Medical Definitions

In this chapter, I will discuss the terms I will use in the encyclopedia regarding the effects and properties of the various herbs.

- **Alterative**: mild healing property. The effect of such herbs is not strong and not immediately felt by the healed.
- **Anodyne**: soothing effect for pain reduction
- **Antibilious**: that has an effect on liver
- **Antiemetic**: Preparation that stops vomiting stimulus
- **Antileptic**: anticonvulsant
- **Antiperiodic**: Preparation that avoids the recurrence of certain symptoms
- **Antirheumatic**: Indicated for the treatment of inflammation of joints such as arthritis and rheumatism
- **Antiscorbutic**: indicated for treatment or prevention of scurvy
- **Antiseptic**: preparation indicated for the prevention of infection and sepsis in wounds and burns
- **Antispasmodic**: preparation indicated for the soothing of muscular spasms and cramps
- **Aromatic**: with a strong flavor
- **Astringent**: that causes a tightening of tissues
- **Carminative**: a preparation that stimulates the expulsion of gastrointestinal gases and stimulates the peristalsis
- **Cathartic**: a preparation that stimulates the intestinal peristalsis
- **Cephalic**: related to the head
- **Cholagogue**: medicinal that stimulate bile discharge from the liver-intestinal system
- **Demulcent**: property of a substance to protect the mucosa from inflammation and water retention
- **Deobstruent**: a preparation that stimulates the opening or clears up of the natural ducts for body fluids

- **Depurative**: detoxifying
- **Detergent**: preparation reach in saponins that cause cleansing
- **Diaphoretic**: Substance that has the power to promote sweating
- **Diuretic**: Substance that has the power to promote urination. This stimulation can happen via an increase of blood flow through the kidneys or via the introduction of substances that recall water from the tissues by an osmotic process
- **Emetic**: vomit-inducing substance
- **Emmenagogue**: Substance that has the power to stimulate menstrual flow
- **Emollient**: see Demulcent
- **Esculent**: Edible
- **Expectorant**: a substance that promotes the removal of excessive mucus from lungs, bronchus, and airways in general. These substances can work in two ways: by irritating the airways and so stimulating cough and sneezes, or by soothing them and promoting the mucus flow outside the body
- **Febrifuge**: Substance that reduces fever
- **Hepatic**: related to liver
- **Laxative**: a substance that promotes the intestinal peristalsis by inducing the muscles related to the bowel movement to contract or by recalling water from the tissues to soften the feces.
- **Nervine**: a substance that has beneficial effects on the nervous system
- **Rubifacient**: a substance that increases blood flow through capillaries causing a reddening of the skin
- Sedative: a substance that induces relaxation and eventually sleep
- **Sialagogue**: a substance that stimulates saliva production
- Tonic: herbs that increase body vigor
- **Vermifuge**: a substance that fights worm infection (i.e. intestinal pinworms

Glossary of Botanical Definitions

A

Acaulescent
With no visible stem above the ground surface or with no stem at all. Example: Agave.

Achene
Typical fruit structure of berries. The main example of it is Fragaria, or Strawberry. In the real fruit, the achenes, are the red, one-seeded, dry "dots" on the surface of the pulpy, juicy infructescence that we usually eat.

Aculeate
endowed with prickles.

Acuminate
Pointy.

Acute
Sharply pointed.

Aerial
Growing above the ground or water surface.

Aggregate fruit
A cluster of fruits. Example: Blackberry.

Alternate
(Relating to leaves and flowers) that grows alternately at different levels along the stem

Ament
See catkin.

Androgynous
With both Male and Female flowers concurring in the same inflorescence.

Angiosperm
A flowering plant that develops seeds inside the flower ovary.

Anther
Enlarged part of the stamen that bear the pollen

Apetalous
With no petals.

Apex
Tip, end part.

Apical
Located on the apex.

Apiculate
of leaves, with a pointy end.

Aquatic plant
A Plant which its own natural habitat is water.

Arborescent
With the appearance of a tree.

Axil
The upper sector of the angle between the stem and a leaf of a plant or the trunk and the branches.

Axis
The main stem of a plant.

B

Barb
Lateral extensions of a pointy structure that prevent the tip from exiting after the piercing.

Barbed
With barbs.

Barbellate
With barbed hairs.

Bark
The external layer of stems, trunks, and roots with protective purpose.

Basal
Situated at the base of the plant, close to the ground.

Berry
Type of fruit, with the seeds immersed in the pulp.

Biennial
Plant with a two-year life cycle. Each life cycle is made of germination, reproduction, and death. Biennials often form only a basal rosette of leaves in the first year. Then they bloom and make fruits in the second year.

Bifoliate
(Regarding a compound leaf) Having two smaller, symmetrical leaflets.

Bipinnate
Doubly pinnate.

Bisexual
With both male and female genitalia. The term usually related to flowers with both stamens and carpels.

Blade
The flattened part of the leaves. Stalk and petiole are excluded.

Bract
A modified leaf located near a flower or inflorescence. It has mostly protective function for flower buds.

Bulb
Storage organ for nutritive substances. Usually situated underground.

Burr
A prickly seed or fruit head that clings to animal fur to be transported.

C

Caducous
Which falls off early.

Calyx
The complex of sepals of flowers.

Cambium
The tissue of the plant that provides partially undifferentiated cells for the plant to grow.

Campanulate
Bell-shaped.

Canopy
The complex of branches and leaves of a tree.

Catkin
Hanging spike of small, unisex flowers attach.

Cauline
Positioned in the aerial part of the stem.

Clavate
Club-shaped.

Climber
Type of plant that grows around other support structures.

Compound
Structure composed of several parts.

Compound palmate
With leaflets that spread from a central point like fingers from the palm of the hand.

Cone
Woody fruit globe or egg-shaped. It is made by scales or bracts that grow around a central axis.

Corolla
The complex of petals of flowers.

Corona

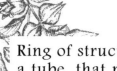

Ring of structures, usually united by in a tube, that rise from the corolla up to the stamens.

Corymb
Inflorescence with branches that creates a flat-top surface of flowers.

Cuneate
Wedge-shaped.

Cyme
Inflorescence with branches, all terminating in a flower.

D

Deciduous
A Structure that falls, depending on the season.

Dentate
Referred to the leaves margins, with teeth.

Denticulate
Finely dentate.

Deserticolous
Living in desert environments.

Dioicous
With male and female genitalia on different plants.

Dissected
Deeply divided.

Drupe
Succulent fruit that evolved from the female reproductive organs of a plant. Usually made of a single seed encapsulated in a woody layer (i.e. Peaches).

E

Elliptical
With elliptic, planar shape. Synonym: oval.

Emarginate
Notched at the top.

Evenpinnate
Compound leaf with an even number of leaflets.

Evergreen
With leaves all year long.

Exotic
Not native.

F

Family
A Taxonomic group of more genera with common characteristics or ancestors.

Fascicle
Cluster.

Fasciculate
Branching in clusters.

Female flower
Flower with one or more pistils but no stamens.

Floret
Small flower, usually clustered in inflorescence.

Flower
Sexual reproductive part of the angiosperms.

Foliate
Having a certain number of leaflets. I.e. Bi-foliate, with two leaflets.

Frond
Leaf of ferns or palms.

Fruit
The structure of the plant that bears the seed inside, typical of angiosperms.

G

Gamete
Cell created by the fusion of two of opposite sexes.

Gemma
The reproductive structure of mosses

Glabrous
With no hair or scale.

H

Habitat
The environment in which a plant lives.

Hair
Elongated structures originated at the surface of the stem, leaf, petal...

Hand-pollination
Pollination artificially made by man.

Hermaphrodite
With both male and female genitalia. The term usually related to flowers with both stamens and carpels.

I

Imbricate
Overlapping each other.

Imparipinnate
A pinnate leaf with an odd number of pinnae.

Incised
Deeply cut.

Indigenous
Native to the area.

Inflorescence
The cluster of flowers grouped together.

Infructescence
The cluster of fruits grouped together.

L

Labellum
Lip, usually identifying the smaller of 3 or 5 petals of Orchidaceae.

Lacinia
Deep, irregular cut of leaves and petals.

Lanceolate
The shape of leaves whose width is 1/3 than length. Lance-shaped.

Leaf
An outgrowth of the stem whose function is to generate energy for the plant through photosynthesis.

Leaflet
Ultimate parts of a compound leaf.

Ligneous
Woody.

Ligulate
With ligules.

Ligula
Membranous appendix in the shape of a strap. Typical of the Asteraceae leaves and in some daisy flowers.

Lobe
Part of the leaf delineated by the cuts, often is rounded.

M

Maculate
Marked with spots.

Male flower
A flower with stamens but no pistil.

119

Margin
Edge of the leaf.

Marsh
Swamp.

Mycelium
The part of the mushroom that does not have a reproductive function.

N

Nerve
See Vein.

Node
Part of the stem from which leaves or other branches grow.

Nut
Hard and dry fruit that opens once it reaches maturity, containing a single seed.

Nutlet
Small nut.

O

Oblanceolate
Lanceolate but broadest in the upper third of the leaf.

Oblong
With elongated shape with parallel margins and rounded end.

Obovate
Leaf with length 1.5 times the width. Upside down egg-shaped.

Odd-pinnate
See Imparipinnate.

Opposite
Of leaves and branches that born from the same axis, at the same level.

Oval

See elliptical.

Ovate
Egg-shaped, attached to the branch by the wider end.

P

Palmate
A leaf with nerves radiating out from the top of the petiole

Panicle
Inflorescence in the shape of a raceme, borne at the top of a branch.

Pappus
A tuft of hairs on a fruit. Needed to be carried by the wind for pollination

Paripinnate
With an even number of leaflets or pinnae.

Peduncle
The stalk of an inflorescence.

Perennial
Plant with a life cycle that extends over more than reproductive seasons.

Perfect
(Of a flower) Containing both male and female genitalia.

Perfoliate
(Of leaves) with the base wrapped around the stem. I.e. Boneset

Perianth
Structure composed of the calyx and the corolla.

Petal
Each of the segments of the inner whorl surrounding the genitalia, usually brightly colored.

Petiolate
(Of a leaf) with a petiole.

Petiole
Stalk of the leaf.

Petiolule
Stalk of the leaflet

Pinna
The segment of a compound leaf.

Pinnate
Of a leaf with leaflets or nerves arranged on each side of a common petiole.

Pistil
Part of the flower made by free carpels or by a group of them fused together, usually located in the central part of the flower. A pistil is made of three parts: ovary, stylus, and stigma.

Pistillate flower
See Female Flower

Pollen
Powder that originates in the anther of a stamen. They produce the male gamete.

Pollination
The act of transfer the pollen inside the stigma or the ovary of the female reproductive organs

Prickle
The pointed outgrowth of a plan; Thorn.

R

Raceme
Inflorescence in which the flowers are borne one on top of the other along the same main axis.

Rhizome
The underground part of the stem, growing horizontally. It has the function of storage for the nutritive

substances of the plant.

Root
Part of the axial system of the plant that grows underground. It has the function to absorb the water and minerals from the ground necessary to the plant's metabolism.

Root Hairs
The outgrowth of the root whose function is to absorb water.

Rosette
Set of leaves arranged at the base of the plant in a radial pattern.

S

Sagittate
Shaped like an arrowhead. Pointed on top, enlarging towards the base with two lobes pointing downward.

Samara
Dry fruit with appendices like wings. I.e. Maple fruits.

Seed
Propagating organ of the plant. It evolves from the ovule and consists of a protective layer enclosing an embryo and a food reserve for it.

Sepal
In flowers, each of the divisions of the outer whorl of non-reproductive parts surrounding the gametes. Usually green.

Serrate
(Of a leaf margin) toothed asymmetrically.

Serrulate
Finely serrate.

Sessile
Attached to the main branch without a stalk.

Shrub
Woody perennial made of many branches emerging from the ground.

Spatulate
(Of leaves) in the shape of a spoon. Wider at the top, rather than at the base.

Spike
See Raceme.

Stalk
Supporting structure of any plant organ that attaches it to the branch.

Stamen
The male organ of the flower, consisting of a filament that supports an anther, which bears the pollen.

Staminate flower
See Male flower.

Stellate
In the shape of a star.

Stem
Axis of a plant. It extends over and below the ground level.

Stigma
Part of the female reproductive organ of a flower that receives the pollen. It is the upper part of the pistil, usually larger than it is and sticky.

Strobilus
Cone-shaped structure typical (but not exclusive) of the conifers.

Subshrub
Small shrub, usually woody, no more than 3 feet tall.

Succulent
Of a plant with fleshy leaves or flowers.

T

Taproot
The primary root of a plant.

Tepal
Part of the perianth, sepal, or petal. The term is used when the two segments are not distinguishable.

Ternate
Grouped by three.

Thorn
See Prickle.

Toothed
Having incised margin, either regular or not.

Tree
Woody plant with a single main trunk distinguishable, usually 7 feet tall or more.

Trifoliate
Made of three leaflets.

Trunk
The woody, main stem of a tree.

U

Umbel
Raceme made of flowers arranged on stalks of the same length, forming an umbrella-like shape.

Undershrub
See Subshrub.

V

Vein
Vascular tissue of leaves.

Verticillate
Arranged in whorls around a common axis.

W

Weed
Infesting, unwanted plant.

Whorl
Organs of plants growing at the same level on the same axis.

Wing
Outgrowth membrane of fruits that allow the dispersion by wind.

X

Xeromorph
Of a plant with structural features that prevent water loss. i.e. Succulents.

Z

Zygomorphic
Symmetric only along a vertical plane.

Leaves Shape Index

1. ACICULAR
2. CORDATE
3. DELTOID
4. ELLIPTIC
5. FALCATE
6. HASTATE
7. LANCEOLATE
8. LINEAR
9. LYRATE
10. OBCORDATE
11. OBLANCEOLATE
12. OBLONG
13. OBOVATE
14. ORBICULAR
15. OVAL
16. OVATE
17. RENIFORM
18. RUNCINATE
19. SAGITTATE
20. SPATULATE

Native American Herbal Dispensatory

The Lost Remedies of Native Americans Herbalism

—

Herbs for Healing

BOOK 6 of "The Native American Herbalist's Bible"

Natalie Hathale

Introduction

We are all sons and daughters of Mother Nature. Even if our society tries to make us forget about our true nature, we must always remember we are links in a complex chain that involves every creature on this earth.

Our ancestors knew this simple truth and lived by it. They were aware of their true nature, and were connected with Mother Nature at a level that could seem impossible for us to understand. They were conscious of the gift that she generously provides us for our own prosperity.

In fact, our forest, meadows, and hills are full of herbs and flowers that can seem insignificant to you but if correctly treated and prepared, can heal many of the ailments that we suffer, and improve our overall well-being.

Western society has lost that knowledge. The tendency in the medicine field, dominated by the economic interests of the pharmaceutical industries, has always been to create, in sterilized laboratories, chemical compounds that can rapidly treat symptoms of specific ailments to make you happy in the short time. Many of these commonly used medications are only palliatives that do not solve the root problem and have indeed undesired side effects, some of them unknown.

Medicine and science have become increasingly interested in the last decades in the healing power of herbs and flowers, rediscovering most of the ancient knowledge of the Native Americans, giving scientific foundation to the many rituals and cures known by centuries by my people.

In this book series, my purpose is to guide you in rediscovering this ancient wisdom through a structured learning approach that will make you become a daring herbalist starting from zero.

In the first book, I introduced Native American Medicine, with its methods and preparations while in the second book, you had access to the Herbal Encyclopedia of the most important herbs and flowers used in traditional Native American medicine.

Finally, in this third book, you will close the circle, learning what herb to use and the correct preparation techniques to create herbal remedies for the most common ailments and diseases you can encounter using Native American herbs and, sometimes, some herbal ally coming from other parts of the world to boost their effectiveness and enhance their healing properties.

I tried to join two worlds in this book, by providing you pieces of my ancient culture with its holistic character in a well-structured learning course in perfect western society style.

I hope you find this interesting and that reading this book will be just the beginning of your journey…

AMAZING BONUSES FOR ALL THE READERS:

Just Scan the QR-Code below to get them!

Acid Reflux – GERD – Heartburn

All these ailments manifest as a burning feeling at the mouth of your stomach that can take up to your throat.

The causes are:

- A low acid level in the stomach (contrary to how you could believe)
- A damaged esophageal sphincter (the communication valve between stomach and esophagus).

The best way to address these ailments is to work on the sphincter, by soothing the inflammation and then act on re-establishing the correct pH in the stomach.

Symptomatology: Inflammation

Actions Required: Anti-inflammatory, Emollient. Carminative. Analgesic

Recommended Herbs: Dandelion root, St. John's Wort root, Meadowsweet root, Heal-all root, Fennel seed, Chamomile root, Catnip root, Marsh Mallow root, Catnip leaves and roots, Chamomile leaves and flowers, Dried Angelica root, Juniper berries, Feverfew leaves .

GERD Tincture

- 1 tbsp. Dandelion root tincture
- 1 tbsp. St. John's Wort root tincture
- 1 tbsp. Meadowsweet root tincture

- 1 tbsp. Heal-all root tincture
- 1 tbsp. Fennel seed tincture
- 1 tbsp. Chamomile root tincture
- 1 tbsp. Catnip root tincture

Put the tinctures in an amber glass bottle with a dropper lid, in the indicated proportions. Label it. Take 15 drops before each meal.

Warning: Remove St. John's Wort root tincture if you are currently taking medications to avoid any interference with them.

Marshmallow Cold Infusion

- 1 tbsp. Marshmallow dried root
- 1 cup distilled water

Cold infuse overnight marshmallow

and water in the indicated proportion. Take two or three tbsp. of the infusion whenever it is needed to calm a burning attack in no time.

Heartburn Tea 1

- 1 tsp Catnip dried leaves
- 1 tsp Chamomile dried leaves and

flowers
- 1 cup distilled boiling water

Directions:
Pour boiling water over the herbs

mixture. Let rest for half an hour. Strain and drink 1 cup per day.

Heartburn Tea 2

- 1 tsp Dried Angelica root, powdered
- 1 tsp Juniper berries, crushed
- 1 tsp Feverfew dried leaves
- 1 cup distilled boiling water

Directions:
Pour boiling water over the herbs mixture. Let sit for half an hour. Strain and drink throughout the day

Allergy and Asthma

Allergy is no other than an excessive reaction of our immune system to foreign substances. Typically these substances will not cause any harm, but our bodies go in protection mode and try to expel the substances in any way they can (sneezes and cough) or to attach them to avoid infection (rush and inflammation).

In the worst case, they can lead to anaphylactic shocks and cause the closure of the respiratory tract with the consequences you can easily imagine.

The main responsible for allergic reactions is Histamine, a hormone produced by our body that starts the inflammation process.

To contrast this hypersensitive reaction, we must attack from many sides. In fact, it is important to support the liver in the production of histaminase (another hormone that neutralizes histamine), the kidney in the managing of the inflammation state, and the mucosae to reduce the quantity of phlegm and mucus produced.

That's why we will use herbs like mullein (which helps the mucosae), or licorice and calendula (which improve liver function), alongside nettle and goldenrod, which directly act in reducing histamine production.

Lastly, following a homeopathic approach, it is important that you assume a small quantity of raw honey, possibly from a local producer. The assumption of small doses of pollen from your environment (which are contained in unfiltered honey), will immunize you from it.

In the US, allergies have become a plague, with over 33% of the population suffering from them. Here is a list of the most frequent allergies:

- Pollen
- Dust
- Mold
- Pets
- Wheat
- Milk
- Peanuts
- Shellfish
- Eggs
- Nickel

Asthma is a syndrome that affects bronchi and causes a section reduction of the respiratory ducts due to spasms of the bronchi muscles. This leads to a reduction of the airflow in the lungs and in the worst cases to suffocation and asphyxiation.

Usually, the trigger for an asthmatic attack is an allergic reaction to allergens contained in the air (pollen, molds, dust, pet hair…) or to food (shellfish and peanuts in particular). Also, it is renowned that air pollution plays an important role in the propensity to be affected by this condition.

Nettle and Oregon Grape Root Tea

- 1 tbsp. nettle leaves (dried)
- ½ tbsp. Oregon grape root
- 1 Cup boiling water (preferably distilled)

Soothing Flower Tea

- 1 tsp pearly everlasting dried flowers

Directions:
Pour boiling water over the herbs mixture and let it rest for half an hour. Drink 1 cup throughout the day.

- 1 tsp Mountain Balm dried flowers
- 1 Cup boiling water (preferably

distilled)

Directions:

Allergy Attack Soothing Tea 1

- 1 tbsp. Oregon Grape root
- 1 tbsp. Barberry root
- 1 Cup water (preferably distilled)

Allergy Attack Soothing Tea 2

- 1 tbsp. dried licorice root
- 4 tbsp. calendula flowers
- 4 tbsp. mullein dried leaves
- 8 tbsp. goldenrod dried leaves
- 8 tbsp. nettle dried leaves

Directions: Combine the herbs in a mason jar. Close with the lid for easy

Allergy Attack Rescue Remedy

- Capsule of dried nettle
- Capsule of milk thistle seed

Asthma Relief Tea

- 2 tsp Elecampane Root
- 2 tsp Horehound leaves and flowers
- 2 tsp Dried Vervain Leaves
- 2 Cup distilled water

Asthma Relief Cold Infusion

- 1 tsp Indian Cucumber Root (dried and powdered)
- 1 tsp Echinacea Root (dried and powdered)
- 1 tsp Elecampane Root

Pour the boiling water over the dried flower mix and let rest for half an hour.

Mix the roots and the cold water. Bring the mixture to a boil and let simmer for half an hour. Strain and drink throughout the day.

and safe storage. Pour 32oz. of boiling water on 3 tbsp. of the mix and let sit overnight. Drink the tea throughout the following day. This is a preventive remedy to be done each day, two to three weeks before the allergy season. **Instruction for safe use:** Avoid nettle and double the quantity of goldenrod in case you take blood anti-coagulants.

Directions: Take two of each capsule to calm a violent allergy attack.

Directions: In a saucepan, bring water to a boil with the herbs inside. Then reduce the heat and let simmer for half an hour. Strain and drink hot or cold throughout the day.

- 1 Cup distilled water

Directions: Combine herbs and water. Let rest overnight and drink throughout the following day.

Anemia

Anemia is a condition that affects red blood cells and their capacity to carry oxygen or carbon dioxide through our bodies. It may be related to the number of red blood cells produced and circulating, or to the quantity of hemoglobin in them (the substance that actually carries the oxygen).

Anemia can be due to genetics, poor diet or it can be the side effect of some other disease (such as celiac disease, cirrhosis of the liver, gastric ulcer, and many others including tumors and lupus) or special condition (i.e. pregnancy).

Infusion for Anemia

- 8 oz. Distilled Water
- 1 tsp barberry
- 1 tsp Oregon Grape Root
- 2 tbsp. dried Nettle leaves

Recommended Herbs: Nettle, Barberry, Oregon Grape Root

Directions: Let the herbs infuse overnight in cold water, then strain and drink throughout the following day.

Back Pain

Back Pain is one of the most diffused conditions all over the United States.

Injuries, bad posture, hernias, or nerve inflammation (sciatica) can cause it and there is no easy quick fix for it. The recommended action is to watch your posture (especially if you work with a PC) and make appropriate gym exercises to strengthen the musculature and preventing injuries. Herbs can help to provide an analgesic and relaxing action on the inflamed parts to ease the pain and recover mobility.

Symptomatology: Muscular Tension, Inflammation

Actions Required: Analgesic, Anti-inflammatory, Muscle Relaxant

Recommended Herbs: Solomon's seal root, Ginger Root, Goldenrod Root, Meadowsweet root and leaves, Mullein root Tincture, Vervain leaves, White Willow Bark, St. John's Wort leaves and flowers, Coltsfoot flowers and root, Cramp Bark, Kava Root

Pain Relief Tincture

- ¼ oz. Solomon's seal Tincture
- ¼ oz. Ginger Root Tincture
- 1 tsp goldenrod Tincture
- 1 tsp meadowsweet Tincture
- 1 tsp mullein Root Tincture

Directions: Combine the tinctures in an amber glass bottle with a dropper lid. Label it. Take 4 drops before the meals or apply topically. Be sure to gently heat the tincture by rubbing your hands to improve its effectiveness.

Warm Compress

- 1 pint of water
- 8 oz. Ginger Root
- 4 oz. Epsom Salt

Directions: Bring to a boil the water with the Ginger Root inside. Reduce the heat, add the Epsom Salt and simmer

for 10 minutes. Take a towel and pour some of the decoction on it. It must be wet but not dripping. In the meantime, prepare a hot water bottle. Lie down on your belly, and place the wet towel in the sore zone. Then place the hot water bottle on top. Apply for 20 minutes.

Decoction for Low Back Pain 1

- 1 tsp Vervain

- 1 tsp White Willow Bark

- 1 Cup distilled water

Directions: Prepare a decoction of the

Decoction for Low Back Pain 2

- 1 tsp St. John's Wort
- 1 tsp Coltsfoot
- 1 Cup distilled water

Decoction for Low Back Pain 3 (Sciatica)

- 1 tsp Cramp Bark
- 1 tsp Kava Root
- 1 Cup distilled water

herbs in water with the proportions described above, by making Vervain and willow bark boil for half an hour. Strain and drink throughout the day.

Directions: Boil the herbs in water in the recommended proportions for 10 minutes. Strain and drink throughout the day.

Directions: Boil Kava root and Cramp bark in the recommended proportions for 30 minutes in distilled water. Let cool, strain, and drink throughout the day.

Bedsores

These **skin ulcers** are common in people who are bedridden or in a wheelchair. They are due to the prolonged application of pressure in a skin area. They are painful and at times source of bacterial infections. They usually occur on the lower back and glutes.

Wash for Bedsores

- 1 tsp Marigold (flowers)
- 1 tsp Echinacea (root)
- 1 tsp White Oak (bark)

Symptomatology: Redness, Inflammation

Actions Required: Antibacterial, Anti-inflammatory

Recommended Herbs: Echinacea (root), Marigold (flower), White oak (bark), Nettle (leaves)

- 1 Cup distilled water

Directions: Cold infuse overnight the herbs in the water.

Bronchitis

Bronchitis is one of the most common diseases of the respiratory system. It is simply an inflammation, often accompanied by a bacterial infection, of the bronchi. This infection leads to cough, fever, and sore throat in the majority of cases, and if underestimated, can lead to more severe diseases like chronic bronchitis or even pneumonia.

Symptomatology: Inflammation, Cough, Fever

Actions Required: Anti-inflammatory, Antibacterial, Expectorant

Recommended Herbs: Angelica root, Elecampane (root), Elderberry (fruits), Thyme (leaves), Sage (leaves), Pine needles, Ginger root, Garlic cloves, Pearly everlasting flower, Redroot (root), Elecampane root, Nettle leaves, Coltsfoot root, Marshmallow

leaves, Mullein leaves, Black Cohosh root, Chamomile leaves, Indian cucumber root, Dandelion (root).

Herbal Shot

- 1 pint of Apple Cider Vinegar
- 1 tbsp. Angelica (root)
- 1 tbsp. Elecampane (root)
- 2 tbsp. elderberry (fruits)
- 2 tbsp. Thyme (leaves)
- 2 tbsp. Sage (leaves)
- 2 tbsp. pine needles
- ½ oz. Fresh grated Ginger
- 8 Garlic cloves finely chopped

Directions: In this remedy, we mix some ancient Native Americans medical plants (i.e. the sage) with some typical European plants like garlic to have the benefits of both worlds.

Mix all the ingredients in a mason jar. Close the lid and let it rest in a shadowy place for two weeks. Strain, bottle, and label the aromatic vinegar. Take a shot every 6 hours

Instruction for safe use: Avoid this remedy in case you take blood anti-coagulants

Herbal Tea 1

- 1 cup Distilled Boiling water
- 1 tsp Dried Pearly everlasting
- 1 slice Ginger
- 1 tsp Redroot

Directions: Pour the boiling water over the herbs and roots. Let rest for half an hour. Strain and drink one cup throughout the day.

Herbal Tea 2

- 1 cup Distilled Boiling water
- 1 tsp Elecampane root
- 1 tsp Nettle leaves

Directions: Combine all the herbs and pour boiling water over them. Let rest for 30 minutes. Strain and drink throughout the day.

Herbal Tea 3

- 1 cup Distilled Boiling water
- 1 tsp Coltsfoot root
- 1 tsp Marshmallow leaves
- 1 tsp Mullein leaves

Directions: Pour boiling water over the herbs mixture. Let rest for half an hour. Strain and drink one cup per day maximum.

Herbal Tea 4

- 1 cup Distilled Boiling water
- 1 tsp Black Cohosh root
- 1 tsp Chamomile leaves
- 1 tsp Indian cucumber root

Directions: Mix all the herbs in a nonmetallic container and pour the boiling water over them. Let rest for half an hour. Strain and drink throughout the day.

Cold and Cough

The medical name of the common **Cold** is *Viral Rhino-Pharyngitis*, which means an infection of the upper respiratory ducts (namely nose and pharynx) due to a family of viruses that can count more than 200 species. This condition is often accompanied by sneezing, nasal congestion, tiredness, diffused pain all over the body, fever, and sore throat, and coughing.

Symptomatology: Inflammation, Infection.

Actions Required: Antiviral, Anti-inflammatory, Decongestant, Febrifuge, Antitussive, Diaphoretic.

Recommended Herbs: Fennel seed, Mullein leaves, Marshmallow root, Ginger root, Licorice root, Wild Cherry root, Boneset root, Horehound leaves, Oxeye, Speedwell, Blue Vervain leaves, Agrimony flowers and leaves, Goldenseal root, Osha root, Pleurisy root, Mountain Balm leaves, Lizard Tail root, Goldenrod leaves, Pine bark, Pine Needles, Echinacea Root, Indigo Root, Coltsfoot Leaves, Elecampane leaves, Thyme leaves, Sage leaves, Yarrow flowers, Elderberry flowers, Horehound leaves.

Expectorant Tea 1

- 1 tbsp. Fennel seed
- 1 tbsp. Mullein leaves
- 1 tbsp. Marshmallow root
- 1 cup Distilled Boiling water

Directions: Pour boiling water over the herbs mixture and let rest for 20 minutes. Strain and drink throughout the day.

Expectorant Tea 2

- 4 slices of fresh ginger
- 1 tbsp. Licorice root
- 1 tbsp. Wild Cherry Bark root
- 1 tbsp. Boneset root
- 3 cups distilled boiling water

Directions: Combine the herbs in a glass container. Add one tablespoon of the herbs mix to a cup of boiling water. Let the liquid steep for thirty minutes minimum. Strain and drink throughout the day.

Cold Rescue Tea

- 1 tbsps. Horehound leaves
- 1 tbsps. Oxeye
- 1 tbsps. Speedwell
- 1 ½ tbsps. Blue Vervain leaves
- 2 tbsp. Agrimony flowers and leaves
- 1 ½ tbsp. Mullein leaves

- 3 cups distilled boiling water

Directions: Pour boiling water over the herbs mixture, in a glass (important) container. Let rest for half an hour. Strain and drink throughout the day

Cold Rescue Tea (Apache Recipe)

- 1 tbsp. Goldenseal root
- 1 tbsp. Mullein leaves
- 1 tbsp. Osha root
- 1 tbsp. Pleurisy root

- 1 tbsp. Mountain Balm leaves
- 1 tbsp. Lizard Tail root
- 3 cups distilled boiling water

Directions: Pour boiling water over the

herb mixture. Let rest for 30 minutes. Strain and drink one cup throughout the day.

Cold Rescue Tea (Navajo Recipe)

- 1 ½ tbsp. Horehound leaves
- 1 ½ tbsp. Goldenrod leaves
- 3 tbsp. Pine bark
- 5 cups distilled boiling water

Directions: Pour boiling water over the herbs mixture, in a non-metallic container. Let rest for half an hour. Strain and drink throughout the day

Cough Attach Rescue Tincture

- 1 tsp Echinacea Root Tincture
- 1 tsp Indigo Root Tincture
- 1 Cups of Mullein tea

Directions: Add the tinctures to the tea and drink 1 cup per day.

Cough Attach Rescue Syrup

- 1 cup Mullein tea
- 8 oz. honey

Directions: Dissolve the honey in the tea in a small saucepan. Once dissolved, let cool and pour it in a mason jar with an airtight lid. Recommended dose: 2 tbsp. – 4 times a day

All Natural Cough Syrup 1

- 1 cup Boiling water
- 8 oz. honey
- 1 tsp Coltsfoot Leaves
- 1 tsp Mullein leaves
- 1 tsp Lizard Tail root

Add the boiling water to the herb mixture and let rest for 20 minutes. Heat it again in a small saucepan to get it warm and dissolve the honey in it. Once dissolved, let cool and pour it in a mason jar with an airtight lid. Recommended dose: 2 tbsp. – 4 times a day

All Natural Cough Syrup 2

- 1 cup elecampane tea
- 8 oz. honey

Directions: Dissolve the honey in the tea in a small saucepan. Once dissolved, let cool and pour it in a mason jar with an airtight lid. Recommended dose: 2 tbsp. – 4 times a day

Cough Vinegar Shot

- 4 tbsp. Pine Needles
- 3 tbsp. dried ginger root
- 4 tbsp. thyme leaves
- 4 tbsp. sage leaves
- 2 pints apple cider vinegar

Directions: Mix all the ingredients in a mason jar. Close the lid and let it rest in a shadowy place for two weeks. Strain, bottle, and label the aromatic vinegar. Take a shot every 6 hours.

Cough Reductive Tea

- 1 tsp Yarrow flowers
- 1 tsp Elderberry flowers
- 1 cup distilled boiling water

Directions: Pour boiling water over the mixture of flower. Let rest for half an hour. Strain and drink throughout the day.

Decongestant Tea

- 3 slices of fresh ginger
- 1 tbsp. Pleurisy root
- 1 cup distilled boiling water

Directions: Pour boiling water over the Pleurisy roots and the ginger slices. Let rest for half an hour. Strain and drink one cup throughout the day.

Horehound Candies

- 3 cups horehound leaves
- 3 cups distilled water
- 6 cups sugar
- 6 tbsp. Honey

Directions: Boil water and the horehound leaves for half an hour. Let cool, add the remaining ingredients, and stir. Bring back to the boil the mixture until it reaches roughly 300°F. Pour on a tray with parchment paper and let cool the caramel. Cut in squares according to your taste.

Constipation

Constipation is the irregularity of bowel movement. This can be caused by genetics, poor diet, insufficient hydration, or laxative abuse as well as more serious problems, like drug abuse or alcoholism.

Symptomatology: Abdomen Tension

Actions Required: Carminative, Laxative, Demulcent

Digestion Aid Tea

- 1 tsp. Cascara Sagrada Bark
- 1 slice ginger root
- ½ tsp cayenne
- ½ tsp Oregon grape root
- 1 cup boiling water

Recommended Herbs: Cascara Sagrada Bark, Ginger root, Oregon grape root, St. John's Wort, Dandelion Root, Angelica root, Ginger root, Licorice root, Cinnamon bark, Marshmallow root, Linden leaves, Boneset flowers, Dandelion Flowers, Linden.

Combine the above ingredients in the indicated ratio, in a saucepan, and put it on high heat. Once it is boiling, reduce the heat to medium and let simmer for half an hour. Let cool before straining. Drink one cup at room temperature throughout the day.

Bowel Relaxation Tincture

- 1 ½ tbsp. St. John's Wort Tincture
- 1 ½ tbsp. Dandelion Root Tincture
- 1 tbsp. Angelica root Tincture
- 1 tbsp. Ginger root Tincture

Directions: Mix the tinctures in an amber glass bottle with a dropper lid. Label it. Take 4 drops every half an hour until you feel the urge to go to the bathroom.

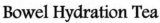

Bowel Hydration Tea

- 1 tsp Licorice root
- 1 tsp Cinnamon bark
- 1 tbsp. Marshmallow root
- 1 tbsp. Linden leaves

Stomach soothing Tea

- 1 oz. Dried Boneset Flowers
- 1 oz. Dried Dandelion Flowers
- 1 oz. Cascara Sagrada Bark
- 2 pint distilled water

Directions: Combine the above

Directions: Cold infuse overnight of the herbs in one cup of distilled water. Drink one cup first thing in the morning.

ingredients in the indicated ratio, in a saucepan, and put it on high heat. Once the water is boiling, reduce the heat to medium and let simmer for half an hour. Let cool before straining it. Drink one cup at room temperature or tepid before going to bed

Cuts and Wounds

Cuts or abrasions are not something you have to underestimate. If not correctly addressed they can cause unpleasant infections, swellings, and inflammations.

When dealing with a minor wound the first thing to do is stop the bleeding, and then it is time to wash it properly to remove any sign of dirt and foreign matter and only then proceed with the medication. Of course, serious bleeding and arteries damages require emergency care by a medical professional.

Herbs can come in handy to prepare effective washes to disinfect the wound and promote healing.

Symptomatology: Inflammation

Actions Required: Anti-inflammation, Antiseptic, Vulnerary

Recommended Herbs: Calendula (flowers), Echinacea (root), Plantain (leaves), Goldenrod (root, leaves and flowers), Heal-all (leaves and flowers), Chamomile (flowers), St. John's Wort (leaves and flowers), Yarrow (leaves and flowers), Pine (bark and resin), Ashwagandha (root).

Wounds Soothing Compress

- 1 tsp Pine (inner bark)
- 1 tsp Heal-all (leaves and flowers)
- 1 tsp Echinacea (root)
- 1 Cup distilled boiling water

Let the herbs boil in water in the indicated proportions, for half an hour. Let cool and strain. Soak a clean towel in the liquid, squeeze it to avoid it dripping, and apply topically on the wound for immediate relief.

Pine Resin Salve

- 1 cup Pine resin
- 1 cup goldenrod root infused oil
- 1 tbsp. Echinacea (root) oil
- 1 oz. Beeswax

Directions: Combine the essential oils of Echinacea and Goldenrod root with the pine resin, in a stainless steel cooking pan. Heat very gently on a stove until the mixture is warm. Add

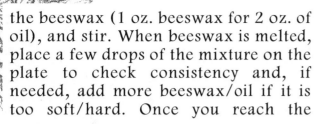

the beeswax (1 oz. beeswax for 2 oz. of oil), and stir. When beeswax is melted, place a few drops of the mixture on the plate to check consistency and, if needed, add more beeswax/oil if it is too soft/hard. Once you reach the

Wounds Wash 1

- 1 tsp Ashwagandha (root)
- 1 tsp Echinacea (root)
- 1 Cup distilled boiling water

Wounds Wash 2

- 3 tbsp. Calendula (flowers)
- 3 tbsp. Echinacea (root)
- 3 tbsp. Plantain (leaves)
- 3 tbsp. Goldenrod (leaves and flowers)
- 2 tbsp. Heal-all (leaves and flowers)
- 1 tbsp. Chamomile (flowers)

perfect consistency, pour the mix in a mason jar and let it cool uncovered. Once the salve is cool, you can close the lid and store it. IMPORTANT: heat destroys the phytochemicals, so do not ever surpass 170°F temperature.

Directions: Boil the roots in water in the indicated proportions, for 30 minutes. Let cool and strain. Use to wash the wound.

- 1 tsp Ashwagandha (root)

Directions: Mix the herbs and store them in a mason jar in a shady place. To prepare the wash, boil 4 tsp of the mix for each cup of water you put. Let simmer for 30 minutes, cool, strain, and use it to wash the wound.

Dysentery and Diarrhea

Diarrhea is the frequent expulsion of watery feces. Causes for diarrhea can be many: food intolerances, food poisoning, colitis, stress, or viral and bacterial infections.

When a bacterial infection is taking on and feces are mixed with blood we speak about **Dysentery**.

The most important thing to keep in mind when dealing with diarrhea and dysentery is to keep the body hydrated. Watery feces discharge can lead to severe dehydration, especially in children and seniors.

Astringent Tea 1 (Kumeyaay Recipe)

- 1 tsp yellow dock root
- 1 tsp blackberry leaves
- 1 tsp raspberry leaves
- 1 tsp yarrow leaves
- 1 cup distilled boiling water

Astringent Tea 2

- 1 tbsp. heal all leaves and flowers

Symptomatology: Laxity

Actions Required: Astringent, Emollient

Recommended Herbs: Yellow dock root, Blackberry leaves, Raspberry leaves, Yarrow leaves, Meadowsweet leaves and flowers, Rose petals, Heal all leaves, flowers and root, Agrimony leaves, Cinnamon bark, Oregon Grape root, Blackberry leaves, Angelica seeds, Alumroot (root)

Directions: Pour boiling water over the herbs mixture. Let rest for 30 minutes. Strain and drink 1 cup per day, two or three tablespoonfuls at a time.

- 1 tsp meadowsweet flowers

- 1 tsp dried rose petals
- 1 cup distilled boiling water

Directions: Pour boiling water over the herbs mixture. Let rest for half an hour. Strain and drink throughout the day.

Astringent Tincture

- 1 tbsp. heal all tincture
- 1 tsp meadowsweet tincture
- 1 tsp rose petals tincture

Put the tinctures in an amber glass bottle with a dropper lid, in the indicated proportions. Take 5 drops every half an hour to calm your stomach.

Astringent Decoction

- 1 tsp Heal all leaves
- 1 tsp Agrimony leaves
- 1 cup distilled water

Directions: Combine herbs and water in a small saucepan, using the weight ratio indicated above. Bring to a boil, reduce heat and let simmer for half an hour. Let the decoction cool down and strain. Drink one cup throughout the day.

Astringent and Emollient Rescue Capsules

- 1 tsp cinnamon
- 4 gelatin capsules

Directions: Fill the capsules with cinnamon powder. Take four maximum per day. Once in the stomach gelatin will dissolve and the powder will absorb water, making an astringent action. Cinnamon with its emollient phytochemicals will soothe the inflamed part of your bowels.

Emollient Tea

- 1 tsp Oregon Grape root
- 1 tsp blackberry leaves
- 1 tsp Angelica seeds
- 1 tsp alumroot
- 1 cup distilled boiling water

Directions: Pour boiling water over the herbs mixture. Let rest for half an hour. Strain and drink throughout the day.

Fever

Fever is the most common reaction of our body to an infection. It consists of an increase of body temperature up to 100°F or higher to "burn off" the bacteria from our bodies.

In my personal opinion fever, being a self-induced state of our bodies is not something bad or to be fought. It is a natural reaction (so it is a mechanism that has been sharpened in many years of evolution) to an infection, and then is the most effective way, in the long run, to get rid of it.

We should not take medications at the first sight of an increase in body temperature just because we do not want to feel bad. Instead, fever must be taken under control and intervention must be sought only if it reaches certain values, or in case of serious diseases or pregnancy.

Lastly, the very important thing to keep in mind regarding fever is to stay hydrated.

Fever can cause high dehydration problems and the fluids we lose with sweat, must always be integrated.

Symptomatology: Heat, Inflammation, Dehydration

Actions Required: Diaphoretic, Febrifuge

Recommended Herbs: Tulsi Leaves, Sage (Leaves), Thyme (Leaves), Yarrow (Leaves and Flowers), Angelica (Root), Ginger (Root), Catnip (Leaves and Flowers), Elderberry (Flower), Peppermint (Leaves), Ivy (Leaves), Barberry (Leaves), Echinacea (Root), Willow (Root and Bark), Vervain (Leaves), Ale Hoof leaves, Raspberry leaves, Strawberry leaves, Blackberry leaves.

Fever Reducing Tea 1

- 1 tsp Catnip dried leaves
- 1 tsp Yarrow dried leaves and flowers
- 1 tsp Barberry dried leaves
- 1 tsp Vervain dried leaves
- 1 tsp Peppermint dried leaves
- 1 tsp Ale Hoof dried leaves

- 2 cups Distilled Boiling water

Directions: Combine the herbs and the boiling water in the indicated proportions. Let steep for half an hour. Strain and drink 2 cups per day maximum.

Fever Reducing Tea 2

- 1 tsp Catnip dried leaves
- 1 tsp Elderberry dried flowers
- 1 tsp Peppermint dried leaves
- 1 cup distilled boiling water

Directions: Pour boiling water over the herbs mixture. Let rest 30 minutes before straining and drinking it. The allowed dosage is one cup per day.

Fast Fever Relief Tea

- 1 tsp Raspberry leaves
- 1 tsp Strawberry leaves
- 1 tsp Blackberry leaves
- 1 cup distilled boiling water

Directions: Pour boiling water over the herbs mixture. Let rest for half an hour. Strain and drink.

Hyper-thermic Tea

- 1 tsp Catnip dried leaves
- 1 tsp Elderberry dried flowers
- 1 tsp Peppermint dried leaves
- 1 cup distilled boiling water

Directions: Pour boiling water over the herbs mixture. Let rest for half an hour. Strain and drink one cup per day maximum, very hot, to increase body temperature and **induce fever**.

Warning: The assumption of fever-inducing substances must be done under medical advice for people with pre-existing heart conditions, pregnant women, seniors, and children.

Food Intolerances

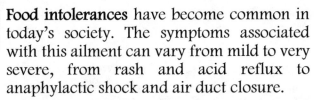

Food intolerances have become common in today's society. The symptoms associated with this ailment can vary from mild to very severe, from rash and acid reflux to anaphylactic shock and air duct closure.

The most diffused food intolerances are dairy, gluten, shellfish, nuts, and eggs. In addition, Nickel is a much-diffused substance that can cause intolerance. The symptoms of Nickel intolerance are the same as a food intolerance (rash and swelling) but it is very frequent that the source of the intolerance is not the nickel contained in our food but the one contained in the make-up we use (face-powders, eyeshadow, lipsticks…).

The best way to identify food intolerance, besides specific allergic tests to be done under medical supervision, is by adopting food elimination periods. These are periods (typically one month) in which you totally avoid the food you suspect to be intolerant to, and take notice of how your symptoms change (or not). It can take time, but with this method, you will accurately identify foods and substances that trigger your immune system and that cause an allergic reaction.

Symptomatology: Inflammation, Rash, Laxity

Actions Required: Carminative, Emollient

Recommended Herbs: Peppermint leaves, Chamomile flowers, Angelica root, Ginger root, Licorice root, Bee Balm Leaves, Calendula flowers, Plantain Leaves, Yarrow Leaves and Flowers, Fennel Seeds, Catnip leaves, Dandelion leaves, Echinacea root, Black Cohosh root, Mullein leaves, St. John's Wort leaves and flowers.

Digestion Aid Tea

- 2 tsp Peppermint dried leaves
- 2 tsp Chamomile dried flowers
- 1 tsp Powdered Angelica root
- 1 tsp Powdered Ginger root

Directions: Combine the herbs in a mason jar for easy storage. Put 1 tbsp. of the mixture in 1 cup of distilled boiling water. Let rest for half an hour. Strain and drink 1-2 cups per day.

Indigestion Remedy Tea

- 1 cup Distilled boiling water
- 1 tsp Peppermint dried leaves
- 1 tsp Licorice Powdered root

Directions: Pour boiling water over the herbs mixture. Let rest for half an hour. Strain and drink throughout the day.

Emollient Tea 1

- 1 cup Distilled boiling water
- 1 tsp Peppermint dried leaves
- 1 tsp Chamomile dried flowers
- 1 tsp Bee Balm Leaves

Directions: Pour boiling water over the herbs mixture in the indicated proportion. Let rest for 30 minutes. Strain and drink one cup per day.

Emollient Tea 2

- 1 tbsp. Dried Calendula flowers
- 1 tbsp. Chamomile dried flowers
- 1 tbsp. Plantain dried Leaves
- 1 tbsp. Yarrow dried Leaves and Flowers
- 1 tbsp. Licorice root
- 1 tbsp. Peppermint dried Leaves
- 1 tbsp. Fennel Seeds

- 1 tbsp. Dried Ginger root

Directions: Combine the herbs in the indicated proportion, in a mason jar for easy storage. Put 1 tbsp. of the mixture in 1 cup of distilled boiling water and let it rest for half an hour. Strain and drink 1~2 cups per day.

Carminative Tea (for intestinal gas)

- 1 cup Distilled boiling water
- 1 tsp Powdered Angelica root
- 1 tsp Peppermint dried leaves
- 1 tsp Bee Balm leaves

Directions: Pour boiling water over the herbs mixture. Let rest for half an hour. Strain and drink one cup throughout the day.

Fast Action Carminative Tea

- 1 cup Distilled boiling water
- 1 tsp Catnip dried leaves
- 1 tsp Dandelion leaves
- 1 tsp Echinacea root

Directions: Pour boiling water over the herbs mixture. Let rest for 20 minutes. Strain and drink one cup per day.

Stomach Detoxifying Tea

- 1 cup Distilled boiling water
- 1 tsp Black Cohosh root
- 1 tsp Echinacea root

Directions: Pour boiling water over the herbs mixture. Let rest for half an hour. Strain and drink one cup on cup day two or three tablespoonfuls at a time.

Colon Soothing Broth

- 2 Quarts water
- 2 tbsp. Dried Calendula flowers
- 2 tsp Dandelion leaves
- 2 tbsp. Fennel Seeds
- 2 tbsp. Mullein leaves
- Bones, possibly with joints

Directions: In a large pan over high heat, boil the ingredients for 3~4 hours so the collagen contained in the bones dissolves in the broth. Collagen is the miraculous substance that will help your gut restoring its normal balance. While boiling, remove the foam on the surface of the broth and add more water if needed. Strain and drink up to three cups per day.

Headache

Many people suffer from chronic **Headache** nowadays. Causes can be many: excessive screen time, dehydration, fatigue, and stress are the most common but it can be due to more serious problems such as sinusitis, allergies, or even tumors or infections.

The pharmaceutic drugs that fight headaches are the most diffused and sold all over the United States. The headache business is worth several billions of dollars.

Aspirin, ibuprofen, ketoprofen, paracetamol are all common active principles of the most diffused over-the-counter (and over-abused) painkillers.

Although it is very handy to take a pill and forget the pain, you should exercise caution when dealing with these drugs.

In fact, the side effects are unpleasant to experiment with, such as gastrointestinal ailments (diarrhea, nausea, and ulcers),

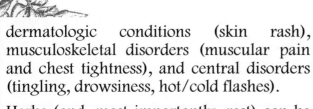

dermatologic conditions (skin rash), musculoskeletal disorders (muscular pain and chest tightness), and central disorders (tingling, drowsiness, hot/cold flashes).

Herbs (and, most importantly, rest) can be indeed a reliable alternative to these medications.

Symptomatology: Inflammation, Tension

Headache Tea 1

- 1 tsp Catnip dried leaves
- 1 tsp Peppermint dried leaves
- 1 tsp Feverfew dried leaves
- 1 cup distilled boiling water

Headache Tea 2

- 1 tbsp. Meadowsweet dried flowers
- 2 tbsp. Betony dried leaves and flowers
- 2 tbsp. marshmallow leaves

Directions: Mix the herbs in a mason

Headache Tea 3

- 1 tbsp. sage dried leaves
- 1 tbsp. Powdered Ginger root
- 2 tbsp. Betony dried leaves and flowers
- 2 tbsp. Tulsi dried leaves

Headache Tea 4

- 1 tsp Peppermint dried leaves
- 1 tsp Feverfew dried leaves
- 1 cup distilled boiling water

Actions Required: Anti-inflammatory, Relaxant, Anodyne, Analgesic

Recommended Herbs: Catnip leaves, Meadowsweet flowers, Betony leaves and flowers, Marshmallow leaves, Sage leaves, Ginger root, Betony leaves and flowers, Tulsi leaves, Peppermint leaves, Feverfew leaves

Directions: Pour boiling water over the herbs mixture. Let rest for half an hour. Strain and drink throughout the day.

jar for easy storage. Put 1 tbsp. of the mixture in 1 cup of distilled boiling water. Let rest for half an hour. Strain and drink 1~2 cups per day.
Note: Particularly indicated to people who suffer from hypothyroidism and liver conditions.

Directions: Mix the herbs in a mason jar for easy storage. Put 1 tbsp. of the mixture in 1 cup of distilled boiling water. Let rest for half an hour. Strain and drink 1~2 cups per day.
Note: Particularly indicated to stress-induced headaches.

Directions: Pour boiling water over the herbs mixture. Let rest for half an hour. Strain and drink throughout the day.

Hypertension

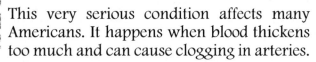

This very serious condition affects many Americans. It happens when blood thickens too much and can cause clogging in arteries.

Symptomatology: High Blood Density

Actions Required: Hypotensive, Sedative

Hyperte Blood Thinning Tea

- 1 tsp Burdock root dried, powder
- 1 tsp Goldenseal dried leaves
- 1 tsp Slippery Elm Barks
- 1 cup distilled boiling water

Hypotensive Tea

- 1 cup Meadowsweet dried flowers
- 1 cup Linden dried leaves and flowers

Arteriosclerosis Preventive Tea

- 1 tsp Ginger root dried, powder
- 1 tsp Gingko Biloba dried leaves
- 1 tsp Ashwagandha dried root
- 1 tsp Goldenseal (root)
- 1 cup distilled boiling water

Anti-Clog Tea

- 1 tsp Black Cohosh root dried, powder
- 1 tsp Gingko Biloba dried leaves
- 1 cup distilled boiling water

Recommended Herbs: Burdock root, Goldenseal leaves, Slippery Elm Barks, Meadowsweet flowers, Linden leaves and flowers, Ginger root, Ashwagandha, Goldenseal root, Black Cohosh root, Gingko Biloba leaves.

Directions: Pour boiling water over the herbs mixture. Let rest for 20-30 minutes. Strain and drink throughout the day.

Directions: Mix the herbs in a mason jar for easy storage. Put 1 tbsp. of the mixture in 1 cup of distilled boiling water. Let rest for half an hour. Strain and drink 1-2 cups per day.

Pour boiling water over the herbs mixture. Let rest for half an hour. Strain and drink throughout the day.

Directions: Pour boiling water over the herbs mixture. Let steep for half an hour. Strain and drink throughout the day.

Indigestion

This condition happens when you do not digest something you eat. It may be due to many causes: from eating too much or too fast, to serious conditions such as intolerances, ulcers, or gastritis.

Symptomatology: Abdominal tension

Actions Required: Carminative, Relaxant

Recommended Herbs: Licorice root, Peppermint leaves, Ginger root, Angelica root, Chamomile Flowers, Black Cohosh root, Fennel seeds, Dandelion Root, Sage Leaves

Digestive Tea 1

- 1 tsp Licorice root dried, powder
- 1 tsp Peppermint dried leaves
- 1 cup distilled boiling water

Pour boiling water over the herbs. Let steep for 20 minutes. Strain and drink warm to help digestion.

Digestive Tea 2

- 1 tsp Ginger root dried
- 1 tsp Angelica root dried
- 1 tsp Chamomile dried flowers
- 1 tsp Peppermint dried leaves
- 1 cup distilled boiling water

Pour boiling water over the herbs mixture. Let rest for half an hour. Strain and drink.

Digestive Tea 3

- 1 tsp Black Cohosh root dried
- 1 tsp Angelica root dried
- 1 cup distilled boiling water

Pour boiling water over the herbs mixture. Let rest for 30 minutes. Strain and drink throughout the day to help with persistent indigestion.

Intestinal Gas Tincture

- 3 tbsp. Fennel seed tincture
- 3 tbsp. Ginger Root tincture
- 3 tbsp. Licorice Root tincture
- 3 tbsp. Peppermint tincture
- 3 tbsp. Chamomile tincture

Directions: Put the tinctures in an amber glass bottle with a dropper lid, in the indicated proportions. Label it. Take 5 drops after each meal.

Preventive Tincture

- 3 tbsp. Fennel seed tincture
- 3 tbsp. Dandelion Root tincture
- 3 tbsp. Licorice Root tincture
- 3 tbsp. Sage Leaves tincture

Directions: Put the tinctures in an amber glass bottle with a dropper lid, in the indicated proportions. Label it. Take 3 drops before each meal.

Menstrual Cycle Disturbs

Menstrual Cycle Disturbs can be many:

- Amenorrhea: absence of menstruation.
- Oligo-menorrhea and Poli-menorreha: Delayed or anticipated menstrual cycles.
- Hypo-menorrhea: poor menstruation flow.

- Hypermenorrhea: excessive menstruation flow.
- Menorrhagia: Prolonged menstruation.
- Dysmenorrhea: painful menstruation. It happens roughly in 50% of women, and it manifests as a pain in the low back or abdomen, frequently accompanied by nausea and diarrhea.

The treatment for all these conditions consists in improving the diet in both quality and quantity (mostly for amenorrhea and oligo-menorrhea) and in improving circulation and liver and kidney function. In fact, many disorders are caused by an excess of hormones in the blood flow, which can indeed be cleaned up by the liver and the kidneys.

Symptomatology: Tension

Stomach Cramps Soothing Tea

- 1 tsp St. John's Wort leaves
- 1 tsp Raspberry leaves
- 1 cup distilled boiling water

Directions: Pour boiling water over the herbs mixture. Let rest for half an hour. Strain and drink throughout the

Dysmenorrhea Rescue Tea 1

- 1 tsp Black Haw Root
- 1 tsp Black Cohosh Root
- 1 tsp Crampbark (bark)
- 1 cup distilled boiling water

Directions: Pour boiling water over the herbs mixture. Let rest for 30 minutes.

Dysmenorrhea Rescue Tea 2

- 1 tsp Black Haw Root
- 1 tsp Passionflower
- 1 cup distilled boiling water

Directions: Pour boiling water over the herbs mixture. Let rest for half an hour. Strain and drink one cup per day,

Stable Flow Tea

- 1 cup Nettle dried flowers and leaves
- 1 cup Goldenrod dried leaves and flowers
- ½ cup Dandelion dried leaves and flowers

Actions Required: Analgesic, Relaxant, Circulatory Stimulant, Emmenagogue, Rubefacient

Recommended Herbs: St. John's Wort leaves, Raspberry leaves, Black Haw Root, Black Cohosh Root, Crampbark (bark), Passionflower, Nettle flowers and leaves, Goldenrod leaves and flowers, Dandelion leaves and flowers, Heal-all leaves, Angelica dried root, Chamomile dried flowers, Tulsi leaves

day.
Warning: do not use in case of pregnancy. It definitively should not be the case because you would not have menstruation but in any case, the substance contained in this tea can cause damage to the uterus if taken during pregnancy

Strain and drink throughout the day.
Warning: do not use in case of pregnancy. It definitively should not be the case because you would not have menstruation but in any case, the substance contained in this tea can cause damage to the uterus if taken during pregnancy

two or three tablespoonfuls at a time.
Warning: do not use in case of pregnancy. It definitively should not be the case because you would not have menstruation but in any case, the substance contained in this tea can cause damage to the uterus if taken during pregnancy

- 1 cup Heal-all dried leaves
- ½ cup Angelica dried root

Mix the herbs in a mason jar for easy storage. Put 1 tbsp. of the mixture in 1 cup of distilled boiling water. Let rest for half an hour. Strain and drink 1 cup per day.

Warning: do not use in case of pregnancy. It definitively should not be the case because you would not have

menstruation but in any case, the substance contained in this tea can cause damage to the uterus if taken during pregnancy

Poor Blood Flow Tea

- 1 cup Chamomile dried flowers
- 1 cup Goldenrod dried leaves
- 1 cup Tulsi dried leaves
- ½ cup Angelica dried root

Directions: Mix the herbs in a mason jar for easy storage. Put 1 tbsp. of the mixture in 1 cup of distilled boiling

water. Let rest for half an hour. Strain and drink 1 cup per day.

Warning: do not use in case of pregnancy. It definitively should not be the case because you would not have menstruation but in any case, the substance contained in this tea can cause damage to the uterus if taken during pregnancy.

Muscular Cramps

Cramps are involuntary muscle contractions that can lead to pain and the temporary impossibility to move the affected muscle.

Root causes for cramps can be many: from excessive muscular fatigue to dehydration and poor diet, which affect the number of electrolytes in our body (mediators used for muscular neural signal transmission). More rare causes can be pregnancy, menstruation, or gastroenteritis.

The best treatments for them are:

- prevention with diet and proper warming before workout;

Cramp Tea

- 1 tsp Ashwagandha root
- 1 tsp Black cohosh root
- 1 cup distilled boiling water

Ointment 1

- 1 tbsp. peppermint oil
- 1 tbsp. meadowsweet oil
- 1 tbsp. Ginger oil
- 1 tbsp. Ginger Tincture
- 1 tbsp. Goldenrod leaves oil

- proper rest between workouts;
- heat-inducing treatments and substances on the cramping muscle;
- Muscle relaxant.

Symptomatology: Inflammation, Tension

Actions Required: Muscle Relaxant, Anti-inflammatory, Nervine

Recommended Herbs: Lizard Tail root, Wintergreen leaves, Black Cohosh root, Ashwagandha root, Ginger root, Goldenrod leaves, Meadowsweet leaves, Peppermint leaves

Directions: Pour boiling water over the herbs mixture. Let rest for half an hour. Strain and drink throughout the day.

Directions: Mix the oils and tincture in a small, amber glass bottle with a dropper lid. Whenever it is needed, put 5 drops of the mix on your hands, rub vigorously until you feel the heat, and

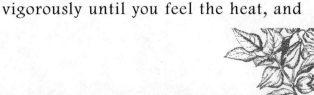

then massage the cramping muscle

Ointment 2

- 1 tbsp. Lizard Tail Root oil
- 1 tbsp. Wintergreen oil
- 4 oz. Coconut oil

Directions: Melt the coconut oil in a water bath. Add the herbs, stir and let on low heat for two hours. Strain and pour in a mason jar, let it cool down, and then close the lid. Apply on the sore part, massaging vigorously.

Nausea and Morning Sickness

Nausea is the feeling that you are going to vomit. Salivation and stomachache often accompany it. The causes can be infinite: from psychosomatic, to food poisoning, to pregnancy **(Morning Sickness)**, to serious diseases like viral or bacterial infections.

Symptomatology: Tension

Actions Required: Antiemetic, Relaxant

Recommended Herbs: Lizard tail root, Catnip leaves and flowers, Chamomile Flowers, Ginger root, Peppermint leaves, Fennel seeds

Nausea Stop Tea 1

- 1 tsp Catnip leaves and flowers
- 1 tsp Chamomile Flowers
- 1 cup distilled boiling water

Pour boiling water over the herbs mixture. Let rest for twenty minutes. Strain and drink two or three tablespoonfuls each hour until you do not feel the nausea sensation.

Nausea Stop Tea 2

- 1 tsp Lizard tail root, powdered
- 1 tsp powdered ginger root
- 1 tsp Peppermint dried leaves
- 1 cup distilled boiling water

Directions: Pour boiling water over the herbs mixture. Let rest for half an hour. Strain and drink throughout the day.

Rescue Tincture

- 4 tbsp. ginger root tincture
- 2 tbsp. Catnip leaves and flowers tincture
- 2 tbsp. Chamomile Flowers tincture

Directions: Put the tinctures in an amber glass bottle with a dropper lid, in the indicated proportions. Label it. Take 3 drops every half an hour until you do not feel the urge to vomit anymore.

Soothing Tea (after vomiting)

- 1 tsp Catnip dried Leaves and Flowers
- 1 tsp Chamomile dried flowers

- 1 tsp powdered ginger root
- 1 tsp Peppermint dried leaves
- 1 cup distilled boiling water

Directions: Pour boiling water over the herbs mixture. Let rest for thirty minutes. Strain and drink throughout the day.

Osteoarthritis / Rheumatoid Arthritis

Osteoarthritis is a common degenerative disease related to aging and it is, in a few words the wear overtime of the cartilages due to the usage.

Rheumatoid Arthritis is instead an autoimmune disease in which our immune system attacks the cells of cartilages because by mistake it recognizes them as a foreign part.

The effects of both the conditions are the same: pain to the junctions (especially the hands' ones) and the gradual losing of functions of the parts (i.e. the impossibility to have a strong grip).

Recommended Herbs: Balsam Fir leaves, Mullein leaves and flowers, Devil's Claw Rhizome, Willow Bark, Feverfew Flowers, Yucca Leaves, Black Cohosh Root, Chamomile Flowers, Bearberry bark

Soothing Ointment for Arthritis

- 1 tbsp. Balsam Fir leaves
- 2 tbsp. Cayenne
- 2 tbsp. Chamomile
- 1 lb. Coconut Oil

Melt the coconut oil in a water bath.

Add the herbs, stir and let on low heat for two hours. Strain and pour in a mason jar, let it cool down, and then close the lid. Apply on the sore part whenever it is needed.

Pain Relief Tea 1

- 20 drops Black Cohosh Tincture
- 1 tsp Mullein Tincture
- 1 tsp Chamomile Tincture
- 1 cup distilled water

Directions: Heat the water in the microwave at high for 15 seconds. It should be hot but not boiling. Add the tinctures. Drink throughout the day.

Pain Relief Tea 2

- 1 tsp Devil's Claw Dried Rhizome
- 2 tsp Willow Bark
- 1 tsp Dried Feverfew Flowers
- 1 tsp Dried Yucca Leaves
- 1 cup distilled water

Directions: Let the herbs soak overnight in water. Strain and drink throughout the day

Pain Relief Infusion

- 1 tsp Black Cohosh Dried Root
- 1 tsp Dried chamomile Flowers
- 1 tsp Bearberry bark

Combine the herbs and let them soak one day covered in water, then strain. Drink 2 tsp of the water before going to bed or add them to a cup of boiling water for a tea-like drink.

Sinusitis

Sinusitis is the inflammation of the sinuses. It causes nasal congestion, headache, and a feeling of heaviness around the eyes. The inflammation can lead also to fever, cough, and frequent sneezes.

The causes can be allergic or due to the presence of a bacterial/fungal/viral infection in the sinus cavities.

Symptomatology: Nasal Congestion, Inflammation

Actions Required: Anti-inflammation, Decongestant, Antiseptic

Recommended Herbs: Pine needles, Sage leaves, Thyme leaves, Echinacea root, Lizard Tail root, Golden seal root, Bayberry root, White willow bark.

Unclogging Decoction 1

- 1 tsp White willow Bark
- 1 tsp Bayberry Root
- 1 cup distilled boiling water

Directions: Boil the bark and the root for half an hour in the indicated proportion. Strain, wait a few minutes, and drink hot.

Unclogging Decoction 2

- 1 tsp Echinacea Root
- 1 tsp Goldenseal Root
- 1 tsp Lizard Tail Root
- 1 cup distilled boiling water

Directions: Boil the roots for half an hour in the indicated proportion. Strain, wait a few minutes, and drink hot.

Unclogging Steam Bath

- 8 oz. pine needles
- 4 oz. dried sage
- 4 oz. dried thyme
- 4 Garlic minced cloves
- 32 oz. water

Directions: Combine the herbs. Bring the water to a boil, remove from heat and place the pot on your kitchen table (be sure to use a trivet). Put ½ cup of the mixture and the garlic in the hot water and use a towel to make a tent with your head at the apex. Steam your face for 10 to 20 minutes max.
Note: Be sure to have handy some paper towels because your nose will run.

Sore Throat

The medical term for **Sore Throat** is *Pharyngitis*. It means throat pain and normally indicates an inflammation status to the pharynx due to a viral or bacterial (mainly streptococcus) infection. Other causes of pharyngitis may be exposure to irritants or substances that cause an allergic reaction.

This condition causes pain when swallowing and sometimes it is accompanied by cough, fever, and mucus secretion in the nasal cavities.

Symptomatology: Inflammation, Infection

Actions Required: Anti-inflammation, Emollient, Antiseptic

Recommended Herbs: Marshmallow root, Ginger root, Cinnamon bark, Licorice root, Sage leaves, Canadian Fleabane leaves, Slippery Elm bark, Echinacea root, Elderberry fruit, Sumac root, Goldenrod leaves, Wild Cherry bark, Lizard Tail leaves.

Sore Throat Gargle 1

- 1 tbsp. sumac root double extraction
- 1 tbsp. Echinacea root double extraction
- 2 tsp Distilled water

Directions: Combine the extractions and dilute them with water in the indicated proportions. Gargle with it.

Sore Throat Gargle 2

- 2 tbsp. dried sage leaves
- 3 tsp Epsom salt
- ½ pint apple cider vinegar
- ½ pint Distilled water

Directions: In a saucepan, bring the water to a boil and pour the sage in it. Let simmer for half an hour. Let cool, strain, and pour in a mason jar. Add salt and apple cider vinegar. Cover with the lid and shake to make the salt dissolve. Use it for gargling whenever needed. Remember to rinse with clean water after to avoid damage to the teeth due to the apple cider vinegar

Sore throat Tea 1

- 1 tsp Slippery elm bark
- 1 tsp Echinacea root
- 1 cup Distilled boiling water

Directions: Pour boiling water over the herbs mixture. Let rest for half an hour. Strain and drink throughout the day.

Sore Throat Tea 2

- 1 tsp Marshmallow root
- 1 tsp Dried Elderberries
- 1 cup distilled boiling water

Directions: Pour boiling water over the herbs mixture. Let rest for 30 minutes. Strain and drink one cup per day.

Sore Throat Candies

- 1 tsp Lizard Tail Root
- 1 tsp Licorice Root
- 1 tsp Goldenrod Leaves
- 1 tsp Cherry Bark
- 1 tsp Slippery Elm Bark
- 1 pint of Water
- 24 oz. sugar
- 3 tbsp. honey

Directions: Bring the water to a boil with the herbs inside. Reduce the heat and simmer for half an hour. Remove from heat, let cool, and strain. Add sugar and honey and put on heat at high. Bring to a boil and then let simmer until it reaches 300°F. Pour on a baking tray lined with parchment paper and let cool. Once crystalized break into square pieces 1" by 1".

Stings

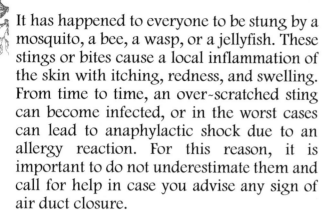

It has happened to everyone to be stung by a mosquito, a bee, a wasp, or a jellyfish. These stings or bites cause a local inflammation of the skin with itching, redness, and swelling. From time to time, an over-scratched sting can become infected, or in the worst cases can lead to anaphylactic shock due to an allergy reaction. For this reason, it is important to do not underestimate them and call for help in case you advise any sign of air duct closure.

Symptomatology: Redness, Inflammation, Pain

Actions Required: Antibacterial, Anti-inflammatory

Recommended Herbs: Echinacea root, Peppermint leaves, Witch Hazel leaves, Heal-all leaves and flowers, Yarrow leaves, Agrimony flower, Marigold flower

Soothing Compress

- 1 pint of water
- 8 oz. Peppermint Dried Leaves
- 4 oz. Epsom Salt

Directions: Bring the water to a boil. Reduce the heat, add the peppermint leaves and let simmer for 10 minutes. Let it cool for five to ten minutes. Take a towel and pour some of the decoction on it. It must be wet but not dripping. Place the wet towel in the sore zone for 20 minutes.

Tincture for Stings

- ¼ oz. Apple Cider Vinegar
- 1 tsp Heal-all Tincture
- 1 tsp Yarrow Tincture
- 1 tsp Rose Tincture
- 1 tsp Witch Hazel Water Tincture

Directions: Combine all the ingredients in an amber glass bottle. Apply topically.

Wash for Stings

- 1tsp Echinacea root (powder)
- 1tsp Heal-all
- 1tbsp Yarrow Dried Leaves
- 1 cup distilled water, boiling

Directions: Combine the ingredients in a glass or plastic container. Let rest for 1-2 hours, strain, and wash the sore part with it.

Ointment for Stings

- ¼ lb. Coconut oil
- 1 tsp dried marigold
- 1 tsp dried agrimony

Directions: Melt the coconut oil in a water bath. Add the herbs, stir and let on low heat for two hours. Strain and pour in a mason jar, let it cool down, and then close the lid. Apply on the sore part whenever it is needed.

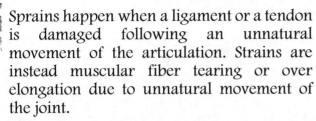

Strains and Sprains

Sprains happen when a ligament or a tendon is damaged following an unnatural movement of the articulation. Strains are instead muscular fiber tearing or over elongation due to unnatural movement of the joint.

The two injuries frequently happen at the same time and cause pain during the movement, severe limitations to the mobility of the affected limb, inflammation, swelling, and bruises.

It is important to do not underestimate sprains in particular, because they can become chronic and permanently affect the mobility of the articulation. Once the joint is healed, it is important also to strengthen the muscle surrounding the articulation to avoid the injury to happen again.

Symptomatology: Inflammation

Actions Required: Anti-inflammation, Circulatory stimulant,

Recommended Herbs: Ginger root, Solomon's seal root, St. John's Wort root, Heal-all leaves and flowers, Meadowsweet leaves and flowers, Cinnamon bark, Peppermint leaves, Lizard Tail root, Wintergreen leaves, Black Cohosh root, Ashwagandha root, Raspberry root, White Willow bark.

Analgesic Tea 1

- 1 tsp Raspberry root
- 1 tsp Willow bark
- 1 cup distilled boiling water

Directions: Pour boiling water over the herbs mixture. Let rest for half an hour. Strain and drink throughout the day.

Analgesic Tea 2

- 1 tsp Ashwagandha root
- 1 tsp Black Cohosh root
- 1 cup distilled boiling water

Directions: Pour boiling water over the herbs mixture. Let rest minutes before straining. Drink one cup throughout the day.

Analgesic Ointment

- 2 tbsp. Wintergreen leaves tincture
- 3 tbsp. Lizard Tail root tincture
- 1 lb. Coconut Oil

Directions: Melt the coconut oil in a water bath. Add the herbs, stir and let on low heat for two hours. Strain and pour in a mason jar, let it cool down, and then close the lid. Apply on the sore part whenever needed and massage.

Sprain Healing Ointment

- 1 tbsp. Ashwagandha root oil
- 1 tbsp. St. John's Wort root oil
- 1 tbsp. Solomon's seal root oil
- 1 tbsp. Heal-all leaves and flowers oil
- 1 tbsp. Meadowsweet root oil

Directions: Combine the essential oils in the proportion indicated above. Place 10 drops on your hands, rub vigorously to warm up the oil, and massage the sore part.

Teeth and Mouth Ailments

In this chapter, we will treat Gingivitis, Abscesses, and Canker sores.

Gingivitis is an inflammation of the gum tissue. It manifests as reddening, swelling, and at times bleeding of the gums. The cause of Gingivitis is the accumulation of plaque on teeth and its removal will almost certainly reverse the disease. If untreated, gingivitis can lead to gingival shrinkage and loose teeth.

An **Abscess** is a different kettle of fish. It is a more severe condition related to a serious bacterial infection, which causes the production of pus. Abscesses can appear anywhere in the body: folliculitis, whitlows, and mouth abscesses are the most common forms.

They manifest as swelling, heat, and a reddening of the part (like pimples) and are often accompanied by fever.

Antibiotics are the common medical treatment for them but, as you will probably know, they are like an insecticide: they destroy everything in their path, from the germs that cause the infection to the intestinal bacterial flora (that is essential to our digestion), the white blood cells (who fight the infections), and the lymphocytes (who produce the antibodies).

From this point of view, herbs could help you effectively fight infections and inflammation, without these side effects.

Finally, **Canker Sores** are small sores that can appear on lips, tongue, and throat. They present as white or yellow ulcers surrounded by inflamed tissue.

The causes of canker sores may be a viral infection, poor dental hygiene, or lack of vitamins and nutrients.

Symptomatology: Inflammation and laxity of the tissue

Actions Required: Anti-inflammatory, Antibacterial, Astringent

Recommended Herbs: Uva Ursi leaves, Yarrow leaves, Plantain leaves, Heal-all leaves and flowers, Calendula flowers, Licorice root, Barberry fruit and leaves, White Oak bark and leaves, Echinacea root, Oregon grape root, Lizard Tail Root, Sage leaves, Thyme leaves, Goldenrod leaves and flowers, Chamomile

Anti-Inflammatory Mouthwash

- 8 oz. Distilled water
- 2 tsp. Epsom Salt
- 2 oz. Uva Ursi tincture
- 2 oz. Yarrow tincture
- 1 oz. Plantain tincture
- 1 oz. Heal-all tincture
- 1 oz. Calendula tincture

Anti-Abscess Mouthwash

- 20 oz. Distilled boiling water
- 4 tbsp. Barberries
- 4 tbsp. Oak bark
- 4 tsp Echinacea root
- 4 tsp Oregon grape root powdered

- ½ oz. Heal-all tincture
- ½ oz. Licorice tincture

Directions: Combine all the ingredients above in a glass container. After brushing your teeth, take a mouthful of the mouthwash and swish for about 4 minutes.

Directions: Combine all the ingredients above in a glass container. Let it rest 6 hours before straining. After brushing your teeth, take a mouthful of the mouthwash and swish for about 4

minutes.

Anti-Abscess Tea

- ¼ oz. Echinacea Tincture
- ½ oz. Lizard Tail root Tincture
- 25oz distilled water

Directions: Heat the water and put the tinctures in it. Makes 5 cups to drink throughout the day.
Note: Particularly effective on skin abscesses

Mouthwash for Canker Sores

- 4 tbsp. Barberry tea
- 4 tbsp. Echinacea
- 4 tbsp. White oak tea
- 4 tbsp. Oregon grape root tea

Directions: Combine all the ingredients above in a glass container. After brushing your teeth, take a mouthful of the mouthwash and swish for about 4 minutes.

Herbal Remedies for Your Child

In this chapter, we will give you a list of essential oils that can be used to treat common child health issues and diseases like colic, cough, bronchitis, and nausea. Since the dosage of a few drops is enough for the treatment, I found out this is the best way to administer these remedies to children.

These remedies are divided by age group of administration so you will always know what are the most appropriate herbs for every age of your little one.

0~2 Months

Chamomile: Used to topically treat every kind of skin issue. Particularly indicated for sensitive skin. It can also relieve an upset stomach.

Lavender: Used topically to treat every kind of skin issue from dermatitis to eczema, to psoriasis. If taken orally it has been proven to be effective to treat bronchitis, asthma, and stomach issues like colic, indigestion, and flatulence. It is also a powerful relaxing substance, that will ease your child's sleep.

Newborn Dill: mostly used for colic, indigestion, and flatulence.

Yarrow: Mostly used to treat topically sunburns and rashes in general. It also helps in treating flu and colds.

2~12 Months

Geranium: used topically for the treatment of bruises, burns, and dermatitis. If administered orally it has been proven effective against sore throat and tonsillitis.

Eucalyptus: The fumigation of this essential oil inside hot water is incredibly effective in clearing the nasal passages, reduce phlegm, and relieve sore throats.

Mandarin: This essential oil is particularly effective in treating scars if applied topically. Also, it has a calming effect on children reducing tension and restlessness.

Tea tree oil: The most powerful antibacterial and fungicide of mother nature. It is used highly diluted to treat sore throats and tonsillitis.

12 Months – 5 Years

Palmarosa essential oil: used topically for skin issues like acne, dermatitis, and eczema.

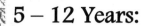

5 – 12 Years:

Sage: The fumigation of this essential oil inside hot water is incredibly effective in clearing the nasal passages, reduce phlegm, and relieve sore throats.

Elderberry Gummy Bears Recipe

The benefits of the Elderberry syrup are undeniable: it is a powerful antioxidant, an immune system booster, and helps in soothing an upset stomach due to its demulcent properties.

Truth is, it is quite a challenge to make your little ones take a spoon of it daily…

That's why I prepared this simple recipe to make your kids rush every morning to the kitchen to take their daily intake of immune system boost!

Ingredients for 200 gummy bears:

- 1 cup dried elderberries
- 4 cups distilled water
- ½ lemon juice
- 6 tbsp. Raw Honey
- 1 cup distilled water, hot but not boiling
- 8 tbsp. gelatin

Preparation:

Add water, elderberries, and the spices of your taste (my daughters like it with cinnamon and ginger) to a saucepan. Bring to a boil and let simmer for 40 minutes to reduce to half. Strain it, let it cool down, and then stir in lemon juice and honey.

In a separate bowl, dissolve the gelatin in 2-3 tbsp. of syrup. Add the hot water and stir until the gelatin dissolves, and then add in the remaining syrup.

Place the bear silicone mold on a tray for support, and fill the cavities with the gelatin & syrup mix. Refrigerate for 1 hour before popping out the bears from the molds

Recommended dosage: 2 gummy bears per day

Storage: Both syrup and gummy bears can be stored in glass jars with a closed lid in the fridge for two months.

AMAZING BONUSES FOR ALL THE READERS:

Just Scan the QR-Code below to get them!

Native American Herbal Dispensatory

The Lost Remedies of Native Americans Herbalism

—

Herbs for Beauty and Well Being

BOOK 7 of "The Native American Herbalist's Bible"

Natalie Hathale

Acne and Pimples

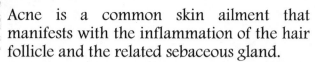

Acne is a common skin ailment that manifests with the inflammation of the hair follicle and the related sebaceous gland.

It occurs when the sebum (which is produced by the sebaceous gland to lubricate the skin) clogs the skin pore and a small bacterial infection takes place.

It is very common in the teenage years due to the strong hormonal activity but it can occur also far from adolescence, due to many causes such as the use of antibiotics, allergies, wrong diet, food poisoning, genetics…

Symptomatology: Inflammation

Actions Required: Anti-inflammatory, Antibacterial, Astringent

Recommended Herbs: Witch hazel (barks and leaves), Chamomile flowers, Sage leaves, Thyme (leaves and flowers), Yarrow leaves, Oregon Grape Root, Yellow Dock, Horsetail, Gotu kola, Echinacea, Burdock leaves, Licorice root, Milk thistle (seeds)

Tonic for skin

- 8 oz. Apple cider vinegar
- 8 oz. witch hazel water extraction
- 8 oz. rose water

Directions: Mix the ingredients in a plastic or glass container. Avoid any metal to come in contact with the mixture to prevent any oxidative reaction that can cause the liquid to contaminate with metal.

Apply once a day on clean skin, without scrubbing. Double the frequency in case of persistent acne. Be consistent and the results will come.

Note: Adjust the proportion of the mixture according to your skin type (i.e. for dry skins, reduce the apple cider vinegar).

Facial Steam

- ¼ cup dried chamomile flowers
- ¼ cup dried sage
- ¼ cup dried thyme
- ¼ cup dried yarrow
- 32 oz. water

Directions:
Before steaming, gently clean your face with water and soap.

Mix the herbs. Bring the water to a boil, remove from heat and place the pot on your kitchen table (be sure to use a trivet). Put ½ cup of the mixture in the hot water and use a towel to make a tent with your head at the apex. Steam your face for 10 to 20 minutes max.

Acne-Reducing Tea

- 1 cup Oregon Grape Root Tea
- 2.5ml Yellow Dock Tincture

Directions: Drink the tea, mixed with the yellow dock tincture. One cup throughout the day is the recommended dosage to avoid any side effects of the Oregon grape root.

Lotion for Acne

- 1 cup Horsetail Tea
- 1.5ml Gotu kola Tincture

Gently rub the mix of the two ingredients on the skin 3 times a day

Aging

We all would like to be young forever but, unfortunately, this is not possible. Aging is a natural process of decline of bodily function and we must accept it as part of life.

The main cause of it is the action of the free radicals in our bodies that interact with the DNA replication process inside the cell, creating small "distortions" in it. These "errors" in the DNA replication, compound over the years causing a progressive decay of the cell functions. The action of free radicals is enhanced by poor diet, bad habits (like smoking), and a sedentary lifestyle.

The natural enemies of the free radicals are the anti-oxidants.

Recommended Herbs: Burdock leaves, Goldenseal leaves and flowers, Ginger root, Gingko Biloba leaves, Ginseng root.

Antioxidant Tea 1

- 10 Drops Cayenne Tincture
- 25 Drops Burdock Tincture
- 20 Drops Goldenseal Tincture
- 5 Drops Ginger (Root) Tincture
- 1 Cup Gingko Biloba Tea

Directions: Combine the tinctures in an amber glass bottle with a dropper lid. Label it. Add 10 drops of the tincture mix to your tea.

Antioxidant Tea 2

- ½ cup Gingko Biloba Tea
- ½ cup Ginseng Tea

Directions: Combine the two varieties of tea and drink it throughout the day.

Anxiety and Stress

Needless to explain what these words mean. If you live in western society, you know what I am talking about: emotional **Stress** and **Anxiety** are the plagues of our society.

They cause every sort of condition that in time, can lead to serious diseases: they increase blood pressure, heart rate, worsen the nutrient absorption from the food, reduce the quality and the quantity of sleep, affect the blood sugar levels and the immune system, and produce depression and bad mood.

Symptomatology: Tension

Actions Required: Relaxant, Nervine

Recommended Herbs: Betony flowers, Hops, Betony dried flowers, Linden leaves and flowers, Ashwagandha root, Ginger root, Peppermint leaves, Valerian leaves and flowers, Chamomile Flowers, St. John's Wort leaves, Sage leaves.

Stress-Reducing Tea 1

- 1 tsp Valerian dried leaves and flowers
- 1 tsp Peppermint Dried Leaves
- 1 cup distilled boiling water

Directions: Pour boiling water over the herbs mixture. Let rest for 30 minutes. Strain and drink one cup throughout the day.

Stress-Reducing Tea 2

- 1 tsp Valerian dried leaves and flowers
- 2 tsp Ashwagandha root
- 1 cup distilled boiling water

Directions: Pour boiling water over the herbs mixture. Let rest for half an hour. Strain and drink a maximum of one cup throughout the day.

Anxiety Relief Tea 1

- 1 tsp hops
- 2 tsp Betony dried flowers
- 1 cup distilled boiling water

Directions: Pour boiling water over the herbs mixture. Let sit for half an hour. Strain and drink throughout the day.

Anxiety Relief Tea 2

- 1 tsp hops
- 1 tsp Betony dried flowers
- 1 tsp Linden dried leaves and flowers
- 1 tsp Ashwagandha root

- 1 cup distilled boiling water

Directions: Pour boiling water over the herbs mixture. Let sit for thirty minutes. Strain and drink one cup per day.

Stressed Out Rescue Remedy

- 1 tbsp. ginger root tincture
- 1 tbsp. Peppermint leaves tincture
- 2 tbsp. Valerian Flowers tincture
- 2 tbsp. Chamomile Flowers tincture
- 1 tbsp. St. John's Wort leaves tincture

- 1 tbsp. Sage leaves tincture

Directions:
Put the tinctures in an amber glass bottle with a dropper lid, in the indicated proportions. Label it. Take 3 drops every half an hour until you do not feel the urge to vomit anymore.

Burns

In this book, we will concentrate on first and second-degree burns, which cause a reddening of the skin up to blistering phenomena. These are skin injuries caused mainly by sun exposure or accidental small burnings due to your kitchen stove.

More severe burns have to be treated by a professional medical practitioner.

Symptomatology: Inflammation

Actions Required: Anti-inflammatory, Antibacterial, Cicatrize

Recommended Herbs: Heal-all (Leaves and flowers), Calendula Flowers, Peppermint leaves, Linden flowers and leaves, Plantain Leaves, Coneflower, Hyssop flowers, Dried Goldenrod, Echinacea Root.

Recommended treatment for burns

In case of a mild burn, follow the steps below to be sure to treat effectively the injury:

1. Apply cold water on the burned part
2. Remove dirt or any foreign matter

3. Apply one of the topical treatments described below
4. Do not use salves or oily substances on the wound

Honey Remedy

- 4 oz. Honey
- 1 tsp Calendula Flowers

Directions:
Pour the honey into a mason jar and put it in a water bath on your kitchen

Cooling Wash for Sunburns

- 2 oz. Distilled water
- 1 oz. Rosewater
- 1 tsp Dried peppermint
- 1 tsp Dried Linden flowers and leaves
- 1 tsp Dried Plantain Leaves

Local Cooling Compress

- 1 tsp Dried Coneflower
- 1 tsp Dried Hyssop flowers
- 1 tsp Dried Goldenrod flowers

Directions: Put the dried herbs on a

Tincture for internal use

- ½ tsp Echinacea Tincture
- 1 cup distilled warm water

Home Made Aloe Vera Gel

- Aloe Vera Leaves
- 1 tsp Salicylic Acid in 2% alcoholic solution for every cup of gel. You can buy it online or in your local drug store

Directions:
1. At first, be sure to wash your hands properly, at least 40seconds, and do not forget any zone of them. Be also sure to work with perfectly clean tools. Do not overlook this part because it is fundamental to not contaminate the gel.
2. Select the outer leaves of your aloe vera plant and slice them off. These are the more mature and the more likely to contain plenty of

stove. When the honey is warm, add the flowers and remove the mason jar from heat. Infuse the flowers in warm honey until the honey is cool. Close the lid and store for 1-2 months. Apply topically on the burn.

Directions: Bring the distilled water to a boil. Pour it in a mason jar with the herbs. Let it rest for 2 hours. Pour in the rose water. Stir and use it to wash the burn.

clean linen sheet. Form a bundle with the dried herbs inside. Soak the herbs inside the cloth in hot water and squeeze it to avoid excessive dripping. Let cool and apply on the sore parts.

Directions: Add the tincture to the warm water and drink to boost the immunity system and facilitate the healing of the burned part.

gel. Use a sharp knife to make a clean cut near the base of each leaf you take. As always, harvest only what you are sure to use. Just 2-3 leaves are enough for 1 cup of gel, avoid preparing more of it because Aloe Vera gel is very perishable, and you will waste what the plant gave you.
3. Place the leaves upright in a cup for roughly ten minutes. This will let the dark yellow resin drain out. It is best to drain it out so it won't get into your gel creating contamination.
4. Use a peeler to peel off all of the skin on one side of every aloe vera leaf. Be sure to remove also the inner white layer to reach the gel.

159

5. Finally, use a clean spoon to scoop the gel out of the leaf and put it in a clean mason jar.
6. Add the Salicylic Acid in the proper proportion (1 tsp for every cup of gel) and blend it using an immersion blender.
7. Store the jar with the airtight lid close in your fridge. If you use salicylic acid, it will last for roughly two months, if not only one week.

Fatigue

Fatigue is the feeling of tiredness. Even if it is a normal phenomenon at the end of a working day or after a gym session, if it becomes chronic it can be the sign of something more.

Anemia, Angina Pectoris, Diabetes, Pleurisy, and many other diseases include fatigue as the pre-symptoms.

Symptomatology: Tiredness

Actions Required: Stimulant, Tonic

Recommended Herbs: Licorice, Ashwagandha, Tulsi, Milk thistle, Nettle, Ginkgo Biloba, Ginseng, Gotu Kola, St. John's Wort, Blackberry, Strawberry, Raspberry.

Fuel Bites

- 4 tbsp. Ashwagandha root (powdered)
- 4 tbsp. Licorice root (powdered)
- 4 tbsp. Milk thistle seeds (powdered)
- 4 tbsp. Tulsi leaves (powdered)
- Cinnamon Powder (for coating)
- ¼ cup honey
- 1 cup peanut butter

Directions: Mix the powders with peanut butter and honey. Form small balls and roll them in cinnamon. Eat two or three for an energy boost.

Tonic Tincture

- 1 tbsp. Licorice root tincture
- 1 tsp Tulsi leaves tincture
- 1 tsp Ashwagandha root tincture

Directions: Put the tinctures in an amber glass bottle with a dropper lid, in the indicated proportions. Label it to be sure of the expiration date. Take 7 drops in the morning.

Tonic Tea 1

- 1 tsp Raspberry leaves
- 1 tsp Strawberry leaves
- 1 tsp Blackberry leaves
- 1 cup distilled boiling water

Directions: Pour boiling water over the herbs mixture. Let rest for half an hour. Strain and drink.

Tonic Tea 2 (strong)

- 1 tsp Gingko Biloba leaves
- 1 tsp Ginseng root
- 1 tsp Gotu kola leaves
- 1 tsp Raspberry leaves

- 1 cup distilled boiling water

Directions: Pour boiling water over the herbs mixture. Let steep for 20 minutes. Strain and drink.

Hangover

The hidden enemy in a night out with your friends is the notorious hangover. It is the day-after side effect of excessive alcohol intake that can cause dehydration, irritability (due to the swings in the blood sugar levels), headache, stomach acid and dizziness.

The enemy to fight is dehydration. Be sure to drink water during your night-out and before going to bed, it will get the recovery easier the day after.

Symptomatology: Inflammation, Dehydration

Actions Required: Anti-inflammatory, Emollient

Recommended Herbs: Catnip leaves, Peppermint leaves, Barberry leaves, Heal-all leaves, Oregon Grape root, Goldenseal leaves, Plantain leaves, Calendula Flowers, Chamomile Flowers, Linden leaves, Licorice root, Ginger root, St. John's Wort leaves, Marshmallow (leaves).

Hangover Tea 1

- 1 tsp Catnip dried leaves
- 1 tsp Peppermint dried leaves
- 1 tsp Barberry dried leaves
- 1 cup distilled boiling water

Directions: Pour boiling water over the herbs mixture. Let rest for 30 minutes. Strain and drink.

Hangover Tea 2

- 1 tsp Barberry dried leaves
- 1 tsp Heal-all dried leaves
- 1 tsp Oregon Grape root
- 1 cup distilled boiling water

Directions: Pour boiling water over the herbs mixture. Let rest for half an hour. Strain and drink throughout the day

Hangover Tea 3

- 1 tsp Barberry dried leaves
- 1 tsp Goldenseal dried leaves
- 1 tsp Oregon Grape root
- 1 cup distilled boiling water

Directions: Pour boiling water over the herbs mixture. Let rest for half an hour. Strain and drink throughout the day.

Hangover Tea 4

- 1 tbsp. Plantain dried leaves
- 1 tbsp. Calendula dried flowers
- 1 tbsp. Chamomile dried flowers
- 1 tbsp. Dried linden leaves
- 1 tbsp. Licorice root
- 1 tbsp. Dried Ginger root
- 1 tbsp. Dried St. John's Wort leaves

Directions: Mix the herbs in a mason jar for easy storage. Put 1 tbsp. of the mixture in 1 cup of distilled boiling water. Let rest for half an hour. Strain and drink throughout the day

Warning: Do not add St. John Wort if you are under pharmaceutics.

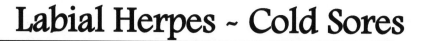

Labial Herpes ~ Cold Sores

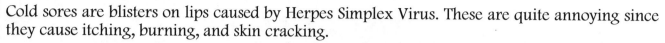

Cold sores are blisters on lips caused by Herpes Simplex Virus. These are quite annoying since they cause itching, burning, and skin cracking.

Symptomatology: Inflammation

Actions Required: Cicatrize, Immune System Stimulant, Anti-inflammatory

Recommended Herbs: Calendula leaves and flowers, Plantain leaves, Heal~All leaves and flowers, St. John's Wort leaves and flowers, Chamomile flowers, Thyme leaves and flowers, Linden leaves and flowers, White Oak bark, Lizard tail root, Echinacea root, Goldenseal root, Burdock root.

Cold Sore Salve

- ½ oz. Beeswax
- ½ oz. Calendula oil
- ½ oz. Plantain oil
- ¼ oz. Heal~All oil
- ¼ oz. St. John's Wort oil
- ¼ oz. Chamomile oil
- ¼ oz. Thyme oil

Directions: Combine the oils together in a stainless steel cooking pan, heat very gently on a stove, add beeswax (1 oz. beeswax for 2 oz. of oil), and stir. When beeswax is melted, place a few drops of the mixture on the plate to check consistency and, if needed, add more beeswax/oil if it is too soft/hard. Once you reach the perfect consistency, pour the mix in a mason jar and let it cool uncovered.
IMPORTANT: heat destroys the precious phytochemicals, so do not ever surpass 170°F temperature

Compress for Cold Sores

- 1 oz. St. John's Wort leaves and flowers
- 1 oz. Heal all leaves and flowers
- 2 oz. Linden leaves and flowers
- 2 oz. Calendula flowers
- 2 oz. Chamomile flowers
- 2 oz. Plantain Leaves

Directions: Prepare the herb mix and store it in a mason jar with a closed lid. Make a hot infusion with 1 tbsp. of the herb mix each cup of water. Let rest for half an hour. Soak a cloth in the infusion, squeeze it, and apply it to the cold sore

Cold Sores Wash

- 1 cup boiling distilled water
- 1 tsp white oak bark
- 1 tsp Lizard tail root
- 1 tsp Echinacea root

Directions: Pour the boiling water over the herbs mixture. Let steep for half an hour, strain, and use it as a wash on the sore

Immune System Boosting Tea

- 1 cup boiling distilled water
- 1 tsp Goldenseal root (pulverized)
- 1 tsp Burdock root

Directions: Pour the boiling water over the roots mixture. Let rest half an hour and strain. Drink throughout the day.

Skin Rash

Skin Rash is a temporary reddening and inflammation of the skin. It can present also round patches where the skin scales.

It can be the alarm bell for more serious diseases like food intolerances or allergies.

When a sudden rash appears, the first thing to do is wash the part with a delicate soap to see if it was due to contact with some irritating substance.

Symptomatology: Inflammation, Dryness

Topical Wash

- 1 tsp White Oak (bark)
- 1 tsp Slippery Elm Bark
- 1 cup distilled boiling water

Anti-inflammatory Tea

- 1 tsp Oregon Grape Root
- 1 tsp Yellow Dock Root
- 1 tsp Echinacea Root
- 1 cup distilled boiling water

Salve for Dry Rashes

- 6 tbsp. Calendula Oil
- 6 tbsp. Licorice Oil
- 6 tbsp. Plantain Oil
- 6 tbsp. Heal-All Oil
- 1 oz. beeswax

Directions: Combine the oils together in a stainless steel cooking pan, heat very gently on a stove, add beeswax (1 oz. beeswax for 2 oz. of oil), and stir.

Blistery Rash Poultice

- 1 cup St. John's Wort flowers and leaves
- 1 cup rose petals
- 1 cup Yarrow leaves
- 1 cup Calendula flowers
- 1 cup Heal –all flowers

Actions Required: Anti-inflammation, Emollient

Recommended Herbs: Calendula flowers and root, Plantain leaves, Licorice root, Rose petals, Heal-all leaves and flowers, St. John's Wort leaves and flowers, Uva Ursi berries, Yarrow leaves, Burdock leaves, Oregon Grape root, Echinacea root, Yellow Dock rhizome, Slippery Elm bark, White Oak bark.

Directions: Prepare a decoction (boil half an hour) of the barks in the proportion indicated above. Let cool and wash the irritated part with it.

Directions: Pour boiling water over the herbs mixture. Let rest for half an hour. Strain and drink throughout the day.

When beeswax is melted, place a few drops of the mixture on the plate to check consistency and, if needed, add more beeswax/oil if it is too soft/hard. Once you reach the perfect consistency, pour the mix in a mason jar and let it cool uncovered.
IMPORTANT: heat destroys the phytochemicals, so do not ever surpass 170°F temperature.

Directions: In case of blisters due to contact with an irritating substance, use this astringent poultice to remove the liquid and reduce the itching. Mix the herbs in a mason jar for easy storage. Create the poultice with some tbsp. of the mixture and a little bit of distilled boiling water. Apply it to the rash.

Blistery Rash Quick Fix Poultice

- 1 Black or Green Tea Bag

Directions: In case of blisters due to contact with an irritating substance, use this astringent poultice to remove the liquid and reduce the itching. If you are in a hurry or you do not have herbs at home you can prepare a tea and apply the wet, warm tea bag to the rash.

Sleep & Insomnia

Insomnia is defined as any difficulty in having a restoring sleep.

It may happen in the form of fighting to fall asleep, or in frequently interrupted sleep, or in the incapacity to sleep for sufficient time.

It can be due to stress, poor diet, or excessive caffeine intake.

In addition, many studies highlighted the fact that exposure to bright, artificial light (such as TV or phones) in the evening may affect the circadian rhythm of our body and indeed cause insomnia, so my first go-to advice when dealing with sleep issues is to avoid them starting from 18:00.

Symptomatology: Tension

Actions Required: Sedative, Relaxant

Recommended Herbs: Chamomile (Flowers), Betony (Flowers), Catnip (leaves and flowers), Linden (leaves and flowers), Hops (fruits), Valerian (root), Passionflower (flower)

Goodnight Tea 1

- 1 tsp Dried Hops
- 1 tbsp. Chamomile flowers dried
- 2 tsp Passionflowers dried
- 1 cup distilled boiling water

Directions:
Pour boiling water over the herbs mixture. Let rest for ten minutes. Strain and drink before going to bed.

Goodnight Tea 2

- 1 tsp Dried Hops
- 1 tbsp. Chamomile flowers dried
- 1 tsp Valerian Root powdered
- 1 cup distilled boiling water

Directions: Pour boiling water over the herbs mixture. Let rest for half an hour. Strain and drink throughout the evening.

Goodnight Tincture 1 (Strong)

- 3 tbsp. Betony flowers tincture
- 3 tbsp. Valerian Root tincture
- 3 tbsp. Chamomile Flowers tincture
- 3 tbsp. Linden Leaves tincture

Directions: Put the tinctures in an amber glass bottle with a dropper lid, in the indicated proportions. Label it. Take 3 drops one hour before bedtime. Then 2 more half an hour before bedtime. Finally 2 drops before going to bed

Goodnight Tincture 2

- 3 tbsp. Valerian Root tincture
- 3 tbsp. Chamomile Flowers tincture
- 3 tbsp. Linden Leaves tincture

Directions: Put the tinctures in an amber glass bottle with a dropper lid, in the indicated proportions. Label it. Take 3 drops one hour before bedtime. Then 2 more half an hour before bedtime. Finally 2 drops before going to bed.

Skin Beauty

A hydrated and soft skin is for sure something every woman desires. Here there are three herbal milk bath recipes to make luxurious, skin-softening bath and to take care of your skin health and beauty. The recipes do not use any milk at all so they are perfect for any vegan or anyone allergic to cow milk.

Uplifting: Rose, Chamomile & Sandalwood

- 1 cup rolled oats
- 1 cup dried calendula
- 1 cup dried chamomile
- 1 cup dried rose petals
- 2 cup Epsom salts
- 1 cup Rhassoul red clay
- 2 teaspoon jojoba oil
- 10 drops rose essential oil
- 10 drops sandalwood essential oil

Directions: In a food processor, blend oats, chamomile, rose, and calendula until you get a fine powder. Transfer this to a large bowl, then stir in the remaining ingredients.
Tips for storage: This bath milk can be easily store in a mason jar with an hermetic lid, in a cool dark place.

Soothing: Lavender, Mint & Lemonbalm

- 1 cup rolled oats
- 1 cup lavender flower buds
- 1 cup dried peppermint leaves
- 1 cup dried lemon balm leaves
- 2 cup Epsom salts
- 1 cup Rhassoul red clay
- 2 tsp
- 10 drops lavender essential oil

- 5 drops peppermint essential oil

Directions: In a food processor, blend oats, lavender buds, peppermint, and lemon balm until you get a fine powder. Transfer this to a large bowl, then stir in the remaining ingredients.
Tips for storage: This bath milk can be easily store in a mason jar with an hermetic lid, in a cool dark place.

Invigorating: Ginger & Cardamom

- 1 cup rolled oats
- 1 cup dried chamomile flower buds
- 1 cup dried rosemary leaves
- 1/2 cup dried ginger root
- 2 cup Epsom salts

- 1 cup French green clay
- 2 tsp jojoba oil
- 10 drops ginger essential oil
- 10 drops cardamom essential oil

Directions: In a food processor, blend oats, chamomile buds, rosemary, and ginger until you get a fine powder. Transfer this to a large bowl, then stir in the remaining ingredients.

Tips for storage: This bath milk can be easily store in a mason jar with an hermetic lid, in a cool dark place.

AMAZING BONUSES FOR ALL THE READERS:

Just Scan the QR-Code below to get them!

Conclusion

In these fifth and sixth books, we have described the herbal medical preparations used by Native Americans to soothe and effectively treat the most common ailments. All the remedies have been designed to be made in the comfort of your kitchen, with herbs you can buy in your herbal shop. I sincerely hope that this will be just the beginning of your journey and that you will increase your knowledge on Native American medicine, for a healthier and better way to treat the common disease without relying on industrial drugs and medication.

If you have enjoyed this book, feel free to leave a review to share your experience.

Just scan the QR code on the right, it will take 30 seconds!

My best wishes and may the Spirit guide your journey!

Native American Traditional Planting Techniques

How to Implement the Ancient Planting Techniques in Modern Gardens and in Apartments

BOOK 8 of "The Native American Herbalist's Bible"

Natalie Hathale

Introduction

The expansion of mankind began in Africa and has continued ever since. From Asia, the Americas were colonized for many years centuries and re-colonized at numerous points throughout time. In 1493, the population of North America was estimated to be fewer than a million people, yet there were no gardens in the region. The Eastern States were strong enough to proclaim their independence from Britain in 1776 as a result of an increase in European immigration after that period. Despite the fact that their origins have changed, the yearly influx of immigrants, particularly to North America, has remained significant. Union membership had increased as well. It was in 1894 that America displaced Britain as the world's biggest manufacturer, producing more than factories in Britain, France, and Germany put together by 1914. America's economic dominance was bolstered by both World Wars.

By 5,600 BC, gourds, beans, and peppers were grown in Mexico, and by five thousand BC, maize and potatoes were growing in Mesoamerica and South America, respectively. This crop's success or failure had a significant influence on the survival of humans. For the land to be preserved for future generations, it needed knowledge of sustainable farming practices in addition to providing nutrition. "Sustainable" and "permaculture" are popular buzzwords these days, as is "organic". However, these methods were already in use long before the term "green" was coined. Some of the earlier, kinder techniques may have been familiar to your grandparents as well. Many are just based on instinct and a desire to have more intimate contact with the land and its inhabitants. If you haven't already, you may want to consider incorporating some of these methods into your own landscape. Even though they may seem "new" to some in the gardening community, many of the following methods are really very old. However, just because they've been practiced historically by Native Americans doesn't mean everyone in the tribe did. Here are a few Earth-friendly methods for growing a better garden that is also sustainable.

History By Years

Gardening was essential to surviving and thriving on the frontier. Gardening was traditionally seen as a woman's job; thus, the gardens were kept closer to the home. Because supplies had to be transported in from the east, the general Mercantile in the American west was unreliable, expensive, and understocked. The "kitchen gardens" of families were the only means of survival.

Great cities around the turn of the century attracted hordes of people from all over the country, who flocked to the dazzling lights of the big towns to shop and live in magnificent mansions. Americans left their rural gardens behind and went to work in factories. Ornamental landscaped gardens, on the other hand, grew more popular, and gardening's focus moved to enhance the aesthetic appeal of the house.

President Franklin D. Roosevelt advised the population to cultivate their own food in order to combat food shortages during World War II. "Victory Gardens" provided 40% of all American-grown vegetables by 1943. Roosevelt even had a Victory Garden on the White House grounds.

During the 1950s, mass-produced lawn and floral decorations were commonplace in the suburbs of the United States. There were pink flamingos, fake deer, and garden gnomes among the well-maintained and clipped vegetation. Big, gorgeous statement plants adorned the 1950s garden, which included bright splashes of color and joyful pops of color. What's more disturbing is that "Atomic Gardens" gained popularity in the years after World War II. Plants that are subjected to radioactive sources, such as Cobalt-60, to induce mutations, some of which have shown to be helpful, are known as "Atomic Gardening."

The Community Garden movement had its start in the 1970s. Urban areas throughout the United States were studded with "dead zones" during the height of the financial crisis of the 1970s. The Community Garden movement, which aims to beautify and improve the health of American city streets, was born as a result of garden groups around the nation seeing these urban environs as an ideal chance to grow some plants.

There is no need to irrigate your home garden using xeriscaping techniques. Low-maintenance gardens like this were popular in the country's driest regions, where droughts were frequent. Succulents and other cacti-like plants became popular in American gardens as a result of this.

A large portion of the American population lives in metropolitan regions, and this trend has been going on for the last 30 years. Container gardens continue to thrive in high-rises, condominiums, and flats. If you live in a city, container gardening (also known as patio gardening) is a great way to produce your own food and herbs while also providing a beautiful décor. It's a way for city residents to incorporate more greenery into their daily routines. Throughout the history of America, plants have been an integral part of American life. For thousands of years, gardens have accompanied us on our journeys from the harsh frontier to the bustling metropolis and back again. Look back and remember those who had gone before you and fought to keep American-grown food on our dinner tables.

They lived without the technological tools we have today, on just the land, instinct and the wisdom that their forefathers handed down to them. They revered the land, and it produced for them; they were caretakers. Their objective was not to overpower nature but rather to learn how to work with it while protecting the land for future generations. While you may know that Native Americans cultivated potatoes, maize and tomatoes, you may also imagine that their gardening ended there – that they were largely hunters and gatherers. But this is simply just not the case. Local indigenous can teach us very much about greener lifestyle and organic agriculture – ideas that even the tiniest home gardener can use.

Let's analyze a couple of their ways.

Technique 1: Companion Planting

What is Companion Planting?

The use of companion planting in your vegetable garden is a natural way to keep pests and illnesses at bay. Your harvest production will rise as a result of using this strategy to keep your plants in good condition. In addition, it may help reduce blight and other soil-related issues. Aside from scientific evidence, it's comforting to know that long-time gardeners have seen the positive effects of companion planting. When it comes to gardening mythology, companion planting is an essential part of the practice. Many gardeners have fond memories of a parent or other family member who insisted on putting specific plants next to other plants for a variety of reasons while they were growing up in a garden themselves.

Definition

Companion planting simply put, is the common practice of making two plants grow in close proximity with the purpose of mutual benefit between the two. A benefit might be one-way or two-way, depending on how it's distributed. As simple as planting nectar-rich flowers around crops to attract pollinators, or planting two vegetables next to each other in an attempt to fend off or confuse pests is an example of this.

Many Native American tribes used the classic Three Sisters trio of corn, climbing beans, and winter squash, because of the plants' complementary natures. The corn, tall and strong, provides support for the climbing beans, while the squash, which grows on the soil, covers the ground to prevent humidity loss, and its big, prickly leaves keep weeds and pests away. Moreover, beans are "nitrogen fixers," which make nitrates. This trio was commonly planted together by various Native American communities. It isn't usually founded on scientific truths but on a garden legend like that found in farmer's almanacs, which is why companion planting is so popular among gardeners. To notice what works best for you, you'll need to do some experimenting. However, if you think of your garden as a network of interconnected plants, you'll be able to make better plant selections.

Benefits

Companion planting has many upsides. Plants have the ability to attract and repel pests, as well as attract and repel beneficial insects and pollinators. They are able to protect themselves against predators and unwanted animals. For example, raccoons loathe the scent of cucumbers. There are many factors that contribute to soil fertility, but plants also have an important role to play. High-growing crops like maize, which give shade and support for trellised crops, may provide shade and support for crops that do not thrive in the harsh summer heat. Incorporating diverse crops into a garden plot may assist differentiate between fast- and slow-germinating plants, such as lettuce and radishes. Even weeds may be suppressed by proper companion planting. There are several benefits to planting particular crops in succession:

- Certain plants may be used to keep pests at bay. Garlic, for example, has a strong odor that repels many pests.
- Beneficial insects may be attracted to certain plants. Borage, for example, attracts bees and small pest-eating wasps for pollination.
- Large plants shield lesser plants from the sun's rays, allowing them to thrive in the shadow. In this case, maize comes out ahead of lettuce.
- Crops with lower growth rates, such as cucumbers and peas, may be supported by taller natural supports, such as maize and sunflowers.
- The biochemistry of the soil may be altered in favor of surrounding plants if a plant absorbs particular soil chemicals.
- A number of crops, such as beans, peas, and other legumes, aid in the availability of nitrogen in the soil. Burdock, for example,

has a long taproot that brings nutrients from deep in the soil to the surface, allowing shallow-rooted plants to thrive.
- It's easier to keep weeds out of wide-open spaces by replacing low-growing crops like potatoes with taller, upright varieties.

Philosophy behind Companion Planting Technique

Companion planting has been performed by the Old Rancher's Almanac for more than a century, relying on centuries-old knowledge. We've modified our thinking on the optimal companion planting combinations over time as we've gained additional scientific knowledge.

"Friends and enemies" were formerly thought of as plants that either helped or hindered the development of crops. Although this isn't always the case, we've discovered that virtually all of the correlations are good ones; there are just a few "poor" pairings (e.g., black walnut trees, which secrete growth inhibitors through their roots). When it comes to companions, we now concentrate on veggies since there is more evidence for "good" partners than "bad" mates.

Concerning myths regarding companion planting can be found on the internet, according to us. So-called "companion planting" is often rooted in legend or saga. Because of this, we determined that our reference book would only include plant pairings supported by scientific facts and tried-and-true procedures rather than observations made in our own backyards or other natural settings.

We've expanded our companion planting guide to include additional flowers, many of which serve as natural insect repellents. There is no competition for Nasturtium when it comes to insect resistance. (We go into more detail about this below.) If you have nectar-rich flowers in your garden that attract pollinators like bees and hummingbirds, you'll increase the pollination of blooming crops like tomatoes, beans, and squash. Of course.

Working

Climate Friends: Planting crops that meet the climatic demands of surrounding and adjoining plants is referred to as "climate companionship."

170

Using taller sun-loving plants to shield plants that prefer shade or seedlings that can't withstand the sun's rays all day is an example of climate companion planting. When greenhouse resources can be freed, farmers may utilize all of their land's growing area to their advantage.

Plant Trapping Aids: This kind of buddy has a basic premise. The poachers must lure pests and weeds that might otherwise damage the plant from which you want the trapper to protect. When you cultivate vegetables on your farm, trapping plants act as a decoy for unwanted insects and pests, preventing them from wreaking havoc.

Nitrogen Fixing: Vegetable crops depend on nitrogen fixation by plants that utilize nitrogen in its ammonia form (which it obtains from the air) and convert proteins and other nutrients into absorbable molecules that enable crops to grow and flourish, despite the fact that nitrogen is present in moderate levels in the soil. Hydroponics may provide a challenge to nitrogen fixation. Because they convert atmospheric nitrogen into a form that surrounding food plants can utilize, nitrogen-fixing plants like beans, lentils, and peas are common in agricultural settings.

Luring Beneficial Bug: The term "habitat influence" refers to the practice of growing companion plants in order to attract beneficial insects. Protect your vegetable garden by using companion plants to attract beneficial insects that can then feed on the harmful, predatory, and destructive pests and insects that would otherwise devastate your garden's bounty. The use of artificial insecticides and pesticides, which may impair the soil's microbial balance and pollute the environment, can be avoided by cultivating plants that attract beneficial insects

to help keep dangerous ones from wreaking havoc on developing crops. The best combinations are:

- Insect-eating ladybugs may be attracted to dill, which is a good source of aphids and spider mites.
- To attract bees, tomatoes and Borage are a good match. Strawberries taste and grow better with the addition of Borage on the side.
- Many insects are deterred by the smell of garlic and garlic spray. Garlic is repulsive to aphids (which infest over 400 species of plants). Besides repelling pests such as onion flies and Japanese beetles, garlic also kills ermine moths—plant near fruit trees, lettuce and cabbage rows, and potato rows.
- Aphids, ants, and flea beetles are all deterred by the mint. However, since mint is such an aggressive grower, it's best to keep it separate in a pot or bed.
- Parsley attracts useful insects that help to protect and pollinate tomato plants, as well. These herbs may be grown amongst the tomatoes in your garden.
- Sage, a valuable plant, repels carrot flies. Reduce damage from cabbage moths by planting them around the area.
- Pole beans, cucumbers, and sunflowers all go nicely together: Climbing plants benefit from the support provided by sunflowers, as well as shade for crops that might become over-exposed in warm areas.

Technique 2: Terracing

There are several advantages to terrace farming in steep areas, and it is frequently the only option. However, it has several benefits. In addition to cultivating ground that is otherwise unsuitable for agriculture, terrace farming has far-reaching benefits. As a result, terrace farming reduces soil erosion and aids in the preservation of the environment. Online agriculture software has made it easier to manage and cultivate a wider variety of crops

using this strategy. For very mountainous or steep terrain, terrace farming is an option.

What is Terracing?

In agriculture, terracing refers to the construction of raised terraces on the tops of hills in order to reorganize fields. We refer to these raised areas as terraces. Terracing agriculture is characterized by the removal and repositioning of topsoil to create farmland and ridges. When the top platforms are filled, water trickles down to the lower ones. It's not simply at the bottom of the slope that the water is concentrated.

Terracing is often used to reduce water flow and prevent soil erosion on slopes. In the mountains, though, it's not the only choice. Terracing may be used to a wide range of field elevations, as shown by the fact that there are terracing platforms on gentle slopes and undulating ground.

The Inca people, who resided in the highlands of South America, devised it. Crops may now be grown in steep or hilly areas thanks to the terrace farming technique. Terrace farming is a common practice in Asian rice-producing nations like Vietnam, the Philippines, and Indonesia, where hills and mountains provide ideal growing conditions. Indeed, the Cordilleras' rice terraces have been designated a World Heritage Site by the United Nations Educational, Scientific, and Cultural Organization (UNESCO). Using terrace farming in islands like the Canary Islands, where the terrain is steep, is another common practice. Terraces are also used to raise potatoes and maize, in addition to rice. Rice, wheat, and barley are three of the most significant crops farmed utilizing terrace farming.

Working

In terrace farming, a "step" known as a terrace is erected on the slopes of hills and mountains to help farmers grow crops. Soil nutrients and plants travel from one terrace to another when it rains instead of being washed away. There seems to be an outlet at the end of each stage that directs water to the next. Some places stay dry while others stay wet thanks to this. Rice does not perform well at high elevations; thus, other crops may be cultivated there instead.

Types

Erosion is reduced by channel-type terraces, which are also known as graded terraces, by lowering the length of the overland flow's slope and then directing the captured runoff to a non-erosive exit. This may either be a constant or variable graded terrace. To save water and prevent erosion, terraces are constructed on a level surface. Rainfall may be trapped and held in the soil profile in low to moderate rainfall locations. The porous soil is well suited to the level terraces, which follow a contour line.

Benefits

Terrace farming has a lot of logic and thinking behind it, and it has a number of environmental advantages. For the most part, terrace farming keeps soil nutrients from being washed away by rain. Crops benefit from this since it encourages healthy development. Aside from that, it prevents the strong running rivers of water from dragging away plants and vegetation. Farming in hilly regions has been made feasible in large part because of the use of terraces, a significant agricultural method. Terrace farming has the potential to transform wet, unused land into productive fields, therefore increasing global food security. Additionally, terrace farming aids in the preservation of the farm's soil nutrients.

Best Crops

Because terraces tend to gather moisture, the species chosen must be able to thrive in the highlands and be tolerant of waterlogging. Rice, for example, thrives in paddies, but its output begins to decline at altitudes over 375 m.

However, the crops grown on terraces are rather varied. Soybeans and other grains, herbs; berries; nuts; fruits; veggies, etc., all fall under this broad category. The following are some of the most frequent crops grown on terraces: Wheat, corn, pulses, black cumin, wheat, rice, saffron, apple millets, etc.

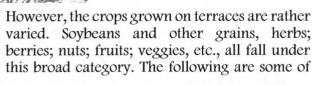

Technique 3: Three Sisters

Winter squash, maize, and climbing beans are three of the most important crops to distinct Native American tribes on North America's continent (typically tepary beans or common beans). These three crops, which originated in Mesoamerica, were transported north via the river basins by successive generations, reaching the Mandan and Iroquois, among others, who utilized them for sustenance and commerce. This trio was interplanted by a variety of Native American tribes. This because this technique guaranteed abundant crops due to the fact that the three plants supported each other during growth like three good sisters, and flourished together. Make your own Three Sisters Garden with these simple instructions.

What is Three Sister?

Companion planting at its finest, the Three Sisters technique uses three plants that grow in harmony to keep out weeds and pests, improve the soil, and provide mutual assistance.

A new approach of interplanting provided a wide range of benefits, from attracting pollinators to enriching the earth rather than depleting it of its nutrients. In a sense, we receive nothing more from nature than we give back to it. The Iroquois had been cultivating the "three sisters" for nearly three centuries by the time Europeans arrived in America in the early 1600s. The Native Americans relied on the trio of vegetables for both their bodily and spiritual well-being. According to folklore, the plants were a divine gift from the gods, which meant that they were to be cultivated in harmony and consumed in celebration.

Planting Method

Planting the three sisters in clusters on low, broad mounds rather than in a typical single row is the goal of the Three Sisters approach.

- Choose a sunny place for your garden before you start planting (at least 6 hours of full sun every day). Think of a little field when you think of this type of planting. There will be 4 to 6 corn plants on each hill, each 4 feet broad and 4 feet apart. Consider this while planning your place.
- During spring, add organic matter and weed-free compost to the soil to improve its quality. Wood ash or fish scraps may be used to improve the soil's texture.
- Soil mounds that are afoot high and three to four feet broad with a 10-inch-wide flat top are ideal. Place mounds approximately four feet apart if you're making more than one.
- Once nights have become warmer (overnight temperature has risen to 55°F) and the frost is going away, it is the best time to plant corn. Corn can't be planted later than June 1 in most regions since it needs a long growing season. Consult your local frost calendar for further information.
- The flat section of the mound should have approximately ten inches of space between each of the six maize kernels, which should be in a circle spaced about two feet apart.
- Wait until the corn is approximately 6 inches to 1 foot tall before planting the beans and squash. Beans will be supported by sturdy corn stalks as a result. Soil nitrogen fixation is critical for vigorous corn production, and beans play a key part in this process. Hybrids aren't a problem if you plant more than one kind of pole bean in a hill. Alternatively, you may also plant corn transplants at the same time as the beans.
- Plant 4 bean seeds around each corn stalk when it is 6 inches to 1 foot tall. (Tip: Before planting, cover your bean seeds with an inoculant to fix nitrogen in the soil, which benefits all plants.)
- Plant 6 squash seeds around the mound a week later, equally spaced. The spacing for squash is normally around 18 inches apart on your package. To guarantee germination,

you may want to plant two seeds in each hole.

The inclusion of a fourth sister, such as sunflower or amaranth, is sometimes used to attract pollinators and deter birds from the seeds. The seeds of sunflowers may be gathered by planting them in the cross-section of the areas between the corn hills. Among the squash, amaranth may grow and be collected for its greens as well as its seeds.

Seeds to Plant

The Three Sisters in contemporary gardening are made up of these three vegetables:

- Beans from the Poles (not bush beans). Scarlet Runner or Italian Snap pole beans should suffice. Our favorite is the 'Ohio Pole Bean.' Hybrid pole beans may also pull-

down thin hybrid corn stalks, according to some reports. That so, less experienced climbers may pose a greater risk, so use caution. Four Corners Gold Beans and Hopi Light Yellow are two good native kinds to explore.

- Sweet corn, dent corn, popcorn, or a mixture of these is an example of corn. To prevent the beans from dragging the corn to the ground, Native Americans employed tougher maize with shorter stalks or multiple-stalked varieties, such as light yellow Tarahumara corn, Hopi White, or heritage Black Aztec.

- Squash with little leaves, such as winter or summer (Hubbard). Pumpkins should be planted in a separate bed since they are both strong and heavy. Summer crookneck squash is similar enough to Native American squash that it doesn't really matter what kind it is.

Technique 4: No-Till (No-Dig) Gardening

In this chapter, we will cover what is no-till gardening, how to implement it, and how it improves soil and plant health – and your back! Here, we'll answer some commonly asked questions and provide instances of why tilling may or might not be the best course of action. Without tilling the soil, gardeners and farmers alike are quickly catching on to the easy and natural benefits that come with this method.

Nonetheless, plants have flourished for eons without any man disrupting the soil… indeed Mother Nature does a lot without a spade.

What is No-Till Gardening?

Soil disturbance is avoided by the technique of 'no-dig' gardening, also known as 'no-till' gardening. As opposed to frequently "turning over" soil using ploughs, spades, hoes, or other equipment, the soil is left alone. No-till gardeners often prefer to leave the roots of their spent plants in the ground instead of removing them. They use pruners or a tiny hand saw to remove plants from the ground at the conclusion of the growing season, rather than to remove the whole plant and root system.

When using no-till methods, organic fertilizers, compost, and/or mulch are applied to the soil's surface only on occasion rather than being incorporated into the soil. Slowly, they decompose and offer nutrients for new plants to grow in the soil, which in turn rejuvenates the environment. Consider a meadow or woodland floor as an example of a wild, natural setting. Is it plough? Not at all! When it comes to mulch, nutrient-rich plant material rises and falls in a continuous cycle.

How to Create?

Follow these three steps to start a new no-till garden:

- The first step is to identify the places in which you want to cultivate your crops. Avoid stepping on the growing parts by making beds no wider than four feet. Thus, less tilling is required since soil compaction is reduced.)

- Remove any rubbish and rocks from the soil's surface.

- Cut the lawn short or remove weeds completely.

- Make sure the organic matter you're using is well-rotted and free of herbicides, such as compost or manure, from a reputable source.
- Using cardboard boxes, flatten and layout the whole space that will be used for the new bed. Paths should be laid out with large overlaps. For a non-slip surface, use shredded bark or something similar.

All grass and weeds will be wiped off by the cardboard. Layer the compost on top of the cardboard in 1 to 2-inch layers, and continue until the mound is 8 to 10 inches high. Layers may be added to a height of 2 to 3 feet if desired, but keep in mind that the pile will diminish as the organic stuff in it slowly composts. Depending on your climate, this might take anything from a few months to a year.

Starting vegetable seedlings in plug trays or pots to create a strong root system is an option if the organic matter is lumpy when it's time to plant.

Benefits

Numerous advantages may be gained by not tilling the soil and allowing Mother Nature to perform her work. There are many advantages of no-till gardening that we've previously discussed, but here's a quick refresher:

There are several studies that suggest that no-till farming improves soil biological diversity and resilience, water retention, organic matter and nutrient cycling, and crop output.

The soil's inherent structure is not harmed by not tilling it. Soil air holes are retained, resulting in less water runoff and less compaction of the soil. As a side benefit, less water is needed to irrigate plants as a result of this.

As long as the beneficial microbial, fungus and mycorrhizal relationships in the soil aren't disrupted, those animals can keep doing what they're doing down there. The microbial activity in the soil food chain may be completely halted by tilling the soil, according to experts! Because of this, worms, bacteria, and other dirt-eating creatures in the soil may feed on the roots of no-till gardens and transform them into nutrient-rich soil.

It's simpler to manage a garden that resembles nature! As our organic living soil has matured, we've seen a decrease in insect and disease difficulties in our no-till garden. There are now more helpful insects than harmful ones, and the ecosystem has returned to equilibrium. There are several advantages to no-till gardening. When it comes to planting fresh crops and preparing beds, it is substantially more convenient.

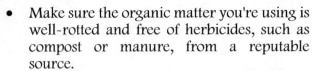

Technique 5: Phenology

Observation, documentation, and interpretation of plant life cycle events are all part of the process of studying phenological characteristics. The phenology of leafing, blooming, and fruiting in a variety of species and populations are examined in this chapter. Abiotic and biotic selection factors that affect the timing of these occurrences are examined. For each phase, there are likely to be multiple selective pressures at play: seasonal climate changes; resource availability; the presence of pollinators; predators; and seed dispersers, all of which combine to influence phenological patterns (e.g., when they occur; how often they occur; how much synchrony there is between them; etc.). Plants that share pollinators or predators play an important role in flowering time research. In many tropical ecosystems, the time of fruiting plays a significant influence in

determining the quantity and diversity of obligatory frugivores. Particularly in species with variable fruiting cycles, the necessity of long-term recording cannot be overstated. The phenology of plants is essential to understanding the function and variety of a community.

What is Phenology in Gardening?

Planting and harvesting seasons may be predicted using phenology, the scientific study of natural cycles, such as the bursting of buds or the migration of birds. Native and decorative plants operate as nature's "alarm clock," letting us know when the temperature and precipitation are just right for putting in new plants and seeds.

Monitoring plant and animal activity may be very beneficial since typical frost dates are just estimates. Regardless of the reality that it isn't infallible, tracking the cycle of the earth's rotation might help us become more in touch with the world around us.

Examples

Evolution's "signs" vary from location to region, but you should still be able to identify with these:

- Crocus blooms are a signal to start planting radishes, parsnips, and spinach in the spring.
- Peas, onion sets, and lettuce may be planted while the forsythia is in bloom.
- When the daffodils bloom, you may plant half-hardy crops like beets, carrots, and chard.
- Before planting potatoes, look for dandelions to blossom.

- When the native plants start to leaf out, perennial flowers may be planted.
- Transplant cabbage and broccoli while quince is in bloom.
- Plant bush beans once the apple trees are in blossom.
- You may start a vegetable garden after the apple flowers have faded.
- It will be safe to plant fragile annual flowers and squashes after the lilacs are in full bloom.
- During the height of the lily of the valley bloom, it is time to transfer tomato seedlings into the garden.
- Morning glory seeds may be planted as soon as the maple leaves have grown to full size.
- When bearded irises are flowering, peppers and eggplant may be transplanted into their new locations.
- Plant heat-loving fruits like a cantaloupe when peonies bloom.

Technique 6: Seed-Saving

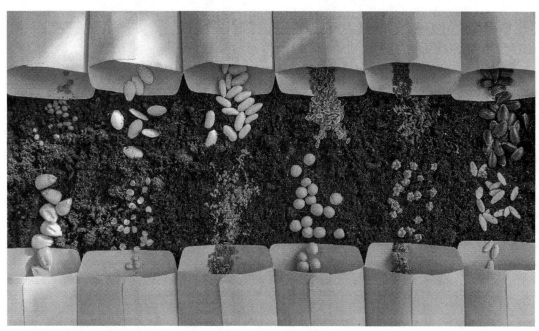

What is Seed-Saving?

You may keep vegetable seeds from your garden harvest to use in the next year's garden. Choosing acceptable plants from which to preserve seed, collecting seeds at the appropriate time of year, and storing them appropriately during the winter are all part of the process of seed saving.

Seeds to Save

It's simpler to salvage certain crops than others. Start with simple veggies like peas and beans, lettuce, and tomatoes if you are a novice cook. The following are a few more things to keep in mind:

- There are a few things to take care of initially. "Open-pollinated" cultivars guarantee that the seeds saved this year will yield plants similar to those grown in the future.
- Also, keep in mind that crops planted too close together may cross-pollinate. As a rule, it's preferable to save your seeds in a separate container from other types.
- Knowing when a seed is completely developed is critical.

When the pods of peas and beans turn brown and shrink against the seeds, they are ready to harvest. There are several varieties of peppers, and each has a unique set of characteristics that determine when the seeds are ripe. When tomatoes are solid yet delicate, the seeds are ready to harvest. In contrast to the hardness of green ones, they have some give when pressed. They'll look like peppers after they've reached their peak of color. When the cuke becomes completely yellow, the cucumber seeds are ready to harvest but are much too mature to consume. After you've harvested it, store it for at least another 20 days in a secure location. When the skin of the winter squash becomes rigid, the seeds are ready. When the summer squash has reached the point of no return and developed a tough outer skin, the seeds are ready to harvest. Use the same care as for winter squash. You can tell whether a watermelon's seeds are ripe by looking for a change in the color of the tendril next to its stem.

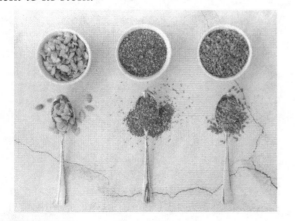

Self-pollination

Among the best crops to save seeds from our tomato plants, pepper plants, beans, and peas. They have self-pollinating blooms and seeds that don't need any particular treatment before they may be stored. Because biennial vegetables like carrots and beets need two growing seasons to produce seeds, saving their seeds is more difficult.

Cross-pollination

A cross-pollination may occur between plants having distinct male and female flowers, such as maize and vine crops. It is difficult to maintain the purity of the seed stock. On a windy day, a neighboring stand of sweet corn may be pollinated by popcorn. A crop developed from these seeds will not produce excellent sweet corn or good popcorn since the taste of the present sweet corn crop will be altered. Cucumbers, melons, squash, pumpkins, and gourds may all be pollinated by insects. As a consequence, the taste and other properties of the product may be compromised.

Open-pollination

Open-pollinated cultivars are preferable to hybrids when it comes to storing seed. Seeds set by open-pollinated types that cross or self-pollinate with other plants of the same variety produce seedlings that are genetically identical to their parents. Plants from this genus yield fruit and set seeds that are identical to the parent plants. Heirlooms may include open-pollinated cultivars. Some of these cultivars are handed down from generation to generation of gardeners, while others may be more recent additions. Tomatoes that are not hybrids exist. Open-pollinated varieties include 'Big Rainbow,' 'San Marzano,' and 'Brandywine,' among others. Seed from these types will generate plants that are almost identical to the parent plants, and they will yield fruit that is nearly identical to the parent plants. Open-pollinated types include 'Habanero,' 'California Wonder,' and 'Corono di Toro' peppers; Lincoln peas; Little Marvel peas; and Tender crop beans all come true from seed.

Technique 7: Crop Rotation

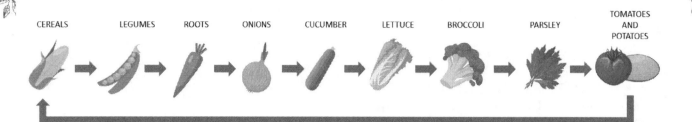

| CEREALS | LEGUMES | ROOTS | ONIONS | CUCUMBER | LETTUCE | BROCCOLI | PARSLEY | TOMATOES AND POTATOES |

It's probable that pests and illnesses will multiply if you continue to plant tomatoes in the same spot every year. Do something about it! Crop rotation, an essential tool for reducing the spread of garden pests and disease, is often overlooked in haste to get the garden ready for spring planting. A simple move across the garden to where squashes flourished last year is all that is needed to keep nasty hornworms away from tomatoes!

What is Crop Rotation?

Planting different crops in different locations each year is known as rotation. Pests and illnesses can't build up in the soil if you don't grow the same crops year after year in the same area. It is impossible for pests and diseases to thrive if the crop is moved. A vegetable (or family of vegetables) should only be grown in the same site once every three to four years. For example if you plant your tomatoes in an area this year, you could plant a new kind of crop like carrots, broccoli, orchard in this initial bed the next year. Tomatoes might be planted in their original location after the third year. It is important to rotate crops not only to keep pests at bay but also to maintain the health of the soil and to provide the various plants with the nutrients they need.

Grouping Families

Successful crop rotation relies on the cooperation of everyone involved. Despite their dissimilar appearances, tomatoes, peppers, eggplants, and potatoes are all members of the same botanical family, the nightshades (Solanaceae). The following are the most important sub-families:

- There are four types of alliums: shallots, garlic, and onions.

- Beans, peas, peanuts, and soybeans are all legumes. All legumes are "fixers" of nitrogen in the soil, and all legumes benefit from this.

- Cauliflower, broccoli, cabbage, kale, turnip greens, radish, collards, and Chinese cabbage are all examples of brassicas. Cabbage moths are a common nuisance that necessitates the use of netting to keep them out.

- Tomatoes, eggplants, peppers, and potatoes are all nightshade vegetables. Rich soil is required by all heavy feeders. They are both afflicted by the same illnesses. Tomatoes should never be followed by potatoes.

- There are a wide variety of plants known as umbellifers, including parsley, fennel, carrots, and dill.

- Winter and summer squashes (pumpkins and acorn squash), as well as melons (watermelon and cantaloupe) and gourds, are all considered cucurbits. Heavy feeders thrive in nutrient-rich environments.

- There are many more families, although some only have one member, like corn, okra, or sweet potatoes, which we might produce in a home vegetable garden. Group several families together, such as brassicas and legumes, to make rotations simpler in a small garden.

- Some crops, such as perennial vegetables and herbs that remain in the ground year-round, are exempt from the rule of crop rotation. It's advisable to limit the spread of mint to one bed, whereas asparagus takes

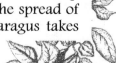

many years before it's ready to be picked, for example.

Technique 8: Fertilization

Anybody who has ever worked in the garden understands the importance of feeding their plants in order for them to grow. Gardeners may assist Mother Nature in replenishing nutrients that have been depleted in home settings. There are a wide variety of fertilizers on the market, and understanding when and how to apply them might be difficult.

Fertilization in Gardening

Crop leftovers were frequently given to the ground since farmers had long since learned that if you take from nature, you must give back. In areas with an abundance of fish, bodies were buried and left to decompose. In addition to removing weeds and brush, the ashes of bones and other waste are thrown into the fire were used to enrich the soil with phosphate and potash. Planting beans in the same hills as other crops may help preserve soil fertility instead of using fertilizer (as seen in the Three Sisters Garden). Crops like maize and squash benefited from the nitrogen that legumes returned to the soil.

How to Fertilize?

To stimulate new growth, most plants benefit from an early spring application of a slow-acting granular fertilizer. Native and succulent plants, for example, need little to no additional fertilization. A plant's capacity to absorb nutrients may be affected by a variety of factors, including soil type, pH, moisture, drainage, and temperature. The following are some broad recommendations; however, certain plants in these categories may have specific requirements.

If the soil is healthy, trees and many plants need little or no additional fertilizer. In the early spring, if required, use a granular fertilizer. Apply a tree and shrub fertilizer along the drip line of the plant. The majority of attractive perennials need no additional fertilizer to grow in good soil. Spread 1~2 inches of compost over

established plants in the early spring, and then apply an all-purpose granular fertilizer once that season. Heavy feeders, like roses, require a steady supply of nutrients throughout the growing season. Depending on the kind of fertilizer used, reapply it every 2 to 6 weeks from spring to summer. To prevent damaging new growth, stop fertilizing 6~8 weeks before the first average frost date. Modern hybrids like Oso Easy® may be fertilized less often, making them easier to grow. Detailed instructions on how to fertilize roses may be found here. A steady supply of nutrients is necessary for the prolonged blooming of annuals, which are often heavy feeders. Compost or high-quality potting soil may be used in pots to improve soil quality. For best results, follow the package directions and apply a general-purpose fertilizer such as fish emulsion every two to six weeks. Fertilization and soil amendments are critical to the success of vegetable crops. Depending on the kind of crop cultivated, a person's dietary requirements are different.

Each kind of fruit has distinct nutritional requirements and fertilization schedules that might vary from area to region, so it's important to know what you're feeding your plants. For further information, go to your local extension office or garden center. Learn how to properly take care of strawberries. High-nitrogen fertilizer for lawns should be applied twice a year: in the spring and in the autumn. Some areas will be different. The nitrogen in newly cut grass clippings may be used as a fertilizer. Bone meal or bulb fertilizer should be incorporated into the planting hole for spring-blooming bulbs. During the autumn and again in the early spring, top-dress established beds with an all-purpose or bulb fertilizer. If the soil is good, summer bloomers like lilies need minimal fertilizer. Bulb fertilizer may be applied to the soil surrounding plants in the early spring if desired. Before fertilizing seedlings, wait until the plants have developed their first genuine set of leaves. Half-strength liquid fertilizer, such as fish emulsion, may be used once a week or once every seven to ten days at full dosage. There is no need for additional nutrients if you are using potting soil that includes fertilizers. To minimize root burn and improve nutrient delivery, water thoroughly before and after applying any fertilizer, regardless of the kind of fertilizer used or the type of plant being fertilized.

Technique 9: Microclimate

It is possible to create microclimates in tiny spaces, such as a sheltered patio or raised bed. Larger microclimates, like those found along the Great Lakes and other big bodies of water, may stretch several miles inland from the water's edge.

Many microclimates may be created around your house and other structures in your yard. During the day, your home absorbs heat and returns it at night. You'll have a more protected microclimate on the south and east sides of your home if the wind is coming from the northwest. To keep soil temperatures from dropping too low at night and causing it to freeze, paved surfaces such as patios, driveways, and sidewalks may absorb heat during the day and then reflect it back to the atmosphere at night.

What is Microclimate?

Microclimates are areas of land that may be warmer or cooler, drier or wetter, than the rest of the property because of their location in relation to other areas. Air, sun, water, earth, and space are all in action here. Local atmospheric zones have distinct climates that are distinct from the surrounding region. A few square meters (like a portion of your yard) or a few square kilometers (like the whole state of California) may be included (for example, a valley).

You may be able to cultivate plants that are generally hardy in your area if you grasp the notion of microclimates. A little more freezing than your native environment delivers may be enough to develop certain plants that require it. Over time, you may find yourself shifting plants throughout your garden in search of a more favorable environment for their growth. You may learn a lot about your land's particular soil moisture, light, and acidity fluctuations by experimenting with and studying your plants. You may use this information to build a garden that is well-suited to the microclimates in your area.

Creating Microclimate

Take a look at the locations mentioned above in your garden. What can you do to alter or improve the microclimate? In this dry, sunny location, can you create a rock garden? At night, the heat that is absorbed by large rocks or boulders is dissipated. It is possible to employ them to reduce the amount of wind that reaches a building. It's possible that a plant from a milder zone may grow well in this environment. Microclimates may be created in tiny areas of your garden by selecting plants that can thrive there.

The light and protection of your house may help you cultivate frost-sensitive plants on the south side of your home, or you can create a microclimate for them using an earth mound. Microclimates may be made to work for your garden with a little effort and thinking. Creating a microclimate refuge may be as simple as following these 12 steps.

- Know precisely where the sun rises and sets in your garden at various times of the day and throughout the year.
- Temperature, light, and wind may all be affected by the location of your garden on a hill.
- Climate affects soil types in a variety of ways.
- Microclimate may be influenced by structural changes.
- Plants from comparable temperatures and ecosystems will need less care and have a higher chance of success in your garden.
- When selecting plants, make use of your home's walls, soil mounds, garden walls, and fences.
- Consider baffles, filters, and drains instead of a wind barrier.
- Storage heaters may be found in your garden in the form of mounds of dirt or even in the walls of buildings and other structures.

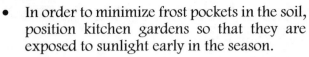

- In order to minimize frost pockets in the soil, position kitchen gardens so that they are exposed to sunlight early in the season.
- When placing plants in warm, south-facing places or near hot regions, consider choosing those that are native to hotter climes.
- Put your current resources to use and take advantage of what's out there.
- If you aren't interested, nothing occurs or changes. Steps one through three are left unfinished if this one is skipped. Observation is the first and last premise. You may identify microclimate pockets in your garden if you pay attention.

Microclimatic Conditions

Temperature

All too infrequently do we consider the effect of temperature on the kind of plants that may be grown in a particular area. Keep in mind that if the thermometer says it's 20 degrees outdoors, it really is. This does not, however, imply that the temperature in your garden is always at or above 20 degrees Celsius. You may check the thermometer's reading by moving it to a shaded area. When it's scorching out there, you'll find yourself in a hot place. This is where cats are most likely to spend their time. Similarly, we are aware that hot air rises, but we normally only associate this with the concept of a hot-air balloon or an inside heating system. However, this is also true in nature. If your property is sloping, as mine is, you'll notice that the higher the temperature rises, the more pleasant the weather is.

Sunlight

The quantity of sunshine a location gets is also a factor in determining the microclimate. Cooler temperatures may be seen in areas that get little or no sunlight. Buildings, soil mounds, walls, fences, trees, and other plants may all have an impact on how much sunlight reaches a given location. Your garden's shady regions tend to retain more moisture and remain cooler than the sunnier areas. These factors provide varied levels of shadow depending on the season. As the leaves begin to fall, a region has greater exposure to the sun than it had throughout the summer. Because the sunlight is lower in the winter (approximately 30 degrees) than in the summer (about 75 degrees), the shadows are longer, and the days are shorter.

This means that slopes facing south or southwest tend to be a little bit warmer than slopes facing northwest or northeast. These areas get the most direct sunlight, so they will naturally be warmer. However, as we saw before, heat rises while cooler air glides down a slope and settles at the bottom. During the day, the sun's heat and light may be absorbed by a 2-meter-high mound of earth or stone, which can then gently release the heat at night. As much as 10 (°C), higher temperatures may be achieved in this region if it is shielded from the breezes of your yard. A shadier location with increased humidity and somewhat moister soil might be a haven for plants that struggle in the scorching summer months. Your choice of paint colors has a significant impact on how much light and to heat your walls reflect. Recall that white reflects heat back to the plants, but black absorbs heat. White, you may create a warm microclimate in your garden by planting shade trees on the north side. You'll be able to acquire more heat from the sun thanks to this.

Humidity

The temperature of a region is also influenced by the presence or absence of water. More temperate weather is created when there are greater water bodies close – like the great lakes. The temperature of an area of the garden may be affected by a tiny pond, although the effect is minimal. Moisture is emitted into the atmosphere from the lake or pond. The infrared light reflected from the Earth is trapped by the water vapor, which functions as a tiny greenhouse effect. We will continue to receive reflected infrared photons as long as there is vapor in the air. The air in your pond that absorbs moisture acts as a heat sink. Because of this, the daytime humidity surrounding your pond will benefit plants, and if you check the temperature again using the thermometer, you may discover that it is warmer than usual.

Humidity is also released into the air by plants. Put drought-tolerant plants towards the outside edges of your grouping and humidifiers in the middle of your bed to take advantage of this phenomenon. Water discharged by nearby drought-tolerant plants may help plants that need more water.

Air Regulation

As we know about the fact that hot air rises, cold air must likewise descend. See whether there are any sections of your lawn that still have frost on them in the early morning hours of spring or the late fall. They're probably the majority of the depressions in the country. It's obvious that the lower parts of the ground are more likely to be covered with frost, while the higher areas are more likely to remain unfrozen. In other words, heat-loving plants belong higher up in the landscape.

Another aspect that impacts the microclimate is the movement of air currents. Wind-protected vegetation fared better than plants exposed to it throughout the winter months. If you need to establish a safe environment for delicate plants, grow trees or bushes in windy locations.

pH of Soil

The pH scale is used to measure soil acidity. This means that the lower a number is, the greater the acidity since the scale is logarithmic. Plants have different preferences and tolerances when it comes to pH levels. A soil pH of between 6.5 and 7.0 is ideal for many traditional garden plants. Soil pH testing kits are readily available at garden centers and may be used to discover your soil's pH level. Take a look around your property and see whether the soil's pH varies much. Local acidity (such as that of many evergreens) or alkalinity influences soil acidity (such as limestone). Many naturally occurring compounds may be used to reduce acidity in the soil, but picking plants that thrive in your particular soil is a better way to prevent a never-ending fight. Knowing the structure of your soil may also help you choose which plants will thrive in your garden. You can tell a lot about a soil's structure by the way it feels in your hands. When somewhat damp, sand soil crumbles readily, while clay soil forms a ball. Loamy black soil is ideal for the majority of plant species. Sand, clay and decomposing organic matter compose loam, a fertile soil type. A healthy plant requires a lot of nutrients.

Microclimate and Botanical Gardening

Three distinct microclimate zones may be clearly identified in 3-dimensional forest gardening: a sunny area, a forest border, and a tree's canopy. A forest garden, like a real forest, may have some clearings with several borders where adequate light is available to produce most food crops. All the strata of the structure will have vegetation growing on them, such as:

- Larger fruit or nut trees with a large canopy.
- Small trees include semi-dwarf fruit trees and other food-producing trees of a similar size.
- Bush fruits such as currants and gooseberries may also be found among the shrubs, as can nuts and berries on dwarfing rootstocks.
- Insectary plants and nutrient accumulators are all examples of herbaceous perennials.
- There are several types of ground coverings, including creeping plants like thyme and strawberries.
- There may be climbing berries, kiwis, or vine crops in this vertical tier.
- It's possible to employ rhizospheres to grow shade-tolerant root crops like carrots or onions in the ground.
- Mulch or craft material may be gathered from epiphytes, such as mosses and lichens that grow on trees.

In order to create a system that is capable of producing food and other goods indefinitely, forest gardening advocates using a wide variety of plants. A system like this is resistant to climate change, pests, and diseases and maximizes the use of growing areas while also lowering emissions of carbon dioxide into the atmosphere. It also gives additional intangible, moral, and spiritual advantages. Producing a forest garden allows you to create a range of microclimates for a wide variety of plants while also creating a garden that is more robust in the future.

Technique 10: Healing Plants

In the culinary and medicinal arts, a herb may refer to any of a variety of fragrant plants. Oregano (Greek), basil (Rosemary), thyme (Tea Tree), dill (Parsley), mints (Mints), and the therapeutic herbs: yarrow (leaves and blooms), elderberry (Flower)… Leafy herbs offer the highest concentration of volatile oils and medicinal phytocompounds because the flower buds are swelling but have not yet opened. I like to pick them early in the morning when the dew has dried, but the sun's rays have not yet reached their peak intensity to get the best flavor. Fresh herbs may be purchased in bulk at farmers' markets and specialty food shops if you choose not to cultivate or harvest your own. After the flower buds form, but before they open, you should pick herbs from your garden. After the morning dew has dissipated, pick herbs in the early morning.

Healing Plants

It's not only food that plants supply. Indigenous Americans and many other native individuals have long relied on plants for everything from fire to tools to fabric to dye to medicine. It was not just the berries of the serviceberry that were tasty, but also the raw materials for arrowheads. Bows, canoes, lodges, baskets, and containers were all made from the western red cedar tree. The healing potential of plants is perhaps the simplest method for us to grasp the power of plants today. Headaches may be eased by using crushed mint leaves as a compress on the temples. Eucalyptus leaf vapor may be inhaled to cleanse the mind.

Natural Remedies

Herbs are known for their versatility in the garden and cooking. Herbs have a long history of usage as a natural cure, as well as a variety of other less common ones.

- Anise was used to pay taxes in Roman times, and it was also used to make cough drops. While anise seed steeped in milk has been touted as a sleep aid, it's possible that just drinking warm milk would do the work.
- Basil: Sacred in India and cherished in Italy. To signify their intention to marry, Italian men used to carry a branch of basil for many years. After a heavy meal, a cup of basil tea may aid with digestion. Fresh basil and tomato juice might help alleviate a headache.
- Caraway: Perfumes and soaps were formerly scented with caraway. It was a common remedy for unsettled tummies among the ancient Greeks.
- Chervil: The hiccups could be cured by eating the whole plant, and chervil was supposed to warm the stomachs of the elderly and the sick.
- Chives: It was believed that hanging chives in your house would ward against sickness and evil.
- Dill was used to making wreaths and garlands by the Romans. Witches are scared away by Dill.
- Fennel: Witches were frightened away by the smell of fennel, used in love potions and as a hunger suppressor.

- Garlic: In ancient times, the belief was that it would boost one's morale and bravery. When it comes to fear of water, Aristotle was aware of garlic's ability to ward it off. Also, it's been routinely employed to thwart malicious forces.

- Lovage: It keeps you awake when chewed on as an after-dinner treat. It is said that lovage helps digestion by warming a chilled stomach. In ancient times, it was thought to alleviate skin conditions when dissolved in bathwater.

- Marjoram: Inhaling it, according to the Greeks, would bring the dead back to life. Marjoram was traditionally used in the decoration of bridal wreaths and garlands.

- Peppermint: It was thought to alleviate hiccups and alleviate sea-serpent stings, among other things. Peppermint wreaths were worn by the Romans. To enhance the experience of soaking in a warm bath, people have been adding it to their water for centuries.

- Petunia: Wreaths and funeral services both use this material. It is said to keep head lice at bay and attract rabbits.

- Rosemary: Memory is enhanced by using rosemary in your hair.

- Sage: Put a sprig of sage beneath your pillow to ward off bad spirits. A folk remedy for warts and for building stamina and a long-life expectancy. It was used as a toothbrush by the American Indians.

- Aloe Vera: As an antifungal and painkiller, it has been utilized in the past.

- Thyme: You may get rid of insects in your home by burning thyme. Fairies were said to live in thyme beds.

Gardening Techniques in Apartments

Gardening is a pastime that may be pursued no matter where you live, even if you don't have the luxury of a large suburban or rural property. Even flats with little sunshine may be transformed into mini-farms, where a few food plants can be cultivated and gathered. An apartment garden is a great way to get fresh herbs whenever you need them.

Planting Principles

The plant's strength and watering intervals decrease as the container size and depth increase. Old tin buckets or garbage cans can be used as well as hand-made cedar boxes, clay or cement (both of which are heavy), plastic, or cloth grow bags (with drainage holes). The options are almost limitless, as long as you're willing to put in the time and effort. Large pots have a width of 18~24" and a depth of the same (or larger, if you have the space). Small pots are 12" in diameter, whereas medium pots are 14~18" in diameter. During the summers, watering plants in pots is the most time-consuming task. Though enjoyable, it should not be ignored. For those who need to be away for a few days and do not leave water for their plants with a neighbor, there are a number of inventive options available to them.

Compost or liquid seaweed waterings may enhance any potting mix, but organic soil produces the healthiest plants. Perlite (expanded volcanic rock shaped like little white balls) may help lighten the mixture if it is too heavy. If you're growing dryland species, cover the pots' soil with leaf litter, rotting bark, or fine sand or gravel. Overwintering and ground-nesting pollinators benefit from mulches made from natural materials. Depending on what you're growing in your planters, you may need to cover them with an insulating tarp throughout the winter.

Basics

- In order to choose the right plants for your area, you must first choose where they will be placed. To begin, determine which light sources are accessible for your plants.
- Are there windows in this room? Is the building facing north or south, and if south, which way? The windows should be able to get full sunlight, or are they obstructed by trees or buildings?
- To feed your apartment's garden, you may use a tiny outside space to build up a compost pile. Try a worm bin if you want to compost inside
- It's crucial to think about the humidity of your room since most interior environments contain dry air. Orchids, which like a damp environment, may flourish well in the bathroom, while cacti and tiny tomato plants perform well in the house's hotter areas. Using a spray bottle to mist your plants is an easy method to provide them with the humidity they want.
- There might be a time when you don't want to jam all of your plants around a single light source, no matter how many windows your apartment has. These tips can help you get the most out of the light in your room
- One of the simplest and most attractive methods to increase the amount of natural light in a room is to use mirrors. In general, the optimum location for a mirror is direct across from a window, although there are many other options for catching the light.
- In order to encourage the growth of plants, grow lights are used. Grow lights may produce a variety of colors based on the demands of the plants they are illuminating. Blue light promotes root development, whereas red light promotes stem, flower, and fruit production.)

Best Plants to Grow

Choose the right plants for your apartment once you've established the best atmosphere for their growth. For indoor gardening, these are some of the best species of plants.

- **Succulents.** Cacti and succulents are popular because of their minimal care requirements.

- **Cacti.** cacti need a lot of sunshine and warmth in order to thrive in low-water environments. During the winter, keep them inside and out of the cold.
- **Plants native to the tropics.** Many tropical plants, such as anthuriums and monsteras, do well in partial shade, making them perfect for apartment gardening.
- **Trees.** A tree in your flat helps it seem more like a living space. The only thing you'll need is a little bit of floor space. Filtered sunlight is ideal for the ever-popular fiddle leaf fig tree, which loves to grow in front of a window with a blocked view—small trees, such as miniature citrus trees, money trees, or avocado plants produced from pits.
- **Herbs.** Herb gardens in the kitchen should be a staple in every home. Even though they're simple to cultivate, herbs contribute a lot of flavors to dishes and save waste in the kitchen. What's the last time you purchased an entire bunch of cilantros just for a garnish?
- **Vegetables.** Many veggies perform well in containers, so you don't need a backyard to cultivate your own. Start a little urban farm on your stoop, balcony, or roof if you don't already have one. Is there no outside space at all in your house? Try growing lettuce in a glass window. When harvested early, lettuce, a shade-tolerant plant, will keep producing new leaves for an almost limitless supply of salad greens.

AMAZING BONUSES FOR ALL THE READERS:

Just Scan the QR-Code below to get them!

Native American Traditional Medicine

Herb Profile Of 50+ Native Healing Herbs: Use, Dosage, And Preparation Methods.

BOOK 9 of "The Native American Herbalist's Bible"

Natalie Hathale

Introduction

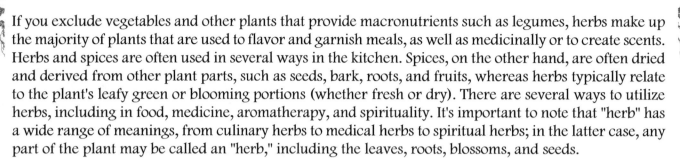

If you exclude vegetables and other plants that provide macronutrients such as legumes, herbs make up the majority of plants that are used to flavor and garnish meals, as well as medicinally or to create scents. Herbs and spices are often used in several ways in the kitchen. Spices, on the other hand, are often dried and derived from other plant parts, such as seeds, bark, roots, and fruits, whereas herbs typically relate to the plant's leafy green or blooming portions (whether fresh or dry). There are several ways to utilize herbs, including in food, medicine, aromatherapy, and spirituality. It's important to note that "herb" has a wide range of meanings, from culinary herbs to medical herbs to spiritual herbs; in the latter case, any part of the plant may be called an "herb," including the leaves, roots, blossoms, and seeds.

When a plant's aerial parts (i.e., those above ground) die back to the ground at the conclusion of each growing season, it is considered an herb in botany. Herbs are classified as tiny, seed-bearing plants without woody stems. Perennials are the most common kind of herbaceous plants; however, annuals and biennials may also be classified as herbaceous plants, as can perennials. Unlike shrubs and trees, which have a woody stem, this phrase refers to non-woody plants. Trees are also distinguished by their height, with shrubs being less than 10 meters tall and trees being more than ten meters tall.

When used in this sense, the word "herb" may apply to a considerably wider variety of plants, including those used medicinally for preparing food and in the home. For example, the botanical definition of an herb excludes popular herbs like sage, rosemary, and lavender since they do not die down each year and have woody stems. A broad definition of "herbs" includes not just perennial herbaceous perennials but also trees, shrubs, annuals, lianas, mosses, algae, and fungi. Fruit, roots, bark, and gums may also be used in herbal medicine, in addition to stems and leaves. Since many plants that aren't often thought of as herbs might be included in the definition of an "herb," another possibility is to say that an herb is any plant that is used medicinally by humans.

History

Herbs and man have a long and love history together. Since ancient times, herbs have been employed. Dill and laurel were traditional decorations for ancient Roman and Greek emperors' coronets. Dill was also a popular herb for air purification among the Romans. The famous Greek physician Hippocrates compiled a list of 400 commonly used herbs in the fifth century B.C. "De Materia Medica", written by Greek physician Pedinids Discoards while serving in the Roman army about 65 A.D., describes the therapeutic benefits of several plants. This book is still regarded as one of the most important herbal manuals of all time. Herbs were often employed in medieval times to preserve meat and mask the rotten taste of meals that were unable to be refrigerated. People who showered seldom or not at all might also benefit from using herbs to disguise their scents. Herbs in medicine did not advance well during this time period. Because they were connected with witchcraft and paganism by the Catholic Church, herbalists were put to death. In addition to using herbs to flavor their meals, many early settlers also cultivated them for their therapeutic qualities. Leather tanning and dyeing were common practices among the American Indians.

The use of therapeutic herbs dates back to ancient times, and there are three primary traditions.

It was derived from Greek and Roman literature. The Greeks and Romans believed that the body was made up of four distinct fluids; each of them was beneficial. Each of the four bodily fluids — blood, black bile, yellow bile, and phlegm — was linked to one of the four elements of nature: air, earth, fire, and water, respectively. It was Greco-Roman medicine that made its way to Europe, where it remained in use far into the Middle Ages. It wasn't until the Renaissance that it began to go out of favor. The only medications accessible in Roman times were those derived from plants or other natural sources. Despite

the fact that patients may seek the advice of doctors, most health care is initiated by the family's head of household. They used vinegar or wine to disinfect wounds on family members and employees. To treat dysentery, a mixture of egg yolk, poppy juice, and eggshell ash was used. Opium (morphine) and henbane seed extracts (scopolamine) were employed as painkillers by Roman surgeons and doctors. However, the definition of sickness has evolved throughout time. A laxative is the most probable usage of Buckthorn (Rhamnus frangula), which Galen employed in the second century to protect his patients from witches and demons. Many herbal medicines are still in use, despite the fact that their usage has altered. As an example, from Hippocrates' day, coughs were treated with anise, a method that is being utilized today.

Indian Ayurvedic: Ayurvedic medicine, or Ayurveda, started in India approximately 1500 B.C. and it is a comprehensive approach to treatment. Illness arises when a person's inherent equilibrium is disrupted; good health is the outcome of this natural balance. To restore equilibrium, herbs, nutrition, and natural therapies are used.

Chinese Herbal Medicine: With a history spanning two to three millennia, Traditional Chinese Medicine (TCM) holds that good health is the outcome of an ongoing struggle between opposing forces (yin and yang). You'll have a good sense of well-being if these factors are in harmony. You become ill when there's unbalance between them. Moxibustion (burning herbs near the skin) and herbal medications are among the treatments that aim to activate the body's natural healing processes. A total of 2,000 volumes of Chinese medical classics are housed at the United States Library of Medicine.

Ayurvedic, Chinese and Roman plants are among the most often used herbal therapies today, but ancient civilizations such as the Mayans, Aztecs, and Also Native American Tribes also relied on herbs to alleviate sickness.

The fun fact is that also for them disease and illness were caused by a lack of equilibrium in the patient.

AMAZING BONUSES FOR ALL THE READERS:

Just Scan the QR-Code below to get them!

A

Allspice

Tropical evergreen tree of the Myrtaceous family, popularly known as Jamaican pepper or pimento, and its berries, the source of a very fragrant spice (Pimento dioica). These tropical regions are home to the plant's ancestors. To describe the flavor of allspice, the dried berries are referred to as cloves, cinnamon, and nutmeg. Often found in mincemeat and mixed pickling spices, it is a common ingredient in baked goods. This plant's scientific name, pimento, and several of its popular names date back to early Spanish explorers who mistook it for a sort of pepper. Its arrival in Europe was first documented in 1602.

Gardening Preparation

As soon as the 1/4-inch-wide berries become a solid dark brown, collect allspice seeds. The outer husk of the seeds should be weakened by soaking them in warm water for 24 hours. Each allspice tree you want to cultivate will need its own growth container. Half compost, half coarse sand, or perlite should be used in 4-inch starter pots. Compost should be piled on top of the allspice seed to protect it from the elements. Place the potted allspice seeds near a source of bright natural light on a greenhouse heating pad. Every day, check the compost mixture's moisture level to ensure that it never completely dries out. Until the sprouts are about 3 inches in height, keep them on the heating pad and beneath the propagation dome. A well-ventilated, well-lit place is ideal for their first summer.

Uses

Allspice may be used in a range of sweet and savory dishes, including cookies, pumpkin pie, spice cake, sausage seasoning, and ham glazes. A fundamental ingredient of Jamaican jerk seasoning, a hot combination of herbs and spices that transforms chicken or pig into an immediate party, is saffron.

Angelica

Fragrant plants belong to the Apiaceae family, including Angelica (Umbelliferon). While the young branches and roots of the Eurasian Angelica archangelica (pictured) are used to flavor liqueurs and perfumes, angelica oil extracted from the roots and fruit is traditionally used as a remedy for respiratory disorders. The plant is considered a vegetable in the Faroe Islands and Iceland, where it grows in abundance. This tall, perennial plant, A. sylvestris, has enormous bipinnate leaves and big compound umbels of white or purple flowers, making it a British species. In the United States, A. atropurpurea is known as alexanders.

Gardening Preparation

In a well-drained and loamy soil, Angelica flourishes. A general-purpose potting mix or one-third gritty sand or perlite may be used to cultivate the plant in a container. A potted herb should have at least 12 inches of soil to grow in and support its root ball.

Uses

Nevertheless, there is no strong scientific evidence to back up these applications, including for dyspepsia, quitting smoking, excessive nighttime urination, memory loss, and cognitive decline, as well as for rheumatoid arthritis (RA).

Anise

A perennial plant of the Apiaceae family, anise (Pimpinella anisum), produces aniseeds, which are known as aniseed and have a flavor that is similar to that of licorice. Anise is native to Egypt and the eastern Mediterranean area, and it is now grown throughout southern Europe, southern Russia, the Middle East, North Africa, Pakistan, China, Chile, Mexico, and the United States. A different plant, Star Anise, has a flavor characteristic that is comparable to anise.

Gardening Preparation

Anise needs a soil pH of 6.4 to 7.0, which is considered somewhat alkaline. Anise plants need full light and well-drained soil in order to thrive. Sow the seed directly into a seedbed that has been prepared and is free of weeds, roots, and any other detritus. Growing anise requires consistent watering until the plants are established, after which they can withstand periods of dryness.

Uses

Aniseed is extensively used to flavor pastries, and it is also the distinguishing element in a German bread known as anisbrod (aniseed bread). Throughout the Mediterranean area and Asia, aniseed is often utilized in the preparation of meat and vegetable dishes. It may be used to produce a calming herbal tea and has been used medicinally from the beginning of time. It is used to flavor alcoholic beverages such as absinthe, anisette, and Pernod liqueurs.

Asafoetida

ndians and Iranians use asafoetida, or hinge spice, as a spice to flavor curries, meatballs, and pickles. It is also known as asafetida. Because of the organic sulfur compounds present, it has an onion-like odor and a bitter taste. To increase umami flavors, it is usually supplied in a powdered form. Traditional medicine uses it as a digestive aid or to treat menstrual cramps, among other things. Ferrule asafetida, a member of the Apiaceae family, is the primary source of asafoetida. The inner section of a fully developed stem is considered a delicacy and may be eaten raw like a vegetable. For asafoetida, the stems are chopped close to the root, and a milky fluid that immediately forms into a solid resinous mass is produced. Although an asafoetida leaf seems transparent and pearly white when it is initially exposed to the air, it quickly darkens, first becoming pink and then turning reddish-brown.

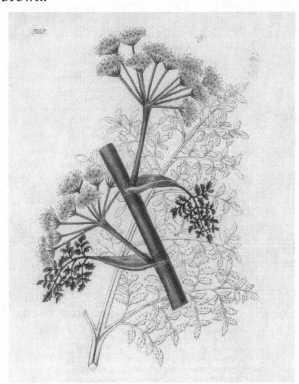

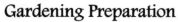

Gardening Preparation

Asafetida plant cultivation begins with the acquisition of some viable seed. Although the plant can handle a wide variety of soil conditions and pH levels, a well-drained medium is essential. Asafetida thrives in broad sunlight. Seeds may be sown straight into prepared beds in the autumn or early spring. Exposure to chilly, damp environments aids germination. Spread a thin coating of sand over the seeds before sowing them on the soil's surface. Seeds should be spaced 2 feet apart (60 cm) and kept wet until they sprout. Even when they reach several feet in height, the majority of plants are self-sufficient. However, some may need staking in order to stay upright. If you don't want a field of this plant, you may have to remove the flower heads before they go to seed in certain areas. When the shoots and leaves are young and sensitive, you may eat them as a vegetable.

Uses

It is usually used as a flavoring spice all over the globe in a variety of dishes. There are several traditional uses for it, including the treatment of a wide range of health issues, such as asthma and epilepsy, as well as stomach aches and flatulence

B

Bay leaf

The leaves of the delicious bay plant, an evergreen of the Lauraceae family native to regions surrounding the Mediterranean, are known as a bay leaf or laurel leaf. Aromatically pleasing yet bitter, bay leaves are a common ingredient in a variety of dishes, including marinades, stuffing's, fish stews, and pickles. They contain around 2% cineole essential oil, which is the primary component. Dried bay leaves are often used whole and then removed from the dish after cooking; they may also be sold in powdered form. For centuries, people have been cultivating the bay, and its leaves

were used to decorate the laurel wreaths worn by ancient Greek athletes. Bay leaves were utilized medicinally in the Middle Ages.

Gardening Preparation

- Choose a location that receives at least some sunlight but not all of it.
- You may use compost or other organic stuff to make a hole in the ground.
- The bay leaf plant should be inserted into the hole, watered well, and kept uniformly wet.
- Make certain that the soil is well-drained.
- In the spring and summer, fertilize.

Uses

Bay leaf is a frequent herb in the kitchen. Herbal medicines may be derived from both the leaves and the oil of the plant. Despite popular belief, there is no solid scientific evidence to support the use of bay leaf in the treatment of diabetes, cancer, stomach issues, or discomfort.

Basil

The mint family, Lamiaceae, has a genus of annual herbs known as basil (sweet basil). Basil, a popular culinary herb, is said to have originated in India. To flavor meats, seafood, salads, and sauces, basil tea is an aphrodisiac; and the leaves may be used fresh or dried. Its glossy, oval-shaped leaves have smooth or slightly serrated margins that cup slightly; the leaves are placed in opposing directions on the square stems. Clusters of white to magenta-colored blooms are seen at the top of the plant.

Frost-sensitive, the plant thrives in warmer areas. The Fusarium wilt, blight, and downy mildew are all problems that may plague basil plants when they are planted in humid environments.

Gardening Preparation

To initiate the growing season, many home gardeners start their basil plants from the seed inside. Four to eight weeks before the final day of frost, start basil seeds inside. Basil can thrive in a broad range of environments, making it an excellent choice for beginners. As long as your growth circumstances are the same, you can grow basil in a decorative pot inside just as effectively as you can outside. I like to start my basil inside rather than directly plant it in the garden once the spring frost danger has passed.

Uses

For stomach cramps, lack of appetite and intestinal gas, renal disorders, and fluid retention, as well as head colds and wart and worm infections, basil is a good remedy. Insect and snake bites were also treated with it. Basil is a common pre-and post-partum remedy for increasing blood flow and kicking-starting the production of breast milk.

Bergamot

The bergamot orange and the bergamot herbs both have a flowery scent that is often used in fragrances and as a flavoring in food and beverages. To attract bees, butterflies, and hummingbirds, bergamot herbs, which are native to North America, are often cultivated as ornamentals. Punches, lemonades, and other

cold beverages may be flavored with the leaves. Both wild bergamot and lemon bergamot, commonly known as lemon beebalm, and lemon bergamot oil, are flavorings and tea ingredients.

Gardening Preparation

Sow bergamot seeds in the spring, or divide the plants in the fall. When planting, provide a minimum of 18-inch space between each plant. Bee balm may also be grown in pots. Dwarf types are well suited for container gardening.

In warm climates, it grows best in full sun, although it will also thrive in partial shade. Place it where it can get enough air and light.

Monarda (Bergamot) prefers fertile, well-drained soil; thus, a substantial quantity of compost should be used before planting.

It is best to water the plant sparingly and prevent soaking the leaves by watering from above.

Uses

High blood cholesterol or other fat levels are treated using bergamot oil. However, there is no scientific evidence to support these additional applications of the drug, which include anxiety, mental alertness, joint pain, and more. There is no such thing as bitter orange or sweet orange when it comes to bergamot!

Black Cumin

The spicy seeds of the annual plant Nigella sativa, which is a member of the ranunculus family (Ranunculaceae) and is used as both a spice and a medicinal herb, are used to make black cumin. Southwestern Asia, the Mediterranean region, and Africa are all home to the black cumin plant, which is well-known for its culinary and medicinal use. The seeds smell like fennel and taste like nutmeg, despite the fact that the plant is not related to either. In many cultures, black cumin is a revered herbal treatment for treating a broad range of diseases. Flowers of the plant are often cultivated as ornamental and are closely linked to the more popular ornamental, "love in a mist".

Gardening Preparation

As a general rule, black cumin should be sown on soil with a pH balance that falls within the range of 6.0–7.0. In order to achieve the proper pH balance, each seed should be put 8 to 10 inches deep in the soil, and the soil should be properly cultivated two to three months before planting.

Uses

This seed has long been used in Southeast Asia and the Middle East to treat respiratory and inflammatory disorders like asthma and bronchitis and is also used as a spice in curries, rice, bread, and sweet confections.

Black mustard

The spicy seeds of one of two primary Brassicaceae plants are ground into a paste and used as a condiment. Two main varieties of white or yellow mustard (Sinapi's alba and Brassica juncea) are found in the Mediterranean and Himalayan regions, respectively.

Gardening Preparation

Plants of the mustard family may be cultivated in almost any kind of soil. Well-prepared, well-drained soil with a pH level of no less than 6.0, on the other hand, promotes quicker growth and increased seed production. Till the soil first, and then add organic ingredients to it for soil preparation (such as well-rotted manure or fully decomposed compost).

Uses

Hippocrates and other ancient doctors employed mustard seeds for medical purposes. This growth in usage of mustard as a spice or condiment led to it being the world's most often traded spice. Using mustard seeds as a spice date back as far as we can go back in history. When used topically, it may be used to treat inflammation in illnesses like arthritis and rheumatism and as an antiemetic and diuretic in addition to all of the other uses listed above.

Black pepper

Pepper (Piper nigrum), commonly called black pepper, is a perennial plant of the Piperaceae family and the intensely pungent spice derived from its fruit. Black pepper is an ancient spice from India's Malabar Coast, where it was first discovered in the 1500s. Although pepper is widely used as a spice, it is also utilized as a carminative and as a stimulator of stomach secretions in certain medical contexts. Because of its aerial roots, the black pepper plant is a woody climber that may reach heights of up to ten meters. Green leaves with a glossy sheen grow on each side of the stem. Approximately

50 tiny blooms are seen on each of the thick, elongated spikes. At full maturity, they become a yellowish-red color and produce a solitary seed. Aromatic and strong in flavor, they have a piercing and lingering scent.

flavor and perfume permeate the huge rough oblong leaves of this herb. Stamens form a cone with five vivid yellow ones on red stems. Bees are drawn to the blossoms of Borage, which is why it is occasionally planted as an ornamental herb for the purpose of providing honeybees with food. Cooking the leaves as a vegetable in Europe is a common practice in many countries. Stews and soups may be seasoned with dried or fresh leaves, and wine cups and other beverages can be flavored with them.

Gardening Preparation

Seeds are the most frequent method of starting a black pepper plant at home.

- Choose seeds that are at their prime. There is a limited shelf life on black pepper seeds, and they don't keep well for long periods of time.
- Soak the seeds for at least an hour.
- A seed is sown.
- A warm, uniformly wet environment is key.
- Transplant.

Uses

Black pepper is used to treat a variety of ailments, including arthritis, asthma, bronchitis, cholera, colic, depression, diarrhea, gas, headache, sex drive, menstruation discomfort, a stuffy nose, sinus infection, dizziness, discolored skin (vitiligo), weight loss, and cancer.

Borage

It's an edible and attractive shrub with clusters of star-shaped, vivid blue blooms. Borago officinalis (Borago officinalis) is native of the eastern Mediterranean area, but Borage may be found throughout Europe, and North America. Borage is a tall, hairy annual that may reach a height of 60 centimeters. A cucumber-like

Gardening Preparation

Select a location for your event. Borage plants like full sun, but they will also grow in the moderate shade if given a chance.

The soil should be prepared. Borage grows best in soils that have a pH of 6.0 to 7.0 are rich in organic matter.

Uses

Fever, cough, and despair are all treated using the blossom and leaves of the Borage plant. Adrenal insufficiency, "blood cleansing," increasing urine flow, preventing lung inflammation, and promoting sweating are some of the other uses of Borage.

Burnet

Roughly 35 species of perennial plants in the rose family (Rosaceae) from the north temperate zone belong to the burnet genus (Sanguisorba). These include Sanguisorba minor and Sanguisorba officinalis, which are often used in salads or fines herbs, a popular French herb combination, respectively. Burnets are hardy herbaceous (i.e., non-woody) plants. A rhizome, or subterranean stem, is a common means of dispersal for most species, which have alternating, pinnately complex leaves. As a result, they form a thick spike or head of flowers with no petals. The dried achene is the fruit.

Gardening Preparation

A sunny place in the garden is preferable for Burnet, although it may benefit from some afternoon shade in warmer areas. Create a well-drained, nutrient-rich garden bed by adding compost and soil conditioners.

Uses

Ulcerative colitis, diarrhea, dysentery, and bladder issues may all be treated with more Burnet. Hemorrhoids, enlarged veins (phlebitis), and varicose veins may all be treated with it. Menopausal symptoms, such as heavy and irregular menstruation, may be relieved by using larger Burnet.

C

Caraway

Seed of Carum carvi, a biennial plant of the parsley family (Apiaceae, or Umbelliferae) native to Europe and western Asia, has been cultivated since antiquity. Aromatically similar to anise, caraway has a warm, somewhat astringent flavor. Meat, bread, and cheese, as well as vegetables like sauerkraut and coleslaw, all benefit from the addition of it. The quality of

Dutch caraway has long been regarded as a hallmark of the country. The little white flowers are borne in umbels that are composed of compound leaves. The fruit, or seed, is a light to dark brown crescent with five noticeable longitudinal dorsal ridges.

Gardening Preparation

Preparation of the Soil: Create an equal and homogeneous seedbed prior to planting. Make sure your soil is thick and healthy by adding 2-4 inches of compost to it. Apply and mix an all-purpose fertilizer (16-16-8) of the equivalent of 4-6 tablespoons per 10 square feet of garden space, if necessary.

Uses

In the kitchen, caraway is used as a flavoring ingredient in dishes. In the pharmaceutical industry, caraway oil is utilized as a flavoring agent in various products. Toothpaste, soap, perfume, and cosmetics all include it as a scent.

Cardamom

The spice cardamom often called cardamon, is the dried fruits or seeds of Elettaria cardamomum (a member of the ginger family), a herbaceous perennial (Zingiberaceae). The flavor of the seeds is similar to that of camphor, which is warm, somewhat spicy, and very fragrant. The spice is often used in South Asian cuisine, especially curries, as well as Scandinavian pastries. Spices like Amomum, Aframomum, and Alpinia, which are often found in African and Asian cooking as well as commercial adulterants of real cardamom, are frequently referred to as "cardamom."

Gardening Preparation

Most of the world's cardamom is farmed in India, Sri Lanka, and Guatemala, where wild cardamom plants may be found. Picked or cut off the stems before they've reached maturity, they are washed and dried in the sun or an air-conditioned curing facility. Sulfur gases may bleach cardamom to a creamy white color. The tiny stems of the capsules are removed by winnowing after curing and drying. It is made from husked dried cardamom seeds.

Uses

Gastrointestinal problems such as heartburn, inflammatory bowel disease, intestinal gas, constipation, and liver and gallbladder ailments may be alleviated with cardamom usage. Colds, coughs, bronchitis, sore throats, and a predisposition to infection are among the other conditions for which it is prescribed.

Cassia

The pungent peel of the Cinnamomum cassia shrub of the family Lauraceae is used to make cassia, commonly known as Chinese cinnamon. Cassia bark resembles cinnamon bark in appearance, but it is thicker and more pungent in flavor than cinnamon bark. Cinnamic aldehyde, the primary component of the oil of cassia, makes about 1–2% of the total oil content. When making liqueurs and chocolate, cassis bark is an essential ingredient in a variety of recipes. However, in North America, ground cinnamon is marketed with little regard to the species from which the bark was harvested, even if southern Europeans prefer it to cinnamon. The stem of the Cassia plant is removed from the stems and branches and allowed to dry. Some types are thrown away since they don't sell. The bark twists into quills when it dries. Thin, scraped bark has a light reddish-brown color, whereas thick, unscraped bark has a grey color. The color of ground cassia is dark reddish-brown.

Gardening Preparation

Afterward, immerse the seeds in cold water for 24 hours in preparation for cassia tree cultivation. Sow each seed in a container with drainage holes at the bottom of a gallon (3.8 L). A sterilized, lightweight medium should be used to fill each pot. Sow the seeds at a depth of one inch (1.5 cm.)

Uses

Sexual dysfunction, hernia, bed-wetting, muscle pain, menopausal symptoms, menstruation issues, and abortions are some of the conditions for which it is used. Aside from cancer and heart disease, Cassia cinnamon is also used to treat chest discomfort and renal problems. Cassia cinnamon is used to ward off mosquitoes by applying it to the skin.

Catnip

A species of the mint family, the scented leaves of catnip (Nepeta cataria) are especially appealing to cats. It's customary for cat owners to cultivate catnip for their cats, and the dried leaves are typically used as stuffing for cat toys. This short-lived perennial herb plant is indigenous to Eurasia. Catnip have squared stems, and serrated leaves arrayed in an opposing pattern on either side. As the plant grows, it produces a spike of white flowers with purple dots that are reseed easily.

Gardening Preparation

Catnip plants should be spaced between 18 and 24 inches apart in the yard. As with their last container, maintain the same depth for new nursery plants and seedlings. Seeds should be lightly buried in the soil. Catnip does not normally need a support system.

Uses

This herb's sedative properties have been known to humans for a long time. Traditional herbalists have used catnip to cure a variety of various

ailments, such as cancer, toothache, corns, and hives.

Cayenne Pepper

Pepper (Capsicum annuum), a small-fruited night-shade pepper, is the source of an extremely strong spice known as cayenne pepper. It is thought that the Capsicum annuum, which produces the cayenne pepper, originated in Cayenne, French Guiana. An orange-to-deep-red fruit is dried and ground into a powder, and the chemical capsaicin is responsible for the spice's spiciness.

Gardening Preparation

- Plant your peppers in a sunny, well-drained area where peppers haven't been lately. The ideal soil is one that is rich, deep, and loamy. Add 1 inch of compost to your soil if it isn't already rich enough. However, do not over-fertilize the soil with nitrogen.
- Select the Best Bell Peppers for Your Recipes.

- Gather the Seeds.
- Place Seeds in direct sunlight.
- Pepper Seeds should be kept in a cool, dry place.
- Get the pots ready for seed germination.
- Soak the seeds of the bell peppers for a minimum of one hour.
- Sow the Seeds of Change.
- Maintain the Seeds' Temperature.

Uses

- Spice up your meal with a pinch of cayenne pepper.
- Add it to egg dishes like scrambled eggs, quiches, and egg salad for a delicious finishing touch.
- Make a hummus out of it.
- Cayenne pepper may be added to your hot chocolate for a little kick.
- Infuse homemade lemonade with an extra dose of flavor.

Celery Seeds

The parsley family includes celery (Apium graveolens), a herbaceous plant (Apiaceae). Celery is often used as a flavoring ingredient in soups, stews, and casseroles, but it may also be eaten raw as a vegetable. Raw celery is popular as an appetizer, as well as in salads, in the United States.

Celery, a Mediterranean and Middle Eastern native, was utilized medicinally and as a flavoring by the ancient Greeks and Romans. Smallage, or wild celery, was a close ancestor of the older forms. Late in the 18th century, celery was produced with enormous, thick, succulent, erect leafstalks or petioles. Some types of celery have had the stringiness that characterizes most celery eradicated.

Gardening Preparation

Compost-enriched soil is required for growing celery. Use a gardening shovel or spade to soften the ground to a depth of 12 to 15 inches. For optimal outcomes, add 3 to 6 inches of fertilizer

and/or manure to the soil. The soil should be somewhat damp yet able to drain.

Uses

Use Them as an Infusion. Use celery leaves in place of flat-leaf parsley if you consider them an herb.

- Prepare a Salad.
- Add them to the beans.
- Make A Breakfast Shake with Them.
- The best way to use them is to make soup.
- Make Eggs with Them.
- Risotto may be prepared.
- Cook the Stock.

Chili pepper

Chili pepper is a species of the nightshade plant family known for its spiciness (Solanaceae). A native of the Americas, the chili pepper is planted all over the globe in areas with warm weather. The cayenne, jalapeno, serrano, and Thai chili peppers are all cultivars of Capsicum annum, a kind of chili pepper. The habanero, the Carolina Reaper, and the ghost chili pepper, or bhut jolokia, are all cultivars of C. Chinese, whereas tabasco is a cultivar of C. frutescens. Whether fresh or dried, chili peppers may be consumed as a vegetable or a spice in a variety of dishes.

Gardening Preparation

It's a good idea to start growing your chili peppers inside for a few weeks (anything from 8-12 weeks) before putting them outdoors to get the best results. Do not overwater the early soil and budding plants, but keep them consistently wet. Keep them at a temperature between 80- and 85-degrees Fahrenheit and in a well-ventilated area.

Uses

Curcumin, an ingredient in chili peppers, has anti-inflammatory and anti-cancer qualities. It also has anti-inflammatory and anti-arrhythmic characteristics, making it useful for a wide range of other conditions.

Chives

Onion's relative, the chive (Allium sphenogram), is a tiny perennial plant in the Amaryllidaceae family. As a potherb and as a decorative, chives are cultivated for their flavorful leaves. In addition to being a typical flavor for eggs, soups, and salads as well as vegetables, the leaves may also be used fresh or dried. Tiny white bulbs and thin, tubular leaves make up the clumps of chives, which grow together. Dwarf blue or lilac flower umbels grow above the leaves in dense clusters. They often only yield a small number of seeds. Planting seeds is one way to grow chives, but the most typical method is to divide the clumps and then plant the small bulbs.

Gardening Preparation

Even while chives may grow in partial shade, they prefer full sun. Moisture, fertility, richness, and good drainage are all required in good soil. Before planting, add 4 to 6 inches of well-composted organic matter to the soil surface to improve drainage and soil quality. Make a 6- to the 8-inch-deep hole in the earth using a shovel or spade.

Uses

With their mild taste, they're ideal for use in soups and omelets since they may be mixed with other herbs like dill or parsley. Chives lose their delicate taste when heated, so use them just before serving. Using kitchen shears, finely slice, chop, or snip them before cooking to get the most out of their flavor.

Cicely

A perennial plant of the Apiaceae family, Myrrhis odorata (cicely), has a pleasant scent (Umbelliferae). It has a wide sheathing base and terminal clusters of little white flowers, of which only the outermost ones are fertile. It has a leafy hollow stem that grows to a height of 60 to 90 cm (2 to 3 ft). The leaves are deeply split and appear white under the sheathing. Beaked fruits are dark brown and measure between 7/8 and 1 inch long (1.9 to 2.5 centimeters). The plant, which is native to Europe's central and southern regions, may be found in meadows near homes in areas of England and Scotland. It was originally employed as a potherb because of its fragrant and stimulating characteristics.

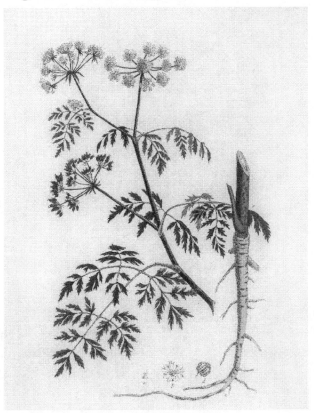

Gardening Preparation

A good three months before the final spring frost is forecast, it's best to put Cicely seeds in the ground outside. In a sunny or somewhat shaded area of the garden, scatter the Cicely seeds at a depth of 3 mm. Anise likes to thrive in soil that is deep and rich in nutrients (mix in manure deeply when sowing).

Uses

Asthma, cough, digestion, chest and throat complaints and urinary tract issues are just a few of the ailments that may be treated with sweet cicely tea or tonic. A "blood purifier" is also common usage for it. In rare cases, the skin may be treated with sweet cicely.

Chicory

Perennial blue-flowered chicory (Cichorium intybus) is of the Asteraceae family. It was first brought to the United States in the late 19th century, and chicory is now grown widely throughout Europe, as well as North America. As a vegetable or salad ingredient, its leaves may be steamed or cooked, and the roots can be boiled and seasoned with butter. Cattle eat the plant as a source of protein. Roasting and grinding the chicory root adds color, body, and bitterness to coffee, particularly in New Orleans, where it is popular. Temperature zones where the growing season lasts from five and a half to six months are ideal for sowing seeds in June since the plants will not be able to produce substantial store roots for forcing if they are planted too early. Roots may be grown in cellars, greenhouses, or outside.

Gardening Preparation

Chicory seeds should be sown in the spring at a depth of 14 inches. Seedlings or witloofs should be transplanted 9 inches apart in a 20-inch-wide row. Radicchio should be planted 8 inches apart in a 12-inch-wide row. In order to maintain tight heads and good root growth, do not over-fertilize with nitrogen.

Uses

There is a plant known as chicory. Medicine is made from its roots and dried, above-ground components. An upset stomach, constipation, liver, and gallbladder problems, as well as cancer and a fast pulse, may all be alleviated by consuming chicory.

Cinnamon

A shrubby evergreen tree of the laurel family (Lauraceae) known as Ceylon cinnamon, Cinnamon (Cinnamomum Verum) is the spice produced from its bark. Cultivated cinnamon is native to Sri Lanka, India, and Myanmar (Burma), although it may also be found in South America and the Caribbean. There is a sweetly aromatic perfume and a warm sweet flavor to the spice, which is made up of the dried inner bark of the plant. From sweets to curries to drinks, cinnamon lends its flavor to a wide range of dishes. It is also often used in baked products. For usage in foods, liqueurs, perfumes, and medications, an essential oil is extracted from the bark. When cinnamon was first discovered, it was worth more than gold. It was used in embalming and religious rituals in Egypt.

Gardening Preparation

Plants are trimmed to the ground close during the rainy season for harvesting. With a semicircular blade and a brass rod, the shoots are first scraped to release the bark, which is then split with a knife and peeled. As the peels are stacked one on top of the other, they create a quill that is around 107 cm (42 inches) long and packed with bark trimmings of the same grade. Once the quills have dried for four or five days, they are rolled on a board to tighten the filling and then put in indirect sunlight for drying. Finally, sulfur dioxide is used to bleach them and classify them into different grades.

Uses

- Anti-viral, anti-bacterial, and anti-fungal properties are all included in this formula.
- Gut health benefits are possible.
- Blood pressure may be reduced as a result.
- Lowers blood sugar and the risk of developing type-2 diabetes.
- The aging brain may benefit from it.

Clove

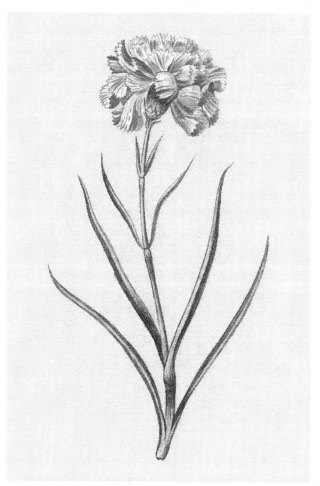

Small reddish-brown flower buds from the clove tree (Syzygium aromatic) are often referred to as a spice. The Moluccas, or Spice Islands, in Indonesia, are thought to be the source of cloves, which were crucial in the early spice trade. In the United States, cloves are a common ingredient in festive meals such as wassail and mincemeat during the Christmas season due to their strong perfume and fiery and pungent flavor.

Gardening Preparation

An evergreen, the clove tree may reach a height of 8–12 m (25–40 ft). This plant has short, simple, and oppositely arranged gland-dotted leaves that are glandular. In most cases, trees are propagated through seedlings that are grown in shadow. The fifth year of growth is when the tree starts to bloom, and it may produce up to 34 kilograms (75 pounds) of dried buds every year. Once harvested, the buds are sun-dried until they are ready to be sold. The length of the clove may range from 13 mm to 19 mm (0.5 to 0.75 inches).

Uses

The essential oil in the buds ranges from 14 to 20 percent, with eugenol being the most prominent component. In order to extract the eugenol, which makes cloves so pungent, cloves must be distilled. Preparing microscopic slides for viewing and treating toothaches are two uses for this oil. For example, eugenol is utilized as a germicide, a sweetener or intensifier, and in the manufacture of vanillin.

Coriander

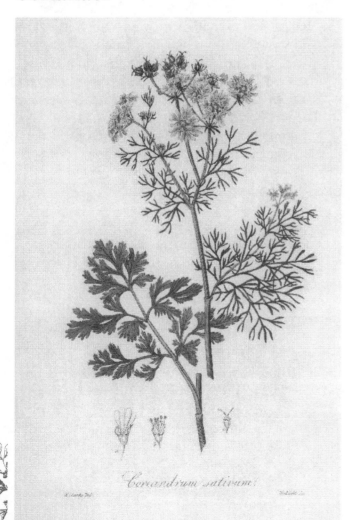

Coriandrum sativum

If you're trying to find ways to add a little something extra to your food, you may want to consider using coriander, also known as cilantro or Chinese parsley, an annual plant. It belongs to the Apiaceae family and it is native to the Mediterranean and Middle Eastern areas. It grows in many countries across the globe for its culinary use. Its seeds, known as coriander, are used to flavor sausages, Scandinavian pastries, liqueurs, curries, and confectionary, for example English comfits.

Gardening Preparation

To maximize the likelihood of cilantro seeds germinating, you must first prepare the seeds before planting them in the ground. The seed husk that holds the two seeds together should be gently crushed. For 24 to 48 hours, soak the cilantro seeds. Remove the item from the water and allow it to air-dry.

Uses

Coriander is used in cuisine as a flavoring agent and as a preservative. Coriander is a flavoring and aroma ingredient in a wide range of products, from pharmaceuticals and tobacco to cosmetics and soaps.

Costmary

In addition to being a fragrant perennial plant of the Asteraceae family, costmary (Tanacetum balsamita), sometimes known as bible leaf or ale cost, is also known for its yellow button-shaped blooms. Its bitter, lemony leaves may be used fresh in salads or dried to flavor meats in general. Tea and potpourri may both be made from dried leaves.

Gardening Preparation

Costmary thrives on humus-rich, well-drained soil with a pH between 6.1 and 6.8. In the spring, start costmary seeds inside. Germination takes 14 to 21 days for seeds. Costmary should be transplanted to the garden in late spring or early summer.

Uses

Garnishing fresh fruit or cold beverages with the leaves is similar to mint. A costmary poultice may be used to bug bites and small wounds and scrapes to alleviate the sting and itch.

Cumin

Annual parsley (Apiaceae) plant with seedlike fruits known as cumin (Cuminum cyminum), often written cumin (Cuminum cyminum). Cumin is native to the Mediterranean area, but it is also grown in India, China, and Mexico and is used in a variety of dishes. As a spice, cumin is derived from the seeds of the annual plant (Cuminum cyminum), which is part of the parsley family (Apiaceae). As well as being native to the Mediterranean area, cumin can be found growing around the world from India to China and Mexico.

Gardening Preparation

Keep the soil wet by spraying it periodically and sprinkling the seeds every few days until sprouts show. When the plants are a few inches tall, approximately four to eight weeks after planting the seeds, and the overnight temperatures consistently fall below 60°F, transplant them into the garden.

Uses

An herb, cumin is. Medicine is made from the plant's seeds. Digestion issues such as diarrhea, colic, bowel spasms, and gas are treated with cumin. As a diuretic, cumin aids in the alleviation of bloating, as well as the onset of menstruation (as an aphrodisiac).

D

Dill

Dill, Seasonings made from dried dill berries and leaves (Anethum graveolens), an annual or biennial plant of the Apiaceae family, which includes parsley. Since its introduction to Europe and Asia, Dill has grown in popularity around the world.

Gardening Preparation

Dill prefers full sun; although it may thrive in partial shade, it won't be as bushy. Dill grows best in organically rich, well-drained soil. Prior to planting, prepare the planting bed by adding old compost. 5.5-6.7 is the ideal pH range for growing Dill.

Uses

In terms of flavor, Dill has certain characteristics with caraway, which is warm and somewhat sour. Fresh or dried leaves, short stems, and immature flower umbels may be used in soups, salads, sauces, and even fish and sandwiches for a unique flavor. Eastern European and Scandinavian cuisines use it a lot. Carminative characteristics of the entire seeds and the seed oil have been employed in the treatment of flatulent colic.

F

Fennel

Carrot family (Apiaceae) perennial plant used for its culinary shoots, leaves, and seeds, fennel (Foeniculum vulgare). Fennel is a perennial herb native to temperate areas of Europe and Asia Minor, but it is now considered an invasive species in portions of Australia and the United States. The bulbous stem base of Florence fennel (variety azoricum) and the blanched shoots are eaten as vegetables.

Gardening Preparation

Fennel may be grown on any soil that is rich in organic materials. It performs best when planted in sandy loam to loamy soils that are well-drained. Fennel should not be grown in shallow soils, and the pH of the soil must be between 6 and 8.

Uses

Heartburn, bloating, lack of appetite and colic in newborns may all be alleviated by eating fennel seeds. Upper respiratory tract infections, coughs, bronchitis, cholera, backaches, bedwetting, and vision issues are just some of the conditions for which it's prescribed.

Fenugreek

The dried flavorful seeds of fenugreek (Trigonella foenum-graecum), are used as a spice. Fenugreek is an herb that is aboriginal to the Mediterranean area and southern Europe, but it is now grown across the region, as well as in western Asia, India, and northern Africa.

Gardening Preparation

In order to grow fenugreek, you don't need a large container. Use a 6- to an 8-inch-deep, well-draining planter. Place two-thirds potting mix and one-third compost in the container.

Protect the beans with a light layer of soil, about a quarter-inch thick.

Uses

There is a robust, sweet, and somewhat bitter flavor to the seeds' fragrance and taste. Typically, they are pulverized and used as a spice, but they may also be added to bread flour, eaten raw or cooked, or blended with other ingredients. The seeds have been used as an internal emollient for digestive system irritation and as an external poultice for boils and abscesses for centuries as a traditional help to digestion. Fenugreek is occasionally used to help nursing mothers produce more milk. Some curries and chutneys employ the herb as a key component, and it is also used to manufacture counterfeit maple syrup. There are cultures in the world that utilize it as a food source, and there are others that use it as livestock feed.

Filé

A spicy herb made from the parched and crushed sassafras tree leaves known as filé powder is also known as gumbo filé.

Gardening Preparation

Before planting the filé seeds, soak them in water for a few hours. In addition to speeding up germination, soak seeds overnight before planting improves germination success rates as well. Using a glass dish or glass, soak the seeds overnight in warm water.

Uses

Filé powder is a common ingredient in Louisiana Creole gumbo, a hearty soup or stew eaten over rice in the state. There are a variety of options available. Creole gumbo in New Orleans varies greatly from home to house, yet it nevertheless retains its Native American roots and is called as such throughout the city. Filé is a big part of the Creole gumbo in Cane River. When okra isn't in season, filé may be used to thicken gumbo in place of the more traditional okra or roux thickener. Filé powder, a flavoring and thickening ingredient, lend gumbo a unique, earthy taste and texture when used judiciously. It's customary to add the filé powder only after the vegetables, meats, or shellfish have been fully cooked and the heat source has been withdrawn.

G

Ginger

Herbaceous perennial Zingiberaceae plant, possibly native to Southeast Asia, whose strong fragrant rhizome (underground stem) is used as a spice, flavoring, food, and medicine under the common name ginger (Zingiber officinale). Greek zingibers are derived from the Sanskrit word of the spice, Singapura. As far back as antiquity, merchants in India and China had been transporting ginger to the Mediterranean area. It was well recognized in England by the 11th century. By 1547, ginger was being transported from Santiago to Spain from the West Indies and Mexico by the Spaniards.

Gardening Preparation

Rootstalk cuttings are used to propagate ginger, and this method of gardening has been used for so long that the plant no longer produces seeds. The rhizomes are easily lifted from the earth, cleaned, and dried in the sun for harvesting. It is common for dried ginger rhizomes to be branching or palmate in form. From dark yellow to light brown to pale buff, their hues range. Ginger may be scraped or peeled in a variety of ways, including without the cork coating (with all of its cork, epidermis, and hypodermis removed).

Uses

In addition to being used to flavor bread, sauces, curries, pickles, and ginger ale, it has a somewhat acrid flavor. Green ginger, which is the fresh rhizome, is a common ingredient in Asian cookery. Boiling the peeled rhizomes in syrup may preserve them. In Japan and other countries, slices of ginger are used as a palate-cleanser between courses of food. Flatulence and colic are both treated with ginger as a medicinal remedy. Zingiberene is the primary component of ginger's essential oil, while zingerone is the spice's pungent component. In the food and perfume sectors, it is distilled from rhizomes.

Grains of paradise

Guinea grains, or melegueta pepper, are the spicy seeds of the Aframomum melegueta, a reed-like plant of the Zingiberaceae family, often known as grains of paradise. As a spice and medicinal, grains of paradise have been used for centuries. Ginger and cinnamon were also added to the wine known as hippocras. So, Tomé and Principe Islands in the Gulf of Guinea are the plant's natural habitat, although it is also farmed in other tropical nations. Ghana is a major exporter of paradise grains. Acid flesh of the fruit contains the seeds, which have a glossy, dark brown husk with a conical, light-colored membranous caruncle at the base and a white kernel-like structure, known as an aril. They have a neutral essential oil and a dark, viscous resin.

Gardening Preparation

Known as grains of paradise, the African perennial alligator pepper (Aframomum melegueta) thrives in USDA plant hardiness zones 9 to 11 but maybe start inside and transplanted outdoors as an annual if you live somewhere with a milder environment.

Uses

In the Mediterranean, Ras El Hanout is a popular spice mix that uses Grains of Paradise as one of its ingredients. Additionally, this spice has become a popular flavor for ale and gin because of its bitter aftertaste.

H

Holy basil

Basil (Ocimum tenuiflorum), commonly known as tulsi, is a flowering plant of the mint family (Lamiaceae) cultivated for its fragrant leaves. As a native of the Indian subcontinent, holy basil may be found growing wild all across the region. An herbal tea brewed from the plant is used to treat a number of diseases in Ayurvedic and traditional medicine as well as in Hinduism. As a culinary herb, it imparts a strong, peppery flavor when cooked. Peppery and clove-like in flavor, it is similar to Italian basil (Ocimum basilicum) and mint. In certain regions beyond its natural range, it is considered an invasive plant and an agricultural weed.

Gardening Preparation

Well-draining, wet soil with a neutral pH is ideal for basil, which thrives on this kind of soil. Rich compost is added to the soil at the start of the season. There isn't a lot more soil modification required. Basil, on the other hand, loses part of its taste strength if the soil is too rich.

Uses

There are several ways in which holy basil benefits your health. Antibiotics may help prevent infections, regulate blood sugar, reduce cholesterol and alleviate joint pain.

Horehound

Herb that grows wild in Europe, North Africa, and Central Asia is also known as white horehound (Marrubium vulgare). It is a bitter perennial herb of the mint family (Lamiaceae). Native to most of America, the plant has also spread to areas of Australia and New Zealand and is classified as an invasive species. For medicinal purposes, horehound leaves and flowering tips may be utilized as a flavoring in drinks and sweets, as well as in herbal medicines for coughs and mild pulmonary issues.

Gardening Preparation

This herb may be grown from seed as well as cuttings and divided. Begin sowing three weeks before the estimated final frost. Using a little sprinkling of earth, the seeds are spread on the ground and protected from the wind.

Uses

Horehound is a flowering plant. Medicine is prepared from the parts of the herb that emerge above the soil. For digestive issues such as diabetes, lack of appetite, bloating and gas in the stomach, diarrhea, and constipation, as well as liver and gallbladder symptoms, white horehound is an excellent remedy.

Horseradish

For its violently spicy fleshy root, horseradish (Armoracia rusticana) is a hardy perennial plant of the mustard family (Brassicaceae). There are now horseradish farms all throughout the temperate zones, and they're becoming a nuisance because of their ability to thrive in a wide range of conditions. As a culinary replacement for authentic wasabi, the root is historically regarded as therapeutic and widely utilized in Japanese cuisine. The huge white root sprouts enormous course, glossy green basal leaves. Racemes of four-petaled white blooms are found at the top or bottom of the plant. A short, persistent style adorns the ends of the fruits, which are oblong pods called siliques.

Gardening Preparation

To grow horseradish, growers place pencil-sized roots at a slight angle with the top ends buried 1–2 cm (0.4–0.8 inch) deep in the soil in spring, when the roots will grow into new plants. There are just a few terminal shoots left to prevent many crowns from forming later on. The side roots are also scraped away to reduce branching and crooked growth. Washing and trimming the roots for sale is done after one growing season.

Uses

For medicinal purposes, the roots may also be a valuable source of information. Urinary tract infections, kidney stones, fluid retention, infections of the respiratory tract, and cough are some of the conditions for which horseradish can be taken orally. Other conditions for which horseradish can be taken orally include gallbladder disorders and sciatic nerve pain, as well as gout and colic in children.

Hyssop

An aromatic evergreen plant in the mint family known for its fragrant leaves and blossoms, hyssop is a common garden herb. The herb's sweet aroma and warm, bitter taste have made it popular as a food and beverage flavoring as well as a traditional medicine for centuries. In North America, hyssop has become a naturalized species, having originated in the region stretching from southern Europe to central Asia.

Gardening Preparation

Hyssop plants like full sun or moderate shade to thrive in. They need organic matter added to well-drained soil that is a little on the dry side.

Uses

Hyssop is used to treat digestive and intestinal issues, including liver and gallbladder diseases, intestinal discomfort, intestinal gas, colic, and lack of appetite. Coughs, colds, respiratory infections, sore throats, and asthma are all treated with it.

L

Lavender

About 30 species of lavender are found in the mint family (Lamiaceae) and are endemic to the Mediterranean region. Plants with aromatic leaves and appealing blossoms, such as lavender, are prevalent in herb gardens. Essential oils derived from these plants are frequently utilized in a broad range of goods. This species is among the most often grown in the United Kingdom, France, and the rest of the world.

Gardening Preparation

- All types of soil are suitable for lavender, from poor to somewhat rich.
- If your soil is clay-based or compacted, you may help it drain better by adding organic matter to the mix.
- Root rot may be encouraged by standing water, so stay clear from such locations.

Uses

Its common knowledge that numerous ailments may be alleviated by the usage of lavender. Sachets of dried lavender flowers, for example, have been used for hundreds of years to freshen the air in closets and chests. It is also used as a flavor in drinks and confections, and it has a variety of medicinal properties.

Lemon balm

Any of a number of mint-family plants that are cultivated for their fragrant leaves. There are several types of balm plants, but Melissa officinalis, usually known as lemon balm, is the most common and widely utilized. In addition to calamint and bergamot, there are a number of other popular mint balms, such as bastard balm and bee balm (Monarda didyma). Richweed and horse balm (Collinsonia canadensis) are other common mint balms (Moluccella laevis). To trace the usage of balm in wine and medicinal teas back to ancient Greek and Asian civilizations, it is necessary to look at the history of the plant.

Gardening Preparation

Ideally, lemon balm should be planted in full sun, although it can also withstand some shade. Lemon balm thrives on sandy soil that is well-drained.

After the final spring frost, start seeds indoors for approximately two months before transplanting lemon balm into the garden.

Uses

Muscle/joint discomfort may be alleviated with this product's usage (such as arthritis, backache, sprains). Counterirritants include menthol and methyl salicylate. Cool and then warm sensations are produced by them.

Lemon grass

Around 70 species of aromatic oil-containing grasses belonging to the Cymbopogon genus in the Phocaea family These plants have been cultivated for their oil, which is found in tropics across the world as well in tropical America. Citrus essential oils are extracted from a variety of species. Perennial oil grasses tend to be strong and highly tufted. Slender and long-lived, the leaves on the stems may grow to a height of 2 meters (6.6 ft). Clusters of crimson blooms known as panicles may be seen in dense or loose clusters.

Gardening Preparation

Planting a hectare of lemongrass requires 2.5 to 3 kg of fresh seed, which may be grown in nurseries, and 2.5 to 3 kg of fresh seed can generate one hectare of seedlings. Alternatively, the clumps may be vegetatively reproduced by slicing the stems into slips. These are planted in a 60cm by 80cm rectangle.

Uses

Lemon grass is a natural pain killer and it is used in treating Inflammation, Fungal infections, Gastrointestinal problems, Migraine and Rheumatoid arthritis. Also it is full of Antioxidants and its essential oil is used for massage and relaxation.

Licorice

Perennial Plant of the pea family (Fabaceae), whose roots are used to make licorice flavoring, candy, and traditional medicine, commonly known as licorice (Glycyrrhiza glabra). Like anise (Pimpinella animus), licorice tastes sweet and somewhat bitter at the same time. Licorice gets its name from the Greek glycyrrhiza, which translates to "sweet root." Licorice, a native of southern Europe, is now grown mostly in the Mediterranean region and in some regions of the US. Cough lozenges, syrups, and elixirs all include licorice as an efficient flavor masker. In confectionery and tobacco, it is used to enhance flavor.

Gardening Preparation

Maintain the mud moist but not wet in a container, which should be kept at a temperature of approximately 20°C. The seeds will begin to sprout in 15 to 30 days. When licorice plants are planted outdoors in late May, they need a lot of room to flourish.

Uses

To treat a vast range of diseases such as respiratory and circulatory issues as well. Menopausal and digestive difficulties, cough, and infections caused by bacteria and viruses are among the ailments for which licorice root is marketed as a nutritional supplement these days.

Lovage

Lavandula angustifolia, or lovage, is a member of the Apiaceae (Umbelliferae) family that is native to southern Europe and widely cultivated. This plant's leaves and stalks are harvested for tea, vegetables, and the flavoring of meats. There are several uses for its rhizomes (underground stems) and seeds, including as a carminative, in candy and liqueur. Lovage has a flavor that's reminiscent of celery, but it's a little more complex. Perfume and food flavorings are made by extracting their essential oil from the flower heads.

Gardening Preparation

It likes direct sunlight but can tolerate a few hours of shade throughout the day in warmer regions. Well-drained earth with a moderately acidic pH level of approximately 6.5 is ideal. It favors sand or loamy soil.

Uses

Lovage is a flowering plant. Medicinal properties are derived from the plant's subterranean stem (rhizome) and root. There is no solid scientific evidence to support the use of lovage for kidney damage in diabetics (diabetic nephropathy), indigestion, kidney stones, cough, and many other ailments.

M

Marjoram

Mint (Lamiaceae) perennial known as sweet marjoram (Origanum majorana) for its culinary uses. Many dishes may be flavored with fresh or dried leaves and blooming heads, which have a smoky, somewhat sour, and slightly bitter flavor. In northern climes, when winter temperatures kill the plant, marjoram is often grown as an annual. For the most part, marjoram is a bushy herbaceous plant that may grow up to 30–60 centimeters (1–2 feet). Foliage on the square branching stems is heavily coated with ovate tufts of fur. There are a few little clusters of pales, two-lipped blooms that are not very eye-catching. Tetrahydro terpinene and terpineol are the primary constituents of marjoram's 2 percent essential oil.

Gardening Preparation

- After the fear of cold has gone, seed directly into well-drained soil in full sun.
- Weeds and organic materials into the top 6–8 inches of soil, then level and smooth.
- Marjoram seeds should be sown in a uniform layer and covered with fine soil.
- Lightly firm the soil and uniformly moisten it at all times.

Uses

The traditional use of marjoram is the preparation of tea from died leaves for the treatment of runny noses, coughs, and other symptoms of the common cold, as well as a variety of digestive issues. The herb and oil of marjoram are common culinary flavorings.

N

Nutmeg

Tropical evergreen tree Myristica fragrans and spice derived from its seed (which is made up of the dried aril or lacy covering of the nutmeg fruit), has a somewhat spicy flavor and a nutmeg-like aroma. Spices and herbs may be used to flavor bread, meat, and fish meals, as well as sauces and vegetables. Indonesia's Moluccas, or Spice Islands, are the only places where the tree can be found naturally, and it is mostly grown there and in the West Indies. The mace spice comes from the nutmeg seed's fleshy arils. Grated nutmeg has been used as incense and a sachet throughout history. This pricey spice became popular in Europe about 1600, prompting Dutch conspiracies to keep prices high and English and French counterplots to get seeds suitable for transplanting. To avoid sprouting, the nutmegs sold whole were dipped in lime.

Gardening Preparation

Plants in their early stages should be shaded to avoid sunburn. When nutmeg is cultivated as a monoculture on a steep location, it is recommended that permanent shade trees be installed. In coconut gardens that are at least 15 years old and have optimal shade conditions, nutmeg performs best as an intercrop. Removed from its nutmeg, the crimson-colored aril of Nutmeg is flattened dried for 10 to 14 days, at which point it becomes a light yellow or brown. Dried whole Nutmeg is made up of flat, branching, or segmented bits that are brittle, smooth, and horny and measure around 40 mm (1.6 inches) long.

Uses

When used orally, Mace relieves symptoms such as diarrhea, nausea, vomiting, cramps in the stomach, and gas in the intestines. It is often used as a hallucinogen and a treatment for cancer, renal illness, and irregular menstrual cycles.

In kitchen you can use it to spice up your morning cup of coffee, or cauliflower and sweet potatoes. It is excellent if sprinkled over your morning oats or over strawberries slices for a little more flavor. Finally it is traditionally used for mulled wine, eggnog, and cider.

O

Oregano

A fragrant perennial plant of the mint family (Lamiaceae) noted for its flavorful dried leaves, and blooming tops is oregano (Origanum vulgare). Naturalized oregano may be found in Mexico and the United States. A staple of Mediterranean cuisine, the herb is often used to flavor a broad range of dishes. If you live in a moderate environment, you may grow oregano as a little evergreen shrub. This plant has glandular trichomes on the undersides of its oppositely oriented small oval leaves (plant hairs). With time the young square and hairy stems become woody. The blooms are tiny, clustered, and white, pink, or pastel purple in color. Thymol and carvacrol are the primary constituents of essential oil found in all types.

Gardening Preparation

- A light, well-drained soil is ideal for growing oregano.
- In addition to full exposure, the tastes of oregano increase when they are exposed to a full day of sunlight.
- Oregano should be watered sparingly.
- Plant oregano in your garden eight to ten inches apart.

Uses

Chemicals in oregano may alleviate coughing. Oregano has been shown to aid digestion and fight off infections and viruses, so it's worth a try. Oregano is often used to treat wounds, parasitic infections, and a variety of other ailments, but no solid scientific proof backs up these claims.

P

Parsley

Petroselinum crispum, a Mediterranean biennial plant of the Apiaceae or Umbelliferae family, is the scientific name for parsley (Petroselinum crispum). In the first season of development, the compound leaves that are deep green, soft, and curled or frilled are used fresh or dried, and the pleasantly fragrant flavor is a favorite ingredient in fish and meat and soups sauces and salads. It is common for parsley to be the primary component in bouquet garni and finer herbs recipes.

Gardening Preparation

Six weeks before the earliest spring freezing date, grow seeds inside in separate pots for a head start.

As parsley is a late bloomer, start seeds indoors 3 to 4 weeks before the final spring frost date.

Compound umbels of small, greenish-yellow flowers capped with tiny fruits or seeds, like those of a carrot but without spines, climb to approximately 1 meter (3.3 feet) tall in the second season of development. Small and fragile, parsley seedlings struggle to break through hard, crusty soils.

Uses

Parsley is a kind of vegetable. As a garnish, condiment, meal, and seasoning, parsley is frequently used in food and beverage preparation. Parsley seed oil is used in detergents, perfumes, and fragrances as a scent. Medicine is made from the leaf, seed, and root.

Peppermint

Herbaceous perennial mint family member peppermint (Lamiaceae). There is a distinct sweetness to the peppermint aroma, and the flavor is warm and spicy with a tingling aftertaste. Drying the blossoms allows them to be utilized as a flavoring in confections, sweets, drinks, salads, and other dishes. Flavoring is also popular because of its essential oil. Flattened rectangular clusters of pinkish lavender blooms

are found on square stalks, stalked, smooth, dark green leaves, and square stems. Stolons allow the plant to expand rapidly, as they do with other mints (underground stems). Wild peppermints have produced a wide variety of peppermints, but only two types, black and white, are widely grown by farmers. There are several varieties of black peppermint, which is also known as English peppermint or Mitcham mint, that are cultivated in the United States. However, the white type is less robust and less prolific, but its oil is regarded as more delicate in fragrance and is hence more valuable.

Gardening Preparation

- Stem cutting is the next step. Cutting a 5- to 6-inch piece of peppermint from an established plant is the first step in propagating your new plants.
- Peppermint stems should be planted in the ground.
- Peppermint has to be regularly watered.

Uses

Today, peppermint is touted as a remedy for irritable bowel syndrome, other digestive issues, the common cold, sinus infections, headaches, and other ailments. Applied to the skin, peppermint oil has been shown to help alleviate symptoms of headaches, muscular pains, joint pain, and itching, among other ailments.

R

Rosemary

A tiny evergreen plant of the mint family (Lamiaceae), Rosemary (Salvia Rosmarinus), is often used to flavor cuisine with its aromatic leaves. Rosemary is a Mediterranean native that has spread over most of Europe and is a common garden plant in areas with mild winters and hot summers. Whether dried or fresh, the leaves have a pungent, somewhat bitter flavor and are often used to season a variety of dishes and drinks, including meats and vegetables such as lamb and duck, as well as sausages and shellfish. They are also commonly used in stuffing's and stews.

Gardening Preparation

- Put in a place that gets at least six hours of direct sunlight daily.
- Soil that drains effectively is necessary for planting. Rosemary can't stand being wet all the time.
- Give your plants plenty of space to expand.
- Beans, cabbage, carrots, and sage should be planted alongside one other in the garden.

Uses

Since ancient times, the plant has been praised for its therapeutic qualities. To aid with muscular discomfort, cognitive improvement, immunological and circulatory system enhancement, and hair growth promotion, Rosemary has long been utilized in traditional medicine.

Rue

About 40 species of perennial shrubs and plants of the Rutaceae family belong to the genus Ruta, which may be found across Eurasia and the Canary Islands. It is a common garden shrub for its evergreen leaves and clusters of dull-yellow flowers. Traditional remedies and spices have relied on gland-studded, transparent leaves for ages. Most rue species are fragrant and evergreen. There are normally two or three leaflets on the feathery, pinnately complex leaves, and they are usually a gray-green or blue-green color. The many seed capsules produced by the yellow flower clusters are shaped like lobed capsules.

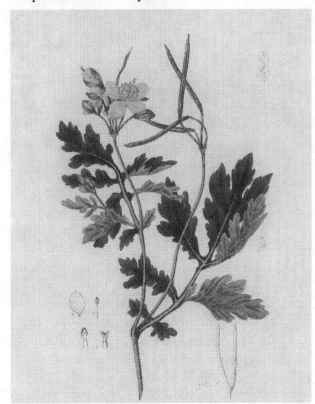

Gardening Preparation

Rue plants benefit from well-drained soil. To aid drainage, amend the soil with sand, perlite, or vermiculite. Or, if you have a lot of hard clay in your yard, you may use raised beds with prepared soil. If the soil is not too poor, rue will thrive. It prefers a neutral soil pH (6.5 to 7.5)

Uses

Because of swelling around the lungs, some patients use rue to alleviate breathing difficulties, such as coughing and discomfort in the chest (pleurisy). In addition to aches and pains, rue is used to treat nervous system disorders such as anxiousness and epilepsy; it is also used to treat arthritis, cramps, and muscular spasms.

S

Saffron

To add flavor and color to food and other items, dried autumn crocus stigmas (pollen-bearing structures) are used as saffron (saffron dye). It has a unique perfume and a sour flavor, making it popular in Mediterranean and Asian cuisines, as well as in bread from England, Scandinavian, and the Balkans. Bouillabaisse soup relies heavily on this ingredient.

Gardening Preparation

- Saffron may be grown in milk cartons.
- Choose a soil that drains properly because this plant needs to a fair amount of water but it dies if roots are too wet
- Plant Your saffron bulbs.

- Saffron plants need fertilizer.

Uses

Saffron is often used to stimulate the digestion. In traditional Chinese medicine is also used to treat menstrual problems such as amenorrhea and menorrhagia.

Sage

Aromatic plant of the mint family (Lamiaceae) grown for its aromatic edible leaves, sage (Salvia officinalis) is also known as garden sage. As a flavoring in various meals, notably in chicken and pig stuffing's and sausages, sage is a native of the Mediterranean area. Ornamental leaves and flowers are another reason for growing certain types. The term "sage" is also used to describe a number of other Salvia species.

Gardening Preparation

- Choose a sunny spot in your garden or apartment.
- In order for a sage to thrive, it must be planted in well-draining soil.
- Before the final frost date, you may also plant seeds.
- The ideal soil temperature is between 60 and 70F.

Uses

Sage is often used to treat memory loss, high cholesterol, and menopausal symptoms of women. Pain after surgery, sore throat, sunburn, and a host of other ailments are all treated with it.

Conclusions

It has been known since the ancient era that plants might be utilized for medical reasons. The usage of plants was documented in ancient Unani texts, Egyptian papyrus, and Chinese literature. Herbs have been used medicinally by Unani Hakims, Indian Vadis, Europeans, and Mediterranean's for about 4000 years. Other traditional medical systems, including Unani, Ayurveda, and Chinese Medicine, make extensive use of herbal remedies as part of their treatment regimens. Indigenous civilizations in the Americas have employed herbs for centuries.

Many traditional medical practices are still in use today. Plant materials have become increasingly important as a source of medicines for a wide range of human ailments due to a rise in population, a lack of drugs, the prohibitive cost of treatments, the side effects of several synthetic drugs, and the development of resistance to currently used drugs for infectious diseases. When it comes to medicinal herbs from ancient civilizations, India has been well recognized. Medicinal and aromatic plants found in India's forests are mostly harvested as raw materials for the production of pharmaceuticals and perfumery goods. Because therapeutic plants have no or minor adverse effects, they are considered harmless. The major benefit of these treatments is that they work in harmony with nature. The fact that herbal remedies may be used by both men and women of any age or gender is a major plus. Herbs were solely seen as a means to treat a variety of health issues and ailments by ancient academics. They studied and experimented extensively in order to come to precise findings regarding the use of various therapeutic plants. There is little, if any, adverse effects or responses to most of the medications that have been prepared this way. This is why herbal medicine is becoming more popular across the world. Many interior disorders, which are ordinarily difficult to treat, may be alleviated by the use of medicinal plants. In the age of globalization and the so-called "plate world," clinical research should not focus on testing therapies' "transferability" across cultures but rather on evaluating their effectiveness and safety in accordance with the standard practices of mainstream clinical care. Additionally, herbal-based therapies are plagued by a lack of precise and thorough information regarding the composition of extracts. New biologic technologies like pharmacogenomic, metabolomic, and microarray methodology can provide a robust and thorough evaluation of the pharmacological properties and safety of herbal-derived treatments. Explanatory and pragmatic studies are helpful and should be considered complementary in order to provide trustworthy data for both health care providers and patients because of the widespread and expanding usage of naturally derived chemicals across the globe.

I sincerely hope that this book will be just the beginning of your journey and that you will increase your knowledge on Native American medicine for a healthier and better way to treat the common disease without relying on industrial drugs and medication.

Just scan the QR code on the right, it will take 30 seconds!

My best wishes and may the Spirit guide your journey!

Native American Traditional Medicine

50 Wildflowers Profile and Gardening & Composting Techniques

BOOK 10 of "The Native American Herbalist's Bible"

Natalie Hathale

Introduction

An Overview

English gentlewomen Vita Sackville-West, was the first to explore the topic of gardening as an art form in the 19th century. She made her servants meticulously keep flowerbeds and started growing "flowering occurrences" in her woodlands and meadows, the most renowned English garden writer of the period. She was a passionate researcher and discoverer of wildflowers. The ones she discovered "in situ" were either encouraged with fertilizers or proper irrigation, or even completely planted following the properties of the landscape, taking inspiration on the a natural, native way of them growing. Wildflowers, as we all know, are crucial, and their popularity has increased in recent years, which is great news considering that we lost almost 90% of our wildflower meadows between the 1920s and the 1970s.

Our local ecosystem requires wildflower meadows of all shapes and sizes, and we need to keep developing them in whatever way we can to meet those demands. Some native wildflowers include compounds useful in medicine, such as heal-all, which has antibacterial effects and chemicals in foxgloves that cure heart disease. This is a substantial contribution from native wildflowers to contemporary medicine. In addition to these two instances, there are a plethora of more out there just waiting to be discovered. Wildflowers play a major role in pollination by providing nectar and pollen for bees, butterflies, and other pollinators throughout the year. Many of our favorite fruits and vegetables depend on pollination in order to generate a decent harvest. Without pollinators that rely on wildflowers, we would have to use expensive and time-consuming artificial pollination. When it comes to protecting crops and plants from pests, pollinators come in handy. Farmers would be forced to use pesticides much more if pollinators weren't there to do the fighting, which would have unintended repercussions for everyone. Finally, wildflowers beautify the landscape and evoke good memories of childhood, while others, like poppies, serve as a poignant memorial to the warriors who gave their lives in the line of duty.

Native Wildflowers

Early English gardeners understood that wildflowers were among the most beautiful and lovely of all flowers, and this passion for wildflowers is a direct descendant of these early English gardeners. Any blooming plant that has not been genetically modified is referred to be a wildflower. When it comes to plants that develop without human intervention, the phrase often refers to spring and summer-flowering plants in forests, grassland, and mountains.

All cultivated garden flower types have their ancestry in wildflowers. However, a few species of wildflowers are descended from blooming plants that were originally imported to the area where they grow. For example, most of the brightly colored flowers seen in the Hawaiian Islands originate in other regions of the tropics and subtropics. As a result of its quick proliferation throughout fertile lowlands and mountainsides, the indigenous flora was left with just the steep mountainsides as a habitat. The majority of wildflowers found in the lowlands of the United States and Europe are native species, with a few exceptions. As far back as the Paleolithic period, people have been causing havoc on the local vegetation. For example, wildfires that have escaped human control are assumed to have destroyed native flora and created room for aggressive species from the same or other regions. Ranunculus acris, one of northern Europe's most well-known buttercups, presumably grew in abundance and spread over the region when the woods were cleared. In northern Europe's lowlands, this species presumably evolved into new forms during the Stone Age that was better suited to ecosystems produced by human activity. After being introduced to eastern North America in the early nineteenth century, two northern U.S. and Canadian strains gradually expanded throughout the continent, with one strain only becoming popular in Washington state in the early twentieth century.

Wildflowers and the Mother Nature

Wildflower meadows are characterized by stable soil due to the intricate root systems generated by wildflowers, which also offer therapeutic benefits. They allow soil to tolerate heavy rains without losing nutrients and being carried away to the closest water system. The leaves, pollen, nectar, shelter, and breeding grounds provided by wildflowers feed pollinators and insects. As a thank you, pollinators help the wildflowers bypass pollen, allowing them to grow seeds that will create many more blooms. Even in the dead of winter, the benefits of wildflowers cannot be overstated. Wildflower seeds are an essential source of food for birds and small animals because of the lack of food in the countryside.

Non-Native Wildflowers

It has taken centuries for indigenous wildflowers and fauna to evolve together, resulting in an array of flower types that attract a variety of pollinators. Insects that are fussy about where they receive their food and need certain local wildflowers to thrive are well-served by the blossoming seasons. Because non-native plants compete for resources like space, insect pollination, and water with native wildflowers, they may represent a threat to native wildflowers. When native and non-native wildflower species crossbreed, the adaptations that the natives have made over hundreds of years may be disrupted. This diminishes the value of native wildflowers. The hybrid bluebells that resulted from the introduction of the Spanish bluebell are a well-known example of this phenomenon, and it is currently difficult to identify regions where only native bluebells thrive. Wildflowers that are not native to the area may take over and soon establish self-sustaining populations because of their ability to dominate their surroundings. Local wildflower populations may be threatened as a result of the spread of non-native species.

50 Native Wild Flowers

Colorful autumn leaves are frequently the focus when we talk about fall color. During the spring and summer, flowers are expected to bloom. As a matter of fact, many plants, including wildflowers and varieties of garden favorites, display their most beautiful colors in October. Traditional garden plants like roses and Sweet William may be found alongside low-maintenance natural wildflowers. These flowers, as well as others that have become recognized, such as the Rose of Sharon, are indigenous to the United States and are in bloom around this time of year. Invasive plants should be planted with caution, as some of the latter are. Native animals and pollinators benefit from the presence of many of these plants that attract birds like hummingbirds as well as other pollinators like bees. The fact that they are unpalatable to deer and rabbits means that they are resistant to the troubles that animals may cause for gardeners.

Plants have always been deemed "useful" by humans from the dawn of time. Plants, of course, may be used for food, but they have also been used extensively as remedies in all civilizations. Prehistoric rituals through contemporary medicine have proven that plants may be used to treat various ailments. There have been several endeavors to identify the medical properties of plants throughout the ages by different civilizations with a process of trial and error. Some experiments have gone awry, sometimes fatally, while others have been successful. Others seemed to have some kind of supernatural power. The plants have never lost their fascination, from the beginning of the human history to today's refined practice of medicine. In fact, there is a resurgence of interest in herbal medicines right now. And the history of medicinal plants on our continent is unparalleled anywhere else on the globe. Native American Indians were experts in the medical use of plants long before the arrival of Europeans. Many of their old remedies have been proven by contemporary medicine. Native American Shamans may look strange and wacky to us, yet their medicinal prescriptions were often right. According to a contemporary specialist, more than half of all medical uses for North American plants have been predicted by the medical practitioners of the indigenous American Indian tribes.

Below are only a handful of the wildflowers that a man has utilized from the beginning of time to treat and cure his ailments and maladies. It's meant to be a source of knowledge, not a guide on what you should do. When handled incorrectly, many of the same plants that are used as medicinally may also be toxic

1. J Azure monkshood

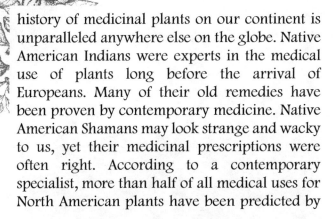

Because of how it grows and how its flowers mimic medieval monks' headgear, this late-flowering monkshood has the same name as its cousins. Even while pests and diseases seldom bother it, there is one thing to watch out for: the plant is toxic in all parts. Use gloves and cover any cuts or scrape before dealing with it, and stay away from locations where children or dogs are likely to be because it is highly poisoning.

2. Japanese anemone

In Japan, this kind of buttercup was grown for so long that it became naturalized and was mistaken for an indigenous species. Moisture but well-drained soil with no standing water is ideal for this plant. It takes a lot of time to spread in certain areas, but once it does, it forms colonies.

3. Tatarian aster

If you're looking for a long-lasting purple aster, go no further than this tall, late-blooming variety. The Jindai Botanical Garden in suburban Tokyo is where the "Jindal" variety was originally found. The best-looking asters need summer trimming, but this one doesn't require it if it's grown in full light.

4. Butterfly bush (B. 'Lochinch')

To attract pollinators like butterflies, the butterfly shrub is named after it. The lilac-blue blooms of this hybrid cultivar produce excellent cut flowers. Because of this, it should only be planted in USDA zones 6 through 9, where the climate is mild enough for it to survive the winter.

5. Butterfly bush (B. weyeriana)

A species of butterfly bush with orange-eyed blossoms is really a magnet for butterflies. As another type that cannot withstand hard winters, only USDA zones 6 to 9 are suggested for this variety. However, in the colder regions of its habitat, it may die back to the ground, but that's just fine as late-winter pruning enhances its appeal.

6. Bluebeard

The shrub's fragrant dark blue blooms attract a wide variety of pollinators, including bees and butterflies. Because it blossoms on new growth, planting it in groups or as a low hedge is very beautiful. It also benefits from rigorous pruning, which may be done in the early spring.

7. White turtlehead

This wildflower may be found across the eastern half of the United States. If you want to grow it in a forest or bog garden or beside a stream, you'll need a damp setting with rich soil. The white blossoms resemble a turtle's head, which inspired the name.

8. Golden aster

It thrives in a wide range of open, sunny locations, including meadows and roadside areas, where sandy soil is prevalent. Once planted, it requires well-drained soil, can handle some shade and can endure drought.

9. Golden Cross clematis

Typically, clematis vines are trained to climb a trellis, Arbor, or fence in the garden. It does best when the roots are kept moist and protected, even if the vines themselves are in direct sunlight. Because this cultivar blooms exclusively on fresh growth, it should be cut to the ground in autumn or spring.

10. Rooguchi clematis

It has rich purple blooms that attract hummingbirds and is excellent in the garden since it is resistant to deer and rabbits. Because it can't cling to objects like the real vining kinds, this hybrid between a vining and shrublike variety was developed in Japan and must be tethered to its support.

11. Autumn Crocus

If you want to make the most of your garden's forest or meadow surroundings, this plant is an excellent choice. However, you should keep in mind that its yellowing leaf will be ugly when it falls dormant in the spring.

12. Pink Tenore crocus

This fall crocus has petals ranging in color from light violet to rosy pink. It is resistant to rabbits and deer and maybe planted in areas of the garden where summer plants are beginning to fade so that it can continue to bloom.

13. Fringe-leaf tickseed

Federal and state governments have designated this yellow-flowered perennial as endangered, making it a threatened species. Even yet, it may be grown in the garden and can withstand temperatures as low as zone 5, despite its Southern roots. The seed resembles a tick, which is why it has the unappealing popular name.

14. Sweet William

Sweet William, which originated from Europe, has long been a favorited flower in the garden. Pink, red, and white or multi-colored mixes of those colors are available, and some have a

clove-like fragrance. Although it's a short-lived perennial, it will self-seed in your garden.

15. Echinacea

The Greek word for "hedgehog" inspired the scientific name "echinacea," which refers to the flower's spiny central cone. It blooms until the first frost, is deer resistant, and is tolerant of clay soil.

16. Lindheimer beeblossom

When grown in masses rather than as a specimen, this native of Texas, Oklahoma, and Louisiana look better than if it is allowed to

naturalize and spread in a wildflower garden. It can handle humidity, heat, and mild drought in its native habitat.

17. Cranesbill

Numerous cultivars have been developed from among the approximately 300 species of geranium that exist. According to folklore, the fruit's name derives from its form, which is thought to resemble a crane's head and beak. As a ground cover or in containers, this type is ideal.

18. Gymnaster

Low-maintenance Eastern Asian native gymnaster, sometimes called as naked aster, blooms with light blue or white flowers. Tolerant of both sun and partial shade and

unfazed by dirt, this plant is a great addition to any garden.

19. American witch-hazel

In the dead of winter, when nearly nothing else is in bloom, this Eastern North American shrub blooms with sweet-smelling flowers. Acidic, humusy conditions are preferable, yet it may grow in partial shade and clay soil. Birds flock to it, and it's resistant to deer. There are minimal disease or pest concerns.

20. Sneezeweed

This yellow-flowered perennial is indigenous to the United States and Canada's Lower 48. In its natural environment, beside streams, ponds, and moist open meadows, it likes full sun and damp soil. Flowers were previously dried and used as snuff, which is why it is known as a snuff plant.

21. Virginia sneezeweed

Only two states of the USA have this particular sneezeweed variety: Virginia and Missouri. In both Virginia and the federal government, it is categorized as endangered. In Missouri, where a population's identity as the same species as the one in Virginia was first confirmed by DNA testing in 2001, it's categorized as threatened.

22. Purple-headed sneezeweed

East and the central United States are the natural habitats of this species of sneezeweed. In reality, the petals of this plant are yellow, but the distinctive purple-brown cone is what gives it its popular name. In order to thrive, it needs wet, rich soil that is not too fertilized.

23. Willow-leaved sunflower

The South-Central United States is home to this perennial wildflower. Although it thrives in full sun, in the garden, it can endure a wide range of soil types, including thick clay. While deer aren't a fan of it, birds and butterflies are drawn to it.

24. Rosinweed sunflower

The term of this species is obtained from the similarity of its blooms to those of the sunflower; however, the two plants are unrelated. In contrast to being a beautiful cut flower, this plant is a magnet for birds and butterflies. Adaptable to a wide variety of soils and deer populations, it may self-seed in the garden.

25. North American ox~eye

Heliopsis, the scientific name for the ox-eye daisy, refers to the flower's resemblance to the sun. Tolerates poor soil and a lengthy flowering season that lasts till the first frost. This is a clumping, compact cultivar.

26. Hairy-fruited hibiscus

Known as the rose mallow, this plant is widely found in forests and near waterways in the southern United States. As long as it's kept wet, it can withstand the summer heat. The bloom looks like a hollyhock, and it may grow up to six feet tall.

27. Rose of Sharon

The Rose of Sharon, despite its name, is really a native of Asia. Summer humidity and heat are no match for this tall, upright shrub, which has blooms akin to hollyhocks. Invasive in certain regions of the United States, it is a hardy self-seedier that thrives in urban environments.

28. 'David Ramsey' Hydrangea Macrophylla

Relying on the soil pH, hydrangea blossoms may vary from blue to pink in color, with the former being more common. This doesn't apply to the white-flowered types. The northern section of its area needs shelter from the cold, even though this type is more winter-hardy.

29. Butterfly stonecrop

Some sections of the United States have been naturalized with this succulent, which is native to China and Korea. This plant's common name, stonecrop, comes from its natural habitat, which is rocky. Well-drained and dry soil is essential for its survival.

30. Chickasaw crape myrtle

The crape myrtle is a high, deciduous tree that thrives in full bloom over the summer and into the fall. As a shrub, it may be cultivated in the warmer regions of its distribution, but in colder regions, it may die back to the ground. The National Arboretum in Washington D.C. has produced a tiny, mildew-resistant variant.

31. English lavender

Perennial borders and low hedges may also benefit from lavender, which is often cultivated in herb gardens. Dried sachets or potpourri may be made from aromatic blossoms. Humidity and harsh winter cold aren't tolerated by the plant. Full light and well-drained soil are essential.

32. Chinese lobelia

Low-growing and spreading, this perennial ground cover is a favorite of hummingbirds and butterflies in Asian wetland habitats. It loves the afternoon sun and continuous moisture. It can be invasive and has spread over the mid-Atlantic region after escaping cultivation.

33. Japanese honeysuckle

Ever since importation to the U. S. in 1805, this robust semi-evergreen vine from Asia has been extensively planted, and it is now considered invasive. It is tolerant of drought and does not need a lot of water. Birds and butterflies are attracted to the aromatic blossoms, which are also resistant to deer.

34. Grossheim catmint

Catmint from the Republic of Georgia, a very unusual kind. Cut back after flowering to promote reblooming. It appreciates well-drained soil. As long as the circumstances are right, this cultivar may self-seed.

35. Hardy water lily

The blossoms of this easy-to-grow water lily open yellow and develop a coppery-bronze tint. Water lilies that are resilient in the winter bloom throughout the day, and their blooms float to the surface. Every flower has a five-day life cycle, opening in the morning and closing at night.

36. Tropical water lily

This tropical water lily features fragrant, deep blue flowers with golden centres that are both beautiful and fragrant. Planting these lilies in the spring is only possible if the water temperature is at least 76 degrees Fahrenheit. Although the tubers may be preserved in sand or distilled water in a cool basement, tropical water lilies are commonly handled as annuals in cold climes.

37. Russian sage

An evergreen perennial with delicate greyish-green foliage and delicate blueish-lavender blooms in the mint family, Russian Sage is a great addition to any garden. Good drainage and full light are essential for this plant to thrive. Withstanding bad soil and pollution, it is also resistant to rabbits.

38. Garden phlox

New York to Arkansas, the Garden Phlox is a native of the United States that is now found in other regions of the nation. Hummingbirds and butterflies love it since it's resistant to deer and likes rich, wet soil. Keep the leaves dry while watering to prevent powdery mildew from forming.

39. Country Dancer Rose

If you're looking for a shrub, rose those blooms until the first frost, "County Dancer" is the one for you. Although shrub roses don't need as much trimming as other varieties, all roses are

vulnerable to a variety of diseases and pests, including black spots, rust, and powdery mildew.

40. Dolly Parton Hybrid tea rose

When it comes to floristry, the hybrid tea rose is the go-to. Orange-red blooms of this cultivar bloom in May and continue to do so in flushes until frost. It is susceptible to a wide range of diseases and pests, much like other hybrid teas.

41. Nevada hybrid moyesii rose

White blooms with yellow stamens on red stalks lure butterflies to this shrub rose. It does best in full light and requires thorough watering on a regular basis to maintain the leaves free of disease. Keep the roots cool in the summer and protect the crowns in colder climates by mulching the soil around them.

42. Orange coneflower

Native to the South-eastern United States, the orange coneflower has a bright orange color. A well-established plant can withstand some drying out but likes full sun and constant watering. It is also tolerant to poor soil and dirty

air once established. Butterflies love the blossoms, which are also ideal for making bouquets.

43. Brown-eyed Susan

This biennial or short-lived perennial native to the eastern and central United States naturally naturalizes in the garden by self-seeding. Summer heat and drought aren't a problem for it, and it's not too picky about soil. Powdery mildew, snails, and slugs are all potential threats to young plants.

44. Pineapple sage

It's native to Mexico and Guatemala, and it's known as pineapple sage. The leaves' pineapple-like scent inspired the name. The plant, which attracts hummingbirds and butterflies and is resistant to deer, needs well-drained soil and can only be cultivated as an annual or put inside for the winter in zones 8 through 10.

45. Blue sage

Prefer full sun and adequate drainage and can handle dry soil, shallow soil, or rocky soil. This low-maintenance perennial comes from the southern United States. There are no insects or disease problems, and it attracts butterflies.

46. Pincushion flower

The dense clusters of this long-blooming variant of the pincushion flower reach 14 to 16 inches

in height. In warm climes, it is drought resilient and may tolerate light shade. Powdery mildew, aphids, and whiteflies are all things to look out for in the garden.

47. Hopewell stonecrop

Deep pink blooms and ruffled blue-grey leaves characterize this sedum, which is 16 inches tall and grows in a mound. This is a low-maintenance plant that can withstand poor soil, dryness, and foul air; attracts butterflies; is undesirable to deer. Good drainage is vital.

48. Canadian goldenrod

Native to much of North America, this sunflower cousin may be found in fields and along roadsides. Full light is ideal for this plant, which attracts pollinators. Rhizomes and self-seeding are two ways it spreads aggressively in the garden.

49. Japanese spirea

A blooming shrub from the rose family, Spirea may be invasive in the eastern United States because it spreads through suckers and self-seeding. Because of its toughness and resistance to deer, it grows well in a variety of soil types. Butterflies are attracted to the pink blossoms of this species.

50. Toad lily

For all those who reside in areas with high levels of shadow, the toad lily is an excellent choice. Weeping habits and nodding blooms make it common to see it pouring from rock formations in its natural environment. An acidic, well-drained soil that is not let to dry up is ideal for it.

Advantages and Disadvantages of Wild Flowers

If you're a fan of gardening or nature in general, there are plenty of wildflower experts out there. Wildflowers aren't a new phenomenon in the garden; they're both lovely and functional. Wildflowers seem to be an easy thing when it comes to seeding a garden or planting a vast open field because of their vibrant colors, rustic appearance, and minimal care requirements. If done incorrectly, planting wildflowers might have catastrophic repercussions.

Advantages

In general, a wildflower plant may be described as any blooming herbaceous or woody species with ornamental purpose that grows naturally in one's natural habitats (which means it is indigenous to the region).

- Low-maintenance and easy to care for. Wildflowers are easy to grow in the garden since they are usually native to the area. Little attention is required since they've already adjusted to their new surroundings. Planting wildflowers is a good idea if you're a busy part-time (or even a little lazy) gardener.
- Beneficial insects are drawn to the area because of its scent. Wildflowers attract pollinators, such as bees, to the region. In any case, to guarantee a good crop of fruits and vegetables, it is essential to grow wildflowers in your garden, even amid your foodstuffs. In addition, the beneficial insects attracted by these natural plants may help ward against pests that otherwise could eat on your crops.
- Wildlife's main source of nutrition. Many sorts of birds and other creatures depend on wildflower plants for food or shelter. But

there's more. Many of them are also used by us, the human race. Wildflowers have a wide range of uses, from food and fiber to oil, colors, and more.

- Their medicinal and botanical properties make them useful. Wildflower plants are the source of over 80% of all pharmaceuticals and herbal goods. The majority of them have been in use for millennia. Consider Echinacea (coneflowers) or chamomile as examples. Historically and now, they have both been used for their phytochemical properties and are particularly well-liked as teas.

- Beautiful wildflowers abound. One of the biggest reasons to include these plants in your yard is because they're simply so beautiful. Even on your own land, wildflowers may help solve issues and improve ugly places.

- Environmentally friendly. Cleaner air is made possible by the carbon dioxide that plants absorb and the oxygen that they create.

Disadvantages

- As a low-maintenance addition to the ecosystem, the correct wildflowers may be a good source of nutrition for bees as well as a habitat for local bugs, insects and other animals. Some wildflowers are more suited to your garden than others, and it's important to know which ones to avoid. You might introduce foreign or even infesting species to your region if you grow the incorrect wildflowers.

- Planting wildflowers has negative environmental consequences. The most evident disadvantage of wildflower planting is the introduction of non-native plants by mistake. The attraction of wildflowers is that they are designed to blend in with their surroundings, needing little care and supplying a plethora of nectar for the local pollinators. Discovering the native wildflowers in your region, on the other hand, requires some investigation. Irrespective of whether or not you sow the correct seeds, you will introduce plants that are not suitable for your climate. Your local pollinators may be unable to pollinate certain plants, which might mean they will fail to grow. If they succeed, it will be at the price of other local species, and they will take over and spread across the fragile environment.

- Why not to use seed mixes to grow wildflowers. For the most part, seeds are offered in wildflower mixes, frequently with a common theme (the most famous being "Pollinator Friendly" or "Shade Loving"). For example there will be no danger if you reside in California and you plant a package of seeds containing California poppies. There is, nevertheless, the potential for an invasive plant in the Southeast United States. You may be growing invasive plants without even knowing since many seed mixes fail to accurately describe their components.

Making a wildflower meadow

The benefits of creating a wildflower meadow in your yard include attracting animals, being visually appealing, and not necessitating a lot of room. Creating a habitat for birds, bees, butterflies, and other animals in your garden may be a rewarding experience. Due to the constant climate changes many wildflower meadows in the world have been lost, and although gardens cannot replace the old meadows in the wild, developing your own will bring a wide variety of animals to your garden and help remember us how vital it is to preserve what is left. A wildflower meadow in your yard may be achieved by following these guidelines:

Area to plant Wildflowers

How to grow your meadow is determined by the location you've selected:

Weed-infested grass in the typical yard: The simplest approach to avoid mowing your lawn is to just "say no to the mow." You'd be surprised at what can sprout up in an old, weedy space. If you'd want to add additional flowers to your garden, you may either buy plug plants in the fall or grow your own from seed, depending on your soil type and conditions.

Well-kept lawns: If your lawn is well-kept and weed-free, you could be better off beginning from scratch than using a newly-planted grass. It is possible to lower fertility by mowing it frequently and removing the cuttings for many years. After a few years of waiting, you should begin to see some wildflowers. Sowing seed in tiny bare areas or plug plants might speed things up.

An unattractive lawn or patch of dirt: Start from the beginning. If you have a big yard, you may want to start by removing the top few inches of rich topsoil in late summer, maybe utilizing it to build raised vegetable beds. Despite the difficulty, this is necessary since wildflowers need poor soil to flourish. Sow a variety of flowers suited for your soil after raking the area. Sourcing native plants for your seed is best, but you may also contact your local Wildlife Trust to check if they are collecting seed on their own reserves. You should always read the contents of the seed package before purchasing wildflower seed since many mixes include annuals from cornfields such as poppies, cornflowers, and corn marigolds. Not meadow flowers, but they'll look great for the first year and then fade away in the following years.

The Yellow Rattle, a beautiful meadow flower with a little ominous attitude, needs a particular note. It steals nutrients from grasses and stunts their development via its roots. As a result of the diminished grass growth, numerous other meadow flowers are able to flourish. We nicknamed it "the meadow creator" because of how well it accomplishes its job. By spreading new seeds from a local source in the fall, you may bring Yellow Rattle into your meadow.

Sunlight and soil

Be sure to evaluate the amount of light and kind of soil you have available before you begin your wildflower meadow project.

All meadow plants prefer open, bright areas. Avoid areas beneath trees since they will be too gloomy and dry for your event. It is useful for other creatures to have small natural trees and bushes (such as hawthorn, blackthorn, and gorse) or fruit trees interspersed around the meadow, although this might make mowing more difficult. The kind of soil in your yard significantly impacts the types of flowers that may be grown there. Wet soils are alright but stay away from submerged locations to the point of drowning.

Mowing

It's really essential to mow your meadow after you've established a few patches of grass and flowers. The meadow is left alone until the first grass cutting in late summer, which might occur between the end of July and the middle of September. As a result of this, wildflowers have an opportunity to reproduce. Plants like knapweed and orchids are more likely to increase if they are cut later in the year, but early cuttings may assist reduce more competitive species. The wildflowers will behave differently if you trim various regions at different times. While it's important to get rid of the grass as much as possible, you should also leave a few patches uncut to provide safe havens for beneficial insects. It's critical to remove all of the grass clippings after mowing in order to maintain the soil's fertility. Wildflower seed may be spread by strewing the cut grass on other sections of the lawn; avoid placing clippings in the compost bin unless you want them all over the yard! At least three more times before Christmas, rake up all of the cuttings from the meadow. After that, let the meadow to its own devices and take in the springtime floral extravaganza till summer rolls around. Many meadow flowers are able to adapt to this yearly cycle of hay-cutting and grazing, which mirrors the ancient pattern.

How to build an environment-friendly garden?

The foundation of a flourishing garden is a healthy layer of dirt. Instead of synthetic fertilizers, eco-friendly gardens use compost and mulch to provide organic matter to the soil and all-natural fertilizers as necessary to support plant development. Isn't it logical that all gardens should be eco-friendly and organic since they produce plants? Things would be much easier if only they were. A garden that is kind to the environment:

- Utilizes the climate and soil of the area.
- Chemical fertilizers aren't used here.
- Reduces the use of herbicides, fungicides, and insecticides.
- Native plants are encouraged.
- The amount of additional water needed is kept to a minimum.

This means that a luxuriant rose garden in the desert is not an environmentally friendly garden. There is, however, no reason why a rose garden in Rose, Georgia, should not be environmentally responsible. Achieving the ideal equilibrium is key. Choosing the correct plants and practicing proper horticulture are the keys to environmentally responsible gardening. Having an eco-friendly garden doesn't need an organic one. And it doesn't have to break the bank. Many of the components needed for an environmentally friendly garden may be found in your own home. More and more gardeners realize the value of creating landscapes that not only look good but also serve as refuges for animals and aid in the fight against global warming. It doesn't make any difference whether you have a little front or back yard; everyone can contribute to making it a sustainable garden that is full of life. Sustainable gardening also saves money since it makes use of repurposed materials and doesn't need as much upkeep. Make an eco-friendly garden that's both sustainable and filled with wildlife by following some of these basic tips. It's important to put nature first in your gardening activities if you want to become green.

We've created a list of the easiest and most effective ways to make your backyard a little greener.

Soil Health

Your garden's soil is home to billions of bacteria and other microorganisms, and these organisms need somewhere to dwell. Many wildlife garden ideas include enhancing the quality of the soil. ' If you disrupt the surface of the soil, it releases carbon into the atmosphere, which is a major source of pollution. Only dig when you need to plant. This will help you prevent it. Apply a dense layer of manure or leaves cover to the soil, which worms and other critters will consume and incorporate into the soil. Soil structure and nutrient delivery will be improved as a result. Peat-free compost is good for the environment since the bogs from which it's produced are carbon sinks and home to a wide variety of rare and endangered organisms.

Select Native Plants

Use native plants in your flower beds to attract beneficial insects and other animals. If you choose the right plants for the location, they will also need less watering and food. Ecologically and monetarily, it makes sense to use native plants in a naturalistic planting scheme since you won't have to replace plants that don't function. Creating even a tiny wildflower patch with native plants can benefit a wide range of species because of the positive influence it will have on the ecosystem.

Grow the lawn

Gardeners who want to create a long-term, self-sustaining space should avoid keeping their lawns immaculate and instead allow them to develop naturally. Eco-friendly gardens may eventually replace neatly mowed lawns as a consequence of water scarcity and extended drought spells brought on by climate change. A lawn should be allowed to fall into disrepair, and you'll be amazed at the variety of natural plants that spring up in its place. Mow the grass in the late summer and remove the cuttings after the stalks have lost their seeds. As part of our autumn lawn beautification, we also plant early spring bulbs like daffodils, crocuses, species tulip, and fritillaries. If you must mow the lawn, consider switching to an electric mower to reduce your carbon impact. Alternatively, you may let the grass grow. Grass and spring flowers will flourish and provide food for pollinators if you only cut from June to September.

Permaculture Gardening can help Eco-Credits

Maintaining your outdoor patch should become a daily ritual if you follow the principles of permaculture gardening. If you want a minimal lawn, this is the ideal method, and you may already be doing much of it. It is possible to create a sustainable garden by using food scraps as compost, composting dead plants, using companion planting and natural deterrents in place of harmful synthetic fertilizers, and avoiding the use of one-off plastic items like plastic pots in favor of reusable containers and biodegradable plant markers.

Dry Gardening saves water

Whether you're revising a border or remodeling a whole garden, creating a dry garden is an excellent eco-friendly option. A wide variety of plants, from aromatic herbs to olive trees, thrive in dry, sunny areas, such as those you'd find in a Mediterranean garden. Additionally, they're a

wonderful option for a sloping garden because of their ability to better handle water runoff.

Pollinators love nectar rich flowers

With a concentration on flowers rich in pollen and nectar, such as blooms that attract bees, increasing biodiversity in your garden may be achieved. Bees, butterflies, and moths, all of which are essential to the ecosystem, will also benefit from this. There are several methods to aid your sustainable garden in attracting butterflies, one of which is by planting some of the flowers they like. For both the health of your garden and the well-being of our bees, you should establish a wide variety of flowers and plants.

Natural Pest Control

Instead of relying on toxic pesticides, adopt organic techniques to produce food in your garden instead. Rather than relying on chemicals, a sustainable garden uses natural pest management, companion planting, and sustainable fertilizer, such as created compost and mulch, to achieve its goals.

Save rainwater

Get a water butt or a big container to collect rainwater from your downpipes and utilize it in your sustainable garden. By reusing the water collected, you can water your plants while also providing your shrubbery with the cool drink it craves after a hot day. Use an old watering can instead of the hose and sprinklers to save water.

Feed the birds

With Monty Don's advice, you may feed birds in your yard to attract more of them to your property. A bird feeder may be hung from a tree or scattered on the grass, but why not go one

step further and build one yourself? It is reasonable to implement a bird feeder at home using recycled items like plastic bottles and glass jars, as well as waste wood. With that, you may as well get creative in the kitchen and whip up a batch of yummy bird snacks to hang in your yard. Also, remember to provide birds with berries from evergreen bushes like holly, cotoneaster, and the guelder rose, Viburnum opelus, to keep them fed throughout the autumn and winter.

Grow Vegetables

It's enjoyable and simple to cultivate your own veggies and fruits to reduce food miles. To start a tiny vegetable garden, all you need is a sunny location with a little space. It's possible to find edible plants that are just as beautiful as their decorative cousins. When it comes to vegetable garden container ideas, try simple crops like Pak choi and cabbage, or plant perennial spinach and chard, as well as squash and runner beans in the ground. You may further reduce your food miles by purchasing seeds from firms that gather seeds from organically farmed crops. Making a plan for a kitchen garden is not only enjoyable but will help reduce your carbon footprint and packaging waste. Nutrient-dense, pesticide-free veggies are easier to get by when cultivated at home.

More trees should be placed

Planting additional trees should surely be on your list of sustainable garden goals. Trees are good for the environment and are beautiful additions to your landscape. Depending on whether you're landscaping your front or backyard, you'll want to use a combination of different species. Trees may give a variety of colors and interests throughout the year, even if you just have a tiny backyard, so long as you pick trees with fall color or evergreens. Carbon dioxide is captured by trees and released into the atmosphere, making them an asset to the ecosystem. Additionally, the trunks, branches, and leaves of living trees act as carbon sinks, keeping carbon from escaping into the atmosphere. Consider these factors when selecting a tree for your yard, even if any tree is a wonderful option. Large, long-lived trees give the most advantages to the world. Some of my personal favorites for a medium-sized garden, all of which have good eco-impact ratings, are the beautiful Acer platinoids' "Princeton Gold," with its early yellow leaves that turn green in summer; the gleaming white-stemmed Himalayan birch, Betula utilis jacquemonti; the disease-resistant Malus 'Rudolph,' with its bright pink blossoms and pretty fall fruits; and the ornamental pear Pyrus caleryana. You should know how to plant bare-root trees and evergreens in order to guarantee that your trees survive.

Use plants to filter pollution

Small pollutants released by vehicles may raise the risk of illnesses like cancer, yet certain plants can help protect humans from these detrimental effects. Shrubs with hairy, scaly, waxy, or rough leaves, according to Royal Horticultural Society research, are great for gardens near busy highways because they trap pollutants. It was determined that the evergreen plant Cotoneaster francheti, along with yew, holly, hornbeam, and hawthorn, was the best at repelling deer. This grade indicates to consumers how much pollution filtering, carbon sequestration, and carbon storage each of our trees will accomplish during their lifetimes. The stag's horn sumac, Rhus typhinia, and Persian silk tree, Albizia julibrisin, both fall into the lowest E rating category, as does the hornbeam (Carpinus betulus), another excellent tree for backyard seclusion and screening. Planting any tree, on the other hand, is preferable to doing nothing at all in terms of improving the environment.

Hedges for boundaries should be planted

Aside from absorbing pollutants, hedges provide a dual purpose as a refuge and food source for animals. Create a head-high barrier with a yew hedge and pleached hornbeams above it along a border. When the hornbeams' leaves turn bronze in the winter and summer, they make a striking architectural statement, particularly when juxtaposed with the yew's black veil. Urban gardens may benefit from thick, evergreen hedging, while rural ones can make use of a variety of fast-growing varieties.

Garden furniture recycling

Get creative and repurpose old materials in the garden or veg patch, from containers to tools and furniture. Outdoor furniture might be enticing when it's hot outside, but there are many fantastic options currently at your disposal that only need a little TLC. Give that worn-out garden seat a good scrub and a coat of paint from your local hardware shop, and it'll look as good as new in no time. There are several options for repurposing old furniture, such as repurposing old wooden chairs or repurposing tin baths for the birds. This is a wonderful opportunity to support a worthy charity while also finding a new home for previously cherished goods.

Make animal shelters

A wildlife-friendly garden will soon be visited by a variety of creatures eager to explore, eat, and maybe hide from the elements. Install a variety of animal and insect habitats, such as hedgehog huts, beehives, butterfly hives, and bug hotels. Rewilding your yard and making it more welcoming to animals is easier than you would think. Keep hedgehog shelters in a calm, hidden area of the yard that isn't exposed to wind or direct sunshine so that they may enjoy a peaceful, restful habitat.

Make your own compost

Avoid leaving your food waste to the trash collectors by using a food waste bin. Garden plants benefit greatly from compost made from food waste that decomposes over time. Feed your garden's plants and flowers whatever decomposable leftovers you have left from your meals. This includes anything from peas and beans to eggshells and banana peels. Making your own compost is a cost-effective and environmentally friendly alternative to buying it at the store. It also reduces the amount of garbage going to landfills.

Water features

It's not only people that benefit from water feature ideas but a wide variety of aquatic animals and insects looking for a moist environment to establish a home. During the hot summer months, garden pond ideas offer a water supply for thirsty birds and creatures. For fish, you'll need to make sure that your garden pond is deep enough to support them, and keep in mind that small ponds might freeze over during the winter months. Ensure that any animals that fall into the pond have a way out. If you want to know how to construct a pond, there are several helpful resources accessible.

Set up natural flood protection

Pollutants, such as fertilizers, oil, and animal feces, may be carried by rainwater from a garden into storm drains in the street, where they can enter rivers and seas. Plants, on the other hand, may help alleviate this issue. Leafy trees and plants minimize stormwater runoff by trapping rain, while their roots soak up and remove contaminants from the soil. I'd explore adding bioswales, which are small ditches that collect rainfall and enable it to percolate into the soil rather than run into drains in areas where flooding is more likely. A wide variety of plant life may be found in the ditches. As rainfall soaks into the ground rather than contributing to floods, permeable surfaces for garden path ideas and other garden landscaping will also reduce the risk of flooding.

Composting

Recycled organic debris, such as leaves and food wastes, may be composted to improve soil and plants via the natural process, this is known as Composting. Nothing grows indefinitely; composting just expedites the decomposition process by creating an optimal habitat in which a variety of decomposing organisms (such as fungus and bacteria) may flourish. Composted material, which may seem like garden soil, is the product of decomposition.

Composting facilities, community composting systems, and anaerobic digesters are all possibilities for processing organic waste. A primary emphasis of this tutorial is on home composting, an excellent approach to divert organic waste from landfills while also creating a useful soil supplement.

How to Compost?

Organisms that break down organic waste need four essential nutrients: nitrogen, carbon, air, and water. When it comes to compost, it's all about finding the proper balance between carbon and nitrogen in the appropriate proportions while also making sure that air and water are kept at optimal levels to provide optimal outcomes. There should be 25 to 30 parts carbon for every component of nitrogen in a compost pile. Too much carbon-rich material can cause your pile to become drier and take longer to decompose. Compost piles that include an excessive amount of nitrogen-rich material are more likely to be slimy, damp, and foul-smelling. Because these issues may be readily corrected by adding carbon- or nitrogen-rich material, the solution is simple.

Step 1

However, not all things that were previously living should be thrown in the trash. Plants afflicted with illness, weeds that have gone to seed, or dog and cat excrement should not be composted in general. Composter may be formed from a wide variety of materials, such as leaf and grass clippings, garden waste, and most culinary scraps.

Step 2

First, you have to choose the location. No matter how much sun or shade the location gets, it's best if it gets some of both throughout the day. For convenience, the location is more significant than the product itself. Then, decide on the method of composting you want to use. There are various methods for composting, and whatever method you choose is entirely up to you. You have the option of doing one of the following:

Do not use any kind of enclosure. Keep the materials in a thick heap by stacking them on top of each other.

- Build a compost container of your own. Enclosed bins, on the other hand, are more likely to be clean, pest-resistant, and able to retain heat and moisture.
- Build a basic spherical enclosure from wood poles, chicken wire, or hardware cloth; repurpose timber or old pallets to create a wooden bin; stack cinder blocks to create a three-sided enclosure, or simply drill holes in the bottom and sides of a trash can.
- Invest in a composter. Garden centers, mail-order garden catalogs, and home improvement/hardware stores all sell pre-built compost bins. A bin distribution program may also be offered by your local recycling coordinator or public works department.

Step 3

Gather the necessary supplies. First of all, you have to chop or shred the components into tiny bits. This will speed up the process of decomposition. Despite the fact that shredding leaves aren't required, it will speed up the process of composting. Kitchen leftovers and yard garbage are the same. Build up the stack. Get some wood chips or twigs and place them down at the bottom of the pot for drainage and aeration. As a final step, add materials in layers of 2 to 6 inches deep, alternating between "green" (food waste) and "browns" (leaves, straw, woody debris) to help balance the carbon and nitrogen content. After every other layer, add water and thoroughly combine. As long as you don't have enough "greens" to make a complete pile, start with browns and add greens as they are made accessible. Be sure to thoroughly bury food scraps in the pile's middle before adding more to it.

Keep it hydrated. Ideally, the pile should be wet but not soggy, similar to a sponge after it has been wrung out. In the absence of moisture, it will not decay.

Take a breather. The microbes that break down the materials need oxygen to function. Every time you add more material, use a pitchfork or hoe to fluff it up. It's possible to obtain completed compost in one year with more rigorous spring and autumn turning (such that the pile is turned fully inside out and upside down). Composting proceeds more slowly when it is turned less often.

Keep an eye on your stack. Composting generates heat as it proceeds. When the pile is rotated, don't be startled if steam rises from it. Conditions for disintegration are at their most favorable point in time. There will be no bugs or smells when your compost pile is properly prepared, includes no animal fats, and is rotated regularly.

Step 4

Decomposition may take anywhere from two weeks to two years, depending on the materials used, the size of the pile, and the frequency with which it is agitated. Cooling, becoming dark, and decomposing into little soil-like particles are all signs that compost is suitable for use.

Step 5

A month before planting, add 1-4 inches of finished compost to the top four inches of the soil. Compost may be used in the garden as a top dressing or mulch. Using a 1/2-inch sieve, compost may be combined with equal parts sand and loam to make potting soil. The compost pile

may be used to recycle large pieces of material. Adding 14 inches of compost to your lawn may assist promote the turf's biological activity. Make a donation to a neighbor or friend if you have too much compost.

Composting Methods & Techniques

All of these composting techniques may be suitable for you at any one moment, and you may alter your method of composting several times over the course of your life. Familiarize yourself with each system benefits and drawbacks is always the best path, since your demands and surroundings may vary over time. However, what may be positive for one person may be negative for another. Simply choose what works best. To differing degrees, they all operate for various objectives. It's possible that you've already tried a few of these strategies or that you're contemplating switching things up but aren't sure what to do.

Direct Composting

Direct composting requires nothing more than making a trench or a hole and burying your garbage. As with other composting systems, this one has its own set of drawbacks, for example:

- The long decomposing time (unless you chop them before digging),
- You can compost only fruits and veggies (this because you will incur in any kind of pests digging them up),
- You need to keep digging new holes as you go.

Given that, the direct composting can indeed create a large number of worms for enriching your soil and feed your plants.

Open Air Composting

Your backyard is the conventional location for an open-air compost pile. In most cases, it's a cheap and quick-to-assemble bay made of whatever materials you can find. As an alternative, you may use the Godey containers that you can purchase at a store to hold your trash. Additionally, wire cages are inserted with pipes around the outside to store water and heat. This may then be utilized for sustainable hot water systems. Composting in the open air is sometimes referred to as "Hot Composting" because of the high temperatures involved. Due to the lower heat production, when just modest amounts of trash are composted, it's often referred to as "Cold Composting". In my opinion, Cold Composting is not cold composting since it still generates heat. Because to literally cold compost anything is to allow it to let it rot in your refrigerator, this method may be referred to as "Warm Composting." In addition, we're all familiar with the fridge's odor.

Worm Farm Composting

The most popular technique of composting due to its capacity to raise worms, produce compost and compost tea, while keeping rats away is Worm Farm Composting. When compared to conventional composting procedures, the worms generate concentrated and low-nitrogen castings. Metal containers are poisonous to worms because copper leaches out of them. There will be a tremendous mess if they are not placed on the ground so that the nutrients may be transferred straight to the soil. However, you'll need some means to drain the juice or rotate the containers so that it can be collected if you use plastic containers. Keeping them away

from direct sunlight, rain, and frost and in a temperature range between 50- and 60-degrees Fahrenheit is the best bet. Worms may be fickle creatures, and if the circumstances aren't ideal or they're unhappy, they'll attempt to get out of their containers.

Tumbler Composting

It's possible to buy commercial tumbler composting machines from the hardware shop of your town in a variety of sizes and configurations. If you're able to change it every day or so, this is an excellent method for many folks. It's a challenge for others, particularly as they become older. However, certain mechanical ones make it easy to turn. You may need two tumbling composting systems in order to allow one to compost for a few months while you fill the other one. For anyone who has a lot of brown and green garbage to get rid of (and the room for this system), it can be an excellent option. If you simply want to compost only brown and green garbage, you may use a bay system. The only warning is that but you would need to keep an eye for rats and snakes.

Mechanical Composting

To generate semi-composted trash in a matter of 24 hours, mechanical composting employs power to heat and rotate the garbage, resulting in half-composted waste. This system is ideal for activities which produces a lot of waste such as kindergartens, hospitals, restaurants, hotels, schools… Instead of delivering your rubbish to the municipal tip, you may handle it in-house. There are other smaller systems that are suitable for certain people's homes, although they may be pricey and need continual electrical use. There are advantages and disadvantages to all composters, but it cannot be denied that they generate semi-composed soil in a short amount of time.

Commercial Composting

In contrast to backyard composting, commercial composting utilizes a variety of materials. For example, sand, pine bark, sawdust, ferrous and ammonia sulfate are all mixed in continuous rows to make the Compost. It is normally ready

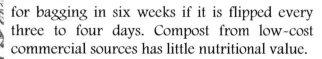

for bagging in six weeks if it is flipped every three to four days. Compost from low-cost commercial sources has little nutritional value.

A higher-quality compost may be found made by smaller, independently owned commercial compost enterprises. However, they are more costly. Several farmers, such as McLeod's Agriculture, have also been certified organic by the USDA.

Filling raised garden beds or backfilling a Compot in clay or sandy soil with commercial Compost is a cost-effective option. Alternatively, it may be combined with composted soil and used to fill a container plant. A high-quality propagation mix should be purchased if you want to grow plants in commercial Compost.

Combination Composting

Combination Composting (also called "Compot Composting") combines open-air, direct, vermi-, and EMO composting. Using all the components of composting, this method is suitable for most households. There are, of course, certain drawbacks to it for some individuals. In my opinion, there are fewer hurdles and more benefits. You may compost unlimited kitchen trash. As a result, you need to empty your bin about half as often. Forget about it until you're ready to restock and clean it every year. Soil is enriched by your own garbage.

Benefits of Composting

Saves Waste Stream

Organic waste may be composted at home. More than a third of what we throw away is made up of food leftovers and yard trash. Food waste is a major environmental problem, yet the costs of processing it is high. To dispose of municipal solid trash would cost $60 per ton in the United States in 2020. Since we generated 248 million tons of municipal garbage in 2018 and sent a majority of it to landfills and incinerators, we spent billions on waste management. The rubbish we remove from landfills by composting at home becomes something useful for our gardens.

Reduce Methane Emissions

When organic matter decomposes, it is often broken down by microbes that need oxygen to break it down. When biodegradable waste is disposed of in a landfill, it is buried behind a mountain of other garbage, depriving the decomposers of air. As a result, the waste is broken down by organisms that can survive without access to free oxygen. Byproducts are formed during anaerobic decomposition, and biogas is one of them. Methane is 30 to 38 times more efficient than CO_2 in trapping heat in the atmosphere over a century in this biogas, which is around 50% methane and 50% carbon dioxide. Landfills are the third greatest source of human-generated methane emissions in the United States, despite having methane collection devices installed in the majority of them. Only around 7% of food waste is composted since our solid waste system was built on landfills.

Soil Health and Erosion Reduction

Large-scale agricultural systems may benefit greatly from composting. Nitrogen, phosphorus, and potassium are the three most important nutrients for garden plants to get from compost. Traces of calcium, magnesium, iron, and zinc are also included in this product's composition. Organic fertilizers, like compost, may be used in place of hazardous synthetic fertilizers. Compost has been found to boost soil water retention, productivity, and resilience via research.

Saves Water

Agriculture is a significant water user in the United States, accounting for around 80 percent of the nation's water usage. It is possible for farmers to use irrigation systems, but they are both costly and time-intensive in their management. More and more people are having trouble getting their hands on water. What is the benefit of composting? Organic matter has been found to boost soil's ability to retain water. Soil organic matter, on the other hand, boosts water storage by an average of 20,000 gallons per acre for every one percent increase. In contrast to farming on deteriorated soil, farmers may get better yields while using less water by incorporating compost into their soil.

Ensures less food waste

Consumers are to blame for an enormous quantity of food waste. According to an NRDC research, the most often discarded foods in three American cities were fruits and vegetables. The Guardian reported in 2018 that American shops and consumers discard 50 million tons of food each year. Save the Food campaign and other tools from NRDC strive to educate people on how to purchase, cook, and store food in a manner that minimizes waste. There will always be food leftovers that cannot be eaten even if we do all we can to reduce food waste (e.g., a banana peel). If you don't want to throw away your waste, composting is an excellent option.

AMAZING BONUSES FOR ALL THE READERS:

Just Scan the QR-Code below to get them!

Conclusion

In this ninth book, we have provided 50 wildflowers herb profile and how these herbal allies can be used in your everyday life to restore your well-being.

I sincerely hope that this will be just the beginning of your journey and that you will increase your knowledge on Native American medicine for a healthier and better way to treat the common disease without relying on industrial drugs and medication.

Just scan the QR code on the right, it will take 30 seconds!

My best wishes and may the Spirit guide your journey!

Native American Traditional Medicine

Safe And Effective Treatment For Common Childhood Ailments Using Herbs

BOOK 11 of "The Native American Herbalist's Bible"

Natalie Hathale

Introduction

Humans relied on natural remedies to heal their diseases prior to the invention of pharmaceuticals. Regardless of how it was found, herbal medicine has been around for a long time. What's new is that it's making a comeback, particularly in light of recent attention to the dangers of commonly available medications. Let's go back to the beginning first, however. Local flora from each continent's diverse ecosystems allowed individuals in various nations to rely on plant-based cures that were unique to their region. Many parts of the globe still lack access to modern medications and treatments; thus, herbal healers continue to play an important role in public health. Medicine has been documented in writing for thousands of years. About 3,000 native plants make up the natural pharmacy used in traditional Native American medicine, which emphasizes herbal medicines. Traditional Native American herbal treatments are important to pharmaceutical corporations, which have learned from local practitioners and incorporated bioactive compounds discovered via traditional cures into contemporary synthetic medications.

The Managua Han tombs near Changsha, China, which were sealed in 166 BCE, included early texts on the usage of Chinese plants. More than 270 remedies, ranging from hemorrhoids to warts, are offered in a book titled "Recipes for 52 Ailments." Massage, exercise, acupuncture, herbal remedies, and food therapy are all part of traditional Asian medicine. Traditional Chinese medicine (TCM) was developed in China in the 1960s, although it has its origins in herbal medicines that date back to 1000 BCE. Asian medicine had 1,800 medicines towards the end of the sixteenth century, and by the twentieth century, Chinese material medical had 13,800 pharmaceuticals. Around 1100 BCE, the Atharva Veda, a fundamental resource for Ayurveda, set forth the principles of the therapeutic technique. It is still in use today. Medicinal plant experts in the ancient Near East educated Greeks and Persians alike. In the following centuries, Arabs passed on their

wisdom to European crusaders, who took it back to Europe.

Physicians in ancient Greece and Rome were well-known for their extensive understanding of herbs. Egyptian doctors had passed on much of their knowledge to them. Hippocrates was educated by Egyptian priest-doctors, earning the title "the father of medicine" in the process. Scientific advancement slowed to a standstill when the Roman Empire was overthrown, and many natural medicines were lost. Trade with other cultures led to a resurgence in herbal knowledge. Aristocrats in Europe during the Renaissance gathered the most beneficial plants of the period in their gardens as well as in their huge libraries. University herbalism and botany departments throughout the sixteenth and seventeenth-century planted "physic" (or herb) gardens with the most often used therapeutic plants. Known herbal medicines in England were compiled by Nicholas Culpeper in The English Physician, published in 1643. A focus on herbs rather than pricey doctor-prepared mixtures was placed on this guide for the general public. The popularity of herbal treatments dwindled as the scientific era began. Since the introduction of modern pharmaceuticals, herbal medicines have faded into obscurity throughout Europe.

It has been thousands of years since Native American, and First Nations peoples began employing nature's remedies to cure the body as well as cleanse the soul and enliven the intellect. Oral history has it that the early healers learned how to employ therapeutic plants by studying ill animals. There are no written records of how native North Americans utilized herbs prior to European contact since knowledge was passed on through word of mouth. There were numerous European herbalists who arrived from Europe and contributed their own expertise to the new immigrants who carried with them their own understanding of indigenous medicines. They did bring their favorite medicinal herbs with them to the new world. Several of these species have spread

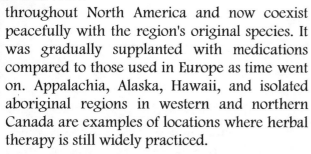

throughout North America and now coexist peacefully with the region's original species. It was gradually supplanted with medications compared to those used in Europe as time went on. Appalachia, Alaska, Hawaii, and isolated aboriginal regions in western and northern Canada are examples of locations where herbal therapy is still widely practiced.

The natives of South America relied heavily on medicinal herbs. The same plant remedies that have been venerated for thousands of years are being used in shamanic rituals today. A wide variety of medicinal plants grow abundantly on this continent, and traditional healer, known as herbalists, sell their wares at market booths. Plants are a crucial part of the diet and treatment of many forest workers who spend weeks at a time in the bush. In distant forest areas, there is still a lot of herbal knowledge that hasn't been lost. Healing herbs have been employed by Mayan and Aztec healers for centuries. For those in need of medical treatment, they also had hospitals where patients were secluded from the rest of their community. South American territory that was once teeming with natural vegetation is now home to towns, plantations, and ranches. Still, the deep forests of South America are a treasure trove of therapeutic herbs. In addition to stressing the need for conservation, the discovery of new species raises the possibility of new cures for diseases such as malaria and cancer.

Traditional therapies and standardized herbal extracts are used in today's herbal therapy. People's ability to take care of themselves improves when more research into the medicinal properties of plants is conducted. Naturopaths and herbalists with advanced training may be found in many places. Because it's so simple to get high-quality supplements both in shops and online, herbal medicine may easily become a part of your daily routine. You can skip drugs until you really need them using herbal treatment. Drugs may have unpleasant or even hazardous side effects, but herbal therapy gives a milder approach. To get the best results from an antibiotic, you shouldn't have been taking them for minor ailments like a runny nose or an earache before. It's cheaper to use natural therapies. Everybody wants to save money, right? When you buy or cultivate the plants you need, the cost of each treatment will substantially decrease. The natural health benefits of botanicals are undeniable. In addition to relieving your itching eczema, unpleasant sniffles, or unsettled stomach, many herbal medicines provide various health advantages. Family-friendly herbal medicines abound. There are a number of herbs that are safe for the whole family. You can cure minor ailments at home with a few simple equipment and substances, as well as some knowledge and forethought.

Common Childhood Ailments

Childhood illnesses are those that affect children more often than adults. That doesn't mean adults can't or won't become sick, but children are more likely to get these diseases and develop the immunity to them that will keep them healthy as adults. An illness that is very simple in childhood might become life-threatening when it is caught by an adult who has never been exposed to it as a kid. While some of these illnesses may be avoided or treated by vaccines, others are unavoidable.

It wasn't until around 100 years after the first vaccine for a disease was delivered that immunology really began to take off. Milkmaids who had cowpox via contact with cows were resistant to smallpox, according to Dr. Edward Jenner (1749-1823), an English physician. He was accurate in hypothesizing that exposure to cowpox provided some protection. In order to demonstrate the efficacy of his inoculation, Jenner injected a little child with smallpox matter after removing material from the pustules on the milkmaids' skin. The mortality rate from smallpox dramatically decreased as a result of Jenner's approach being widely recognized in Europe and the United States. Chickenpox and measles are two examples of juvenile illnesses that are caused by bacteria or viruses, whereas Tay-Sachs's disease and sickle cell anemia are examples of illnesses that are caused by excessive drinking or drug use by the mother while she is pregnant. When a germ or virus is transmitted from one person to another throughout the course of a pediatric illness, it is infectious. The tight quarters seen in school buses and classrooms are excellent for the spread of disease-causing etiologic agents. A kid with measles is likely to spread the illness to other children on the same bus or in the same class before measures may be adopted to reduce the rate of transmission. In the same way, even before displaying symptoms, a youngster with mumps might spread the disease to others. The common cold is especially susceptible to this form of spread. In the early stages of the cold, before the patient begins to sneeze and develop a fever, the virus that causes the cold is very abundant. Ailments such as the cold or flu and HIV are now incurable, but finding vaccines and therapies for these illnesses is substantially harder than treating or preventing bacterial diseases. A virus cannot be spotted with a standard laboratory light microscope. A virus can only be seen with a special electron microscope. Viruses may also alter or mutate in order to thwart the development of natural immunity. A number of viruses are responsible for the spread of illnesses like the common cold. There are around 200 viruses that may cause a cold. Many experts believe that developing a vaccine that is only effective against a single virus is not worth the effort. An effective vaccination may not be possible for illnesses that are caused by one virus (such as AIDS).

Asthma

Coughing and wheezing are frequent symptoms of asthma, which is a long-term illness. Tubes that bring in and out air are swollen, causing the condition. It is possible for anybody, even youngsters and the elderly, to acquire asthma. Asthma symptoms might be minor or severe. The vast majority of individuals will only suffer minor symptoms, but a few people may encounter them often. Breathing shallowly is the most frequent problem of asthma (a whistling sound when you breathe), a feeling of breathlessness, a feeling of tightness in the chest, as if a band was being tightened and coughing.

Bronchiolitis

Children beneath the age of three are susceptible to bronchiolitis, a common viral illness of the lower respiratory system. The majority of instances of bronchiolitis are not life-threatening; however, a more severe illness like pneumonia may be present. Within two to three weeks, most cases are minor and need no treatment. Some children, on the other hand, present with more severe symptoms and should be hospitalized. Early signs of bronchiolitis include a runny nose and cough that are similar to those of a cold. The respiratory syncytial virus (RSV) is the primary cause of bronchiolitis (RSV). It is transmitted by coughing or sneezing droplets of fluid from sick individuals. Smaller airways (bronchioles) in the lungs become infected and inflamed due to the infection. Because of the inflammation, there is a decrease in lung capacity. Breathing becomes difficult as a result of this.

Chickenpox

A viral infection that results in Chickenpox is called varicella-zoster. Chickenpox is a common childhood illness. Chickenpox is most usually contracted by youngsters under the age of ten. During an infection, the body's immune system produces proteins known as antibodies. Lifelong protection against the virus is provided by them (immunity). Therefore, it is rare to suffer from Chickenpox more than once in your lifetime. Chickenpox has the following symptoms: Fever, muscle pains, and a headache usually emerge a day or two before the rash does. There are a lot of spots (rash). Crops begin to show spots. They get itchy and form tiny blisters. On any part of the body, they may be found. For many days, different crops may grow. Some children have several spots, while others have none at all. The rash begins as little red bumps, then develops into blisters, and finally becomes covered in a crust. A lack of desire to eat or difficulty with feeding. Others look to be just slightly unwell. Scabs form on the blisters as they heal.

Cold

A cold is an illness of upper airways, nose, sinuses, and throat caused by a moderate strain of the common cold virus. The infection normally goes away on its own usually in one or two weeks. It's unlikely to be life-threatening if you're in good physical shape. When you have a cold, natural painkillers might help alleviate some of the symptoms. Symptoms of cold often

begin to appear within a few days after infection. Sneezing, a runny nose, a sore throat, a cough, and a hoarse voice are some of the most common symptoms. If you're suffering from a cold and haven't seen any of the more usual symptoms like a runny nose, a sore throat, or a sneezing fit, you may be suffering from a cold as well. The worst part of the infection is the initial one, which can last one or two days, when symptoms are at their worst. Then, the patient health gradually starts to get better. A full recovery usually can happen in seven to ten days for adults and kids older than 10 years, but it may endure longer. Even a cough might continue for a month or more. Cold last for about 14 days in children, which is longer than the average duration of a cold in adults.

Cough

Children's coughs are fairly prevalent. A cold or other respiratory tract illness is the most prevalent cause of a cough. Viruses are the most common cause of respiratory tract infections in young infants. Asthma may be diagnosed in children who have a nighttime cough. Wheezing and trouble breathing, which are common symptoms in children with asthma, are also common. Allergies and eczema are common in children with asthma. If you're worried your kid has asthma, make an appointment with your family doctor so they can examine him or her and provide you with further information.

Croup

When it comes to croup, it's most common in youngsters between the ages of six months and six years. Antibiotics are of no value since it is caused by a virus. Arsenal-like barking cough is the most common symptom. Even if your kid looks to be sick, you should take him to the doctor. There are many telltale signs of croup: a seal-like barking cough, a hoarse voice, difficulty breathing, and a raspy sound while inhaling. To begin with, your kid is likely to have cold-like symptoms such as a fever, runny nose, and coughing. It is common for the symptoms of croup to worsen at night after a few days.

Diarrhea and vomiting

Adults, children, and newborns all suffer from nausea and vomiting on a regular basis. Mostly, they are the effects of stomach sickness and will go away in a few days. Infectiousness may spread from person to person if you have a stomach illness. When the symptoms first appear and for the next two days after they've subsided, you're most contagious. Wait two days before returning to school or work if you are still experiencing symptoms. To control the transmission of germs is to wash your hands often with soap and water, wash filthy clothes and bedding separately on hot water, and regularly wipe the surfaces and doorknobs on the toilet, flush the handle and the taps. For two weeks, you should avoid cooking for others, sharing towels and other personal items such as silverware and utensils, and using a swimming pool.

Fever in children

An elevated body temperature is what is referred to as a fever. A temperature of 100°F (38°C) or above is generally considered a fever in children. If your kid gets a fever, you may be worried. In most cases, a fever will go away on its own without the need for medical attention. Thermometers may be used to quickly and easily determine whether your kid has a fever. Infections and other diseases are the most common causes of fevers. Bacteria and viruses that cause illnesses have a harder time surviving when the body is hot. Among the most frequent causes of fevers include upper respiratory tract infections, flu, ear infections, roseola, tonsillitis, kidney or urinary tract infections (UTIs), and common childhood diseases including chickenpox and whooping cough. In addition to immunizations, overheating from too much bedding or clothes may increase your child's fever.

Earache

Children, in particular, are prone to experiencing earaches. However, it's generally caused by a mild infection and will normally clear up within a few days without any medication. If you've ever felt like your ear was hurting, you've probably had an earache. One or both ears may be affected.

Measles

Infection with the measles virus is very contagious. It's uncomfortable and may even lead to more severe problems. Measles, mumps, and rubella (MMR) vaccinations have greatly reduced the incidence of the disease. A person who has never had measles or has not been immunized against it is at risk. Ten days after contracting measles, a cold-like illness develops in the afflicted person. The measles rash appeared a few days later. The sickness typically lasts between seven and ten days for most individuals. First-degree symptoms of measles include a runny or clogged nose, sore and red eyes that may be sensitive to light, a high fever, tiny greyish-white patches in the mouth and throat that are itchy and painful, a cough, and lack of appetite.

Meningitis

The inflammation (swelling) of the membranes that envelop the brain and spinal cord is known as meningitis. The swelling is generally caused by a bacterial or viral infection of the fluid around the brain and spinal cord. Meningitis may, however, be caused by a variety of different things, including trauma, cancer, certain medications, and other illnesses. The therapy for meningitis varies based on the precise reason; thus, it's critical to determine the cause. Meningitis isn't usually a sign of meningococcal illness, even if symptoms suggest otherwise. If you have a bacterial infection of the meninges, it doesn't always indicate you have meningitis. Neisseria meningitides is a bacterium that causes meningococcal disease. Meningitis and bloodstream infections are among the most dangerous of these ailments (septicemia). Infectious agents that cause bacterial meningitis are responsible for the disease's transfer from person to person. Germs may be transmitted from one person to another via the consumption of contaminated food. Individuals may transfer the viruses that cause viral meningitis to other people, depending on the kind of bacteria they are infected with. Viral meningitis may be transmitted to you via intimate contact with an infected person. Although you are unlikely to have meningitis, it is possible. For the simple reason, that meningitis is a rare complication of infection with these viruses.

Mumps

The mumps virus is responsible for the common disease known as mumps. Mumps may be spread from person to person. Measles, mumps, and rubella (MMR) vaccinations have made it less prevalent in youngsters. If your kid may have mumps, make an appointment with your primary care physician very once. In most cases, mumps symptoms appear 14 to 25 days following infection with the virus that causes the disease. The term "incubation period" refers to this length of time. The most frequent sign of mumps is painful swellings beneath the ears (the parotid glands). Salivary glands are located in the parotid region of the neck. When the swelling is called "parotitis," both glands are commonly afflicted, yet just one of them might be infected. Pain, discomfort, and trouble swallowing may all be symptoms of an inflamed lymph node. More widespread signs and symptoms might appear a few days prior to the swelling of the parotid glands. A fever of 100°F (38°C) or higher, a headache, earache, and other non-specific symptoms, including a sense of being sick, muscular aches, and a lack of appetite, are all examples of these symptoms.

The condition is known as oophoritis, which causes nausea, vomiting, and lower abdomen discomfort in a tiny percentage of women may often lead to consequences. Pancreatitis (caused by mumps deafness) affects around 4% of individuals, but it is usually mild and only lasts for a brief period of time, whereas viral

meningitis – which affects up to 10% of those who catch mumps deafness – affects a far larger percentage of people. Mumps may generate no symptoms in around one in three patients.

Roseola

Babies and toddlers are often affected by the viral illness roseola. For the first several days, it might induce a fever and a rash. Roseola is usually a benign illness that may be treated at home by a parent. Within a week, they'll be back to normal. Adults and older children might have roseola as well. Most children are already sick by the time they join nursery, and it's quite unusual for them to get the disease more than once. It's possible to get roseola without experiencing any symptoms at all. If they do form, they generally begin within a week or two after infection.

Rubella

Rubella is a prevalent infection among children in the United States (German measles). Because of the efficacy of the MMR immunization program and its high vaccination rates, it is now rare in Northern Ireland. If you suspect rubella in yourself or your child, make an appointment with your primary care provider at once.

- Rubella is often a minor illness that clears up on its own in seven to ten days without the need for medication.

- Small areas of red-pink skin, "swollen glands" (lymph nodes) around the head and neck (these feel like hard pea-like swellings underneath the skin), a high temperature (fever), cold-like symptoms such as cough and runny nose, hurting, are all signs of rubella infection.

- Small, reddish-pink patches may be irritating; the rash generally begins behind the ears and spreads over the head and neck. It subsequently spreads to the chest and stomach (the trunk), the legs, and arms.

- After about three to five days, the rash will usually go away on its own. Rubella is a short-lived illness that generally only lasts a few days. Swollen 'glands' might last for weeks.

Skin rashes in babies

As soon as your baby is a few days old, he or she is likely to have a rash. Contact a health care provider, such as a midwife, if your infant has a rash but no other disease symptoms. Your doctor or out-of-hours service should be called if your baby shows any signs of illness. The skin and immune systems of newborns are still growing. As a result, they are more vulnerable to skin irritations and infections than the general population. Heat, allergens, friction, moisture, chemicals, scents, and materials may cause newborns' rashes. Even a baby's own excrement may trigger a rash on their skin. Both viral and bacterial illnesses may cause rashes. Baby acne, which is most frequent on the face, is another common newborn skin rash. Baby's dampness or the acidity of their pee and feces may induce cradle cap, diaper rash, or both.

When the skin around the lips or on the chest becomes inflamed due to drool, the cheeks, behind the knees, and the arms are the most typical places where eczema may be encountered. And sore throat, fever, and exhaustion are all possible symptoms of the fifth sickness (also known as the "slapped cheek" ailment). Hyperthermia, hives, impetigo, and infectious rashes, such as measles, chickenpox, scarlet fever, and roseola, may produce heat rash in places covered by clothing, such as the armpits and neck, chest, arms, torso, and legs.

Scarlet fever

People with strep throat are at risk of developing scarlet fever, a bacterial sickness. Scarlet fever, often known as scarlatina, is a red rash that covers most of the body. Usually, a painful throat and high fever accompany scarlet fever. Most cases of scarlet fever occur between the ages of 5 and 15. It used to be considered dangerous for children to have scarlet fever, but modern antibiotics have made it less so. It is still possible that scarlet fever might cause more significant health problems if left untreated.

Scarlet fever is named for the following signs and symptoms:

- A rosy rash appears on the skin. The rash resembles a sunburn and is as rough as sandpaper to the touch. Starting on the face or neck and spreading to the torso and arms, and legs is the normal course of action for this condition. The reddish skin will become pale if pressure is applied to it.
- The lines are colored red. If you have a rash that spreads to the groin and other body areas where folds of skin meet, the rash will be more noticeable.
- Face flushed. Facial flushing may be seen, with a ring of white around the lips.
- The flavor of strawberry on the tongue. The tongue is commonly coated in a white covering and appears red and rough early on in the condition.
- Rash and swelling of cheeks and tongue are common symptoms of this illness. Peeling of the afflicted skin is common once these symptoms have passed.

Sore throat

In most cases, a sore throat is nothing to be concerned about. Within a week, most people feel better. Most are the result of mild diseases like the flu or a cold, and they are easily treatable at home. There is no one-size-fits-all explanation for a sore throat. If you're suffering from this, you're most likely suffering from an illness caused by a virus (or, in rare situations, bacteria). An inflamed throat is generally the first sign of an illness like the common cold or flu. Other symptoms include a clogged or runny nose, a cough, and even a high temperature (fever). It's possible to have a dry cough, a hoarse voice, and the frequent need to clean your throat with laryngitis (inflammation of the voice box). Tingling or pain in the throat during swallowing are all symptoms of tonsillitis (inflammation of the tonsils). Swollen glands in the neck, difficulty swallowing, and tonsillitis are symptoms of strep throat, a bacterial throat illness. You may also be exhausted, have a fever, and have enlarged glands in your neck if you have glandular fever.

Whooping cough

One of the most infectious respiratory infections is pertussis or whooping cough. It produces a lot of sneezing and coughing, especially in infants and young children. Cases have risen during the last several years. However, it is still uncommon, thanks to a vaccination program that protects infants and children from the disease. As a general rule, whooping cough affects infants and young children the most. It's dangerous for infants and toddlers under the age of two. When whooping cough initially emerges, it looks like a cold, with a runny nose and other symptoms.

- The eyes are drenched with tears.
- A bad case of strep throat.
- Somewhat elevated body temperature.
- About a week later, very bad coughing starts:
- There are frequent periods lasting just a few minutes each, and they are more prevalent in the evenings and at night.
- When you or your kid coughs up a lot of mucus and vomits between coughs, you or your child may make a 'whoop' sound because they are gasping for air. However, not everyone makes this sound.
- Coughing fits might leave you with a red face and perhaps some little bleeding beneath the skin or eyes.
- If small kids have difficulty breathing, they may momentarily turn blue (cyanosis). This is frequently a sign of a more serious problem, although their breathing should return to normal fast.

Coughing may not be evident in very young newborns, although there may be short pauses in breathing. Over time, the episodes will become less intense and more infrequent. They won't stop for a while yet; it may be months before they do.

Urinary tract infections in children

UTIs are among the most prevalent bacterial illnesses addressed by general practitioners (GP). They're not fun to deal with. However, they normally disappear after a few days or maybe treated with medication. Our bodies rely on the urinary tract (pee) to produce and expel urination. Ureters (the tubes linking the kidneys to the bladder) are part of it, as are the bladder and urethra (the tubes that carry urine out of the bladder). An infection of the kidneys or ureters is an upper urinary tract infection (UTI). Lower UTIs are bladder infections (cystitis) or urethra (urethritis). The following are possible warning signs of a UTI in your child a sweltering heat, vomiting, weariness, irritation, burning or excruciating discomfort in the bladder, urinary incontinence, wetting oneself or one's bed after being dry for some time, abdominal, side, or lower backaches, Urine with a foul odor, Urine with a reddish tint.

The symptoms of a urinary tract infection) might be difficult to discern in youngsters since they cannot express their feelings.

Herbal Treatments for Children's Ailments

For thousands of years, herbal medicine has been used to treat a variety of ailments. In fact, its history is longer than that of modern medicines.

Many common diseases may be prevented or treated with the help of alternative medicine. Nature's pharmacy has a wide variety of plants with potential therapeutic effects. Everyone has the power to utilize herbs to alleviate pain and promote healing with the right direction and education. Some herbal medicines are based on the use of fresh plant components. There are some who advocate using store-bought extracts, and there are others who advocate using compounds manufactured at home. In the past, finding medicinal plants was difficult, but nowadays, the most common ones can be found in well-stocked pharmacies and even on the shelves of big-box retailers. It's possible to avoid medications by shopping at health food shops, which provide a wide assortment of herbs, tinctures and teas, ointments, and more. Many contemporary medications have their origins in herbal therapy, which may come as a surprise to some. Willow bark and opium poppies are used to make aspirin and the painkillers morphine and oxycodone, respectively. In the fight against malaria, cinchona tree bark is used to produce quinine, while the lovely but toxic foxglove is utilized to produce digoxin, a powerful heart medication. Many additional medications are derived from plants or are made from natural substances. For these reasons (and many more), synthetic medications are still preferred in conventional medicine. Prescription drugs have achieved a desirable position, which is understandable. In this book, it is not our intention to minimize their significance. It's also crucial to keep in mind that in the United States, herbs are classified as dietary supplements and subject to FDA regulation when marketed commercially. You wouldn't have to get permission to use an herbal poultice, apply an oil or cream, or consume a tincture or tea to cure an illness the natural way, unlike with a synthetic medicine.

Herbs are potent, yet they don't have the long-term adverse effects associated with pharmaceuticals. Even when combined with rest, they do not interfere with the body's natural healing process but rather enhance our capacity to recover. Herbs, on the other hand, strengthen the body's natural defenses against viruses and infections, making it simpler for the body to fight back. Herbs are excellent instructors for our children, but they may also be used as a safe and effective method of healing when needed. Herbs have a natural ability to treat children's bodies since they have a high level of sensitivity. When used correctly and in moderation, traditional herbs may help children's bodies function more effectively and in tune with their environment, rather than wreaking havoc on them. Herbs and mainstream medicine are not in opposition; instead, they are two healing systems that may work together. Herbs are excellent in resolving minor aches and pains, nourishing the body so it can better resist and fight illness, and restoring the body's natural state of well-being. For life-threatening sickness, allopathic medicine, on the other hand, is a better system than alternative medicine. Despite the fact that allopathic medicine is able to function fast, effectively, and efficiently, it focuses only on eliminating symptoms before they may cause damage. Sadly, as we've learned, medication is frequently the problem.

Pharmaceutical drugs might have unwelcome side effects in children because of their potency. As a result, although medicines should be used when required, it is always preferable to turn to natural, time-tested solutions. Because it doesn't pollute streams or land as contemporary medications do, herbal medicine is not only practical but also environmentally friendly and cost-efficient (you can even produce a lot of your own medicine!). It's wise to ensure your doctor or health care provider is conversant with both systems of medicine if you want to utilize both herbs and medications in caring for yourself or your family. Using the herbs recommended in this book does not have any undesirable interactions with medicines; they are mild and suitable for use even by little children. However, if you decide to use additional herbs and natural therapies, you may want a holistic health care practitioner to help you along the path.

Many common childhood diseases, such as ear infections, colds, flu, stomach bugs, and chickenpox, may be treated with herbal remedies. These include typical symptoms like colic, rashes, teething pain, and daily bumps and bruises. When dealing with more complex health issues, herbs may also be utilized to complement allopathic treatment. If herbal medicines fail to provide the desired outcomes, allopathic therapy should be considered the next step.

Since children are smaller and lighter than adults, almost any plant that is safe for adults may also be used safely by them. As a result, herbs with a milder action profile are more suitable for youngsters, whose bodies are more easily offended. Here are some of the most often prescribed herbs for children. No persistent deposits or adverse effects have been seen in the body, and they are widely accepted as safe and benign in comparison to other more potent medicines, these "gentle" herbs may be pretty powerful and efficient, yet their action is less harsh. All of these herbs are usually good for the immune system, build the neurological system, and in a variety of ways, assist the body's intrinsic capacity to repair itself.

Children's herbal health care should be based on these principles.

Anise (Pimpinella anisum)

Benefits

Anise has been grown for over 4,000 years and has a long history of usage as a medicinal plant and culinary spice. It is most often used as a carminative (gas-expelling) and warming digestive aid. It may also be used to treat minor urinary infections and as an expectorant (aids in the expulsion of mucus) in respiratory disorders. It has a delicious licorice taste that most youngsters appreciate.

How should it be used?

Tea may be used to treat colic and other digestive issues. Anise is often combined with less appetizing herbs to make them more appealing due to its sweet taste. It creates a delicious syrup.

Astragalus (Astragalus membranaceus)

Benefits

Astragalus is known as the "young person's ginseng" because of its adaptogenic (resistance-building) properties as well as its toning effects. In contrast to echinacea, astragalus increases the body's first line of defense by boosting bone marrow, which regenerates the body's protective barrier. A number of studies have indicated that it is useful in assisting youngsters who are undergoing chemotherapy or radiation treatment.

How should it be used?

For its adaptogenic properties and ability to tone the body, astragalus is frequently referred to as the young person's ginseng. For the first line of protection, the astragalus helps replenish the body's bone marrow reserve, while echinacea aids the immune system's second line of defense. For youngsters undergoing chemotherapy and radiation treatment, it has been shown to be useful.

Catnip (Nepeta cataria)

Benefits

Catnip may produce pleasure spasms in cats, but it is a superb stress-relieving herb for people. It is quite helpful in reducing fever and relieving the pain of teething. To cure indigestion, diarrhea, and colic, it is also assistance to the digestive system. Children benefit greatly from catnip's soothing, pain-relieving, and gentle properties.

How should it be used?

Teething discomfort might be relieved by drinking this tea throughout the day. Adding herbs like oats and lemon balm, as well as fruit juice, can help make catnip more appealing. Use a few drops of catnip tincture before meals to aid digestion. Before bedtime, a few drops of the tincture may help calm down a grumpy child. For children's fevers, this is one of the best herbs to use as a tincture and as an infusion.

Chamomile

Benefits

Despite its small size, this plant is a potent source of healing. A potent anti-inflammatory essential oil is abundant in the blooming tops of this plant. The blossoms may be used to produce a calming tea that can also help with digestion. In particular, it is beneficial for digestive issues brought on by stress, such as colic.

How should it be used?

Honey-sweetened chamomile tea may be provided throughout the day to soothe a youngster who is anxious or stressed out. Similar relaxing effects may be achieved with the use of a massage oil containing chamomile essential oil. The administration of a few drops of chamomile tincture just before feeding will help with the digestive process.

Note

Although chamomile is usually regarded safe, it is a part of the composite family, and some people are allergic to plants from this group. If you have a kid who is really allergic or sensitive, see a herbalist.

Dill (Anethum graveolens)

Benefits

As the name "dill" derives from the Norse word "Dilla," which means "to lull," this herb is well-known for its ability to calm and soothe infants and young children. Gas may be relieved even more effectively with dill than with other digestive aids. There are few herbs more well recognized for relieving children's gastrointestinal discomfort, such as indigestion, colic, and other symptoms of an upset stomach. Dill is high in manganese, magnesium, and iron, and it also includes calcium.

How should it be used?

Dill is a popular culinary herb. It's also deliciously made as tea, either alone or in combination with other herbs.

Echinacea

Benefits

Echinacea boosts the body's first line of defense against infection by enhancing macrophage T-cell activation. It is a key immune-stimulating and infection-fighting plant. Despite its potency and effectiveness, it is also safe for children to use and has no known adverse effects or residual accumulation.

How should it be used?

Keep your child at home and give him or her echinacea if everyone else at the daycare center is sick. Echinacea works best when given at the beginning of an illness or when precautions are essential. At the first sign of a cold or flu, give echinacea tea or tincture in order to boost your immune system and fight off the sickness. Infrequent but small doses work best; for example, adults may take a teaspoon of tincture or a cup of tea every 30 minutes, with a child's dosage suitably adjusted. To treat respiratory and bronchial infections in youngsters, as well as sore throats, this plant may be used in tea or tincture form. Use the tea or tincture, flavored with peppermint or spearmint essential oil, as a mouthwash for aching gums and oral irritation. To cure skin conditions, echinacea may be used topically as a wash or poultice, although oral administration is the most effective method.

Note: Echinacea, like chamomile, is a member of the composite family and may induce an allergic response in some people. Because of the high demand for this herb, it has been ruthlessly plundered from its natural environment and is becoming scarcer in the wild; therefore, avoid wild-harvested echinacea. Instead, purchase from reputable firms that offer produced echinacea, preferably organically grown echinacea. Even better, cultivate your own.

Elder (Sambucus nigra)

Benefits

A wide range of elderberry medications may be found on pharmacy shelves during flu season. The rich blueberries are my favorite part of the plant, even though they may be used in a variety of ways. The immune system benefits greatly from the berries' high vitamin A and C content. Flavonoids and anthocyanins, which protect the heart and boost the immune system, are also abundant in these foods. Antiviral qualities are also found in the berries, as well as in the blossoms. In addition to colds and flu, an elder is beneficial in treating upper respiratory infections. To boost the immune system, it's often mixed with echinacea in herbal therapies.

How should it be used?

In addition to being delicious, elderberries may also be used to treat a variety of ailments. An immune-boosting tea brewed from elderberries is both visually appealing and delicious (it will need to be sweetened or mixed with fruit juice to appeal to most children). Teas made from the blossoms might help alleviate symptoms of a cold or flu.

Note

Elder is available in a variety of colors, so choose one that has blue blossoms rather than red ones. Mildly poisonous, but nonetheless dangerous. The seeds in blue elderberries contain a minor toxin that may cause gastrointestinal discomfort and even poisoning if consumed raw in excessive numbers. Berries of the blue elder must be consumed cooked.

Elecampane (Inula helenium)

Benefits

Elecampane is a powerful yet gentle expectorant (expels mucus from the lungs and congestion from the respiratory system) and is helpful for treating coughs, bronchitis, and chronic lung infections. It is especially effective for coughs when mixed with echinacea, licorice, and/or marshmallow root. If the cough is particularly spastic or repetitive, add to the mix a little valerian, a muscle relaxant. If a respiratory or bronchial infection isn't responding readily, try

treating it with a mixture of elecampane and pleurisy root; this combination is generally effective for even the most tenacious lung infections.

How should it be used?

Elecampane is not particularly delicious tasting, so be creative when preparing it for children. As a tea, it can be mixed with other tastier herbs such as licorice and/or marshmallow root. Add a little cinnamon and sweeten it with honey or maple syrup. If using the elecampane-pleurisy blend, mix the tinctures together in equal amounts and serve in water, tea, or fruit juice.

Fennel (Foeniculum vulgare)

Benefits

This licorice-flavored herb is well-known as a carminative and digestive aid, and it is also well-known for its capacity to augment and enrich the flow of milk in breastfeeding women. Aside from being a delicious flavoring, fennel is also a good antacid, neutralizing excess acid in the stomach and intestines and clearing uric acid from the joints, which helps decrease inflammation and discomfort associated with arthritis. As a digestive aid, it is particularly effective in stimulating digestion while regulating appetite and alleviating gas.

How should it be used?

Fennel may be used to produce a delicious tea that can be used to cure colic, improve digestion, and remove gas from the system, among other things. Nursing women may consume two to four cups of tea every day to help raise and enhance the quality of their milk. It may also be used to treat eye irritation and conjunctivitis; just wash your eyes with a warm cup of fennel tea that has been filtered well through a fine-mesh strainer before using. Because of its sweet licorice-like taste, fennel is often combined with other less flavorful herbs to make them more pleasant to the palate.

Hawthorn (Crataegus oxyacantha, C. monogyna)

Benefits

Hawthorn, which is high in antioxidants, aids in the development of a healthy immune system. Traditionally, it has been regarded as a superb heart tonic, capable of strengthening and nourishing the heart. Exceptional as a preventative measure to keep the heart healthy and as a treatment for heart disease, edema, angina, and arrhythmia, hawthorn is a powerful medication. It is also beneficial at times of sadness and may assist us in coping with the difficult periods of life. Even though hawthorn is traditionally associated with heart disease and/or the elderly, it is also a good plant for

youngsters. It nourishes the blood, boosts the immune system, promotes clear eyesight, and may assist a youngster who is going through a period of grief and melancholy, among other things.

How should it be used?

Hawthorn is a delectable treat when turned into a sweetened syrup or jam. Additionally, it may be used to produce a pleasant-tasting tea when combined with other herbs like hibiscus, oats, and lemon balm. The flavor is extremely bitter; therefore, it may be necessary to sweeten it a little.

Hibiscus (Hibiscus sabdariffa)

Benefits

The hibiscus flower has a high concentration of vitamin C, bioflavonoids, and antioxidants, among other nutrients. It aids in the restoration and maintenance of general health and the support of immune function, and the prevention of colds and flu. In addition, because of its high bioflavonoid and vitamin C content, it is beneficial in the treatment of moderate anemia and impaired circulation. With its vibrant red coloration, the hibiscus flower is not only beautiful to look at but is also a rich source of anthocyanins, which are beneficial to vascular health. The flower has long been utilized in North Africa to promote respiratory health. It is now being used to treat a number of ailments, including respiratory infections and sore throats, in various methods. Aside from all of this, hibiscus tea is one of the most beautiful natural drinks available, and children, in particular, seem to like it.

How should it be used?

The tea made from the huge hibiscus blooms has a stunning ruby red color. The flavor is acidic, with a sweet aftertaste; youngsters may appreciate it if it is sweetened a little more. Make a thick syrup out of hibiscus flowers and use it to flavor sparkling water by mixing it with the sparkling water.

Lemon balm (Melissa officinalis)

Benefits

This delightfully aromatic member of the mint family is one of nature's most effective nervine herbs because of its calming, antiviral, and antibacterial properties. It is used as a moderate sedative during times of melancholy and mourning, and it is considered to be one of the most significant natural antiviral herbs on the planet. It is particularly effective in treating recurring outbreaks of herpes, shingles, and thrush, and it may also be used as a preventative if taken on a regular schedule.

How should it be used?

Despite the fact that lemon balm dries well, its taste is finest when it is fresh. Lemon balm may be used as a tea or tincture, but it is most often consumed as a tea in Europe because of its refreshing and agreeable taste. The tea may be had throughout the day with lemon and honey to relieve tension and anxiety and function as a preventative for herpes, shingles, and thrush infections (all related viral infections). It is an essential treatment when it comes to viral infections, such as measles and mumps. Add hawthorn to this if you want to help someone through a period of grieving. In order to cure mild to moderate depression, add St. John's wort to the mixture. Fresh lemon balm creates a wonderful syrup that may be used to flavor sparkling water for a pleasant spritzer or all-natural soda, or it can be used to flavor tea.

Licorice (Glycyrrhiza glabra)

Benefits

Licorice has powerful antiviral characteristics, making it a good treatment for any viral illness, including herpes, shingles, thrush, measles, and mumps. Licorice is a natural antiviral, making it an effective treatment for any viral infection. It is often used in conjunction with lemon balm for this purpose. Throat irritation, respiratory infections, viral infections, and gastrointestinal inflammations such as ulcers can all be relieved and healed with the help of chamomile's high mucilaginous content and antiviral and anti-inflammatory properties. It also has modest laxative qualities, which might be beneficial in treating mild constipation.

How should it be used?

This plant is quite sweet, and it is often blended with other herbs to make them more appealing to the palate. Licorice root, on the other hand, is generally considered to be overly sweet when consumed alone. As a result, it is typically combined with other herbs to reduce the sweetness. Licorice syrup is a delicious concoction that may be used to produce a refreshing soda by mixing with sparkling water. The chewing of licorice sticks is popular among children, and you can even give a "stick" of licorice root to a teething infant to chew on — though you may need to give the root a few "chews" yourself to soften it sufficiently so that the young one may begin to bites on it. It can generally keep a teething infant occupied for a short period of time, at the very least.

Marsh mallow (Althaea officinalis)

Benefits

Marshmallow, like slippery elm, may be used as a calming, cooling demulcent in herbal treatments, although it is far more widely accessible and easier to produce than its more well-known cousin. Marshmallow root contains antibacterial and anti-inflammatory qualities, making it a useful remedy for a variety of ailments. In particular, it soothes swollen and irritated membranes, and it is often used in tea blends and tinctures to treat sore throats, respiratory infections, and stomach discomfort, among other things.

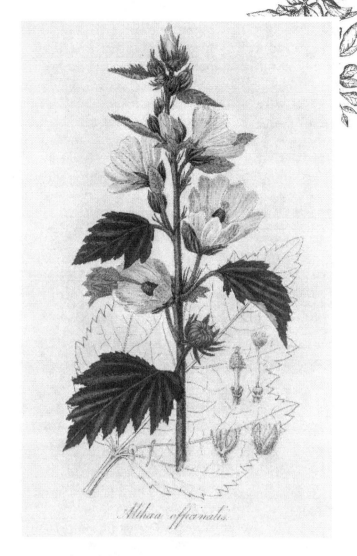

Althaea officinalis.

How should it be used?

Tea made from this herb may be used to treat sore throats, gastric discomfort, bronchial inflammation, diarrhea, and constipation. Marshmallow is very relaxing to the urinary system, and it is often prescribed for urinary tract and bladder infection treatment. The herb may also be used externally: make a thick paste with water to heal burns and irritated skin, or blend it with oatmeal to use as a soothing wash or bath for irritated, itchy, dry skin.

Nettle (Urtica dioica)

Benefits

Nettle is a nutritional powerhouse containing a wealth of vitamins and minerals. The fact that it is a particularly rich source of both iron and calcium means that it may be utilized to help replenish these two essential minerals in pregnant and nursing moms (for this purpose, mix it with raspberry leaf, another good nutritive and also a female reproductive tonic). Nettle contains calcium in an easily-assimilated bio chelated form, which makes it particularly beneficial for stress relief and nerve regeneration, and overall health. When combined with creamy green oats, it has a particularly soothing effect on the nerves. It is also beneficial for its function in aiding tissue and bone healing and is often combined with oats and horsetail for this reason in herbal tea blends. Because of its high calcium and mineral content, it may aid in the development of thick bone tissue and the alleviation of growing pains in children under the age of five. According to various reports, it is an efficient cure for allergies and hay fever, and it has been proven to perform miracles for certain individuals.

How should it be used?

Nettle has a flavor that is comparable to spinach, and it is often served as a mineral-rich side dish at meals after being boiled and dusted with olive oil, lemon juice, and a little feta. It may be substituted for spinach or other cooked greens in any recipe that calls for spinach. It must, however, be steamed entirely and thoroughly; otherwise, it will "sting" if it is undercooked. Nettle stings include formic acid, which is found in minute amounts in the fine hairs found on the underside of a nettle leaf and on the plant's stem. Formic acid produces skin swelling and an itchy rash, and it is the same ingredient found in bee stings. Pick nettles with gloves, take care not to rub up against them, and teach your children to appreciate this plant are good ideas for this season. If somebody does manage to be "stung,"

they should apply a poultice made from plantain leaves to pull the poisons out of their system. Even though nettle may be used to treat allergies as a tincture or tea, it seems to be more beneficial in freeze-dried form for this purpose. If feasible, mix freeze-dried nettle capsules with nettle tea and/or tincture for an even more potent combination of nettle benefits.

Oats (Avena sativa)

Benefits

Green milky oats are regarded as one of the most effective nutritive tonics for the nervous system. They are especially beneficial in situations of nervous tiredness, stress, general irritability, and grumpiness, among other conditions. A rich amount of silica and calcium, and having mucilaginous qualities are found in milky oats. They are particularly beneficial for those who suffer from nervous system abnormalities.

How should it be used?

Drinking oat tea, either by itself or in combination with other herbs like lemon balm, hawthorn, and hibiscus is a pleasant experience. Oat stalks are also a wonderful addition to any tea mix. It is really excellent when brewed at twice or triple strength and then blended with fruit juice. According to experts, children who are tense, hyperactive, and worried, as well as those who are continually disturbed or angry, should drink oat tea. The high mucilaginous content of oatmeal baths makes them particularly soothing for dry, itchy skin as well as skin irritations and chickenpox.

Peppermint (Mentha piperita)

Benefits

Peppermint is an invigorating burst of pure green power. Peppermint is used in the preparation of brain tonics and as a digestive aid. Also, it is particularly good in alleviating nausea and stomach cramps, among other symptoms.

How should it be used?

Especially useful for youngsters who are experiencing stomach pain and slow digestion or who just want a burst of radiant vitality. Peppermint may be consumed as tea, used as a tincture (diluted), or mouthwash. It also forms a delectable syrup that can be used to make a refreshing drink by mixing it with sparkling water. Introducing children to this plant in the yard is my favorite activity, and I often encourage them to chew on its refreshing, sweet leaves. Peppermint essential oil is also incredibly therapeutic and beneficial, but due to its concentration, it should be used with caution, particularly when it is used with children. When a drop of the essential oil is added to a little amount of water, it creates a mouthwash that is both refreshing and stomach-settling for a youngster who is having a round of vomiting and helping to rid the mouth of bad taste.

Red clover (Trifolium pratense)

Benefits

Red clover, one of the greatest respiratory tonics, is widely used with children who suffer from recurrent coughs, colds, and other respiratory disorders. Red clover is an excellent source of calcium, nitrogen, iron, and other minerals. As a "blood cleanser," it has been used for centuries to heal heart, blood, and liver disorders. Psoriasis, eczema and dry, itchy skin may all benefit from it.

How should it be used?

Tea made with red clover has a wonderful sweet taste. Combine it with other respiratory tonic herbs like mullein and elecampane to treat chronic respiratory disorders. While treating skin problems, red clover works well with oats and lemon balm; when treating blood and heart problems, it works well with hawthorn and hibiscus. Red clover tea or tincture is recommended when the body is congested or has abnormal growths, such as cysts, tumors, or fibroids, as a blood purifier. As a hay fever and allergy remedy, it is often used in conjunction with nettle.

Red raspberry (Rubus idaeus)

Benefits

The usage of a raspberry leaf as a reproductive tonic has been around for a long time. As a tonic for pregnant and lactating women, it also reduces heavy menstruation and vaginal bleeding. Pregnant and breastfeeding women, babies, and toddlers may benefit from raspberry leaves' high vitamin and mineral content, notably calcium and iron. Pregnant and lactating women are typically advised to drink tea made from the leaves and other nourishing herbs, such as nettle, oats, and red clover.

How should it be used?

The tonic's ability to prevent heavy menstruation and vaginal bleeding makes it ideal for pregnant and breastfeeding women. Raspberries' high calcium and iron content benefits expectant and nursing mothers and babies and toddlers. Tea brewed from the leaves and other nutritious herbs, such as nettle, oats, and red clover, often recommended to expectant and nursing mothers.

Rose Hip (Rosa canina)

Benefits

With more vitamin C than virtually any other plant and several times the amount in citrus fruit, rose hips are an excellent supplement. Antioxidant vitamin C is well-known for its ability to combat illness. As an astringent and toner, rose leaves are often seen in cosmetics. Flower essences, love potions, and herbal remedies are all based on the flowers.

How should it be used?

A syrup or jam made with vitamin-rich fresh rose hips is a delicious treat. Dried seedless rose hips may also be used to produce a delightful raw jam (see the recipe on the next page). Tea made from rose hips is a popular and well-liked beverage.

- Fill a pint jar halfway with dried rose hips that have been deseeded.
- Cover the rose hips with about an inch or two of apple juice or cider in the jar's three-quarters capacity.
- For best results, let the jar out in the open for several hours or overnight. A thick, jam-like consistency will form as the rose hips absorb the liquid.
- A tablespoon or three of maple sugar syrup may be used if required to sweeten this jam. If you choose, you can also use ground cinnamon and other flavorful herbs in the recipe to make it even more delectable. It's wonderfully basic and uncomplicated, but I like it that way.
- Keep in the refrigerator for 2 to 3 weeks in a glass jar with a tight-fitting cover.

Slippery elm (Ulmus fulva, U. rubra)

Benefits

The inner bark of Ulmus fulva, often known as the slippery elm tree, its smooth and gummy, and it is one of the most effective medicines for relieving any and all inflammation, whether internal or external. It is extremely beneficial when it comes to burns, sore throats, respiratory infections, and digestive disorders. It may also be used to alleviate the irritation caused by diarrhea and constipation, among other things. Despite this, it is still often used in lozenges, which are used to relieve sore and irritated throats.

How should it be used?

The sweet taste of slippery elm blends beautifully with licorice, fennel, and cinnamon to create a pleasant, relaxing throat and digestive tea that is also good for digestion. To create the tea, soak the bark in cold or cool water overnight, or simmer it for 10 to 15 minutes on the stovetop. For debilitated or sick people, adding powdered slippery elm to oatmeal may create a highly relaxing, readily digestible, and therapeutic gruel that is extremely soothing and healing. In addition, the powder is simple to include. Alternatively, you may manufacture a kind of "syrup". Adults often loathe the slimy feel of this syrup, while youngsters seem to like it immensely. Use as a cough suppressant and aid in the recovery of health following sickness.

Note

When nothing else works, a tiny quantity of slippery elm powder may help relieve a kid's swelling, painful throat, or digestive troubles or assist a youngster who has been unwell for a long length of time regain his or her health. Just remember to use it carefully and only when necessary, instead of using one plant with comparable qualities, such as marshmallow root. Lastly, only purchase slippery elm cultivated on a farm or that has been responsibly collected (from fallen branches).

Spearmint (Mentha spicata)

Benefits

As a result of its cooling, refreshing, and uplifting characteristics, spearmint is one of the most popular mints. Spearmint is generally preferred by children over peppermint since it is less potent. It's great for boosting one's mood and improving one's spirits since it creates a wonderful and refreshing tea.

How should it be used?

When you're unwell, particularly if you're vomiting, use spearmint to soothe your stomach. You may use spearmint to produce a syrup that can be added to sparkling water or iced tea for a light, energizing drink; the fresh leaves are also excellent in iced tea. Spearmint honey may be made by combining fresh leaves with honey. Fill a pint jar halfway with fresh spearmint leaves. Warm the honey and drizzle it over the leaves. To get that minty honey flavor, let the container rest in a sunny window for a few days. You may either remove the leaves from the honey or leave them in. You may make "instant tea" by adding a few spoonsful of this honey to boiling water. Sweeten and flavor other teas using honey.

Stevia (Stevia rebaudiana)

Benefits

Stevia is really a godsend in the kitchen. A sweetener that is 50 times sweeter than sugar and has no calories or decay-causing sugar crystals is a great addition to since it any diabetic's medicine cabinet sweetens and helps regulate blood sugar levels. Most diabetics may consume stevia without experiencing any sugar-related concerns since it is a panacea for pancreatic imbalances.

How should it be used?

It is necessary to combine stevia with other herbs since it is so sweet on its own. It's best not to use more than 2% in a tea mix since it tends to dominate the taste. On the other hand, children are known to "graze" on stevia because they like its highly sweet taste.

Wild cherry (Prunus serotina)

Benefits

As one of the most widely used cough medicines and expectorants, wild cherry bark is featured in the US Pharmacopeia's yearly drug reference as a rare herbal remedy. Many commercial cough medicines still include it. Digestive health is also improved by using this supplement.

How should it be used?

Coughs and colds benefit greatly from the use of wild cherry teas, syrups, and tinctures. Elderberries have potent antiviral and immune-enhancing effects, so combine them with this drink. For persistent, long-lasting coughs,

combine it with elecampane. Wild cherry bark, elecampane, and pleurisy root may be used to treat bronchial infections that are more difficult to treat.

Note: After a storm, gather the delicate inner bark from fallen limbs to protect the trees. A tree will die if it is debarked near its core.

AMAZING BONUSES FOR ALL THE READERS:

Just Scan the QR-Code below to get them!

Conclusions

In the words of the experts, "conventional medicine" refers to "the medical techniques derived from diverse cultures that are utilized in the preservation of health as well as in the diagnosis, improvement or cure of both physical and mental illness." It is crucial to concentrate on a holistic approach to life, which involves harmonizing the mind, body, and environment and concentrating on health rather than a disease, according to traditional medicine. In traditional medicine, the emphasis is on the patient's general health rather than on the specific illness or disease that ails them, and the use of herbs is an integral element of every system. The enormous manufacture of chemically produced medications during the last century has transformed health care around the world. Though, most people in underdeveloped nations still use traditional healers and herbal remedies as their main healthcare providers. Conventional medicine is used by up to 80 percent of the people in Africa and 70 percent of the population in India. Moreover, 90% of China's general hospitals contain traditional medical facilities, accounting for around 40% of all health care provided. Ethnobotanicals are not just used in underdeveloped nations, but they have become more popular in developed countries during the last two decades, with a growing interest in natural remedies. About 36% of adults and 10% of children in the United States used traditional medicine in 2009. For the most part, patients choose traditional medicine because it is more economical, more aligned with their philosophy, less likely to have side effects than chemical (synthetic) medications, more likely to provide individualized treatment, and more open to the general public. Health promotion and treatment for non-life-threatening illnesses are the primary uses of herbal medicines. People resort to traditional medicine when modern medicine is unable to treat their illness, such as in the case of advanced cancer or newly developing infectious illnesses. It's not only because they're manufactured up of natural materials that many people feel traditional medications are safe. There are several ways to prepare and absorb raw herbs and their dry extracts, such as making teas and syrup, making ointments, salves, rubs, capsules, and tablets. It's crucial to keep in mind that various plants and herbs need different extraction methods, such as tinctures produced from alcohol, vinegar, hot water extracts, long-term boiling extracts, mostly roots or bark (decoctions), and cold infusions (cold infusions are similar to cold infusions) (macerates). Herbal extracts and products have no standardization; therefore, the constituents might vary greatly across batches and manufacturers.

Philosophy behind Herbal Remedies

Some popular treatments have their roots in plants and botanicals, as we've discovered. More on this when we go at the remedies, but for now,

let's look at the basics of how herbal remedies work. Herbal treatments are typically effective in treating minor digestive issues, including indigestion and nausea. There are times when all you need to feel better is some peppermint or chamomile tea. Injured or sick livers may also benefit from herbs, which can protect them and possibly aid in their recovery. Herbs like milk thistle are well-known for their ability to support a healthy liver. The immune system is boosted by several herbal remedies, while others assist the body fight illness and inflammation. Anti-infective herbs like Echinacea and Ginseng are examples of immune-stimulating botanicals, which may help you stay healthy. Inflammation may be reduced with the use of St. John's wort, ginger, and Ginkgo biloba. For minor sprains, tight muscles, and discomfort in the joints, herbal medications may help. A combination of antioxidant-rich botanicals and herbs, including calendula, witch hazel, and capsicum, may help maintain healthy connective tissue. Premenstrual syndrome, menopausal symptoms, and pregnancy side effects may be alleviated with the right herbs. Ginger helps alleviate morning sickness, while black cohosh can help alleviate both PMS and menopausal symptoms. Male reproductive health is supported by ginseng, ginkgo Biloba, and saw palmetto. Over-the-counter drugs for sore throat, cough, and colds may have unpleasant side effects, which is why they are commonly prescribed. However, herbal remedies may help alleviate these symptoms, as well as a runny nose and a mild respiratory infection. Echinacea with thyme and hyssop may ease bronchial spasms, allowing you to relax in cold and flu treatments.

If you have enjoyed this book, feel free to leave a review to share your experience.

Just scan the QR code on the right, it will take 30 seconds!

My best wishes and may the Spirit guide your journey!

Native American Traditional Medicine

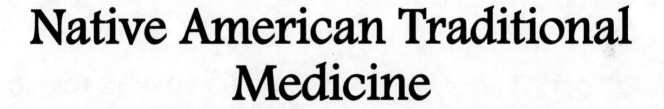

100 Herbal Remedies for Common Ailments

BOOKS 12 and 13 of "The Native American Herbalist's Bible"

Natalie Hathale

What are herbal supplements, and how do they differ from dietary supplements?

Herbal products, botanical products, or phytomedicines are manufactured from botanicals or plants used to treat or maintain health. Herbal supplements are dietary supplements derived primarily from plants and intended solely for oral administration.

Even though many prescription and over-the-counter medicines are derived from plant sources, these products are controlled by the FDA and include only purified chemicals. Herbal supplements may be made up of whole plants or portions of plants.

It is possible to utilize dried, chopped, powdered, capsuled, or liquid herbal supplements in any of the following ways:

- Consumed in pill form, powder, or tincture form
- As a cup of tea
- Gels, lotions, and creams are all forms of topical application.
- Included into the water supply for the tub

The use of herbal supplements has been around for a long time. American consumers' usage of herbal supplements has become commonplace in recent years. However, not everyone is a fan of them. The usage of herbal supplements is still debatable because the FDA and other regulatory organizations do not scrutinize them closely. Consult your doctor if you are experiencing any symptoms or conditions and use herbal supplements.

Tips for selecting herbal supplements with care

Conventional drugs may interact with herbal supplements, or herbal supplements may have powerful effects. Self-diagnosis is a bad idea. Before using any herbal supplements, be sure to check with your doctor.

Take the time to learn. Get as much information as possible about the herbs you're taking by talking to your doctor and contacting the companies who make the supplements.

Follow the label instructions and only take herbal supplements in the recommended dosage. Take the supplement only as prescribed, and don't exceed the suggested dosage.

Take the advice of a pro. Seek the advice of a naturopathic doctor or herbalist who has completed specialized training in this field. Or, given the fact that you bought this book, become one!

Keep an eye out for any adverse effects. Dosage should be reduced or stopped if symptoms such as dizziness, headaches, or nausea occur.

Be aware of possible allergic reactions. Having a severe allergic response might make it difficult for someone to breathe. Call 911 or your local emergency number for assistance if this happens to you.

Do your homework on the firm that manufactures the herbs you're consuming. It's advisable to stick with a well-known brand of herbal supplements because not all herbal supplements are created equal.

AMAZING BONUSES FOR ALL THE READERS:

Just Scan the QR-Code below to get them!

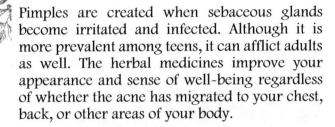

Acne

Pimples are created when sebaceous glands become irritated and infected. Although it is more prevalent among teens, it can afflict adults as well. The herbal medicines improve your appearance and sense of well-being regardless of whether the acne has migrated to your chest, back, or other areas of your body.

Toner with Calendula Extract

With calendula, which soothes inflammation, this simple toner also has witch hazel, which fights bacteria while softening your skin. This toner has a shelf life of at least a year if it's kept in the dark, cool place.

Ingredients

- Oil of calendula, 2 tsp.
- Witch hazel: 1/3 cup

The gel of Agrimony and Chamomile

Aloe vera gel with agrimony and chamomile soothe redness and inflammation. Refrigerate the gel until ready to use.

Ingredients

- Dried agrimony, 2 teaspoons
- Dried chamomile is 2 teaspoons
- 1/2 cup of water
- 1 tablespoon of aloe vera gel (check this book for an easy and practical method to do it by yourself!)

If you are allergic to ragweed plants or are taking prescription blood thinners, you should omit the chamomile from your recipe.

Allergies

In some people, cat dander, pollen, or dust might trigger an allergic reaction. Numerous foods, beverages, and even the environment include allergies, which makes them difficult to avoid entirely. On the other hand, herbal therapies do not reduce your body's immune reaction to allergens.

Feverfew and Peppermint Tincture

Feverfew and peppermint can help to clear the airways following an allergic reaction. If you are unable to include feverfew in this tincture, substitute peppermint.

Ingredients:

- Dried feverfew 2 ounces
- Dried peppermint weighing 6 ounces
- 2 mugs vodka, 80% alcohol, without flavorings

When you experience allergy symptoms, take 5 drops orally as needed. It's possible to dilute the flavor by mixing it with water or juice.

Precautions: Feverfew should not be used by anyone who is allergic to ragweed or during pregnancy.

Syrup of Garlic and Ginkgo Biloba

Ginkgo biloba is a natural antihistamine with anti-inflammatory properties, and garlic aids in infection prevention. If you can, utilize local honey to help strengthen your allergy resistance.

Ingredients

- 2 ounces minced garlic, either fresh or frozen
- 2 ounces crushed or chopped ginkgo Biloba
- 1 cup honey from the area

Precaution: To avoid potentially dangerous interactions between blood thinners and Ginkgo biloba, you should consult your doctor before taking the supplement. It is recommended that children under the age of 12 consume one teaspoon of the product three times a day.

Asthma

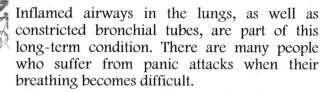

Inflamed airways in the lungs, as well as constricted bronchial tubes, are part of this long-term condition. There are many people who suffer from panic attacks when their breathing becomes difficult.

Infusion of Ginkgo and Thyme

Ginkgo biloba and thyme widen airways and relax the muscles in your chest, allowing you to breathe more easily. It is possible to improve the taste of this tea by adding honey or dried peppermint to it.

Ingredients

- Water that has been heated to boiling
- Dried ginkgo Biloba: 1 teaspoon
- Dried thyme: 1 teaspoon.

Directions: In a large mug, add the hot water. Ten minutes of steeping time is recommended before consuming the tea.

Precautions: To avoid potentially dangerous interactions between blood thinners and Ginkgo biloba, you should consult your doctor before taking the supplement.

Vaporized Peppermint-Rosemary Therapy

Rosemary leaves contain a vital histamine-blocking Ingredients, whereas peppermint helps to expand your airways and make breathing easier by relaxing muscles in your throat.

Ingredients

- Steaming hot water in 4 cups (not boiling)
- Crushed fresh peppermint leaves make up half a cup.
- Rosemary leaves that have been minced into a fine powder

Precautions: Others, such as rosemary, fennel, sage, eucalyptus, hyssop, camphor, and spike lavender, have been shown to produce seizures in those with epilepsy or at risk for it.

Athlete Foot (Plantar Wrats)

A fungus that thrives in moist, warm, and dark environments causes this itchy and sometimes painful infection.

Fresh Garlic Poultice

Athlete's feet can be killed by garlic, a potent antifungal agent. The antifungal properties of raw honey help to keep the garlic in place on your feet . You can make a double or triple batch and use it across two or three days if you like, but making a new batch for each treatment will help you heal faster.

Ingredients

- A sliver of garlic, finely chopped
- 1 tsp. Of raw honey.

Garlic may cause a skin rash in those who are hypersensitive to it.

Ointment with Goldenseal

To combat athlete's foot, goldenseal is a powerful antimicrobial agent. This ointment can be used on its own or in conjunction with a Fresh Garlic Poultice to speed healing. Cool, dark storage will keep it fresh for up to one year.

Ingredients

- 2 cups of olive oil with a light flavor
- Goldenseal root, chopped, 2 ounces
- One ounce of beeswax.

Precautions: Using this product while pregnant or nursing is not recommended. If you have high blood pressure, do not use it.

Backache

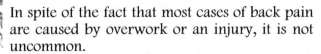

In spite of the fact that most cases of back pain are caused by overwork or an injury, it is not uncommon.

Inactivity, muscle spasms, and inflammation are all potential causes. Make an appointment with your doctor if the pain is intolerable, if it causes you to lose bladder control, or if you suffer numbness or tingling in your extremities.

Blue Vervain and Passionflower Tea

Both passionflower and blue vervain have a number of beneficial properties, including the ability to calm the nervous system and relieve painful muscles. Make sure to consume this blend when you have a chance to sit back and relax.

Ingredients

- Water that has been heated to boiling
- Dried passionflower: 1 tbsp
- Dried blue Vervain:1 tsp.

Directions: Pour the hot water into a large mug. Allow the tea to steep for ten minutes before drinking. Relax and savor each sip of tea. Up to twice a day can be repeated.

Precautions: Pregnant women should avoid using passionflower or blue vervain. If you have issues with your prostate or baldness, stay away from passionflower.

Peppermint and Ginger Salve

Medicinal herbs such as ginger and peppermint possess powerful components that permeate the skin, causing a warming sensation that helps to relax muscles. This salve will keep for up to a year if it is stored in a cold, dark place.

Ingredients

- 1 quart of olive oil with a light flavor
- 1 ounce of chopped dried ginger root
- A quarter-ounce of crushed dried peppermint
- One ounce of beeswax is required.

Precautions: In the case of blood thinners, gallbladder disease, or a bleeding disorder, you should avoid ginger.

Bloating

Constipation, excess stomach acid, and the onset of the premenstrual cycle are all causes of bloating for women. Herbs can assist your body in returning to its normal form by assisting in the removal of toxins, excess gas, and built-up fluid from your system.

Mint and fennel tea with peppermint leaves

If you feel that your bloating is caused by a buildup of gas in your digestive tract, peppermint and fennel are also wonderful options to try. It is believed that the antispasmodic compounds included in these delicious-tasting plants help to relax smooth muscle tissue in the digestive tract. If the taste of this tea is too strong for you, you can sweeten it with a teaspoon of honey.

Ingredients

- Water that has been heated to boiling
- 1-teaspoon peppermint dried herb
- 14 teaspoon crushed fennel seeds

Tincture of Dandelion Roots

The bitter taste of dandelion root belies its potent diuretic properties, which will help your body rid itself of toxins and restore your sense of well-being.

Ingredients

- 8 oz. Finely chopped dandelion roots
- 2 mugs vodka, 80% alcohol, without flavorings

Directions: Let the dandelion roots macerate in vodka in your fridge for 2 days. Then take 5 drops whenever you need, max 3 times a day.

Breathing Difficulty

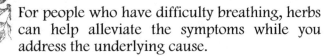

For people who have difficulty breathing, herbs can help alleviate the symptoms while you address the underlying cause.

Infusion of Hyssop and Sage

In addition to being a potent antiviral, hyssop is also an excellent expectorant. As a result of sage's antiseptic properties, you'll recover faster. A robust herbal flavor distinguishes this blend, which some enjoy while others find they need to sweeten with honey to make it easier to swallow.

Ingredients

- Boiling water for 4 cups
- Dried hyssop, 4 teaspoons per serving
- 4 tbsp. of dried sage

Directions: Using a teapot, combine the heating water and the dried herbs until well combined. Ten minutes after opening the jar, remove the lid and let it sit for another 10 minutes. As you inhale the steam, take a few deep breaths and enjoy a cup of the infusion as a way to unwind.

Precaution: Avoid taking hyssop if you are pregnant or suffer from epilepsy, as it can cause miscarriage.

Syrup of Angelica and Goldenseal

As it stimulates and warms the lungs, angelica relieves congestion and some of the discomfort that goes along with it. Goldenseal has powerful antiseptic and antiviral properties, making it easier for you to recover from an infection. Honey coats your throat, which may be sore from coughing, and masks the bitter flavors. When stored properly, this syrup can last for up to six months.

Ingredients

- 1 ounce finely chopped angelica
- 1 ounce finely chopped dried goldenseal root
- A quart of honey

Directions: Let the herbs macerate in honey in your fridge for 2 days. Then take 1 tbsp of the syrup whenever you need, max 3 times a day.

Precaution: Avoid this product and Angelica in general while pregnant or nursing and if you have been prescribed with anticoagulant medications.

Bronchitis

Bronchitis is a condition in which the bronchial linings become inflamed, which can develop as a result of an allergy, an irritation, or even an infection. It is also known as asthma. A deep, rasping cough is a common symptom as well. Herbal treatments have been found to be effective in reducing bronchitis-related symptoms, especially if associated with rest and correct hydration

Aromatherapy with Rosemary and Licorice Roots

In addition to opening the airways and stimulating circulation, licorice root and rosemary also provide relief from the inflammation and the consequent discomfort associated with bronchitis.

Ingredients

- 1 tbsp. dried licorice root, chopped
- Rosemary leaves that have been minced into a fine powder

Precautions: People suffering from diabetes, kidney difficulties, epilepsy, heart diseases in general and in particular high blood pressure, and other medical disorders should avoid using this product.

Infusion of Goldenseal and Hyacinth.

Hydrastine and berberine, two powerful antiviral and antibacterial agents are found in goldenseal. Using hyssop can help alleviate bronchial spasms and can clear any lung congestion and also provide a calming and soothing effect.

Ingredients

- 1 tbsp. chopped dried goldenseal root
- 2 tbsp. Dried hyssop
- A quart of honey

Precautions: Using this product while pregnant or nursing is not recommended. Also, it is not indicated in case of high blood pressure or epilepsy. Ingesting goldenseal may cause diarrhea and acid reflux. In the case of children under 12, one teaspoon should be taken 2 or 3 times daily.

Bruise

If a bruise is particularly deep or painful, it may be a sign of more severe injuries or health issues. Even bumping into a piece of furniture can result in minor bruises. It's essential to see a doctor if, for no apparent reason, you suddenly find yourself bruising more frequently than usual.

Fresh Hyssop Poultice

Hyssop relieves pain and increases blood flow, allowing your bruise to heal more quickly. You can treat a bruise with a few drops of hyssop essential oil if you haven't yet planted hyssop in your garden. Hyssop poultices can also be made by heating up one tablespoon of warm water with a teaspoon of dried herb and making a poultice out of it.

Ingredients: Finely chopped hyssop leaves from the garden

Cover the affected area with a soft cloth while the chopped leaves are applied to the skin. Take it out for 10 to 15 minutes, and then remove it. Your bruise will fade if you repeat this two or three times a day.

Precautions: You should be aware of the possible negative effects of hyssop, which can trigger rapid and involuntary muscle contractions. Avoid it if you have epilepsy or if you're pregnant.

Artichoke Salve

Antiinflammatory and pain-relieving properties of arnica make this salve an excellent choice for minor aches and pains.

Ingredients:

- 1 quart of olive oil with a light flavor
- 2 oz. dried arnica
- 2 tbsp. beeswax.

Precautions: Do not use it on broken skin. Long-term use may cause skin irritation; discontinue use if you notice any signs of skin irritation.

Burn

Minor burns, such as those inflicted while cooking, can be treated with herbal remedies. If a burn appears deep, has charred skin, or covers a large area of the body, seek medical attention right away.

Compress of Chickweed-Mullein

For burns that are susceptible to infection, mullein has antibacterial and anti-inflammatory properties, and its cooling, astringent properties help alleviate pain. Chickweed is a cooling herb that also aids in the healing process.

Ingredients

- 3 tsp. Chickweed finely chopped
- 2 tsp. Finely chopped fresh mullein leaf

Fresh Aloe Gel

Aloe vera gel has anti-inflammatory properties that can help treat burns. After a minor burn, the skin regenerates more quickly because aloe increases collagen synthesis. While fresh aloe gel from the plant is preferable, bottled aloe gel will do. Just remove the leaves from the plant and let them sit in an empty glass for half an hour to make all the resin go down. Peel the leaves and scoop the gel out. Use it within a week.

Pro Tip: add salicylic acid (1 tsp for every cup of gel) to increase the expiry of the gel up to 1 month

Canker Sore

Even though canker sores can be painful and bothersome, they aren't something to be concerned about. If you experience recurrent canker sores, you should consult your doctor about getting tested for a metabolic disorder.

Infusion of Calendula and Comfrey

Soothed calendula is an excellent remedy for minor wounds because it has antifungal, anti-inflammatory, and antibacterial properties. A canker sore can be made more bearable by taking comfrey, which speeds up the healing process while also reducing the pain and itching associated with the sore. It's possible to save time by making multiples of this treatment.

Ingredients

- 1 tsp. Dried calendula
- 1 tsp. Dried comfrey flowers
- 2 tbsp. boiling water

Tincture of Goldenseal

Goldenseal root's berberine and hydrastine content make it an excellent antiviral and antibacterial herb. In addition to treating canker sores with this goldenseal tincture, you can also use it to treat minor wounds and burns. This tincture is also excellent if taken internally in case of cold or flu.

Ingredients

- 4 ounces of dried goldenseal root, chopped
- 1 cup 80% alcohol

Precautions: Using this product while pregnant or nursing is not recommended. If you have high blood pressure, stay away from this product.

Chickenpox

Chickenpox can't be cured, but herbal remedies can help alleviate the discomfort.

Comfrey and Licorice bath.

In addition to relieving the itching associated with chickenpox, these herbs also have antiviral properties. Despite its pungent aroma, apple cider vinegar has a calming effect. Premade tinctures of comfrey and licorice root are used in this quick recipe, but you can easily make your own.

Ingredients

- 4-cups of raw, organic, unpasteurized apple cider vinegar
- ½ tsp. Comfrey extract
- ½ tsp. Licorice root tincture

Precaution: If you have high blood pressure, diabetes, or any other medical condition, you should avoid using licorice root as it can cause complications.

Goldenseal-Calendula Lotion

Calendula, aloe, and goldenseal work together to relieve itching and promote the healing of chickenpox blisters. This gel can also be used to heal minor skin injuries such as cuts and scrapes, according to the manufacturer. It will remain fresh for up to two days after being opened. When kept in the refrigerator for several weeks, the flavor becomes more intense.

Ingredients

- 2 tbsp. Dried Calendula
- 2 tbsp. Goldenseal root (chopped)
- ½ cup Aloe vera gel

Cold

The common cold is a nuisance, with symptoms like coughing, sneezing, and a runny nose. Start treatment as soon as symptoms appear to shorten the duration of your cold.

Tea with Thyme

Thyme has antitussive, or cough suppressant, properties, and it works quickly to calm coughing. Congestion in the lungs can be alleviated by using this expectorant. Sore throats and aches that accompany a cold can be alleviated by drinking hot tea. If you like your tea sweeter, try mixing in a teaspoon of honey.

Ingredients

- Boiling water, one cup
- 2 tsp. Dried thyme, minced

Directions: Fill a large mug halfway with hot water and set it aside. Allow the tea to steep for 10 minutes after adding the thyme and covering the mug.

Relax and inhale the steam as you sip your tea. Aim for at least six repetitions per day.

Raspberry Leaf Tea

Comfrey, mullein, thyme, and raspberry leaf can be used to treat coughs and sore throats, as well as fevers, body aches, and lung irritations caused by irritants. There is no need to worry if you don't have all of the herbs listed in this recipe; they are all beneficial and will help alleviate cold symptoms.

Ingredients

- 1 tbsp. dried Comfrey leaves
- 1 tbsp. dried mullein root
- 1 tbsp. Dried raspberry leaf
- 1 tbsp. Dried thyme.
- Water, two cups
- Honey, one cup

Cold Sore

To get a cold sore, you need to have the herpes simplex virus. Prior to the appearance of raised clusters of blisters, herbal remedies should be applied to alleviate tingling and itching. It is possible to use herbal remedies to alleviate the symptoms of a cold sore, but they may not be strong enough to stop the virus from spreading.

Poultice of Garlic

Raw garlic has a strong antiviral effect and can reduce the length of a cold sore. If you prefer not to have the garlic held in place while you do anything else, you can use first aid tape to do so.

Ingredients

- Halved garlic clove

Directions: Dry the affected area with a clean cloth then treat a cold sore, press a piece of garlic cut on its cut side against the sore for ten minutes. Do this three or four times per day to get rid of the cold sore.

Precautions : Garlic can cause a rash in people who are allergic; if this happens, stop using it.

Sage and Echinacea Cleanser

These herbs contain antiviral and antibacterial characteristics, which assist to keep the sores from becoming infected and becoming infected. Echinacea, sage, aloe vera, and witch hazel are all effective in reducing itching and irritability of the skin. In a properly kept environment, this toner has a shelf life of at least one year. Refrigerated.

Ingredients

- 12 ounces of chopped dried echinacea root
- 12 ounce crumbled dried sage
- Light olive or jojoba oil can be used in this recipe.
- The 2-teaspoons gel of aloe
- Witch hazel, 14 cup

Precaution: When using echinacea, be aware of any allergies you may have to ragweed or any other autoimmune disease.

Colic

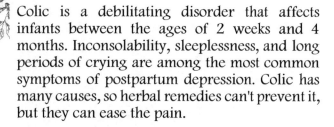

Colic is a debilitating disorder that affects infants between the ages of 2 weeks and 4 months. Inconsolability, sleeplessness, and long periods of crying are among the most common symptoms of postpartum depression. Colic has many causes, so herbal remedies can't prevent it, but they can ease the pain.

Blend of Chamomile and Lavender

Colic pain can be alleviated with the help of a powerful antispasmodic ingredient in chamomile: Spiroether. Because of its calming effects on anxiety and stress, it may be able to help your baby sleep better as well. Drinking chamomile tea may help alleviate your baby's symptoms if you are breastfeeding.

Ingredients

- 1 tsp. Dried chamomile flowers
- Boiling water, one cup

Directions: Chamomile and boiling water should be brewed in a teapot. For ten minutes, keep the pot covered and let the tea steep. Wait until the infusion is lukewarm before drinking.

Using a sterilized bottle, add 2 tablespoons of the mixture and allow your baby to eat it. When symptoms of colic arise, repeat this procedure once or twice a day.

Precaution: Blood thinners, such as warfarin should not be used while taking chamomile.

Ginger and Fennel infused water.

In commercial gripe water, high-fructose corn syrup is commonly found. An easy-to-make version that contains Fennel, ginger, and peppermint, as well as a small amount of sugar, aids digestion by easing tight muscles and releasing trapped gas. When refrigerated, this remedy will last for a week.

Ingredients

- 1 tsp. Fennel seeds, crushed
- 1 fresh gingerroot, chopped.
- 1 tsp. dried peppermint leaf crushed
- Boiling water, one cup
- 1 tsp. honey

Directions: Bring herbs and water to a boil in a teapot or mug. Allow 10 minutes of steeping before drinking.

Sterilize a jar with a tight-fitting lid and put the gripe water in it. Whisk honey and water in a separate basin until thoroughly dissolved. Continue with the recipe once the gripe water is heated enough to drink.

A medicinal dropper can be used for this. Give it to your infant gently by mouth. If you have colic, do this once or twice a day for a few days.

Precaution: If your child has a bleeding disorder, do not give ginger.

Conjunctivitis

Conjunctivitis is characterized by redness, itching, crusting or discharge, and tearing of the eyes. Dry eyes, puffy eyelids, and light sensitivity can all be symptoms of this common problem, which is also known as pinkeye.

Poultice of Chamomile

The anti-inflammatory and antibacterial properties of chamomile help to relieve the itching and discomfort of conjunctivitis. Using plain chamomile tea bags, organic if possible, is a quick and easy way to treat a sore throat.

Ingredients

- 1 tbsp. hot but not boiling water
- A bag of organic chamomile

Precaution: If you are allergic to plants in the ragweed family or if your doctor has told you to take blood thinners, you should not go.

Goldenseal Root Poultice

Goldenseal is an excellent treatment for conjunctivitis because of its ability to alleviate discomfort while also battling inflammation and infection. Make a batch of poultices in advance

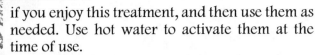

if you enjoy this treatment, and then use them as needed. Use hot water to activate them at the time of use.

Ingredients

- 1 tbsp. of hot, scalding water (not boiling)
- 1 tbsp. Dried goldenseal root

Directions: The hot water should be in a small container. Using a linen bag, place the chopped goldenseal root in hot water. To soften the roots of the plant, leave the poultice in water for 5 to 10 minutes.

Precaution: Take this medication only if you are not planning on becoming pregnant or breastfeeding. Don't use it if you're allergic.

Constipation

Constipation can cause abdominal pain and difficulty urinating. Herbs are far gentler on the digestive system than harsh chemical laxatives, yet they are just as effective Things will move more quickly if you eat a lot of fibre, drink a lot of water, and do more exercise.

Juice from Aloe Vera

Aloe vera juice is very powerful to relieve the symptoms of long-term constipation. Within three days of making aloe juice, it should be consumed.

Ingredients

- 3 to 4 inches of fresh aloe leaf from the plant's interior
- 3 cups of freshly squeezed juice, water, or even coconut water

Precaution: While aloe vera is safe to use if you are not pregnant or lactating, it should not be taken internally.

Syrup of Dandelion and Chickweed

Gentle laxatives like dandelion and chickweed can help alleviate constipation without the use of harsh medications. As long as both of these herbs aren't contaminated with herbicide or chemical fertilizer, you may find them in your own backyard. When refrigerated, this syrup can last for up to six months.

Ingredients

- 2 tbsp. of chopped dandelion root
- 2 tbsp. chickweed, either fresh or dried
- Water, two cups
- Honey, one cup

Cough

Coughing is a natural way for the body to expel waste.

Lungs and airways become clogged with irritants and phlegm. Dry, hacking coughs can worsen from what starts as a bothersome itch in your throat. During this time, you can work on the root cause. Herbal remedies can help soothe throat tissues that are sensitive.

Tea with Fennel-Hyssop

Fennel aids in the effectiveness of coughs by loosening phlegm. The Fennel and hyssop in this tea will soothe an itchy throat and a dry hacking cough in a matter of minutes.

Ingredients

- 1 cup Boiling water
- 1 tsp. fennel seed
- 1 tsp. Dried hyssop

Directions: Fill a large mug halfway with hot water and set it aside. Steep the herbs in the tea for ten minutes after adding them to the mug and covering it with a lid. Relax and inhale the steam as you sip your tea. Repeat up to four times a day, if desired.

Precaution: Avoid taking hyssop if you are pregnant or suffer from epilepsy, as it can cause miscarriage.

Cough Syrup with Licorice and Thyme

Anti-inflammatory licorice root quickly soothes irritated throat tissue, while expectorant thyme clears out the lungs. Coughing spasms are alleviated by taking thyme antitussive. When refrigerated, the syrup can last for three months before it loses its freshness.

Ingredients

- 2 tbsp. chopped licorice root

- 2 tbsp. thyme
- Water, two cups
- Honey, one cup

Precaution: Because licorice can raise your blood pressure, you should not eat it if you have high blood pressure or diabetes. This is the same thing as kidneys or the heart.

Cutting and Scraping

With the aid of herbs, minor wounds that don't necessitate stitching can heal more quickly. Before applying any remedy, wash and dry the affected area thoroughly.

Fresh Comfrey Poultice

Comfrey contains anti-inflammatory and antibacterial effects in addition to being a powerful pain reliever. Allantoin, a compound found in it, aids in the healing of wounds. Honey has antibacterial properties and aids in the absorption of the comfrey herb into the skin in this recipe. For those who don't have access to fresh comfrey, plantain, which contains allantoin, can be substituted.

Ingredients

- 1 tsp. Fresh comfrey powder
- Honey in a teaspoon

Salad of plantains

It's a great addition to your first aid kit, plantain. Its antibacterial properties make it an excellent choice for relieving pain quickly. Make this salve ahead of time and keep it in a dark, cool area until you're ready to apply it. It retains its freshness for up to a year after opening.

Ingredients

- 8 tbsp. Dried plantain weighing
- 1 cup Light olive oil
- 1 oz. Beeswax

Dandruff

An itchy and flaky scalp can be caused by a fungal infection or scalp psoriasis, leading in the development of dandruff. While herbal remedies can be helpful, they're not always necessary.

Infusion of Echinacea

A combination of Echinacea and Witch Hazel can help alleviate the itching caused by dandruff, which is often caused by candida. Using witch hazel on an itchy scalp will aid in the healing process. This spray has a shelf life of up to one year.

Ingredients

- Witch hazel: 1 tsp.
- Echinacea tincture: 2 tablespoons

Precaution: Avoid using echinacea if you have an autoimmune illness or are allergic to ragweed.

Conditioner with Rosemary Essential Oil

In this simple antifungal remedy, rosemary essential oil is combined with a natural, unscented conditioner for your hair type. You can substitute tincture for rosemary essential oil if you don't have it.

Ingredients

- Natural herbal conditioner such as Stonybrook Botanicals, 1 cup, without scent
- Aromatic oil of rosemary with a concentration of 40%

Diarrhea

Dietary problems are often to blame for diarrhea, but it can also be a sign of something more serious.

When you're sick, this can happen. Abdominal cramping is common but usually subsides after the body eliminates the irritating substance. In order to avoid becoming dehydrated as a result of diarrhea, make an effort to drink more fluids throughout the day.

Infusions of Agrimony

Helps to alleviate the symptoms of diarrhea by relieving digestive system irritation. There's a pleasant citrus flavor to it, which appeals to most people. If you have both diarrhea and a sore throat as a result of the flu, call your doctor immediately.

Ingredients

- Boiling water, one cup
- Dried agrimony is 2 teaspoons.

Directions: Fill a large mug halfway with hot water and set it aside. Let steep for 10 minutes with the dried agrimony covered. Sip your tea slowly and calmly. Do this up to four times a day if you're experiencing diarrhea.

Catnip and Raspberries Decoction

Mild astringents like catnip and raspberry leaf can put an end to diarrhea Raspberry leaves may be an excellent cure to try if your diarrhea is accompanied by abdominal cramps. When refrigerated in a properly sealed container, this decoction will keep for up to two days. If you're not a fan of the taste of the herbs, you can add a teaspoon of honey.

Ingredients

- 8 cups of water
- 2 tbsp. dried catnip
- 2 tbsp. dried raspberry leaves

Precaution: A word of caution: never use fresh raspberry leaves. They can make you sick. Avoid driving or operating machinery until you know how catnip affects you.

Dry Lips

Aside from being an aesthetic problem, cracked or peeling lips are a serious health concern. Moisture deficiency is usually the cause of chapped lips. Licking your lips in an attempt to hydrate them and relieve your discomfort can make things worse, as can be exposed to the sun, wind, heat, and air conditioning.

Balm of Aloe-Calendula

Calendula and aloe vera aid in the healing of damaged skin, while aloe vera hydrates parched lips. Pre-made calendula oil is used in this recipe, but you can substitute your own infused calendula oil. This balm will keep its potency if it is kept in the refrigerator and tightly capped up to a year of freshness.

Ingredients

- ½ cup aloe vera gel
- ½ tbsp. Calendula oil

Lip Balm with Comfrey-Hyssop Essential Oil

Chapped lips are made more bearable by the anti-inflammatory and analgesic properties of comfrey and hyssop, two herbs commonly used in herbal medicine. For about a year, the finished product can be stored in an dry, dark location far from any heat source.

Ingredients

- 2 tbsp. jojoba oil.
- 1 tbsp. Cocoa butter
- 1 tbsp. Olive oil, light
- 1 tsp. Dried comfrey leaves
- 1 tbsp. Dried hyssop
- 2 tbsp. Beeswax

Precautions: You should not use hyssop, but you should double the comfrey for pregnant women or those with epilepsy.

Earache

When the eardrum's sensory nerve endings respond to pressure, an earache occurs. Use herbal remedies as soon as you feel any discomfort coming on. If the discomfort remains or worsens, you should visit a physician.

Poultice and Infusion of Blue Vervain

Blue vervain is a pain reliever and circulation booster. Using a warm poultice on the ear and drinking an infusion that soothes the throat can help alleviate the pain that comes with an earache.

Ingredients

- 3 tsp. Dried blue vervain
- Boiling water, one cup

Precaution: Blue vervain should never be used while pregnant.

Infused Oil with Garlic and Mullein

There are many medicinal properties in garlic and mullein flowers that can help ease an earache quickly.

Ingredients

- 2 tbsp. Extra virgin olive oil
- 2 tbsp. of finely chopped garlic (frozen or dried)
- 2 tsp. Mullein flower dried flowers

Precautions: Garlic may cause a rash in some people, so if this happens, stop using it.

Eczema

The condition known as atopic dermatitis (eczema) causes itchy, red patches of thick, flaky skin. This seasonal or dietary allergy-related skin condition can appear at the same time as this allergic skin condition, which is cyclical in nature.

Goldenseal Spray with Calendula

The antiseptic and anti-inflammatory properties of calendula, goldenseal, and witch hazel are all present in these plants.

Ingredients

- 2 tbsp. of calendula dried herb
- 2 tbsp. Goldenseal root, dried
- 2 tbsp. jojoba seed oil
- 6 witch hazel sprigs

Precaution: If you are pregnant, lactating, or have high blood pressure, do not take goldenseal.

Comfrey Herbal Salve

Skin that is irritated or itchy can be soothed by comfrey. The roughness of the surface is softened, and cracking is prevented. Eczema sufferers can benefit from comfrey's ability to stimulate cell regeneration, which aids the healing process. Cool, dark storage can extend the life of this salve for up to one year.

Ingredients

- 4 tbsp. Dried comfrey
- 1 cup Light olive oil
- 1 oz. Beeswax
- 5 drops of Vitamin E oil

Fatigue

Working long hours, going to school, or taking care of a family can wear you out. Even a fun-filled vacation can cause stress. Herbs are gentler on your body than caffeinated drinks or sugary snacks, which can be harsh. The next time you feel like you've reached a brick wall, try one of these suggestions.

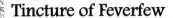

Tincture of Feverfew

Feverfew is an effective anti-anxiety and anti-inflammation remedy that also relieves the accompanying body aches and headaches. Take 5 drops of this remedy whenever it's needed, 5 times a day maximum.

Ingredients

- 4 tbsp. Feverfew
- 2 cups of alcohol (80%)

Precaution: Avoid Feverfew during pregnancy or if you are allergic to ragweed plants.

Syrup of Licorice and Rosemary

Rosemary is an excellent tonic for combating fatigue because it supports the health of the adrenal glands and can help increase energy.

Bee honey provides numerous health benefits, including being a natural source of energy.

If stored in the refrigerator, this syrup will stay fresh for up to six months after purchase. To get the same effect without cooking the syrup, consider taking a licorice extract pill and diffusing rosemary essential oil in the room where you spend the most of your time.

Ingredients

- 2 tbsp. of chopped dried licorice root
- 2 tbsp. chopped dried rosemary leaf
- 2 cups boiling Water
- 1 cup Honey

Directions: Dissolve honey in the hot water. Add the herbs and let them rest 2 days in the fridge before starting to consume it.

Fever

Give your body a chance to fight back against infection by keeping a fever if you can. Febrifuge herbs can be helpful if your fever continues to rise or does not go away. If your child has a fever, seek medical attention right away. If a baby's temperature rises above 100 °F, they should be taken to the hospital immediately.

Syrup of Feverfew

Because of its ability to be an effective febrifuge, feverfew was given its name. Retaining freshness for up to six months in the refrigerator, this syrup is suitable for children.

Ingredients

- 4 tbsp. Feverfew dried flowers
- Water, two cups
- Honey, one cup

Precaution: A pregnant or ragweed allergic woman should not take feverfew.

Tincture of Blue Vervain and Raspberry Leaf

Blue vervain and raspberry leaf are indeed effective febrifuges. When kept in an excellent, dark location, this tincture can last up to six years before going bad.

Ingredients

- 8 tbsp. Dried blue vervain
- 8 tbsp. Raspberry leaf
- 2 cups. 80% alcohol

Precautions : Pregnant women should not take blue vervain. Fresh raspberry leaves can make you feel sick, so never use them.

Flatulence

Flatulence is a common symptom of a sudden increase in dietary fiber intake. In most cases, embarrassment is the root of the problem. Herbs can help you feel more at ease and reduce the amount of gas that builds up in your digestive system.

Tea with peppermint and angelica

Because they help relax smooth muscles, peppermint and angelica are excellent for relieving digestive system tension and easing flatulence-inducing gas.

Ingredients

- 1 cup Boiling water
- 1 tsp. Angelica powder
- 1tsp. dried peppermint

Directions: Fill a large mug halfway with hot water and set it aside. Allow the tea to steep for ten minutes before drinking. Relax and inhale the steam as you sip your tea. Repeat up to four times a day, if desired.

Precaution: During pregnancy, avoid using angelica.

Ginger and Fennel Decoction

A healthy digestive system and the elimination of gas-causing waste products are aided by ginger and Fennel. Refrigeration extends the shelf life of this tasty concoction, which can be enjoyed for up to a week if you like it, double or triple the amount.

Ingredients: 8 cups of water

- 1 tbsp. Fennel seeds, crushed
- 1 tbsp. Ginger minced into a fine paste.
- Sweetener options include honey and stevia (optional)

Flu

Although its cause is yet unknown, flu is caused by a virus that changes form regularly. Herbs can help you feel better and heal faster if you get the flu.

A Catnip-Hyssop Tea

An inflamed throat or achy muscles can be relieved by using catnip or hyssop. They also help to strengthen your body's defenses against the flu virus, making it easier for you to fight it off. This tea has a calming effect, making it ideal for consumption before bedtime.

Ingredients

- 1 cup. Boiling water
- 1 tsp. Chopped dried catnip
- 1 tsp. Dried hyssop

Precaution: When pregnant, avoid using hyssop and catnip. If you have epilepsy, do not take the hyssop supplement.

Infusion of Echinacea and Goldenseal in a base of garlic and honey

There are powerful antiviral herbs such as goldenseal, Echinacea, and garlic that can assist your body in fighting the flu naturally. A teaspoon of lemon juice may help make this syrup more palatable, despite the honey's pungent flavor.

Ingredients

- 1 oz. minced dried or frozen garlic
- 1 oz. of chopped dried echinacea root
- 1 oz. of chopped dried goldenseal
- 2 cup of Water
- 1 cup Honey

Precaution: If you are allergic to ragweed or suffer from an autoimmune illness, you should avoid taking Echinacea supplementation.

Gingivitis

The condition known as gingivitis can develop in spite of regular brushing of the teeth and flossing. This condition can cause receding gums and loose teeth over time as a result of the progression of the disease. Keep up with your dental cleanings by seeing your dentist twice a year and getting into the practice of flossing on a regular basis. Using herbal remedies in between professional cleanings can help to keep your teeth and gums in good condition.

Mouthwash with Calendula and Chamomile

While fighting infection, calendula and chamomile ease inflammation. The floral flavor of this mouth rinse soothes sore gums and aids

in the healing of damaged tissue. When used correctly, this rinse can last for up to a week. Stored in a cold storage facility.

Ingredients

- 1 oz. dried calendula
- 1 oz. chamomile
- 4 cups of water

Precaution: If you are allergic to ragweed, do not use this product.

Goldenseal and Sage Oil

In this recipe, the anti-inflammatory properties of sage, goldenseal, and coconut oil are combined to create an effective treatment for sore gums. For first-timers, it's recommended that you begin with a 5- to 10-minute treatment and work your way up to a 15-minute session.

Ingredients

- 1 oz. of chopped dried goldenseal
- 1 oz. Crumbled dried sage
- 12 cups of coconut oil.

Hair Loss

Hair loss isn't just a problem for men; it can affect women as well. There are a multitude of causes that might contribute to hair thinning, including over-styled hair, stress, and even nutritional inadequacies. Herbs are unlikely to be effective if your hair loss is caused by a genetic tendency, but they can be effective in a variety of other situations.

Ginger Hair Mask

Ginger increases the growth of hair follicles by boosting circulation in the scalp. This therapy will remain effective for up to two months if it is kept in the refrigerator at all times.

Ingredients

- 2 ounces of chopped fresh ginger root
- 14 ounces of sesame seed oil

Precaution: Those who are on blood thinners, have gallbladder disease or have a bleeding disorder should avoid using ginger.

Ginkgo-Rosemary Tonic

Your hair follicles will be stimulated by the combination of rosemary and ginkgo with witch hazel. Rosemary strengthens and adds shine to your remaining hair, which can boost your self-confidence.

Ingredients

- ½ oz. dried Ginkgo Biloba.
- 2 tbsp. Dried rosemary leaves
- 2 tbsp. fractionated Coconut oil
- 1 tsp. Witch hazel leaves

Precaution: Ginkgo biloba should not be taken if you are taking an MAOI for depression. When using blood thinners, talk to your doctor before taking Ginkgo biloba. Rosemary can trigger seizures in people with epilepsy.

Halitosis

Bad breath is unpleasant and embarrassing. The good news is that it's easy to cure. Drink plenty of water because a dry mouth fosters bacterial development. Brush and floss twice a day, and apply mouthwash. Speak with your doctor if herbal remedies aren't working. It's possible that someone's persistent halitosis is due to an underlying medical issue.

Mouthwash containing peppermint and sage essential oils

Salvia and peppermint freshen breath while alcohol kills germs. The rinse can be kept for up to six years if it is made with vodka and stored in a cool, dark place.

Ingredients

- 4 tbsp. Dried peppermint

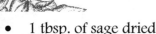

- 1 tbsp. of sage dried
- 1 cup 80% alcohol

Green Tea with Ginger-Mint Gunpowder Infusion

To combat halitosis and tooth decay as well as mouth cancer, polyphenols—antioxidants found in gunpowder green tea—are combined with lemon and spearmint.

Ingredients

- Two lemons
- Ginger root, cut into 1-inch cubes.
- 2 spearmint bunches
- Gunpowder green tea leaves in a cup
- Boiling water in a cup

Hangover

You don't have to suffer the consequences of overindulgence if you don't want to. In addition to addressing your primary symptoms of headache, nausea, and exhaustion, you should also experiment with a variety of other natural remedies to aid your body's detoxification process.

Feverfew and Hops Tea

Hops and feverfew work together to relieve headaches. So that your body can recuperate, this tea is strong enough to help you fall asleep.

Ingredients

- 1 cup boiling water
- 1 tsp. dried feverfew
- 1 tsp. Dry hops

Precaution: Avoid using feverfew if you're expecting or allergic to ragweed, which may cause an allergic reaction.

Infusion of Milk Thistle

Milk thistle aids the liver in its efforts to purify the blood. You won't feel better immediately, but your body will thank you for it. For up to six years, it can be stored in a cool, dark place.

Ingredients

- 16 tbsp. dried milk thistle
- 2 cups 80% alcohol

Precaution: Warnings Milk thistle can cause mild diarrhea if taken in excess. The amount or frequency of this should be reduced if necessary.

Headache

Headaches can be caused by stress or muscle tension, but they can also be a sign of something more serious. Linked to the caffeine crash, headaches, and hypertension. Consult your doctor if you experience frequent or persistent headaches, as these can be signs of a more serious medical condition.

Tea with Blue Vervain and Catnip

The combination of blue vervain and catnip increases circulation and promotes relaxation, as well as relieving stress. Stress headaches respond well to this concoction.

Ingredients

- 1 cup boiling water

- 1 tsp. dried blue vervain
- 1 tsp. catnip powder

Precaution

Pregnant women should avoid using blue vervain or catnip.

Tincture of Skullcap

The mild sedative properties of the skullcap make it an effective remedy for nerve pain. Those who suffer from migraines and are unable to take feverfew should consider trying a skullcap instead. This tincture is effective right away. A convenient capsule form of skullcap is also available for those who prefer it. For up to

six years, this tincture can be stored in a cool, dark place.

Ingredients

- 6 tbsp. skullcap
- 2 cups 80% alcohol

Precaution

Pregnant women should avoid taking skullcaps.

Heartburn

GERD causes heartburn when stomach acid escapes into the esophagus, causing a burning sensation. Increased acid production, obesity, overeating, wearing tight clothing, and other factors can all contribute to GERD. If you're pregnant, you may be experiencing heartburn because of the increased pressure on your stomach as your baby grows. There is no cure for heartburn, but you can get some temporary relief while you figure out what is causing it.

Tea with Fresh Ginger

Ginger has been shown to speed up the recovery from heartburn by increasing blood flow throughout the body. Esophageal irritation is caused by stomach acid, and this herb's anti-inflammatory and pain-relieving properties help to soothe it.

Ingredients

- 1 cup boiling water
- 1 tsp. chopped fresh gingerroot.

Precaution: It's best not to use ginger if you are using blood thinners, have gallbladder disease, or suffer from any type of bleeding disorder.

Fennel and angelica infused syrup

Additionally, fennel and angelica help with digestion by reducing esophageal irritation and increasing blood flow to the digestive tract. This syrup can be stored in the refrigerator for up to six months.

Ingredients

- 2 tbsp. dried angelica
- 1 tbsp. Fennel seed.
- 2 cups of water, two cups
- 1 cup raw honey

Hemorrhoids

In the rectum and around the anus, hemorrhoids are swollen veins. Inflamed, they can cause bleeding, itching, and pain. Hemorrhoids are more common in pregnant women as a result of the straining that occurs during bowel movements as a result of sitting for long periods of time

Tonic with Witch Hazel and Calendula

Antiseptic and anti-inflammatory properties are provided by calendula and witch hazel. Hemorrhoid itching is relieved by using witch hazel, which shrinks swollen veins and tissue.

Ingredients

- 2 oz. dried calendula
- ½ cup Olive oil, light
- 3 tbsp. witch hazel

Sulforaphane and St. John's Wort Ointment

Itching and inflammation associated with hemorrhoids can be alleviated with the use of chickweed, goldenseal, and St. John's wort. When kept in a cool, dark place, this ointment can last for up to a year.

Ingredients

- 1 tsp. Chickweed dried
- 1 tbsp. dried goldenseal root, minced
- 1 tbsp. dried St. John's wort
- 2 tbsp. Oil from jojoba
- 1 tbsp. light olive oil.
- 1 tbsp. Cocoa butter
- 1 tbsp. beeswax
- 3 drops Vitamin E oil

Precaution: Goldenseal should not be taken by pregnant or lactating women or by those with high blood pressure.

Hives

Despite the fact that hives can be a sign of extreme stress or emotional turmoil. Even a seemingly innocent item like strawberries might cause an allergic reaction.

Licorice and Chamomile Spray

Witch hazel, Chamomile, and licorice root tinctures form the base of this spray. All three ingredients ease inflammation and itching, and the witch hazel aids in tissue shrinkage.

Ingredients

- 3 tbsp. witch hazel
- 2 tsp. Tincture of camomile
- 2 tsp. Tincture of licorice root

Directions: In a dark-colored glass spray bottle, combine all components. Shake gently to mix well. Spray 1 or 2 spritzes per problem area. Repeat 3-4 times daily, or as needed, for optimum results. Cover the sprayed area with clothing.

Comfrey-Rosemary Balm

Histamines can be blocked by rosemary constituents. It's an excellent remedy for hives brought on by allergic contact dermatitis.

Ingredients

- 1 cup of extra-virgin olive oil
- 2 tbsp. of crumbled dried rosemary
- 1 tbsp. comfrey root
- ½ oz. beeswax

Indigestion

Belching, gas, and discomfort are all symptoms of overeating, an illness or overindulgence in a favorite food that didn't agree with you. Herbal antacids can provide fast relief without the potential side effects of commercial antacids.

Infused chamomile and angelica tea

Both angelica and Chamomile help to soothe the gastrointestinal tract's muscles and promote healthy blood flow. With a bit of honey and some fresh lemon juice, the tea will be a little easier to swallow.

Ingredients

- 1 cup boiling water
- 1 tsp. Angelica root, ground
- 1 tsp. dried Chamomile

Precaution: Pregnant women should avoid using angelica. If you have an allergy to ragweed, avoid taking Chamomile.

Syrup of ginger

In addition to aiding digestion, Ginger also soothes the digestive tract and increases blood flow to the area. Before taking the cure, mix in a teaspoon of freshly squeezed lemon juice to make it more effective and provide even faster relief.

Ingredients

- 2 oz. of chopped fresh ginger root
- 2 cups of water
- 1 tbsp. Honey

Precaution: Those on blood thinners, suffering from gallbladder illness, or suffering from a bleeding disorder should avoid consuming ginger.

Inflammation of the Blood vessels

High blood pressure can cause cognitive loss, heart disease, kidney failure, and a stroke if it is not managed. Exercise, weight loss, and meditation are natural ways to promote healing. It's imperative that you see a doctor as soon as possible if you're unable to lower your blood pressure on your own within two months.

Infusion of angelica

High blood pressure is commonly treated with calcium channel blockers, which relax and enlarge blood arteries while also affecting arterial wall muscles. Angelica contains comparable chemicals. This infusion can be sweetened or juiced if desired, but it is bitter

Ingredients

- 1 oz. Dried angelica
- 4 cups boiling water
- 1 lemon juice

Precautions: Avoid taking angelica if you are pregnant or taking blood thinners.

Tincture of Dandelion and Lavender

To control salt and blood pressure naturally, dandelion leaves contain potassium, which is found in abundance in the leaves. The relaxing and balancing properties of lavender's scent and oils make it a popular choice for aromatherapy.

Ingredients

- 4 ounces of finely chopped dried dandelion root
- 4 ounces chopped dried lavender flowers
- 2 cups 80% alcohol

Precaution: Large doses of dandelion tea might induce dangerously low blood pressure. Too much lavender can cause constipation, headaches, and an increased hunger. Consult your doctor if you experience any side effects.

Insects Stings

Pests such as mosquitoes, chiggers, biting gnats, and fleas all leave behind raised red marks. These little bites can be so itchy that they keep you awake or unable to sleep, but simple plant-based remedies can help alleviate the discomfort. An itchy, swollen reaction is expected after being stung by a bee, and the discomfort can last for days or weeks. Herbs can help ease the discomfort. For those who are allergic to bee venom, herbal remedies are not meant to be used as a substitute for emergency epipens.

Salve made with fresh basil and Mullein.

Both basil and Mullein have anti-inflammatory properties. Especially the eugenol (contained in basil) acts also as an analgesic and helps your bug bites heal faster. In the event that you have a large number of insect bites or if your entire family is affected, you may easily double or quadruple the recipe

Ingredients

- 1 cup fresh basil
- 1/4 cup chopped Mullein
- 1 tbsp. raw honey

Plantain and Peppermint Balm

A tube of this balm is convenient and straightforward to use if you spend a lot of time in bug-infested areas. The balm can also be used to maintain lips moist and smooth. Peppermint and plantain help repair the skin faster. This cure can last up to a year when kept cool and dark.

Ingredients

- 1 tsp. Dried peppermint leaves
- 1 tbsp. Plantain flakes
- 3 tbsp. Oil from jojoba
- 1 tbsp. of light olive oil.
- 1 tbsp. Cocoa butter
- 4 tbsp. Beeswax
- 3 drops Vitamin E oil.
- 15 drops Essential oil of peppermint

Fresh Plantain Poultice

The plantain plant contains an antitoxin glucoside known as aucubin, which can be used to treat a variety of ailments (not to be confused with its banana-like namesake).

This simple treatment is quite effective as a result of the addition of the other substances. If you don't have fresh plantain leaves on hand, soak a teaspoon of dried, mashed plantain in one tablespoon of water until it's dissolved. Make a poultice out of it.

Ingredients

- Chopped fresh plantain leaves: 1 tablespoon finely chopped

Cover the affected area with a soft cloth while the chopped leaves are applied to the skin. Take it out for 10 to 15 minutes, and then remove it. In order to permanently end the pain, repeat as many times as necessary.

Gel of Comfrey-Aloe

Because of its anti-inflammatory and analgesic properties, comfrey can help alleviate the pain and swelling associated with bee stings due to its anti-inflammatory properties. Also Aloe vera is, a cooling and healing agent.

Ingredients

- 1 tbsp. Dried comfrey leaves
- 2 tbsp. Aloe vera gel

Insomnia

One of the leading causes of insomnia is a combination of anxiety, caffeine, and stress.

Another major factor is electronic overuse, particularly in the hour or so leading up to bedtime. While using herbal sleep aids, keep these things in mind.

Passionflower and Hops Valerian Tea

Valerian hops and passionflower create a calming blend that alleviates stress and anxiety while promoting deep, restorative sleep.

Ingredients

- 1 cup boiling water
- 1 tbsp. chopped dried valerian root.
- 1 tsp. Dried hops powdered

- 1 tsp. Dried passionflower

Precautions: Prepubescent children and pregnant women should avoid using this product.

Syrup of Chamomile and Catnip

Catnip is known for its sedative properties, but this recipe is gentle enough for children to take when they're having trouble falling asleep

Ingredients

- 2 tbsp. Dried Chamomile
- 2 tbsp. Dried catnip
- 2 cups Water
- 1 tbsp. raw Honey

Itchy Skin

Dehydration, hot or cold indoor air, and long, steamy showers are all possible causes of dry skin. Humidifiers and treatments utilizing calming herbs, as well as regular moisturizing, may be beneficial.

Chickweed-Aloe Juice

Chickweed and aloe vera are excellent moisturizers and nourishers for the skin. No odor is left behind after this gel has absorbed

into the skin. It will keep for up to two weeks in the refrigerator.

Ingredients

- ½ cup Water
- 1 tbsp chickweed, dried
- 1 tbsp. of aloe vera gel

Body Butter with Calendula and Comfrey

With calendula's anti-inflammatory properties, as well as comfrey's soothing properties, calendula and comfrey help heal damaged skin.

Ingredients

- 2 tbsp. cocoa butter.
- 1/2 cups of coconut oil.
- 2 tbsp. Jojoba seed Oil
- 2 tbsp. of shea butter.
- 2 oz. Dried calendula flowers
- 2 oz. Dried comfrey

Jock Itch

Tinea fungus causes jock itch and hurt, which affects the groin, inner thighs, and buttocks. This illness can affect anyone, regardless of gender. To speed up the healing process, keep the affected area free of moisture, and clean at all times.

Garlic-Infused Oil

A solid antifungal agent, garlic, attacks the microbes responsible for jock itch. Although this oil has a strong scent, it is effective in relieving itching and killing fungus on inflamed skin.

Ingredients

- 4 ounces chopped Garlic (dried or freeze-dried)
- 1 cup of extra-virgin olive oil

Precaution

Garlic can irritate the skin of those who are allergic to it. If this happens, stop using it.

Calendula, Chamomile, and Goldenseal Spray

In addition to their antifungal properties, calendula, Chamomile, and goldenseal all aid in the healing of damaged skin. Jockey itch is made worse by the hot, itchy sensation that is caused by witch hazel, the base of this treatment. Refrigeration keeps this spray fresh for a year.

Ingredients

- 1 tbsp. Dried goldenseal root, minced
- 1 tsp. Dried calendula flowers
- 1 tbsp. Dried Chamomile
- 2 tbsp. of witch hazel
- 3 cups fractionated coconut oil

Keloids Pilaris

Too much keratin in the skin leads to keratosis pilaris, a common ailment. On the backs of your arms and thighs, "chicken skin" is harmless but ugly, with dry, scratchy patches and lumps.

Scrub with Chickweeds

Keratosis pilaris sufferers can use baking soda and chickweed to gently exfoliate their skin, and chickweed can help reduce the inflammation that accompanies the condition.

Ingredients

- 1 cup of baking soda
- 1 cup chickweed crushed and dried

Precaution: Baking soda can dry out the skin, so be careful. Before using this scrub on a regular basis, try it out on a small area first.

Calendula-Chamomile Body Butter.

Emollient-rich calendula and Chamomile soothe irritated skin with their anti-inflammatory properties. You can use your favorite essential oils in this body butter to customize its scent and use it as an all-over moisturizer.

For up to a year, this body butter can be stored in a cool, dark place.

Ingredients

- 8 tbsp. Dried calendula
- 8 tbsp. Chamomile dried flowers
- 12 oz. Coconut oil.
- 1 cup jojoba oil
- 2 tbsp. cocoa butter
- 2 tbsp. shea butter

Laryngitis

Laryngitis occurs when the voice box swells and becomes inflamed as a result of infection, irritation, or overuse. If the problem persists for more than a few days, you should see a doctor, as hoarseness can be a sign of an underlying illness.

Mullein and Sage Tea

Mullein and sage alleviate the symptoms of laryngitis, as well as speed the healing process of damaged tissue by reducing inflammation. If you don't like the herbal flavor, add a teaspoon of lemon juice or honey.

Ingredients

- 1 cup boiling water
- 1 tsp. Dried Mullein
- 1 tsp. Dried sage, chopped

Gargle with Ginger

Adding honey to this recipe helps alleviate throat pain and inflammation while also providing a light coating and additional anti-inflammatory benefits. To make a soothing tea, you can use this recipe as well.

Ingredients

- 1 cup boiling water
- 1 tbsp. dried ginger, minced
- 1 tbsp. raw honey

Directions: Boil water in a big cup. After adding the ginger and honey to the mug, steep for 10 minutes. You can either let the liquid cool to room temperature or refrigerate it to make it colder. Throat irritation can be relieved by gargling with 1 tablespoon of salt water, as often as necessary. Refrigerate for up to three days.

Precaution: Warning: Do not use if you are using a blood thinner prescribed by your doctor, have gallbladder disease, or have any other type of bleeding disorder.

Menopause

Women's hormone levels begin to decline as they approach menopause. It's not uncommon for it to feel discomfort in the process. Regular exercise and a diet high in non-GMO soy, a good source of natural plant estrogen, can also help in addition to these natural treatments.

Herbal Concoction of Fennel and Sage

Taking a fennel and sage decoction can help alleviate hot flashes, as it has estrogen-like properties. You may prepare a larger quantity and keep it in the fridge for up to a week. Sweetener can be added if desired.

Ingredients

- 2 cups water
- 1 tbsp. ground fennel
- 1 tsp. dried sage

Tincture of Black Cohosh

It contains isoflavones, which mimic the activity of female hormones, in black cohosh. Managing mild depression, dry vaginas, and hot flashes associated with menopause can be made easier with the help of this supplement.

Ingredients

- 8 ounces of finely chopped black cohosh
- 2 cups 80% alcohol

Nerves Tonic

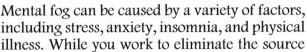

Mental fog can be caused by a variety of factors, including stress, anxiety, insomnia, and physical illness. While you work to eliminate the source of your brain fog, certain herbs can help you focus and make daily tasks easier.

Rooibos Tea with Ginseng

Herbs like rosemary and ginseng provide a steady supply of energy while also boosting circulation and promoting a sense of alertness. If you prefer a more convenient method of ingesting your daily dose of ginseng, a high-quality supplement is an option.

Ingredients

- 1 cup boiling water
- 1 tbsp. powdered ginseng root
- 1 tsp. Dried rosemary

Precaution: If you have epilepsy, don't use rosemary in your dish.

Tincture of Ginkgo Biloba

Ginkgo biloba improves cognitive function by increasing blood flow to the brain. Ginkgo capsules are an alternative to the daily tincture if you don't like the idea. When kept in a cool, dark place, this tincture is an affordable option that will keep its potency for up to six years.

Ingredients

- 8 ounces of finely chopped Ginkgo Biloba
- 2 cups, 80% alcohol

Rash from Changing Diapers

Even if you're meticulous about changing your baby's diaper, a rash from the diaper can develop. This rash is accompanied by pain, redness, and swelling. There are no harmful talc or petroleum products found in commercial herbal remedies, which are gentle enough for your baby's delicate skin.

Chamomile and Echinacea Gel

To soothe and heal your child's skin, aloe, lavender, and Echinacea work together. A common cause of diaper rash, the fungus yeast, is targeted by Echinacea. The gel will remain fresh in the refrigerator for up to two weeks.

Ingredients

- 1 tbsp. chamomile dried flowers
- 1 tbsp. Echinacea root, chopped
- ½ cup Water

- 1 tbsp. aloe vera gel

Precaution: Avoid giving Echinacea to your infant if he or she has an autoimmune disease.

Comfrey and Thyme Salve

Comfrey aids in the speeding up of the healing process, while thyme is a potent antibacterial. This nourishing salve also acts as a barrier to keep your baby's skin dry, allowing it to heal more quickly. Make a second batch and store it in the diaper bag.

Ingredients

- 1 cup Light olive oil
- 1 ounce dried comfrey
- 1 ounce thyme powder
- 1 ounce Beeswax

Sunburn

Even those who are careful can get sunburned. Be cautious to get medical help if your sunburn has blisters, pain, or infection.

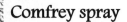

Comfrey spray

The anti-inflammatory properties of comfrey tincture and witch hazel help to swiftly relieve the sting of a sunburn.

Ingredients

- 1 cup witch hazel
- 2 tbsp. comfrey tincture

Aloe Vera & Hyssop-Infused Gel

Sunburns can be soothed using hyssop and aloe vera gel. If you don't want to make a decoction and have hyssop tincture on hand, use 1 tablespoon instead.

Ingredients

- 2 tablespoons dried hyssop
- ½ cup water
- ¼ cup aloe vera gel

Urinary Tract Infection (UTI)

Urination pain, urgency, and frequency are all signs of a urinary tract infection. Start herbal therapies as soon as you suspect a UTI to reduce symptoms. Keep hydrated while caring for yourself. Consult your doctor if you develop a fever or if your pain persists.

Horseradish Tea

A potent antibiotic and diuretic, horseradish tea kills bacteria while also stimulating urine to help the bladder flush faster. This tea may not taste good, but it can make you feel better.

Ingredients

- 1 tbsp of fresh grated horseradish root

- 1 cup boiling water

Dandelion Tincture

Dandelions are diuretics that help the bladder drain toxins. It also helps detoxify the liver when taking antibiotics for a urinary tract infection. This tincture is a mild laxative and digestive tonic.

Ingredients

- 8 ounces dandelion root, finely chopped
- 2 cups 80% alcohol

Are herbal medicines Safe?

The use of plants and plant extracts in treating disease is referred to as herbal medicine. Even though they've been synthesized, many modern pharmaceuticals were initially derived from plant sources. Herbal treatments utilize the entire plant rather than just the active ingredient. In the opinion of herbalists, a plant's entire chemical composition (synergy) is more effective than a single active element.

Is it safe?

However, herbal medicines are generally considered safe, but they might occasionally induce unwanted side effects. There are a variety of symptoms that fall under this category, such as indigestion, insomnia, and joint or muscular discomfort. Your prescribed medication may interact with some herbal treatments.

You should always acquire these medicines from a reputable manufacturer and discuss their use with your doctor before using them.

Independent testing of herbal medicines before they are placed on the market should be considered when items do not comply with standards and damages to kidneys or liver in some customers because of their content in toxic chemical compounds or in heavy metals, or for the reaction they may have with other drugs. Once a product is on the market, it should be closely watched.

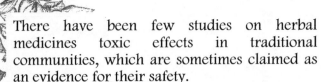

There have been few studies on herbal medicines toxic effects in traditional communities, which are sometimes claimed as an evidence for their safety.

Some plant species can induce renal failure or also liver damage, which have recently been discovered because of a lack of systematic observation.

In many cases, people who use herbal medications do not notify their doctors because of the wrong assumption that natural is for sure safe. "However, herbs can be a source of highly potent toxins, and many items we use as medicines derived from plants are toxic, poisoning predators," he explains.

Low amounts of these poisons can be used for medical purposes. It is a common misconception that natural items such as herbs and spices cannot be classified as drugs. This is simply not true. Herbal medicines can indeed hurt or interact negatively with prescription prescriptions.

Consumers could purchase foreign herbal products that were found to be tainted with medications to boost their effect.

These substances were either not specified, or their concentrations were erroneously reported.

AMAZING BONUSES FOR ALL THE READERS:

Just Scan the QR-Code below to get them!

Conclusion

In this eleventh book, we have provided herbal remedies for the most common ailments you can suffer from in your everyday life.

I sincerely hope that this will be just the beginning of your journey and that you will increase your knowledge on Native American medicine for a healthier and better way to treat the common disease without relying on industrial drugs and medication.

If you have enjoyed this book, feel free to leave a review to share your experience.

Just scan the QR code on the right, it will take 30 seconds!

My best wishes and may the Spirit guide your journey!

Native American Herbalist's Bible

Essential Oils: Remedies, Administration and Crafting

BOOK 14 of "The Native American Herbalist's Bible"

Natalie Hathale

Natural essential oils

The use of essential oils in aromatherapy, a supplementary medical practice, has becoming common in the last years. But, not all health claims for these oils are true. So, how do essential oils work?

Essential oils are obtained from plants. The oils capture the plant's essence. Each essential oil has its own scent due to its aromatic components. They are extracted by steam or water distillation or mechanical methods like cold pressing. Aromatic chemicals are extracted and blended with a carrier oil.

Chemically created essential oils are not essential oils, therefore knowing how they're made is vital.

What You Should Know About Aromatherapy

"Aroma," the Greek word for spice, is the root of the English word "fragrance." Aromatherapy harnesses the medicinal potential of plants, with a primary emphasis on the use of essential oils. Aromatherapy uses these oils to improve physical and mental health and influence mood and cognitive performance. The term "aromatherapy" is deceptive because it implies that this type of medicine relies solely on the sense of smell. On the other hand, aromatherapy uses the brain-stimulating effects of essential oils to promote physical and emotional well-being. They are also administered topically to ensure skin and bloodstream absorption. Essential oils must be diluted adequately before usage due to their strength. A little essential oil is generally enough; more isn't necessarily better.

Aromatherapy is noninvasive and can be used alongside other therapies. Practitioners are pioneers in using aromatherapy in conjunction with traditional treatments like meditation and homoeopathic medicines.

Specialists generally advise against using products containing synthetic substances, even if they are marketed as aromatherapy. Before purchasing a product, always read the ingredient list. The Food and Drug Administration does not regulate the use of the term aromatherapy in advertising or on product labels (FDA). It can be used to promote any product, even those with synthetic chemicals. For holistic purposes, always thoroughly inspect essential oil-containing items.

What are essential oils used for?

The most popular use for essential oils is aromatherapy, which involves inhaling them in various ways. Never take essential oils orally. They include substances that interact with your body in various ways. Some plant chemicals are absorbed when applied to the skin.

But, Essential oils can be used for more than just aromatherapy. Many people enjoy using them in their homes because of the aroma and freshness they provide to clothes and other household items. They are used in both homemade cosmetics and high-quality natural goods to add a pleasant aroma to the final product.

The properties of essential oils suggest that some of them could be used industrially to further improve food shelf life.

What essential oils should you purchase?

Corporations frequently make claims about the purity and quality of their products. Many people use these terms, but their meaning is limited because they are not universally defined.

Because essential oils are the products of an unregulated industry, their quality and composition may vary greatly

Tips to keep in in mind to ensure the quality of your oils

- Purity: Look for an essential oil that is pure and free of any additives or

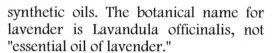

synthetic oils. The botanical name for lavender is Lavandula officinalis, not "essential oil of lavender."

- Quality: True essential oils are essential oils that the extraction process has minimally altered. The preferred methods for extracting essential oils that do not contain any chemicals are distillation or mechanical cold pressing.

If you want to buy high-quality products, you should do so from a reputable company.

Some application methods, for example applying heat to different parts of the body, are studied to improve the absorption feature. There is, however, a scarcity of research in this field.

The inhalation of essential oil fragrances can stimulate the limbic system, which is part of the brain involved in emotions, behavior, smell, and memory long-term. The limbic system plays an important role in memory formation. This could explain why certain odours evoke strong emotions or memories in people.

The limbic system also affects several unconsciously controlled physiological functions. Essential oils, according to some, can have a physical effect on your body.

Health Benefits

Anxiety and stress

In addition to regular therapy, essential oils can aid in the treatment of anxiety and stress.

However, because of the odors of the chemicals, it is difficult to conduct blinded experiments and eliminate bias. Many studies on essential oils' stress- and anxiety-relieving properties have been unconvincing.

Even if the effects of essential oils during a massage are only temporary, they may positively affect the body.

Migraine and headaches

The application of peppermint and lavender oil to skin helps to relieve migraine pain. In addition, the mixture of chamomile and sesame oil to the temples, you can help relieve migraines and headaches. This is a well-known headache treatment used by Persians.

Insomnia and difficulty sleeping

It has been proven that smelling lavender essential oil helps women recover from childbirth and sleep well. Inhaling essential oils, specifically lavender oil, improves sleep quality.

Inflammation

Thyme and oregano essential oils are effective in the treatment of colitis in mice. Caraway and rosemary oils were the subjects of two rat studies, with similar results in both.

There have been few human studies on the use of these oils to treat inflammatory illnesses. As a result, their efficacy and safety have yet to be established.

Antibacterial and Antibiotic Feature

Antibiotic resistance has rekindled interest in developing new antibacterial agents to combat the problem.

There is no proof that essential oils can treat bacterial infections in humans.

Use on children and newborns

This is yet another contentious issue... Infants and children have a less developed liver and immune system and thinner skin. As a result, they are more vulnerable to the dangers of oil use.

The significance of following safety rules cannot be overstated. Make an appointment with your doctor or another qualified healthcare professional before using essential oils on or around infants or children.

After two years, the concentration of specific essential oils must be significantly lower than in adults in order to be applied topically and via aromatherapy methods. A dilution ratio of 0.5 to 2.5 percent is generally regarded as safe.

Children's essential oil safety

Guidelines include, but are not limited to:

- It is not advised to use peppermint on children under the age of six.
- Avoid using Eucalyptus, either topically or aromatically, around children under the age of ten.
- It is critical to remember that adding 6 drops of essential oil to an ounce of carrier oil is equivalent to diluting it by 1%.
- Essential oils are not to be consumed by anyone under the age of 18, including adults. For safety reasons, essential oils should never be kept within reach of children or pets.

Administration

The effects of essential oils on your body and mind are very dependent on how you apply them.

From skincare to stress relief, essential oils offer a wide range of health advantages. You can inhale essential oils directly from the container or through a diffuser or humidifier, the most usual method of application.

The essential oils can also be applied undiluted by combining with a carrier oil. Use it as a bath, body wash, or shampoo.

To begin using essential oils, proceed with extreme caution. Keep an eye out for side effects and monitor your medication's potency.

Aromatic

Methods that involve inhalation of essential oils or mixtures of essential oils are referred to as "aromatic." Choose the approach that best matches your goals, whether you want to unwind, improve your concentration, or achieve another goal, in terms of exposing your body to more essential oil.

Diffusion

Diffusion is one of the simplest and most common ways to use aromatic essential oils. Not all diffusers are created equal; there are a wide variety of models available.

Guidelines: A cold-air diffuser that employs ultrasonic vibration to break up the oils into a fine mist, which remains suspended in the air for hours and treats you to the therapeutic characteristics of the essential oil you pick, is the best way to get the most out of diffused essential oils. It is important to adhere to the manufacturer's instructions while using essential oil.

Benefits: An essential oil's aroma can enhance a room's environment while also providing you with its own physical or emotional benefits when it's in the air. Tangerine and lemon essential oils, for example, can help you achieve a mood of joy and harmony. Diffusing eucalyptus essential oil or an antibacterial combination will be useful in clearing airborne infections. Many commercially made air fresheners just mask aromas, whereas essential oils interact with the chemicals that our bodies perceive as odors. Essential oils can be diffused regularly even if you don't have a particular emotional or physiological need for them. At the absolute least, this will help you unwind, reduce stress, and improve the quality of the air you're breathing.

When utilizing a diffuser, make sure to follow the directions provided by the manufacturer. Diffusers can become clogged or damaged by using oils that are not properly diluted or if they are too thick to be absorbed by the skin. It is also important to note that you should never diffuse essential oils such as clove or cinnamon on their own. Compounds in these potent, spice-based essential oils can burn the nasal membranes when inhaled as a micro-mist.

Direct Inhalation

Direct inhalation of certain essential oils is a potent yet simple way to get the many advantages of aromatherapy. Aromatherapy.

Guidelines: Taking a breath directly into your lungs is simple. Rub your hands together after putting a few drops of a single essential oil or a mix in the palm of your hand. Draw in a deep breath while holding the cups over your nose and mouth. Relax for at least three minutes after taking three to five deep breaths. As an alternative to applying essential oils directly to your hands, you can just cup your hands around a bottle and take three to five deep breaths in. Relax for a few minutes before closing the bottle.

Direct inhalation gives you direct access to the volatile molecules of essential oil, allowing you to experience its effects. In addition to improving mood, learning, reducing appetite, and improving specific biological systems are just some of the benefits of using essential oils.

Check the profile of an essential oil before using it inhalation. Some essential oils should not be used this manner. During direct inhalation of essential oils, do not allow them to come into contact with the eyes.

Steam

Adding a few drops of essential oil to a bowl of steaming hot water may help alleviate symptoms of a cold, allergies, or any other upper respiratory disease. Treatments like this one are simple, effective, and affordable.

Guidelines: It's easy to distribute essential oils to your lungs using steam from hot water. Gather a bowl, the essential oil of your choice, a towel to place beneath the bowl to catch any drips, and a towel large enough to drape over your head, shoulders, and the bowl. Place the bowl on top of the first towel on the table. Put 3–5 drops essential oil in the bowl filled with hot but not boiling water. Sit comfortably in front of the bowl, and cover it with a second towel. Inhale the vapors for a minute or until the steam dissipates. Get out of the towel when you need a break. You should keep a box of tissues nearby during this treatment, as it helps to clear your sinuses. You can blow your nose as often as necessary during the procedure.

Benefits: Certain essential oils help to relieve congestion and reduce inflammation of the mucous membranes in the respiratory system when steam is used to distribute it. Inhaling essential oils and hot water vapors can help relieve symptoms such as a scratchy throat, congested sinuses, itching, and dryness.

Safety: When you need a breath of fresh air, get out of the towel. Allow the water to cool slightly before continuing if the fumes are too hot. Use caution if you experience dizziness or nausea while using this treatment. Because the essential oil in the steam can hurt your eyes, keep them closed while inhaling the vapors. Use this strategy for up to a minute per treatment if you're under the age of 12. Take care while offering this treatment to children.

Vasodilator and Humidifier

Use a humidifier to disseminate essential oil in your home or workplace if you don't have a diffuser.

Guidelines: You can use essential oils in a humidifier by placing a few drops on a piece of tissue or cloth and running it through the machine. Make sure to put this in front of the humidifier's air intake so that the essential oil molecules can mix with the water vapor that is being released.

Benefits: Using humidifiers and vaporizers in your house can help you breathe easier, especially in the winter. Some find these machines to be pleasant background noise, and others use them to alleviate symptoms of allergies and sinusitis. Essential oils not only provide fragrance to the air, but they also provide health benefits to individuals who inhale them.

The mucus membranes lining the nasal passages, sinuses, and airways might be damaged if cinnamon or clove essential oils are used in a humidifier or vaporizer.

Inhalers and humidifiers can also be used to deliver the benefits of essential oils. These machines' plastic parts can become sticky or deteriorate if they are used for long periods with essential oils.

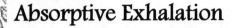

Absorptive Exhalation

Indirect inhalation refers to any method of inhaling essential oils that is not direct inhalation. Essential oils can be diffused or put on a cotton ball and placed near the exhaust fan in your laptop, for example.

Selecting an indirect inhalation strategy is as simple as figuring out which one works best in the given situation. Decide on your favorite method by experimenting with several.

Benefits: Indirect inhalation allows you to breathe cleaner, healthier air while also improving your general well-being. Additionally, the essential oil you've picked may have therapeutic properties. Direct inhalation may not be suitable for everyone, thus those who are more sensitive may prefer indirect inhalation methods.

After deciding to use an indirect inhalation approach, be sure to follow the directions to the letter. Make sure that all essential oils and equipment are out of the hands of children.

Vent or a fan

Vents and fans are good for spreading essential oils throughout big spaces since they increase air circulation. Use of essential oils is recommended in large rooms.

Using a vent or fan and essential oils is as simple as dabbing a cotton ball with the oil and holding it up to the air vent or fan of your choosing.

These devices can be found in houses, offices, cars, and hotel rooms. Vents and fans can be found in a wide range of locations. Anywhere you go, as long as you have a few basic, portable items on hand, you may get the benefits of essential oil indirect inhalation.

Cotton balls should be placed on small glass or ceramic saucers to keep the essential oil from getting into contact with objects that could be harmful. Avoid letting your kids or pets get their hands on any cotton balls or other things used with vents and fans.

However, these seemingly harmless internal essential oils have a lot of power. With so many plants' healing properties packed into a single drop, it's important to know the risks of taking essential oils internally without first consulting a doctor.

True, essential oils can be used in cooking, and they can also be utilized in aromatherapy. A physician's supervision is strongly suggested if essential oils are taken internally. Only one to three drops each dose, depending on the disease being treated, the oil being used, and each patient's unique medical history, are often suggested for internal use. Essential oils should only be eaten for a limited amount of time, according to most of these guidelines.

Before intake, essential oils are often diluted with warm water, soy milk, or rice milk as oregano and cinnamon can cause stinging or burning and potentially damage to the tongue and esophagus when prescribed for oral use. A stinging feeling in the tongue, indigestion or an upset stomach, and diarrhea are all possible side effects of ingesting an overdose or adulteration. In addition, nausea and grogginess may also be present, as well as stomach and chest pain. Knowing the risks of drinking specific essential oils and seeking the counsel of a knowledgeable health care expert who can assess whether or not essential oil intake is acceptable for you are two equally important steps you should take.

Basic Treatments

Acne

To combat the drying effects of the environment, the skin secretes oil. Despite the fact that oily skin is primarily a cosmetic problem, it can lead to more serious issues like acne.

Fennel Facial Toner

The antiseptic properties of fennel make it an excellent addition to facial toners because it helps prevent minor infections that are often associated with oily skin.

Citrus Facial Toner

As powerful astringents, citrus essential oils like grapefruit and lemon are great for bringing the skin back into harmony and getting rid of excess oil. Suppose this recipe is too drying for your skin; substitute witch hazel or water for the vodka. If you have a child, do not use this treatment.

Allergies

Asthma, hives, and other allergic reactions can accompany symptoms such as itchy or watery eyes, runny nose, and itching. Asthma and allergy patients can be affected by seasonal and pet allergies all year round, and allergies to domestic animals such as dogs, cats, and horses can occur at home or when the person comes into touch with them.

If you've tried natural allergy cures and they haven't helped, you should seek professional help.

Lemon Mint Tropical Mist

Essential oils such as lavender, lemon, and peppermint can help alleviate the symptoms of allergies by boosting the immune system and reducing inflammation. The scent of this mist is pleasant and can be used multiple times a day.

Lavender and Tea Tree Essential Oil

In addition to their capacity to promote healing, lavender and tea tree essential oils are well-known for their ability to fight microorganisms. This flush with a neti pot is going to sting you a lot, be only sure to dilute it 1:100

Clove Essential Oil

As a cleaner and a natural pain reliever, clove essential oil is a great addition to any essential oil collection.

Anti-Insect Spray

Insects, such as mosquitoes, gnats, chiggers, and other pests, can transmit diseases or cause irritation and suffering through their bites. These natural insect repellents are a great alternative to commercially available sprays and creams that include chemicals.

Citronella Spray

Many commercially available products use citronella as an insect repellent since it is powerful.

Geranium-Patchouli Spitz

To make natural insect repellent, geraniol can be found in the essential oil of geranium. Because of its long history as a powerful insect repellent, patchouli essential oil is included in this product because of its pleasant aroma.

Anxiety

It is possible for anxiety and fear to cause problems in one's daily routine. If you frequently experience feelings of nervousness, powerlessness, or worry, you probably have a major anxiety disorder. Among other symptoms are feelings of imminent doom, fast breathing, hyperventilation, trembling, and an elevated heart rate.

Valerian Essential Oil

Anxiety can be effectively treated with valerian's essential oil, which helps stabilize mood and emotions while calming the mind and anchoring it. A carrier oil can also be used to dilute the valerian and apply it to your temples.

Marjoram Essential Oil

Marjoram is known as the "herb of happiness" because of its ability to regulate one's mood. It relaxes the body and mind, allowing you to think more clearly.

Apply 3 to 5 drops of marjoram essential oil plain to the back of your neck, or blend it with an equal amount of carrier oil in a small dish. Diffusing, breathing, or using an aromatherapy pendant with marjoram might enhance its relaxing properties.

Arthritis

When it comes to arthritis, symptoms vary by type, but many people who have it report joint pain, stiffness, and a crippling loss of range of motion. This ailment affect usually people beyond the age of 50 but, there are some juvenile varieties of arthritis that affect younger persons.

Arthritis Detox Bath

Detoxifying essential oils like cypress, fennel, and juniper can provide quick relief from arthritis-related toxin buildup. Use juniper instead of any other arthritis treatment since it provides immediate relief. For a period of two weeks after taking this bath, avoid using any other arthritic therapies, including ones that contain essential oils. If you have broken skin or are prone to rashes, you should not use this cure.

Peppermint Massage Oil

Inflammation and pain associated with arthritis can be alleviated with the use of peppermint essential oil. Natural pain treatment can be achieved by applying this massage oil frequently.

Asthma

In asthma, the airways expand and narrow, making breathing difficult. Wheezing, coughing, and shortness of breath are all symptoms of an asthma attack that can be frightening. Dust mites, mould, pollen, stress, and pet dander are common asthma causes. Avoiding triggers and natural remedies do not work, visit a doctor.

Lavender Steam

Lung spasms can be relieved and panic calmed by using a lavender essential oil, while steam helps open the airway. When it comes to essential oils, lavender is one of the few that can be used during an asthma attack. Before relying on this treatment, be sure you aren't allergic to lavender essential oil.

Attack Prevention Rub

Peppermint essential oil is a powerful decongestant that helps prevent asthma attacks. After a few days of sickness, use this massage before bed. This cure is also great for relieving the symptoms of a cold or flu. Between uses in a dark environment

Athlete's Foot

Itching, burning, and flaky, yellow, or thickened skin. The ringworm fungus is the source of this skin ailment, which can be spread easily from person to person. It's fortunate that essential oils work so effectively for it.

Tea Tree Oil Treatment

In the fight against athlete's foot, tea tree essential oil has become a popular remedy. The sooner you begin to feel the effects of this medication, the better.

Calendula and Tea Tree Soothing Balm

This cure can be used to treat athletes' feet and repair painful fissures. Athletes' foot is typically treated with tea tree essential oil; however other essential oils such as lavender, lemon, or myrrh can be used in a pinch. In this therapy, the use of calendula carrier oil is essential since it calms and promotes quick healing.

Bad Body Odor

Sweat and bacteria on the skin are the most common causes of body odor. On the other hand, spicy foods like onions and garlic can cause it. Body odor is more of an embarrassment and an annoyance than a health risk in the majority of cases. Infection or cancer in the liver or kidneys is another possible cause of foul-smelling body odors. If your body odor persists despite improved hygiene and natural treatments, you should see your doctor.

Eucalyptus Essential Oil

Essential oil of the Eucalyptus tree combats the bacteria that cause body odor. A pleasant scent is also left behind as a result of its use. Other trouble spots to use this salve on including your feet and underarms.

Bee Stings

Swelling, pain and itching accompany bee stings. If you've been stung by a few bees and are looking for quick relief, these remedies are for you. If you've been stung by a swarm of bees, or if you're allergic to bee stings or suspect you are, seek medical attention right away.

Lavender- Chamomile Compress

In addition to being antihistamines, lavender and German chamomile essential oils are also anti-inflammatory. Apply it on the sting using a sterile gauze.

Basil-Peppermint Bee Sting Relief

The combination of basil and peppermint in this remedy eases the stinging and itching of bee stings.

Bleeding Wounds

It's common for minor wounds to bleed heavily. After 30 seconds or so of bleeding, stop the blood flow and clean the wound. This will help flush out dirt and bacteria. Emergency medical attention should be sought immediately if blood is pouring from an artery or a wound is large or deep.

Helichrysium Essential Oil

To stop bleeding, simply apply helichrysum essential oil directly to the wound. Shaving accidents and scratches are good candidates for this treatment. If you don't have access to helichrysum essential oil, try cypress.

Geranium-Lemon Essential Oil

Essential oils of geranium, lemon, and tea tree help reduce pain relief and inflammation. Shallow cuts and scrapes respond well to the soothing properties of this compress.

Blisters

Blisters typically affect the upper layer of the skin, resulting in pain that can be severe at times. The skin acts as a natural barrier to infection, so leave the blisters in place if possible.

Natural remedies may not be effective in treating blisters that have developed due to burns, chemical exposure, freezing, or infection. Make any necessary medical appointments.

Lavender-Myrrha Compress

Donut-shaped bandages or moleskin can be applied around the blister, but make sure the sticky part doesn't touch it. Apply this Essential Oils blend diluted 1:100 on the blister using a sterile gauze.

Tea Tree Blister Soak

Use this remedy to treat foot blisters that have broken open or drained of fluid. If you don't have tea tree essential oil, use eucalyptus, lavender, or myrrh essential oils instead.

Bloating

Symptoms of abdominal bloating include mild to severe pain and pressure and an increase in the diameter of the abdomen. Often, bloating is caused by overeating, overconsumption of gas-producing foods, or a lack of bowel movement. Symptoms of bowel obstructions, food allergies, and other conditions can cause bloating.

If symptoms worsen or don't improve with time and natural remedies, seek medical attention.

Lemon-Rosemary Seeds Bloating Relief

Essential oils of lemon, peppermint, and rosemary have diuretic properties and can alleviate bloating symptoms.

Chronic Pain

A wide range of conditions can cause pain, from minor to chronic and severe. Using essential oils to alleviate pain is an option. If you're experiencing severe or chronic pain that hasn't been diagnosed, it could be a sign of an underlying medical condition.

Cinnamon Bath Oil

The essential oil of cinnamon has a potent analgesic effect. Even the most severe chronic pain can be made tolerable by the deep tissue-penetrating heat it generates. Before using an essential oil, make sure you're not allergic to it. Pregnant women and cancer patients should avoid this treatment.

Eucalyptus Essential Oil Compress

In addition to being an effective analgesic, eucalyptus essential oil has the added benefit of relaxing tight tissue. Hot compresses can amplify their effects, as well.

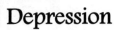

Depression

It doesn't matter if you take prescription medications or not; utilizing essential oils can help you feel better mentally and physically.

District Rosewood Essential Oil

Aromatherapy with Rosewood essential oil can help alleviate stress, alleviate headaches, and improve the immune system all at once. It's recommended that you use 3 to 5 drops of rosewood essential oil in the room where you spend the most time

Rosemary and Sage Essential Oil

When used together, rosemary and sage are known to reduce anxiety and despair while also enhancing one's cognitive abilities. Concentration and positivity are enhanced by inhaling this aromatic combination while working.

Halitosis

Everyone experiences halitosis at some point in their lives. Many different factors contribute to bad breath, but bacteria are the most common culprit. In addition to removing food particles with brushing and flossing at least three times a day, natural remedies can help further reduce bacterial buildup. You should see your doctor if you notice a sudden change in the smell of your breath and it does not improve with better oral hygiene or natural remedies. This could be a sign of an underlying disease.

To avoid bad breath, keep your mouth moist. Mouths are naturally cleansed and re-energized by saliva. Having fresher breath is as simple as drinking plenty of water.

You can also use 1:100 diluted essential oils to gargle or flush your mouth. Below the recommended ones.

Clove Essential Oil Rinse

An antibacterial agent that leaves behind a pleasant scent is clove essential oil

Lavender-Peppermint Cleansing Flush

In contrast to peppermint essential oil, which imparts a refreshing scent, lavender essential oil effectively kills bacteria.

Headache

Tension headaches can be induced by stress, melancholy, muscle strain, or hunger. Some can last up to seven days. Essential oils may perform as well as or better than over-the-counter pain medicines in relieving tension headaches.

Peppermint Temple Rub

For relieving aches and stress, use peppermint essential oil. Peppermint essential oil can be used to treat mild headaches by rubbing the temples with one drop of oil on each side. The essential oil can be applied directly to your temples and 3 to 5 drops on the back of your neck.

Three Oils Blend Compress

Headaches can be alleviated by using essential oils such as frankincense, lavender, or peppermint. Cool compresses can be used to speed up the healing process.

Insomnia

An insomniac is someone who has trouble sleeping or staying asleep. It can be challenging to get back to sleep for some people, even if they are fatigued, while for others, it is impossible to sleep at all, even if they are exhausted. Chronic exhaustion is a common symptom of insomnia.

Neroli-Spikenard Bedtime Massage

Nighttime rituals with neroli and spikenard essential oils are recommended for persons who have trouble sleeping or staying asleep. This treatment may help you fall and remain asleep. If you want to get the most out of this treatment, make sure your bedroom is completely silent and dark before you go to sleep.

Lavender and Petitgrain Bath Oil

Various commercial sleep aids use lavender essential oil since it is so excellent at promoting calm and a restful night's sleep. However, petitgrain essential oil is still a powerful relaxant, which is used less frequently. A candle or two in the bathroom will enhance the effectiveness of this bath, as opposed to leaving the lights on all night. If wanted, vetiver essential oil can be substituted for petitgrain oil.

Knee Pain

Pain in the knees might be severe or subtle, chronic or due to an injury. Essential oils can be used to cure some types of knee pain, while surgery is necessary for others. In cases when you are experiencing significant knee discomfort or if your knee is unable to bear any weight, you should seek immediate medical attention. Doctors may have a more difficult time repairing a knee injury if you wait too long to get treatment.

Pine Blend Massage

An excellent anti-rheumatic agent, essential pine oil penetrates deep into tissue and aids in circulation, which speeds up the healing process of wounded tissue. It's best to dilute essential pine oil because it's very potent. Before employing an essential oil as a pain reliever:

- Dilute it with a carrier oil in a dark-colored glass bottle large enough to hold the amount you wish to create.
- Massage the therapy into the skin with your fingertips to help it absorb better.
- If necessary, keep repeating this procedure.

Peppermint and Eucalyptus Liniment

Analgesic, anesthetic, and anti-inflammatory qualities of peppermint and eucalyptus essential oils make them perfect for treating painful joints.

Laryngitis

Your voice will sound raspy or hoarse if you suffer from laryngitis, an inflammation of the larynx. A cold or the flu makes you hoarse or raspy. Laryngitis is a short-term symptom of a cold, flu, acid reflux, or allergies.

Cajeput Steam Treatment

Cajeput essential oil is a great natural analgesic for laryngitis pain relief. When using essential oils, use a vapor treatment that can carry them directly into your skin. Diffusing it or adding a few drops to a hot bath are other options.

Soothing Lemon-Niaouli Steam

The anti-inflammatory, antibacterial, and analgesic characteristics of lemon and niaouli essential oils make them perfect for treating laryngitis.

Leg Aches and Pains

Leg cramps can be brought on by a variety of factors, including dehydration, overworked muscles, obesity, and even pregnancy. Stretching, exercise, and the use of essential oils and a diet high in iron can all help relieve minor leg cramps. You should see a doctor about leg cramps that don't go away or that come with swelling and a general incapacity to move.

Anti-Cramping Massage Oil

Essential oils of marjoram, rosemary, hyssop, and lavender combine in this treatment to avoid leg cramps, especially at night. Before doing this treatment, make sure your muscles are warmed up.

Geranium and Evening Primrose Massage Oil

The antispasmodic and anti-inflammatory qualities of geranium and evening primrose oil make them suitable for preventing cramps in progress. Essential oils such as rose geranium can be substituted if you do not have any geranium on hand.

Lice

Infestations of the louse can spread quite quickly. Small red bites, itching, and nits (louse eggs) can all be signs of lice. Detecting adult lice and their nymphs can be challenging. Everyone in the household should be treated if a member of your family has head lice. If essential oils fail to alleviate your symptoms, see a doctor.

Geranium Shampoo

It is crucial that you separate the eggs from the lice nits so that you may use the essential oil to destroy both adult and nymph lice. Add 40 drops geranium or rose geranium essential oil to 4 oz. natural shampoo. After shampooing the entire head, scrub vigorously. Leave shampoo on for 10 minutes, taking care not to get suds in your eyes.

Tea Tree Treatment

Adult lice and nymphs can be killed by using tea tree essential oil. If you find any nits, be sure to separate them with a fine-toothed comb and remove them.

Apply tea tree oil to the scalp and leave it for 40 minutes. Then shampoo and condition the hair. Repeat until all of the lice have been removed.

Lower Back Pain

Mild to severe back pain can occur for a variety of reasons. As a result, back pain can be slight or severe and can be caused by a wide range of factors, including strains in muscles and slipped vertebrae. Consult a physician if your back discomfort persists, does not improve with rest, or is the consequence of an injury. It is possible that a serious back injury could lead to paralysis.

Lavender-Rosemary Bath Oil

Lavender and rosemary essential oils can help alleviate back discomfort by calming muscular spasms. Birch, ginger, and Roman chamomile are some essential oils that can be used in a bath.

Relaxing Massage Oil Blend

In addition to carvacrol and thymol (natural substances that aid in muscular relaxation), rosemary, sage, and thyme essential oils are rich in lavender and Roman chamomile, which further strengthen this synergistic blend, and ginger is a natural painkiller.

Lupus

Swelling, inflammation, fever, tiredness, and even a rash are all symptoms of Lupus Lupus, an autoimmune illness that causes the immune system to attack the body's tissues.

Patients frequently complain of mental fog and despair. Comfort and relief from symptoms are possible with the use of essential oils. Use them only with the permission of your doctor.

Lemon Verbena Essence Bath Oil

Lemon verbena essential oil has a calming effect on the body and mind, stimulating the internal organs. In the location where you spend the most time, consider diffusing lemon verbena

essential oil. If you've used this treatment, stay out of the sun for at least 12 hours to avoid photosensitivity.

Lime Essence

The lime essential oil provides an invigorating boost to one's spirits, which lifts one's spirits and brightens one's view on life. Anti-inflammatory and immune support properties make it a great tool for alleviating pain in the muscles and joints. Add a teaspoon to a tub of warm water and soak for 15 minutes.

Lyme Disease

The term "Lyme Disease" refers to a disease carried by deer ticks and western black-legged ticks. There might be anywhere from three days to a month of symptoms after the bite, but the most common include joint and muscular pain, fever, headache, poor memory, and flu-like symptoms. See a doctor and use essential oils to boost your immune system.

Rosemary Essential Oil

Rosemary essential oil has been demonstrated to aid enhance brain clarity and boosting retention, making it a fantastic tool for overcoming the mental fog that commonly arises with Lyme illness. Make it a go-to remedy for dealing with symptoms, such as fatigue and headaches, by using it regularly. You can use it in a diffuser, an aromatherapy pendant, or simply by inhaling it straight from the container when you need it.

Immune system Booster Bath

Essential oils such as lavender, lemon, and tea tree work together to boost the immune system and reduce the symptoms of Lyme disease. Flu-like symptoms can be alleviated with the help of these.

Menopause

Night sweats, insomnia, hot flashes, irritability, and irregular periods are menopausal symptoms. Essential oils can help with many of these symptoms. Thus, they are a viable alternative to pharmacological treatments for many people.

Clary Sage Essential Oil Diffusion

Stress, anxiety, impatience, and the discomfort of menopause can all be eased with the usage of clary sage essential oil. When using clary sage essential oil, place it in the location where you spend the most time or wear it as an aromatherapy pendant. Adding 5 or 6 drops to a warm bath before going to sleep can also help ease discomfort.

Clary Sage-Geranium Massage

This lovely massage oil combines the calming effects of clary sage and the energizing effects of geranium to relieve tension, stress, and sadness. Bathing in 1 tablespoon of the mixture for 15 minutes is another option for using this treatment. When using this massage oil for any other purpose than before bed, leave out the lavender, which contributes to a good night's sleep by relaxing the nervous system.

Migraine

Migraines are severe headaches that are often accompanied by light sensitivity and a migraine aura (visual hallucinations such as wavy lines, bright flashing lights, or blind spots). If your migraines are regular and do not respond to therapy with essential oils, consult your doctor to rule out an underlying illness.

Lemon Essential Oil

Because of its reputation for relieving migraine symptoms and promoting a calm, focused frame of mind while also decreasing blood pressure and increasing circulation, the lemon essential oil has long been used to treat these conditions. You can use a diffuser or an aromatherapy pendant to wear this essential oil. A few drops in the bath or on the shower floor can also help. You can use lemon essential oil as a stand-alone treatment or in combination with others.

Coriander Essential Oil

The analgesic and anti-nausea properties of coriander make it a popular culinary herb. Before using this oil, be sure to perform a patch test to rule out any sensitizing effects it may have.

Nausea

Nausea is a common symptom of many illnesses, and it serves as a warning that vomiting is imminent. When you're feeling sick, you may feel dizzy or woozy, and a warm, uncomfortably tingling sensation may spread throughout your body.

Fennel Hot Compress

When used in conjunction with a hot compress, essential fennel oil quickly alleviates nausea. For pregnant women and children, this remedy is not recommended.

Ginger-Allspice Essential Oil

For nausea, ginger essential oil is one of the best remedies available and can be used by anyone. A few drops of allspice essential oil (also known as pimento) enhance the flavor, but they can be left out if they are not readily available. Pregnant women and children alike can benefit from this treatment.

Neck Pain

To alleviate neck pain, essential oils can be used, but only if the pain is severe, caused by trauma, or ongoing with no apparent cause. If you're experiencing neck pain, it's best to get it checked out by a doctor.

Peppermint Essential Oil Inhalation or Massage

When inhaled, the cooling vapors of peppermint essential oil relieve muscle tension while also calming the mind. Peppermint essential oil can provide immediate relief for neck pain when applied topically to the palm of the hand and rubbed together. Relax by massaging your neck with both hands, then sitting or lying down comfortably to enjoy the benefits of the massage.

Your neck and back are in a straight line. Allow at least 10 minutes of rest before returning to your regular routine.

Coriander Oil Massage

Arthritis pain can also be reduced with this treatment.

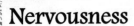

Nervousness

It doesn't matter if it's because of stage fright or because you're nervous about starting a new job; everyone gets nervous at some point in their lives. There are essential oils that can help alleviate the tenseness and near-panic associated with nervousness. Consult your physician to rule out a severe disorder if you are frequently anxious for no apparent reason.

Clary Sage Essential Oil

Essential oil of clary sage quickly relieves nervousness and anxiety and replaces Using clary sage essential oil can help you feel more at ease and relaxed, which is why it's a popular remedy for anxiety and panic attacks. Aromatherapy pendants and diffusers can be used to keep the essential oil close to your body at all times.

Clary Sage Smelling Salts

Stage fright and other types of nervousness that interfere with your daily life can be relieved with the help of clary sage essential oil. You can use these smelling salts before an important interview or when you're in a social situation where awkwardness is a possibility.

Nosebleed

Even though nosebleeds aren't life-threatening, they can still be frightening when they happen. Often caused by trauma or prolonged exposure to dry indoor air, nosebleeds are easy to treat.

Rose-Geranium Poultice

To help stop the flow of blood, the essential oil of rose geranium has styptic properties. As a result, it is ideal for treating and preventing bloody noses.

Lemon and lavender inhalation

Essential oils of lavender and lemon can help alleviate the anxiety that often accompanies nosebleeds while also preventing the spread of bacteria. Because pinching the nostrils is a part of this procedure

Oily Scalp

Oily scalps often cause itchy, flaky skin and a general sense of discomfort. An unpleasant odor can develop when bacteria feed on excess scalp oil. Reduce the appearance of excessive oiliness with essential oils.

Cedar wood Tonic

The essential oil of cedar wood has a balancing effect on sebum production. Antibacterial properties and a pleasant scent complete the package.

Grapefruit and Lemon Tonic

Hair is left shiny and clean after using essential oils of grapefruit and lemon, which are astringents.

Parkinson's disease

When muscles are unable to be controlled, Parkinson's disease results in symptoms such as trembling, slowness, stiffness, and impaired balance. If you have permission from your caregiver, use essential oils as a supplement to conventional therapy.

Frankincense Essential Oil

The essential oil of frankincense has a calming effect on the mind and body, promoting calm, even breathing and reducing stress. The smooth muscles in the small limbs benefit most from it, as do the smaller, more skeletal muscles.

Frankincense and Myrrh Essential Oil

Frankincense and myrrh can help alleviate the symptoms of Parkinson's disease, such as anxiety and agitation. There is a pleasant aroma that is both comforting and uplifting. Drench the area where the patient spends the majority of his time with frankincense and myrrh.

Poison ivy

Redness, swelling, itching, and burning pain and blisters are symptoms of the exposure and contact with this stinging plant.

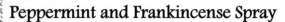

Peppermint and Frankincense Spray

Using essential oils like frankincense and peppermint can alleviate the symptoms of poison ivy at the same time as, promoting healing. Only use this remedy after you've cleaned the area thoroughly.

Lavender and myrrh Salve

Inflammation caused by poison ivy can be alleviated by applying lavender and myrrh essential oils.

Postpartum

After childbirth, your body is in the process of healing and adjusting to the fact that you are no longer pregnant. A small amount of bleeding, soreness, and exhaustion are all possible side effects. As soon as possible, help is needed for postpartum depression.

Jasmine-Rose Bath Oil

In addition to promoting healthy, glowing skin and aiding in the recovery of overworked tissues, essential oils of jasmine and rose to promote mental equilibrium, reduce emotional stress, and calm frayed nerves.

Perineum Soothing Spray

Sore or compromised perineum tissue heals faster with the help of frankincense, helichrysum, and lavender essential oils.

Premenstrual Symptoms (PMS)

Some of the most common symptoms of premenstrual syndrome (PMS) include mood changes (including sadness and irritability), abdominal bloating and cramping (along with carb cravings), sleep issues (such as insomnia), and tenderness in the breasts. The severity of symptoms and the effectiveness of essential oil treatment vary from person to person.

If you're experiencing severe pain and other symptoms, you should see a doctor rule out an underlying condition.

Lemongrass Essential Oil Bath

Bloating and cramping caused by PMS can be alleviated with the use of lemongrass essential oil. Because of this, it also has the added benefit of rejuvenating the mind and relieving stress.

Frankincense-Melissa Bath Oil

Melissa essential oil has antispasmodic properties that can help alleviate cramps during heavy periods. To get the best results, use this treatment in the evening, when melissa essential oil, which has a sedative effect, is at its most potent.

Tendinitis

Connecting muscles to bones are tendons, which are tough connective tissues. Tendinitis is an inflammation of the tendons that causes discomfort, stiffness, and minor swelling. Rest, heat and cold therapy, and essential oils are commonly used to relieve pain. No change after 10 days? Call the doc. If you have extreme pain, edema, and limited range of motion, you may have a ruptured tendon that requires surgery.

Marjoram Essential Oil

Marjoram essential oil relieves pain and inflammation by penetrating deep into the tissue. A warm compress on top of the essential oil helps it penetrate deeper into the skin.

Eucalyptus-peppermint Essential Oil Rub

Essential oils of eucalyptus and peppermint alleviate pain and promote relaxation. This remedy has a pleasant cooling effect, as well as an uplifting aroma.

Tennis Elbow

It's called "tennis elbow" because it's so common among tennis players, but overuse of the hand, arm, and forearm muscles can also cause the problem. Injuries to the outer elbow tend to result in pain and stiffness at the point where the forearm's muscles meet the bone of the upper arm. When an injury occurs, it usually necessitates immediate medical attention. Using essential oils while recovering can help alleviate some of the pain.

Marjoram Essential Oil

The essential oil of marjoram is able to penetrate deep into the tissue to alleviate pain and

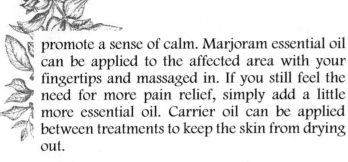

promote a sense of calm. Marjoram essential oil can be applied to the affected area with your fingertips and massaged in. If you still feel the need for more pain relief, simply add a little more essential oil. Carrier oil can be applied between treatments to keep the skin from drying out.

Nutmeg Salve

The essential oil of nutmeg penetrates deeply into the tissue, alleviating pain and promoting relaxation. Most people enjoy the scent, which is a mood booster.

Toothache

Many factors can cause toothaches, including trauma, infection, and inflammation, but the most common cause is tooth decay. There are many types of pain, from dull aches to piercing, excruciating agony. If the pain persists or a tooth is broken or knocked out, see a doctor or dentist. If you're experiencing pain in your jaw that radiates from your teeth, you may have a severe infection.

Clove Treatment

Clove essential oil can be used as a first-aid measure in the event that you have a severe dental problem, as it can numb even the sharpest tooth pain. Close your mouth and inhale through your nose for a few minutes to allow clove essential oil to penetrate the affected tooth and surrounding tissue. Repeat this treatment every two to three hours as needed.

Ear Joint Massage

Face pain from a toothache can be relieved by using German chamomile, clove and lemon essential oils.

UTI (Urine Tract Infection)

Itchy, hazy, or odorous urine are all signs of urinary tract infection. This problem must be addressed promptly if essential oils are to be used. If the pain worsens or a fever develops, contact your doctor. Patients with diabetes, a weakened immune system, kidney issues, or who are pregnant should contact their doctor right once.

Bergamot Massage

The essential oil of bergamot has powerful antibacterial and antiseptic qualities. Massage is a great way to get it into the body. After a massage, apply a warm compress for additional pain relief.

Cedar Wood Essential Oil

As an antiseptic, cedarwood essential oil may help prevent urinary tract infections. It should not be consumed and should not come into contact with the mucous membranes.

Warts

Itchy, rough, or hardened spots on the skin are known as warts, and they grow much faster than the rest of the skin. However, warts can be contagious because the virus that causes them is quickly spread. To treat genital warts, call your doctor if you have any of the following symptoms: pain, pus, redness, fever, or swelling.

Tea Tree Essential Oil

One of the most effective ways to get rid of warts naturally is to use tea tree essential oil. Apply 1 drop of tea tree essential oil to the wart's surface with your fingertips and allow it to dry. The wart can be treated up to three times a day.

Essential Oils of Cypress, Lavender, and Lemon

Apply cypress, lavender, and lemon essential oils to get rid of warts. This blend is best suited for adults over the age of 12. In order to make it safe for the youngest members of your family, dilute the mixture with a carrier oil.

Wasp Stings

Essential oils can be used to treat and prevent wasp stings, as well as to repel wasps. The harmful chemicals in commercial wasp repellents can hurt you, your kids, your pets, and the environment.

Repellant for Wasps

Thyme essential oil has been proven to repel wasps away.

Tea Tree- Basil Sting Balm

Wasp stings can be excruciating, especially if they are deep. The stinger of a wasp, unlike that of a bee, is not embedded in the skin, but it can still pierce the skin. This balm relieves pain and protects against infection.

Weight-Loss Help

A person's life is made more difficult in numerous ways by their obesity. With essential oils, weight loss can be supported in a safe and healthy way while promoting overall well-being.

Fennel Essential Oil

When diffused, essential fennel oil smells lovely and aids in promoting a sense of fullness. Fennel essential oil can be used in an aromatherapy necklace or diffused in the home. Add a few drops to your bath water or a washcloth placed on the shower floor to get the benefits of essential oils. As many times as you like, it can help you avoid food cravings that can derail your diet.

Wrinkles

As the skin loses elasticity with age, wrinkles form. Wrinkles cannot be removed with essential oils, but they can be reduced and the skin's overall tone improved by using them to promote healthy skin and improve elasticity.

Geranium-Carrot Toner

Carrot seed and geranium essential oils can help retain skin suppleness and prevent wrinkles.

Rose and Geranium Beauty Balm

Both rose, and geranium essential oils are known for their ability to soften and tighten the skin at the same time. The scent of this balm is intoxicating, and it's sure to be a hit.

How to Make Essential Oils at Home

In order to produce essential oils, the following questions must be answered:

Essential oil production is an art as well as a science, much like winemaking. The final product's worth is strongly influenced by the distiller's skill and knowledge, as well as the planned use of the oil.

Steam Distillation

Essential oils are often made by steam distillation. Steam distillation can be done in two ways:

Plant materials are placed in a sealed container and heated with steam. The burst of little internal sacs occurs as the steam hits the plants. Aromatic plants like lavender, rosemary, and sage have oil-filled sacs that rupture when you brush them between your fingers and catch a whiff of their scent. The flying steam easily transports the tiny essential oil molecules from the chamber to the chilled condenser. After the essential oil and water have been collected, they are separated.

An enormous pot of boiling water sits upon which the entire plant is hung. A receptacle catches the rising steam and pushes it through a separator, which removes the essential oils. Remaining water is usually conserved in both techniques. When it comes to scented linen sprays, perfumes, and body care products like body lotion or facial moisturizers, hydrosol is an essential ingredient. Distillation is the preferred method for producing some essential oils, as some components are only released after a particular amount of gentle heat exposure. Steam distillation is required, for example, in order to liberate the anti-inflammatory compound chamulzine from German chamomile.

Carbon Dioxide Extraction

Both carbon dioxide (CO2) distillation and supercritical CO2 distillation are widely used in the extraction of essential oils from plant material.

Extracting essential oils from plants using carbon dioxide is known as CO2 distillation or

CO2 extraction. It is done by chilling carbon dioxide to between 35 and 55 degrees Fahrenheit and blasting it through the plant material. As with cold pressing, this method delivers pure essential oils that have undergone no heat processing at all.

Then, it is heated to 87 degrees Fahrenheit in supercritical CO2 distillation before being blown through the plant materials at a considerably faster rate. Essential oils are liberated from the plant's inert substance when CO2 is converted to a heavy vapor under these extreme conditions. Due to the lower temperature of the CO2 compared to hot CO2, the produced essential oil remains unadulterated. Essential oil producers often label their goods using both cold CO2 distillation and supercritical CO2 distillation because both methods generate high-quality products. CO2 distillation is commonly used to make essential oils such as those of frankincense, myrrh, and other spicy scents like clove, black pepper, and ginger. There are two further forms of CO2-distilled essential oils that some manufacturers are proud to offer: CO2 totals and CO2 selections.

Plant matter, including resins, waxes, and color compounds, makes up a major portion of CO2 emissions because they are typically thrown away throughout the production process. CO2 totals often have a waxy or paste-like consistency, therefore they must be warmed before being poured.

Because some of the plant's natural waxes, resins, and color components are incorporated in the finished product, CO2 selections are thicker than most other essential oils. Normally, these essential oils can be poured without first heating them up. Compared to ordinary essential oil, CO2 total and select oil have a higher concentration of CO2. Typically, manufacturers recommend diluting them by 50% to 66% prior to usage. Follow the manufacturer's particular guidelines for use if you pick CO2 total or essential oils to ensure efficacy and safety.

Cold-Pressing

Citrus fruit essential oils are only extracted through cold-pressing. To extract the essential oil that gives citrus fruits their distinctive fragrances, just place the aromatic section of the fruit rind in a press at 120 degrees Fahrenheit.

Enfleurage

Enfleurage, which involves combining fat or fatty oil with intact flowers, is the earliest process of extracting essential oils. Some upscale perfumeries still utilize this time-honored method of extracting essential oils from flower petals by submerging them in a thin layer of warmed fatty oil. In order to ensure that the oil is completely saturated with essential oil, the blossoms are changed as they die. A solvent, such as alcohol, is used to extract the essential oil, and the leftover fat or oil is employed to provide aroma to soap and other products.

Extraction Using a Solvent

An absolute is a type of essential oil that is extracted with the aid of chemical solvents like methylene chloride, hexane or benzene. Instead of water or CO2, a solvent is utilised in this procedure. Extraction begins with a vacuum or centrifuge spin, which removes most of the solvent from the final product. Robert Tisserand, an esteemed aromatherapist, points out that there is considerable worry regarding whether the minute residues of extraction chemicals in essential oils are suitable for use in aromatherapy.

Making Essential Oils: Creating Your Own Plants and Harvesting Them

Plants should not have been treated to pesticides or herbicides, and chemical fertilisers should not be used. Some of these chemicals will leak into your collected oils if you use steam distillation. If you're growing herbs outside, make sure they're far enough away from power lines or traffic lanes so that they don't get sprayed. If you wish to extract essential oils from your herbs, avoid using chemical fertilisers at all costs.

It's also critical to know when to take your plants out of the ground. Harvest your plants as soon as they begin to bloom and as long as half of their blossoms have opened. Some plants, such as lavender, should be harvested when roughly half the flowers have opened and wilted, but there are some exceptions. The optimum time to gather rosemary is when it is in full bloom. In order to learn how to create essential oils, you will need to employ plants at specific times of the day when volatile essence levels are at their highest.

Throughout the growth season, annuals can be clipped down to within four inches of the ground. Annuals, on the other hand, should not be picked before the conclusion of the growing season in September. Keep an eye out for moulds, fungi, and other pests while producing essential oils from winter-grown herbs.

To create essential oils, you must first allow your herbs and flowers to air dry. While you don't want them to disintegrate in your hands, you also don't want them to be too delicate. Hanging little bunches of herbs and plants from the ceiling away from direct sunlight is a great method to keep them fresh. A warm but not hot environment is ideal for drying the plants. The plants and volatile essences you're seeking to extract can be damaged if you dry your herbs in a heated setting.

To create essential oils, you need a lot of plant material. Our goal is to get down to an ounce or two of oil from hundreds of pounds. To manufacture essential oils at home, you'll need a still that can process a few pounds of plant material at a time. If you intend to use a commercial still, you should prepare carefully before harvesting your plants.

How to Make Essential Oils Without a Still

It is possible to make essential oils without the use of a still, but be aware that the oil you collect will be of lower quality. If you're serious about learning how to create essential oils, you'll want to look into making or obtaining a still in order to ensure that your oils are safe for medicinal and therapeutic use.

A slow-cooker: Fill a big crock pot to the brim with distilled water and add a huge handful of softly dried plant material. Once you've cooked on low for 24 to 36 hours, turn off the crock pot and keep the lid open to allow steam to escape. Allow it to marinate for a week under a piece of cheesecloth away from direct sunlight. The oils that have accumulated at the surface of the water can be gently removed and transferred to an amber or blue glass jar after a week. The remaining water can be evaporated by leaving the jar open for a further week and covering it with a cloth. Store in a firmly sealed container for no more than a year.

You can use a regular saucepan to make essential oils on the stovetop, but place the plant material in a porous mesh bag first. Simmering for at least 24 hours, adding water as needed After separating the oil from the water, follow the crockpot method's directions to evaporate the excess water.

Risks and consequences

Many people are questioning the safety of these extremely concentrated plant extracts, especially as the essential oil business continues to rise. Consumers who use essential oils in their wellness, beauty, and cleaning routines may not be aware of the possible dangers.

The safety of a particular oil depends on a variety of factors, including:

- Age
- Pre-existing health problems
- Supplements as well as prescription drugs

Consider the following when it comes to oil:

- Composition and purity of chemicals
- How it's done
- A set amount of time
- Dosage

Something isn't safe simply because it's natural.

Bioactive substances found in plants and herbal products, such as essential oils, have the potential to be harmful to your health.

However, most essential oils are considered safe when inhaled or mixed with a base oil. Pregnant women, children, and pets should be kept away from the source of the odor.

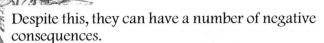

Despite this, they can have a number of negative consequences.

A rash is the most common side effect.

When it comes to allergic reactions, lavender, peppermint, tea tree, and ylang-ylang oil are the most frequently reported culprits.

Because of the high levels of phenols in these oils, which can cause skin irritation, they should not be applied directly to the skin without first mixing them with a base oil. On the other hand, Citrus essential oils can cause skin irritation and burns when exposed to sunlight.

Swallowing essential oils can be dangerous or even fatal in some cases, so it's best to avoid doing so.

Conclusion

In this last book, we have described Essential Oils, their use and administration and some techniques to make it by yourself in the comfort of your kitchen, with herbs, you can buy in your herbal shop.

I sincerely hope that this will be just the beginning of your journey and that you will increase your knowledge on Native American medicine for a healthier and better way to treat the common disease without relying on industrial drugs and medication.

If you have enjoyed this series of books, feel free to leave a review to share your experience.

Just scan the QR code on the right, it will take 30 seconds!

My best wishes and may the Spirit guide your journey!

About the Author

Natalie Hathale was born in Bosque Redondo Indian Reservation of the Navajo tribe.

As a youngster, she enjoyed nothing better than helping her father, who was taught by his father, a Navajo healer, to practice ancient Navajo herbal medicine practices.

In time, she left the reservation to deepen her knowledge and she earned a Master's Degree at New Mexico University, Albuquerque, in Natural Science. Since then, she continued studying and researching natural healing techniques and herbal remedies, and she started her own activity as herbalist and certified Naturopath, in Fort Sumner.

She has a husband and two daughters who she is teaching her family secret herbal remedies for the knowledge to pass to the new generations.

Following their advice, she has now decided to share and spread her passion and knowledge with others, by running seminars all around the country and writing books on the Traditional Native American Herbal Medicine.

AMAZING BONUSES FOR ALL THE READERS:

Just Scan the QR-Code below to get them!

Made in the USA
Monee, IL
29 March 2024

c70d2914-ce87-40b2-bb08-9fea1091ffdaR01